Latter-day Saint
Nurses at War

If I Had a Wish

If I had a wish, then it would be
Peace throughout the world, you see.

If people could see what peace could bring,
We could join hands and together we'd sing.

You wouldn't see children with crying faces,
Happiness would be present in all places.

We wouldn't have to worry about blood and gore,
And my mom wouldn't have to go off to war.

A very long time ago,
People fought with arrows and bows.

Today we use missiles, rockets, and bombs,
We also use many guns and napalm.

Wars cause destruction, as you can see;
If we didn't have wars, we all could be free.

—Natalie Nielsen
daughter of Jay and Deanna Nielsen,
veterans of the Vietnam War and Operation Desert Storm
Salt Lake City, Utah
Fifth Grade
December 1990

Latter-day Saint Nurses at War

A Story of Caring and Sacrifice

Compiled by Patricia Rushton,
Lynn Clark Callister,
and Maile K. Wilson

RSC

Religious Studies Center
Brigham Young University

USA flag cover image, Photodisc Red Collection/Getty Images
Nurse cover image, courtesy of National Archives, image no. 044-PA-204
Cover design copyrighted 2005 by Covenant Communications, Inc.

Published by the Religious Studies Center, Brigham Young University, Provo, Utah
Printed by Covenant Communications, Inc., American Fork, Utah
Printed in Canada

ISBN 0-8425-2611-0

Contents

—INTRODUCTION—

FOR CENTURIES, actions associated with caring and sacrifice have been noted in historical accounts. In biblical times, Rebekah provided sustenance by taking water from the well to give to the stranger, Abraham's servant, and his camels (see Genesis 24:14–21); Jacob worked seven additional years to marry Rachel (see Genesis 29:21–30); Moses advocated for the daughters of Jethro in Midian when he protected their flocks (see Moses 2:16–20); the woman at the Samaritan well provided physical water for Christ, and He offered her living water (see John 4:7–14); Christ healed the blind man at Bethesda (see John 5:5–9); Jesus Christ comforted Martha at the death of Lazarus (see John 11:19–26); and Jesus Christ suffered for mankind in the Garden of Gethsemane (see Luke 22:41–44).

During the nineteenth century, family members and friends cared for those in need, but "nursing" was considered beneath the dignity and social status of all but the lowest working class or prostitutes. For Florence Nightingale to do such menial work would threaten her social standing, but she did it anyway for the benefit of the men she cared for (Helmstadter 2002). During that same century, certain events motivated people to organize acts of caring and sacrifice. These people began to establish standards and values to achieve a common purpose. The people were nurses, the purpose was better patient care, and the setting was the battlefield.

The purpose of this work is to tell the story of Latter-day Saint (LDS) nurses who have served during wartime situations. These nurses have never had the opportunity to tell their story, which has much in common with other stories of nurses who served during a wartime period, but which also demonstrates some unique aspects because of their spiritual and religious perspective.

A LEGACY OF CARING

Since the work of Florence Nightingale, Dorothea Dix, and Clara Barton, professional nurses have been involved in caring for the sick and wounded during military conflicts. Members of The Church of Jesus Christ of Latter-day Saints have cared for the sick and wounded since the establishment of this faith in 1830 and have carried out their duties as part of the military since at least World War I. The collection of these accounts is of great benefit to nurse-historians and others studying those who have served during military conflict. Collecting and archiving these accounts is critical because most of the nurses who served in World War I have died and nurses who served during World War II are now in their eighties, some with fading memory and declining health. Many voices are lost each day as this generation passes.

Nurses have much to gain from learning about their rich historical legacy from courageous women and men who served their country during periods of military conflict. Almost all of the nurses who have contributed to this project have made a statement like "I didn't do anything special. I just did what I had to do." Their stories, however, illustrate their personal growth, their loyalty to their faith and their country, and their valuable contributions to the progress of the nursing profession and to the health and well-being of others.

We asked LDS nurses to share their wartime experiences through audiotaped interviews, accounts written in personal journals, or retrospective written accounts. In addition to these primary sources, secondary sources included newspaper accounts, letters, biographies written by children or spouses, military records and memorabilia, and photographs. For example, one participant shared the letters she wrote home while serving in the European theater during World War II. One, written from somewhere in France on January 27, 1945, reads: "Dearest Mother and Family: Writing by the light of a dim lantern is rather difficult. At least now we have a fire going in the little stove in our tent. We are settled in these humble living conditions [fourteen in one tent], but are thankful that it will not always be this way."

Some of the participants became very emotional as they recalled challenging experiences. As interviewers, we offered support, waited in silence, and then asked them if they wished to continue. Some had never discussed their military service with their families and found it helpful to talk with an interested investigator. Articulating their memories seemed to validate their perceptions and help them draw meaning from their experiences. Many expressed the sense that having this opportunity to share their perspectives was actually therapeutic, although this was not the intent of the project.

HISTORICAL BACKGROUND

It is important to understand from whence the profession of nursing came in order to understand the foundation of professional nursing. "Professional nursing began on the battlefield," says Paul Kerry, professor in the History Department of Brigham Young University. We see evidence for that statement in the lives of Florence Nightingale, Mary Jane Bickerdyke, and Clara Barton.

Florence Nightingale went to Scutari, Crimea, as a representative of the British government in an effort to improve the situation of sick or wounded British soldiers during the Crimean War. She wrote: "We have now four miles of beds—and not eighteen inches apart. . . . These poor fellows have not had a clean shirt nor been washed for two months before they came here, and the state in which they arrive from transport is literally crawling. . . . When one poor fellow who is to be amputated tomorrow, sees his comrade today die under the knife it makes impression—and diminishes his chances. We have Erysipelas Fever and Gangrene" (Florence Nightingale, in Dossey 2000, 125–26).

> The Barrack Hospital sat over a network of cesspools, but sewer lines were blocked and privies overflowed into the hallways. Windows were closed against the cold, wind, and rain, trapping the stench from the sewers together with smoke from the stoves. The water supply was visibly contaminated with organic matter. Not surprisingly, cholera, typhoid, and typhus

> added to the toll of illness and death. (Dossey 2000, 126)

In comparing Nightingale to Vietnam War nurses, Barker suggested that Nightingale might have suffered from post-traumatic stress disorder. She commented that Nightingale suffered somatic symptoms for much of the rest of her life. She never nursed again and was rarely seen in public. However, she was a prolific writer and advocate for the causes of the British soldier, sanitation, and educated nurses (1989, 630).

Nightingale's nursing activities to improve the quality of life for British military men threatened her physical and emotional health, social standing, and family approval; however, she brought cleanliness, reduced infection, and improved ventilation, privacy, and nutrition for those who were ill, and her practice became the basis of the standard of patient care that has continued to the present.

Mary Jane Bickerdyke, another early nurse, was a widow with two sons who supported her family by doing home nursing during the American Civil War. Some of the men at the Union camp in Cairo, Illinois, were ill and dying even before the first battle of the Civil War was fought. Gangwer wrote:

> Believing it was the Lord's work that she was called to do, Mrs. Bickerdyke placed her sons in the care of friends and left her home to take the supplies to Cairo. When she arrived, she was appalled at what she saw. There were three hospital tents crowded with cots; the ground inside the tents was covered with wet, dirty straw. Flies swarmed around the water buckets. The "noxious effluvia" was overpowering.
>
> Mrs. Bickerdyke rolled up her calico sleeves, asked for some able-bodied men to help her, and went to work. Under her orders, they shoveled out the tents, made barrels into bath tubs, and drew fresh water for the drinking buckets. The patients were scrubbed with her yellow soap while she made up the cots with clean linen she had brought. Dirty clothes were laundered or burned, and clean clothes supplied. She enlisted the help of Cairo citizens to set up laundries in the camp as well as kitchens. Special food was prepared for the sick instead of the usual ration of bacon and beans. One of her soldier helpers, a young man named Andy Somerville, told her that she reminded him of his mother and she soon became known as "Mother" Bickerdyke. She has also been called the "angel of Cairo" and a "cyclone in calico." (Gangwer 1998, 11–12)

At one time she ignored the orders of one of the contract surgeons, who then complained to General William T. Sherman. Sherman replied, "Oh! Mother Bickerdyke outranks me. She takes her orders from God" (Gangwer 1988, 12).

Clara Barton also provided nursing care during the Civil War, including in Fredericksburg, Virginia, in May 1864, after the Battle of the Wilderness. During that battle, 21,700 soldiers were either killed or wounded. Barton's description of the situation after the battle speaks to the terrible conditions suffered by military men during the war:

> I saw, crowded into one old sunken hotel, lying helpless upon its bare, wet, bloody floors, five hundred fainting men hold up their cold, bloodless, dingy hands, as I passed, and beg me in Heaven's name for a cracker to keep them from starving (and I had none); or to give them a cup that they might have something to drink water from (and I had no cup and could get none). . . . I saw two hundred six-mule army wagons in a line, ranged down the street to headquarters, and reaching so far out on the Wilderness road that I never found the end of it; every wagon crowded with wounded men, stopped, standing in the rain and mud, wrenched back and forth by the restless, hungry animals all night from four o'clock in the afternoon till eight next morning and how much longer I know not. The dark spot in the mud under many a wagon, told only too plainly where some fellow's life had dripped out in those dreadful hours. (Barton 1922, 277–78)

During the Civil War, Clara Barton independently managed a large-scale war relief operation in which she arranged for huge quantities of supplies to be furnished to the army and the hospitals. She impartially cared for the casualties of both the Federal and Confederate armies, for both blacks and whites. She was frequently in physical danger, being shot at as she tended to those on the battlefield. The ideals of caring for anyone in need, regardless of their physical, social, or financial situation, are the ideals embodied in the organization that Barton helped to organize: the American Red Cross (Donahue 1985, 294).

Those who served as nurses during the American Civil War elevated the standard of patient care in providing comfort and life-saving measures. They sacrificed personal comfort, possessions, and welfare to care for those who served on both sides of the conflict. They added to Florence Nightingale's foundation for modern nursing. Their actions have been described as follows:

> Despite the early skepticism of the surgeons and the general public about the propriety and ability of women to serve as nurses, these women showed the world they had the stamina, commitment, organizational ability, and talent to become a vital force in the nation. They not only opened up nursing as a career for women in America but laid the groundwork for developing the modern hospital. But perhaps the truest measure of their accomplishment is the effect they had on their patients. If some surgeons still retained their prewar prejudices about female nurses, these were offset by accolades from the returning veterans. (Culpepper and Adams 1988, 984)

> Challenges came in many forms, including a lack of acceptance, impossible sanitary conditions, supply shortages, and a general lack of training. Each difficulty produced changes and advances in the nursing field that would affect all future generations of nurses. The methods perfected and the challenges met by these pioneering nurses would set a standard of advancement and excellence in the field beyond anyone's imagining (Purcell 2000, 18).

> The Civil War revolutionized nursing care in the United States. For the first time in American history, well-educated, respectable, middle-class women were encouraged to use their knowledge of nursing to care for ill, injured, or infirm military personnel outside their own circle of family and friends. The war generated an increase in the demand for systematic educational programs designed to inculcate in women a knowledge of the principles of nursing care. Women breached the social barriers to practicing nursing in hospitals, never again to be barred from the wards by social conventions. They won the grudging respect of surgeons and were often idolized by their patients. Many of the women became regional heroines, and a few became national legends. (Rogge 1987, 26)

The nineteenth century also provided examples within the Latter-day Saint community of the caring and sacrifice typical of pre-professional nursing. These examples are accompanied by faith in the power and will of our Heavenly Father to bless His children. One example is that of Amanda Smith at Haun's Mill, Caldwell County, Missouri, on October 30, 1838, and is best told in her own words:

> I suddenly saw the mob coming. . . . I seized my two little girls and escaped across the millpond on a slab-walk. . . . Yet though we were women, with tender children, in flight for our lives, the demons poured volley after volley to kill us. . . . When the firing had ceased I went back to the scene of the massacre, for there were husband and three sons, of whose fate I as yet knew nothing. . . . Passing on I came to a scene more terrible still to the mother and wife. Emerging from the blacksmith shop was Willard, [Amanda's son] bearing on his shoulders his little brother Alma.
>
> "Oh, my Alma is dead!" I cried, in anguish.
>
> "No, mother; I think Alma is not dead. But Father and brother Sardius are killed!"
>
> . . . The entire hip joint of my wounded boy [Alma] had been shot away. Flesh, hip bone, joint and all had been ploughed out from the muzzle of the gun which the ruffian placed to the child's hip through the logs of the shop and deliberately fired. The bones that remained were three or four inches apart.

> We laid little Alma on a bed in our tent and I examined the wound. It was ghastly sight. I knew not what to do. It was night now. . . . Yet was I there, all that long dreadful night, with my dead and my wounded, and none but God as our physician and help.
>
> "Oh, my Heavenly Father," I cried. "What shall I do? Thou seest my poor wounded boy and knowest my inexperience. Oh Heavenly Father, direct me what to do!"
>
> And then I was directed as by a voice speaking to me. The ashes of our fire was still smoldering. We had been burning the bark of the shag-bark hickory. I was directed to take those ashes and make a lye and put a cloth saturated with it right into the wound. It hurt, but little Alma was too near dead to heed it much. Again and again I saturated the cloth and put it into the hole from which the hip joint had been ploughed, and each time mashed flesh and splinters of bone came away with the cloth; and the wound became as white as chicken's flesh.
>
> Having done as directed I again prayed to the Lord and was again instructed as distinctly as though a physician had been standing by speaking to me. Nearby was a slippery-elm tree. From this I was told to make a slippery-elm poultice and fill the wound with it. . . . I made the poultice, and the wound . . . was properly dressed. . . .
>
> I removed the wounded boy to the house of Brother David Evans, two miles away, the next day, and dressed his hip; the Lord directing me as before. I was reminded that in my husband's trunk there was a bottle of balsam. This I poured into the wound, greatly soothing Alma's pain.
>
> "Alma, my child," I said, "you believe that the Lord made your hip?"
>
> "Yes, Mother."
>
> "Well, the Lord can make something there in the place of your hip. Don't you believe that he can, Alma?"
>
> "Do you think that the Lord can, Mother?" inquired the child, in his simplicity.
>
> "Yes, my son," I replied, "he has shown it all to me in a vision."
>
> Then I laid him comfortably on his face and said, "Now you lay like that, and don't move, and the Lord will make you another hip."
>
> So Alma laid on his face for five weeks, until he was entirely recovered—a flexible gristle having grown in place of the missing joint and socket, which remains to this day a marvel to physicians.
>
> On the day that he walked again I was out of the house fetching a bucket of water, when I heard screams from the children. Running back, in affright, I entered, and there was Alma on the floor, dancing around, and the children screaming in astonishment and joy. (Hodson 1996, 78–84)

Another example of caring in early Latter-day Saint history is the brief account of care provided to Joseph Smith after a mob had tarred and feathered him at the John Johnson farm on March 24, 1832. The mobbers dragged him out of the house, tore off his clothes, scratched his body with bare fingernails, and covered him with hot tar and feathers. Unsuccessful attempts were made to pour tar into his mouth and to poison him. Joseph reported, "My friends spent the night in scraping and removing the tar, and washing and cleansing my body; so that by morning I was ready to be clothed again" (Smith 1980, 264). Though Joseph reported this care in the few words characteristic of many plainspoken frontiersmen, the act itself was probably not small. It took all night and required that cooled tar imbedded with feathers be stripped from skin that had been burned and scratched.

Sorensen, in her work on Mormon nursing, notes, "The unquestioned origin of professional nursing among the Latter-day Saints is found in the sisterly acts of pioneer midwives. In Nauvoo, midwives Patty Sessions, Vienna Jacques, and Ann Carling had been set apart by the Prophet Joseph Smith to care for the women of the Church. The work of the midwives continued in the Salt Lake Valley, as they combined faith with practical skills, offering spiritual gifts with physical comfort" (1998, 53). Sorensen continues with a concise summary of pre-professional nursing among Mormon women:

> Social and philosophical upheaval also profoundly affected the daily lives of turn-of-the-century Mormon women. Women had walked

> beside male priesthood leaders through the years of forced emigration, from Ohio to Missouri, Missouri to Illinois, and from Illinois across the country to the Salt Lake Valley. All the while, they re-established homes, cared for the sick, delivered infants, reared children, anointed and buried the dead, and provided for entire households while men were away as scouts, soldiers, missionaries, or polygamist fugitives. Such adversity and responsibility, as well as the pervading characteristic of daily life of essentially separate cultures for men and women, promoted a fierce independence and leadership among Mormon women. Devoted to their faith, their families, and to the success of the Church, women exhibited a social and political progressiveness unique in their history and contrary to their public image. (1998, 55)

ABOUT THIS STUDY

Firsthand accounts appear alphabetically by the nurses' last names. Several common themes emerged as the nurses discussed both their professional and personal experiences. The main theme was "We did what we had to do." Nurses demonstrated strength and courage associated with their spiritual lifestyle. This is perhaps best exemplified in the words of an army nurse serving during World War II spoken with pride: "We had chosen a profession that required our best in brain and brawn." Even fledgling nurses had a sense of mission and purpose, as one stated: "The work and studies were demanding. Our work gave us a warm feeling of helping the war effort. To this day I do not know how we had the strength to do what we did. We gave such support to each other. Being a nurse called for such sacrifice that only the finest type of woman could fulfill."

Professional themes included short staffing, long hours, and insufficient supplies calling for creativity and ingenuity in clinical practice, even for the cadet nurses. One cadet nurse whose brother died landing in Okinawa, wrote in June 1944: "Very few graduate nurses worked in the hospital at this time. Our head nurses, supervisors, and instructors were graduates. The main work force were student nurses in various stages of training. We had excellent and difficult experiences. We worked hard, we became efficient, and grew in responsibility."

Another cadet nurse wrote about the relative lack of effective medications and equipment even stateside during World War II: "They did not have antibiotics when I was a student. Sulfa came in about the time I graduated. Many people died of pneumonia, which was one of the major killers. There were no respirators or anything of that sort. There was none of the wonderful equipment we take for granted today. The IVs and blood transfusions were nothing like they are today. We used very primitive homemade gastric-suctioning machines. For incubators for premature babies, we had a box with a light bulb in it."

Nurses treated victims of shock and trauma, as many of them practiced before the establishment of critical care units in the 1960s. They cared for patients with post traumatic stress syndrome, which was not identified as an official diagnosis until after the Vietnam War. They cared for patients with unusual diseases not typically seen in clinical practice, including jungle rot and other skin conditions typical in the Pacific theater in World War II. Sometimes they were in situations where they were required to provide care that was beyond their scope of practice under very difficult circumstances. Often they had profound emotional experiences. Speaking about receiving 1,062 former prisoners of war at the end of the Pacific conflict in World War II, a navy nurse said: "Soon our patients began arriving, many emaciated and weak, some limping or using crutches. Our few corpsmen hurried up the road with stretchers and carried back the weakest ones. In the meantime, we nurses were assigned patients as they arrived, making sure that they each had a thorough sponge bath and clean pajamas. Then they were promptly transported to the ship (USS *Consolation*) and admitted to the hospital. Many of the former prisoners were American, but some were British, Australian, or from countries where I couldn't understand their language.

But sign language was adequate; smiles and happy gestures let us know that they were just as thankful to be rescued as the ones who tried to express their feelings in words or who quietly shed a few tears."

An army nurse in the European theater during World War II wrote about her typical working day: "Wounded soldiers were admitted by ambulance. My duties were to clean wounds, change dressings, send patients to shower, and then check them for further wounds. That meant seventy-two hours of straight duty that night and the next couple of days until we were exhausted. We worked twelve-hour shifts steady from that time on, until the end of the war [fourteen months later]."

Personal themes included fear of the unknown, a sense of uncertainty, loneliness, ambivalence about military conflict, a sense of appreciation and love for home and country, and concerns for family at home. One nurse wrote: "There were many nights in the Arabian Peninsula when loneliness and missing your family set in, and to me that is the worst feeling that anyone could experience. As Mother Teresa has said, 'Loneliness and to be unwanted is the greatest poverty.' I couldn't agree more."

The German nurse whose comment follows was only seventeen when she was pressed into service as a Red Cross nurse caring for the wounded and dying on the Russian front. Frightened and alone, she expressed the deep uncertainty she felt: "I never would have imagined that while I was on the Russian front, that my life would have taken me where it has. I thought I was definitely going to die. It was to a point that I had given up. There was really nothing whatsoever left for me."

Some study participants made meaning of their war time experiences, and described the lessons learned that profoundly affected their lives. These included living fully in the present, reevaluating priorities, cherishing freedom, valuing home and family, and having faith and trust in God. These were the values they held fast to and which sustained them in difficult times. One perioperative nurse in Operation Desert Storm, who left a wife and four young children, including a newborn, at home, identified the importance of living fully in the present: "Being given four days to get our lives in order was not a lot of time. The lessons learned were that one never knows what tomorrow will bring. Life is fragile, and we should live today as though it might be our last."

Another spoke of reevaluating priorities: "I promised myself that if I made it out of this conflict, if I ever had to choose between time and money, I would always choose time to be with my family and those I love."

For the most part, study participants were very patriotic and spoke of cherishing freedom, even in those instances where they had conflicting feelings about going to war: "We should cherish freedom, and hold it so close and dear to our hearts that we would be willing to give our lives to protect the freedoms our country is based on." Another wrote, "Ever since the day I returned home, I cannot see a flag or hear the "Star-Spangled Banner" without privately coming to attention and paying respect for the symbol that flag represents."

Valuing home and family was a pervasive theme found in the interviews and in the letters written home: "I left my family not knowing if I was going to return. My only prayer the whole time that I was gone, was not that I would be protected, but that my [family] would be well cared for in my absence. . . . My wife said that there was a shield, a protection over our home at all times. That meant a lot to me."

These nurses espoused a spiritual lifestyle, and this was a common thread throughout the interviews. They found strength in their relationship with a higher power and made meaning of their experiences because of their religious beliefs: "We may find times in our lives when we are totally helpless. No matter how much control we think we have over our lives, we must always remember that we have to have faith and trust in God. We are dependent on Him."

A navy nurse who served in World War II in the Pacific theater reflected on her experiences: "You are so aware of the Supreme Power that controls all. I know that God has been good to us for preserving us. There is joy in living—being aware that you are very much alive."

On November 11, 2004, Veterans Day, a note dedicated to nurses was left at the Vietnam Wall. It read, "I don't remember your name, but thanks for saving my life." This indication of how much the quiet, unsung, heroic services of a nurse meant to this veteran is inspiring. These men and women whose stories are chronicled in this text have made a difference in the lives of countless military personnel—and though they may not remember their names, they remember the quiet presence and dedicated and competent care they received from a nurse.

—World War I—

THE TWENTIETH CENTURY was a time of great conflict during which the United States fought in six major military operations: the Spanish-American War, World War I, World War II, the Korean War, the Vietnam War, and Operation Desert Storm (the First Gulf War). In World Wars I and II, as in the Crimean War and the U.S. Civil War, there were more deaths from disease than from combat wounds.

HISTORICAL BACKGROUND

Even before the United States entered World War I, the Red Cross recruited nurses and sent them to the battlefront (Baer 1987). Then, when the United States entered the war, the surgeon general charged the American Red Cross to recruit nurses to serve American troops in France. Their motto was "American Nurses for American Men." In spring 1918 the Red Cross was charged to recruit eight thousand nurses for service to American soldiers. These nurses were outfitted by the Red Cross in uniforms that came to be a familiar image, complete with the Red Cross cape with red lining. These nurses were often housed in Red Cross facilities and supported overseas by the Red Cross (Bledsoe 1997).

Another route was to apply directly to the Army Nurse Corps. Sarnecky notes, "From July to November of 1918, 9,200 new Army nurses joined the corps, another 4,700 transferred overseas, and approximately 1,500 arrived at the Port of Embarkation waiting for transportation" (1999, 92). The army and Red Cross shared responsibilities for care throughout the theaters of operation (Sarnecky 1999, 99).

In 1916 the army and Red Cross collaborated to form fifty base-hospital units. Their staffs were drawn from the large hospital staffs of established civilian universities such as Princeton, Yale, and Harvard. It was felt that units formed in such a manner would have an inherent sense of staff cohesion combined with advanced professional training. This would lead to quicker mobilization and more efficient medical service (Sarnecky 1999, 80–81).

Travel was by train and troopship. There were two million American soldiers in Europe at the end of World War I and twenty thousand Red Cross nurses who joined the Army Reserve to care for the 230,000 wounded Americans (Bledsoe 1997). One hundred ninety-eight nurses died in World War I, many from disease rather than combat-related conditions (Beeber 1996).

The conditions under which nurses worked in the field during World War I were terrible. Hoskins describes battlefront conditions for British soldiers during the Battle of the Somme:

> They took the wounded soldiers to the regimental first-aid post, which was situated about 100 yards behind the trenches. The regimental medical officer then performed the first triage by separating the walking wounded . . . from the severely wounded. . . . The seriously injured were moved on to dressing stations run by the RAMC field ambulance. . . . Here a second triage of the wounded took place, which included the provision of rudimentary first aid, such as antitetanus jabs and the application of field dressings. Very severely wounded soldiers were separated to one side and left to die.
>
> On the first day of the Battle of the Somme, the bodies were piled high in rows as the true extent of the tragedy unfolded. . . . The full complement of nursing staff, which covered several tents, usually consisted of a sister, a staff nurse and two Voluntary Aid Detachments (VADs), which was grossly inadequate for the task in hand. . . .
>
> Surgeons worked on five or six operations simultaneously, and nurses found themselves participating in procedures they were not qualified to carry out, such as the administration of anaesthesia and the closing-off of amputated limbs.
>
> The only analgesia that could be offered to quieten the cries of the wounded was aspirin or morphine. There were no antibiotics to administer prophylactically to prevent gas gangrene, which subsequently accounted for 80% of arm and leg wounds resulting in amputations. (1998, 15)

Instead, nurses continually carried out irrigation of septic wounds in an attempt to prevent gas gangrene, which in the early stages of the war killed as many British soldiers as the bullets themselves. Millard describes the horror of caring for patients who had been exposed to mustard gas:

> Mustard gas produced profound burns and lung damage. Gas cases are terrible. They cannot breathe lying down or sitting up. They just struggle for breath but nothing can be done . . . their lungs are gone . . . literally burnt out . . . some with their eyes and faces entirely eaten away by the gas, and bodies covered with first degree burns. We try to relieve them by pouring oil on them. They cannot be bandaged or even touched. . . . One boy, today, screaming to die. The entire top layer of skin burned from his face and body. I gave him an injection of morphine . . . he was wheeled out just before I came off duty. (Quoted in Beeber 1996, 24)

Long hours, the short staff, and the multiplicity of terrible wounds had their effect on nurses. "As L. Herrick, RN, who had served in Contrexieville, France, put it . . . 'the experience made me different from nurses, and from other women I knew . . . so different that when I returned, for a long time I felt lost—I didn't fit in anymore'" (Beeber, 23).

Letters home from France during World War I expressed love for home, country, and the American soldiers who were fighting in the war.

> The letters reflected the themes of love of country and of the American "boys" who were protecting that country. The nurses projected this sentiment as their reason for being in whatever camp or hospital they served: "What a great privilege it is to be here and take care of our dear American boys"; "our boys deserve everything that can be given them, they are so unselfish always thinking of the boys they left behind and they are the bravest things . . . they have the spirit of 1776 born right in them"; "we can never understand or appreciate what our men, or the men of any other country really undertakes when they are called to arms, until we really live in the camps and know their privations" (Baer 1987, 23).

Letters to St. Vincent's Hospital in New York City refer to the many nonmilitary conditions affecting the troops and the nurses. The military had no experience with housing or caring for large numbers of people. The men lived in open tents. Fire was a constant threat and often destroyed hospital and troop property. The troops were exposed to such diseases as measles, with its associated pneumonia, mumps, scarlet fever, and influenza, and the flu pandemic of 1917.

Many nurses were required to stay in the United States to care for men here, thus making it possible for other nurses to go to the front and for more troops to be shipped overseas. One nurse wrote, "There are some among us who, perhaps, will never experience the excitement of life near the 'front' but will remain quietly behind somewhere and accept whatever of duty that comes our way" (Baer 1987, 19).

Accounts of Agnes Climie's war experience in France were much different in her journal than in her letters home. The letters did not describe the terrible rations and living conditions, the frequent air raids, or the sorry state of the soldiers brought into the hospital from the front. The journal notes that water was carried in buckets, that there was no way to boil water to sterilize it, and that wounds were dressed in cold carbolic lotion and unsterilized gauze and wool.

The actions of nurses during World War I had an impact on the passage of women's suffrage in 1918 and the passage of the British Nurses Registration Act in 1919 (Lorenzton 1995, 28).

Only one account of a Latter-day Saint nurse who served during World War I is currently available to this project. The following experience was contributed by the nurse's family.

Dora Maiben

Dora was always interested in caring and healing. In May 1906, at age nineteen, she entered training at LDS Hospital in Salt Lake City, Utah. Students were paid ten dollars a month for the three-month nursing course.

During World War I, the Red Cross was in desperate need of trained nurses. Dora spent one year at Fort Bliss and Fort Sam Houston in Texas as a Red Cross nurse. As the war was drawing to a close, Dora's group was sent to Europe.

Dora was assigned to Mobile Unit Two, stationed in France. Dora belonged to the Princeton Unit. After arriving at the front, the units would leapfrog each other in truck convoys. As a unit arrived to a new location on the front, they would first evacuate the wounded who could be moved and then set up hospital tents and equipment for the next group to care for the immobile.

Amid the blood and tumult of the fighting of the Argonne Forest (September–November 1918), one of Dora's tasks was to determine which of the wounded had a chance of being saved if quickly transferred by ambulance to a field hospital and which had little or no chance.

After the war ended on November 11, 1918, Dora was transferred to Koblenz, Germany. She worked at Medical Occupation Hospital 29, caring for the American occupation forces from December 1918 until August 1919. Dora gained a reputation among the soldiers for being very matter-of-fact as to what was expected of them. As she approached one of the wards, she heard the hushed warning going around, "Better get back to bed. Here comes Reddy."

Dora was then sent to the Balkans, specifically Serbia near the Turkish border. She worked in a Red Cross school and children's clinic. An epidemic of childhood diseases broke out. In a cart pulled by a donkey, Dora would travel to the outlying rural areas to treat the children. It was in Salonka, Montenegro, that Dora felt she did the most good. The orphanage there was in terrible shape. The children were covered with sores and scabs on their scalps and skin. Dora found that even a simple gift to a child went a long way. To one little girl, Dora gave a set of underclothes. The little girl was so proud that she wore them over her other clothing for all to admire. On occasions when Dora would stay at a private home while traveling, the locals were so interested in this western woman that they observed and examined everything, from her actions to her clothing. The local people seemed very grateful for the healthcare provided. Children often ran ahead of the nurses, calling, "Merican Nursee." The occupation forces also set up soup kitchens for the locals, providing cereal and hot cocoa. The empty milk cans from the States were saved to make cups for the people.

Dora returned to the United States and worked at the Salt Lake City, Utah, Board of Health. Until her retirement at age sixty-five, Dora spent many years as a school health nurse and was remembered for her tireless efforts and concern for the health and well-being of others. Dora passed away on March 11, 1978, at the age of ninety-one.

— World War II —

In September 1939, Germany invaded Poland. By 1941 Czechoslovakia, Norway, Denmark, Belgium, Holland, and France had been invaded by Hitler, and Great Britain was being attacked. The United States entered World War II on December 8, 1941, on the side of the Allies, after Japan bombed Pearl Harbor on December 7. The United States, Great Britain, and France became the Allied Powers, fighting Germany initially and then the Axis Powers of Germany, Italy, and Japan.

HISTORICAL BACKGROUND

In 1940 the American Red Cross organized hospital units to aid Britain and collect information about the effects of disasters such as epidemics, floods, and crowded living conditions. The Harvard Unit was one of these (Fosburgh, 1995). Units were constructed of tents, and the Red Cross took everything necessary to erect, equip, and supply the hospitals for patient care. Gertrude Madley recalled, "We had twenty-two [tents]; ten for patients, one administration, one laboratory, one kitchen and dining room, one laundry, one storeroom, one recreation, and six for living quarters" (Fosburgh 1995, 501). All of the equipment was transported on British ships. American ships could not land at British ports since America was not yet at war. Sometimes the supplies arrived in an organized fashion, and other times they were destroyed upon arrival by German air attacks, or they arrived too late to be of much use. However, the concept of a mobile tent hospital, fully staffed and supplied, continued throughout the conflicts of the twentieth century and into the twenty-first century.

Crossing the ocean in a convoy brought the risk of being sunk by German submarines. The Harvard Unit had two ships destroyed in transit. Twenty-seven nurses were aboard those two ships. A tanker picked up nine nurses, and six other nurses were taken to Iceland. Four more nurses landed in Iceland after spending twelve days in an open boat. These nurses were so ill from frostbite and exposure that they returned to the United States. Four more nurses landed in Ireland after spending nineteen days in an open boat, and two died from the effects of exposure. The two who survived served another year with the Harvard unit. The four remaining nurses were never heard from after their ship sank.

Madley also described the conditions in Britain after their arrival. There was destruction everywhere. The British people bounced back from every attack, carrying on with their lives amidst the physical destruction and emotional trauma. Madley commented on the blessing of being an American: "How fortunate we are that we are privileged to live in a country like America, and how many of us offer up our thanks in prayer. The things we see in the movies and read about in the newspapers, and hear about over the radio, are actually happening over there. Do we ever try in imagination to live that thing through?" (Fosburgh 1995, 504).

Even though the United States did not enter the war until December 1941, nursing shortages had already become apparent by August of that year (Fosburgh 1995). The shortages became problems for both military and civilian institutions and were an impetus to shorten the education and training period of nurses. Fosburgh notes, "United States nurse anesthetists sought to deal with possible manpower shortages concerning military and civilian service as the threat of war mounted. Proper education and adequate facilities for a full education in nurse anesthesia became a legitimate concern to the profession. Furthermore, American Association of Nurse Anesthetists (AANA) leaders sought to gain military recognition of nurse anesthesia being a clinical specialty within nursing, and allow nurse anesthetists to make the most efficient use of the training" (1995, 387).

World War II was the first time in history that a real attempt was made to salvage the critically wounded from the battlefield (Breakiron 1995). Efforts were made to get medical care to the front for immediate stabilization of the wounded before transfer to a stationary hospital. For the first time, nurses were given commissions as officers and salaries of $70 a month. Under the direction of Major Luther H. Wolff, field hospitals also kept extensive records of the work they performed:

> Dr. Wolff wrote often in his WWII diary about how poor the care of the wounded was until nurses arrived. Because of legal restrictions during most of the war, nurses were the only military females allowed to serve outside the continental United States. At their peak, the Army and Navy Nurse Corps had nearly 69,000 recruits. These nurses served at nine stations in 52 areas scattered across 50 nations. Navy nurses served on 12 hospital ships and in more than 300 naval stations. By the time the law was amended in 1944, the first Women's Army and Navy nurses already had seen action on the Philippine Islands of Bataan and Corrigador. Nurses also had waded ashore with the field and evacuation hospitals on the Anzio, Italy, beachhead four days after the invasion of Normandy, France. (Breakiron 1995, 713)

Breakiron noted that these nurses dealt with many difficulties, including filthy facilities that needed to be cleaned with soap and water, water carried in combat helmets, limited supplies or supplies that never arrived, the cleaning and repair of old equipment, the washing and boiling of surgical instruments, and the long hours. They struggled to provide adequate hygiene for themselves and their patients. However, they were instrumental in some innovations. They worked for the first time with antibiotics, principally penicillin and sulfa. They developed the first recovery room close to the operating room to decrease the amount of time and number of nurses it took to help patients recover in the wards. Nurses became autonomous in making routine, emergency decisions and in giving ether-type anesthesia because physicians were either in short supply or working in the operating room. Nurses who were in dangerous situations learned to use weapons to protect themselves and their patients.

Breakiron notes:

> More than 217 Army nurses are buried in U.S. cemeteries overseas. More than 1,600 nurses were decorated for meritorious service and bravery under fire. . . . Twenty-one Army nurses escaped the Philippine Island of Corrigador before it fell to the Japanese, but 11 Navy nurses and 66 Army nurses became prisoners of the Japanese and were interned in the Santo Tomas prison, Manila, Philippines, for 37 months. Thirteen flight nurses crash-landed behind German lines in Albania and were lost for four months before they managed to find their way out. Some nurses were killed instantly when their hospitals sustained direct hits from enemy artillery. Six nurses were killed on the Anzio beach when their hospital was bombed. They lie buried with infantrymen, tank drivers, artillery men, and others in the American cemetery on the Anzio beach.
>
> Some nurses went down with their patients on hospital ships hit by torpedoes. On the night of April 28, 1945, the hospital ship *Comfort* had all her lights burning and her great red cross showing clearly, according to the rules of the Geneva Convention. The ORs were crowded with wounded. The *Comfort* carried no guns, so it was helpless when a Japanese kamikaze pilot circled above and plunged into the ship's superstructure. It tore into the OR and exploded. Six OR nurses were killed, and four were seriously wounded. Those nurses who were still standing continued to work. (1995, 718)

Norman wrote about the seventy-seven nurses who became prisoners of war in the Philippine Islands when the Japanese invaded the islands in 1942 (1999, xii). Norman and Eifried described the fear, deprivation, creativity, and resourcefulness experienced by the group of nurses in order for them to survive their experience and to care for patients. "They endured because they possessed two fundamental virtues. They had each other and they remained faithful to their mission as nurses" (1995, 105).

World War II was the first time American women worked as military flight nurses (Barger 1991). They described the terrible living conditions, the poor food, and the lack of bathroom facilities for women, either on base or at plane stops. They talked about the snakes, lizards, and insects that plagued their lives. They commented on their experiences of trying to stabilize patients and keep them alive while in flight until they could get medical assistance. "Pilots, for example, would land at the nearest base having a medical facility if such a request was made by the flight nurse to save the life of a patient. . . . Concern for their own safety was seldom mentioned by the flight nurses; rather, the safety of their patients was the flight nurses' primary concern" (Barger 1991, 155). They discussed their own conflict with such issues as whether it was morally correct to drop the atomic bomb on Japan or whether they should save themselves before they saved the patients if there was an emergency landing at sea. Flight nurses commented on the vulnerability they felt while at war. They realized they could die or be wounded. "Writing letters to the deceased flight nurse's family and arranging for the notification of parents and the disposition of belongings in the event of death reflected problem-focused coping" (Barger 1991, 156).

Flight nurses used techniques common to other military nurses to deal with their own particular situations. Social support was very important, especially among POW nurses. Health and youthful energy were important resources. Diet, rest, and relaxation when possible were important coping strategies. These nurses learned to be creative and flexible in administering patient care as well as in meeting their own personal needs. Flight nurses were noted for their devotion to country, patients, and each other, as well as for their ability to take care of themselves, to be responsible, to meet expectations, and to endure hardships that nonmilitary nurses would probably never experience.

In November 1943, flight nurse training was changed from six to eight weeks and included curriculum in emergency medical treatment, transporting patients at high altitudes, the use of oxygen on board the plane, antibiotic and blood therapy, ditching procedures, and survival. This training acknowledged the ability and autonomy of nurses to manage treatment of patients on board the plane.

> A public relations document contained in the news film archives explained that during flights a nurse may have to apply splints, administer medications, stop a sudden hemorrhage, treat shock, administer oxygen, or handle any other emergency. The document claimed that "The flight nurse can do anything an MD can do except operate." . . . Nurses increased the caliber of care aboard a plane and contributed mightily to the morale of patients who often were airborne for the first time: "The presence of the nurse quieted their fears." (Stevens, 97)

Some nurses served on active duty in more than one war—sometimes in as many as three different conflicts. Their stories will be presented in the section representing the first conflict in which they served.

Wylma Jane Callahan Ade

Wylma Jane Callahan Ade

I was born in Davenport, Iowa, on March 10, 1920. During World War II, my mother had a flag in her window with three stars on it for the three children [two sons and one daughter] she had in the army. The Gold Star mothers had a gold star for their children that were lost in the service. They started taking some women in the military after I left for the service, but up until that time the only women in the military were nurses.

In 1941 I was at a Children's Memorial Hospital in Chicago on a pediatric affiliation when the bomb was dropped on Pearl Harbor. I was a senior. My main thought was that the war would be over before I could have the chance to go into the army. I think how different that is from the people now. But there is a little renewed interest in the military and public service since September 2001.

When I was in school, the pay for registered nurses was $70 a month, but when I graduated it was increased to $90 a month because by September of 1942 the older nurses were already leaving, and they were having trouble staffing the hospital. When I went in the army as second lieutenant, the pay was $150 a month. That was a lot of money then.

I graduated in 1942 and at that time the war was in full speed, so we only had to take state boards for one day because they wanted to hurry getting us registered. I had already signed up to go in the 31st General Hospital in Denver, Colorado. Because I was affiliated with that hospital, I knew I would eventually be going overseas. However, my first duty was at Fort Leonard Wood in Missouri. It was an engineering camp not too far from St. Louis, Missouri. I was at Fort Leonard Wood for several months. There we did calisthenics, marched, and all the military things, including taking caring of patients in the hospital. The military was getting us ready to go overseas. We did an obstacle course where we had to crawl under barbed wire while machine guns were firing over our heads. I guess they were a safe distance over our head. I was young, but many of the nurses working in the hospital were quite a bit older than I was, and they had to do everything that we had to do. It was hard for the older women.

The medications were very different from what they are today. APCs were the drug of choice. Everybody got it no matter what was wrong. The APCs were aspirin, phenacetin, and caffeine, kind of like Empirin now. We had aspirin and soda: you would give a 5-grain aspirin and 5-grain soda tablets. Sulfa was just being developed in the late 1930s. Germany was where Prontosil and Neoprontisol were really developed, and they were miracle drugs at the time. They were a sulfa-type drug. They were the first things we had to fight infections. Morphine was the drug for pain besides aspirin. We boiled water in little teaspoons and dissolved the morphine tablets and drew it up in our syringes. We probably used codeine for milder pain.

In 1942 penicillin was being developed, but it was a long time before they had the long-acting type. We had to administer it every two or three hours and it was a big job to keep giving penicillin around the clock. There was a lot of gonorrhea with the soldiers, and penicillin proved to be effective in treating it.

After we left Fort Leonard Wood, we went to Camp Carson in Colorado, and that was when the 31st General Hospital was organized. Of course at this time the war was escalating, and we were looking forward to getting on with our duty. When we left Camp Carson, we were up all night at Camp Stoneman in California, where we were issued wool clothes. I am sure that the army knew we were going to the South Pacific, but they issued us all the army wool clothing to take to the South Pacific, where it just mildewed and most was just thrown away because it was useless. My friends who were nurses in France were freezing to death. I have heard many of them talk about how they were so cold and they didn't have anything warm to wear.

After being up all night, we got aboard our ship, the *Klipfontein*, which was a Dutch ship still on its maiden voyage. It was a luxurious ship. We went down to San Diego and picked up about 2,500 marines. The crew on the ship was trained to take care of the people who would ordinarily be traveling on a luxury ship. The dining room had all silver service. It was quite elegant. In the morning they would put out hard rolls and meat and cheese so that we could fix a sandwich. We only had two meals a day, so at lunch we would have tea or hot chocolate and maybe a soup and the sandwiches we had made earlier. In the evening it really was almost a formal dining room. We heard later that the ship never made it home. It was sunk before ever reaching Holland again.

Our destination was Noumea, New Caledonia. Our first area was a beautiful French town named Bougeanvillea; the whole island was covered with red and purple flowers. There was a big navy base there. We were stationed at a little hospital about ninety miles north of Noumea. We were only there for a short time for temporary duty.

We were then sent to the New Hebrides on the island of Espiritu Santo. That was where we were for the next couple of years. We had a big general hospital: one thousand patients the first day. All the islands in the Pacific had many fierce battles going on, like Guadalcanal and Saipan. Those casualties were sent back to our hospital. We had a large group, a large hospital, and we had all the services. There were probably 100 to 130 nurses in my group; we had physical therapists, x-ray technicians, and five Red Cross workers. There were only female nurses in my unit, and our unit was also all white. We had to censor the mail of the enlisted personnel. I don't think the officers' mail was censored. Much of our mail was the one-page V-Mail; it was not so bulky. The five Red Cross workers who were assigned to our unit were friends and all lived together; they would take care of the patients' other needs, such as writing letters to their families, and other things. It was a one-thousand-bed hospital. Some of our doctors were young, and others were experienced surgeons and orthopedic doctors. Our hospital was filled the first day it opened.

We had all kinds of bad injuries. I remember a few of them specifically and how hard we would work to get them stabilized so that they could go home. Later we would find out that they died on the way home. We felt bad about that because we gave them everything that we could to keep them going. We worked long hours. It was like all nursing: you worked until the work was done. We all had to take turns doing night duty. We still didn't have many drugs. We still gave the penicillin around the clock. We had the sulfa drugs too. We were able to take care of some infections that we would not have been able to earlier on.

When I was in my school of nursing, there were no aides or corpsmen to help us. The student nurses did everything; we cleaned the bedpans and took the flowers out at night to water them. Nursing was completely different then from what it is now. In the army we did have corpsmen and we had a very good relationship with them. They were good, dedicated men working to help us. Some of the patients were in critical condition. We did work hard on some of them just to get them stabilized because we were a long way from home. Down in the South Pacific it was probably a two- to three-week trip to get back to the States.

We had a lot of orthopedics and gunshot wounds. Some were self-inflicted because they wanted to go home. They probably had good reason to want to go home. The islands were not that pleasant. It was hot and sweaty, and the food was not very good. Wherever they were, it was grim. It was so different invading those islands than the hand-to-hand combat that you usually think about in war. They had to go island by island and take each one separately.

One of my most memorable patients was a fellow named Updike. He was seriously injured. He was there a long time before we got him stabilized and ready to go home. As far as I know he made it home. It was hard to get information back because there were so many ships taking people back and forth that it was just a fluke if you heard from anybody. In Espiritu Santo we worked just like we would in the States and did everything that we could for the patients. I don't remember ever having a shortage of medications or dressings. It seems like we had everything that we needed.

The military would fly in the wounded, but most of them came by ship. There was a big harbor and a navy base. Whenever we wanted a good meal, we would go out with someone in the navy because they always had better food. I didn't drink milk, I didn't eat eggs, and I didn't like beer, so it wasn't a hardship to me as far as food was concerned in the army. We had raisin bread once a week, and one of my friends would pick the raisins out of mine because I don't like raisins.

In Espiritu Santo there were no Anopheles mosquitoes, so we didn't have to take Atabrine as a malaria preventative. Many of the other nurses on the other islands had to take Atabrine, and it turned their skin yellow. We did have a mosquito net, and there were mosquitoes, just not Anopheles mosquitoes.

We had a limited knowledge of how the war was progressing. We were in radio contact, so we knew what was generally going on in the different battles. After being on Espiritu Santo in 1943 and 1944, we were transferred to Hollandia, New Guinea, for several months. Hollandia was where General MacArthur had his big home on a high peak so he could look out on the ocean. When we were in Hollandia, New Guinea, there were some navy and marine officers there who were sure the war was going to be over soon. I think they knew something about the atomic bomb. I think they knew there was something special in the works because they wanted to bet us that the war was going to be over soon. We were just as sure that it wasn't going to be.

After we were in Hollandia about three months, we were sent to Luzon, Philippines. There were still some of the Japanese army fighting in the hills around us while we were there, and it was considered an active war zone. That was where the Japanese came in when they invaded the Philippines and continued on to Manila, Bataan, and Corregidor. The Japanese occupation lasted until the early part of 1945.

The war just seemed to get progressively worse as we moved on. The first time that we heard about V-E Day (May 7, 1945) was around Mother's Day. We were happy that the war was over in Europe. I was in the Philippines on V-J Day (September 2, 1945). Every morning songs that were popular in the States, like "Sentimental Journey," were played over the loudspeaker. Then we heard, "Now hear this, now hear this!" and we waited to hear what was going to be announced. I remember when they announced the war was over in Japan. That was a very happy day, but we didn't think that affected us much because we were still busy.

I heard over the loudspeaker that the war was over, and then we got a little camp newspaper that was just a one- or two-page sheet. I suppose more information came to us after the first bomb fell. We had been waiting all summer for something to happen. Every day when they alerted us over the loud speaker, we kept thinking that something was going to happen. We were probably getting ready to go home. We had been overseas since 1943, but every day was a busy day just like it was for everybody else. You have certain things you have to do everyday, so you keep going.

I still have a camp newspaper that was published when the war was finally over. It is kind of hard to remember what I heard then about the bomb being dropped and what I have heard since. I picture the big atomic bomb with the big umbrella. I don't remember when we first knew that there was an atomic bomb or of the devastation in Japan. It is only now, sixty years later, that I fully comprehend all the atrocities of that war. As I read about the experiences of the people who were prisoners in the Philippines and how the Japanese people treated them, I really feel we got off pretty easy. I feel sorry for the devastation of the atomic bomb, but I don't think that the people in the United States really comprehended what they were doing to us, even though they saw the things happening at Pearl Harbor. That was terrible, but it was only the beginning. Wherever there were prisoners of the Japanese for the next three years, it was incomprehensible how they were treated.

We were on a hospital ship for a month coming home. Something happened to the ship's rudder, and we were out in the middle of the Pacific Ocean going around in circles until they got it fixed. It was pretty rough coming home. We were mustered out at Fort Sheridan. We got a lot of money because we hadn't been paid for a long time. We left in December, and it was cold. We must have looked like poor people from Europe. We had carried our wool clothes all through the South Pacific, and we didn't have any warm clothes by the time we got home. We had a lot of money in our pockets, but we probably looked pretty sad. I came home on Thanksgiving, and the war was over in August. I was on leave until February, so we were still considered in the army until the middle of February.

My dad was a rural mail carrier, and one of the regrets that I have in my life was that when I came home from the army he wanted me to wear my uniform and go on the mail route with him, and I didn't do it. I was just glad to get out of my uniform. I did go on the mail route with him. He was extremely proud of me. For three years everybody on his mail route had to hear about me. I am sure that everyone on the mail route knew all about his three children who were in the service. It would have given him so much pleasure if I would have worn my uniform so he could show me off, but I didn't do it, and it is too late now.

When I was discharged from the army, they gave me bars to symbolize the medals for which I was qualified. One is from being in the American theater, USAFFE, and the Bronze Star. I will have a Bronze Star on the Philippines victory medal because they were still shooting there. I never picked my medals up because I never thought the medals that go with them were important, but now I want to leave a legacy for my children and grandchildren. I recently wrote to my congressman to get them. Hopefully they will soon be on their way.

Then I got married in 1947 and joined The Church of Jesus Christ of Latter-day Saints in 1952. I was Catholic at the time of the war, and I had the opportunity to go to church. Espiritu Santo was a French island with a French coffee plantation owner, just like in the movie *South Pacific*. There was a little Catholic church that we would go to. I remember hearing that there were Mormon church services on Sunday afternoons at about 3 o'clock. I know there was a nurse and some corpsmen who were Mormon. I know that there were Mormons in my group, and I know that they did meet.

When I was in the Philippines, I didn't drink beer or smoke. I thought I was doing all the work while everyone was outside smoking. I decided to join them. It wasn't easy to start smoking. You choke and cough, and you really have to be determined to abuse yourself like that. My main thought was that I was working the floor while everyone was getting a break. I was never a heavy smoker, but one year at Christmas time I added up all the money I was spending on cigarettes, and it was about a dollar a week, and I thought with that I could buy a package of cookies and the whole family could enjoy a treat. In March 1952 we heard about the Church. If the missionaries would have come around and told me I could not smoke or drink coffee (I had been drinking coffee my whole life), I would never have listened to them. But by then I wasn't smoking. I have always been glad I did quit smoking. It was foolish to ever get started in the first place.

I went to church more while I was in the army than I did growing up. In Espiritu Santo we went to church more than we did other places. When you are working you don't necessarily get every Sunday off to go to church, and I don't remember going to church in the Philippines. I think that I was always fundamentally a good person, but I don't think that I was real religious at all during that time. We never had a lot of religion in our home while I was growing up. After my husband and I got married and joined the Church, it became a big part of our lives. There was not even a Mormon Church in Davenport, Iowa, until after we moved away. I don't know what I would do with my time and money if I wasn't able to serve the Lord.

We were living in Davenport, Iowa, when we joined The Church of Jesus Christ of Latter-day Saints. We started to go to church in March and were baptized in May 1952. I had a strong testimony from the very beginning.

I would like to tell my children and grandchildren that I am happy I had a chance to serve. I never felt like my experiences were more than any ordinary job that anyone else does. I know that when we are helping we are happy. I feel fortunate to do as much as I can do at age eighty-two. I don't know that I have had many trials, and I have been incredibly blessed. I think that I was blessed to recognize the truthfulness of the gospel. I know it has been a blessing to my children and grandchildren.

Laura Ellen Alley

I graduated in June 1944 from LDS Hospital School of Nursing. I enlisted with a friend of mine on March 1, 1945, and was sent to camp at Fort Lewis, Washington. We went up to Fort Lewis, which was absolutely wonderful. We were treated just like the troops. We went out on bivouac, and we were there for a month. We had to do drills, and we had to learn some army law and things like that.

After that thirty days we were sent to Macaw General Hospital in Walla Walla, Washington, where I was assigned to the orthopedic division. At that time we were working twelve-hour shifts for six or sometimes seven days a week. We were short of help. When I was in orthopedics, these kids would come from the front in casts that had never been changed, or with wounds that looked abscessed. They weren't healed when they got to me, but they were in fairly good shape. As soon as they got there, we would cut off the casts and start looking at the wounds, and they were full of maggots. I just nearly died. I will never forget that experience when we cut away the cast. One fellow who had on an airplane splint was the worst. The wounds that I saw with the maggots were clean and not infected. The maggots just happened because of the conditions they were in: the doctors didn't put them there. We cleaned the maggots out of the wound because they were far enough along so that they were doing okay. When I came home and was working at the hospital in Salt Lake, the patients had severe osteomyelitis. The doctors were beginning to use a lot of antibiotics, but they weren't as effective in these kind of cases as maggots.

I worked in the orthopedics division for about a month, and then I was transferred to the paraplegics and quadriplegic wards, where I stayed until I was transferred again. I had a wonderful experience with those boys. Most of them were about nineteen or twenty-year-old boys. We cared for them and tried to get them up into chairs, swimming, and out into the social life.

It was the last of September 1945. I volunteered to go overseas once a month. Finally, as the war tapered down over there, we were sent to Birmingham General Hospital, Van Nuys, California. Macaw was closed at that time because of the war closing up a little. We stayed with those boys, and they made a lot of progress down there. It was really a pretty good experience. By that time we were working eight-hour shifts, which was standard in nursing, but we still sometimes worked six or seven days a week.

In March 1946 they said that they were going to close Birmingham, so I elected to come home.

All of them [the patients] were so young (I was twenty-two). Most of them were my age or younger. We had two or three who were older—in their late twenties. This one fellow was paralyzed from the waist down, but he had a lot of spasms, and he used to bend over into fetal position and couldn't help it. He would cry. So all of us spent a long time trying to help him through this. We had an older man from California who was in his late twenties or early thirties, and he wouldn't let anybody but me shave him because I did such a good job.

We had the old Stryker frames; they were just coming out at the time. You had to be sure that the patients were tied in, and we had to turn them every two hours. We had several patients' legs fall out of the frame when we turned them. Before we used Strykers, we used manpower. We just turned them. I remember when I came home from the service, my sister-in-law Virginia said to me, "My gosh, you have the most wide, powerful upper body that I ever did see." It was from lifting those kids. We had to turn those Stryker frames frequently. We had a young man who came from the Pacific zone and had malaria quite bad. He was on a Stryker frame (he was a paraplegic). When he would begin his chills, a couple of us would have to lie across his body to keep him on top of the frame because he would shake so violently.

Antibiotics were new in nursing—at that time we had just started giving penicillin. We had some sulfa that we used, but the penicillin was the thing. We used to fill a syringe and then just change the needles and give them each 1 cc. Streptomycin, I think, came out at that time too. The Wangensteen suction was improved a little bit at that time. It was the two-bottle stomach suction. The Stryker frames were made wider after the war ended. The care of paraplegics and quadriplegics also improved because caregivers realized that patients needed to be up and more active.

We used to load a government van up with the kids and take them out to the diners. All the restaurants and show places down there catered to these kids and built ramps for their wheelchairs and put them up at the tables. They were very helpful.

There was one paraplegic whose father was very wealthy. This independent young man came down to Birmingham while we were there to demonstrate to the boys what they could do. He had his own car, and he would show them how he could get in and out of his car and show them different techniques he developed to help himself. He got sick with kidney problems while he was there. We kept him for several days until he could move on. He did a lot to show the boys how independent they could become and how to get around much better.

I wasn't aware of any nurses or boys who were LDS. They did have a church and a Protestant chaplain, as I remember. We just all went to the church.

I think my life was different because I served those thirteen months. I got a lot of good nursing experience. I developed a lot more patience and understanding of some of these people who had such terrible wounds and accidents. My skills developed considerably in taking care of post-op patients. I don't think the nurses who didn't serve in the war ever realized the importance of turning patients and making them get up, and making them breathe and all of that. That was one thing we really starting doing with the patients and getting them ambulatory a little bit faster.

I'm glad I stayed in nursing. I haven't been disappointed with any of that.

Alice Lofgren Andrus

Alice Lofgren Andrus

On December 7, 1941, I vividly remember that I was a junior student nurse on duty in an outpatient clinic at the Los Angeles County General Hospital. Sunday was seldom busy, so while we were between patients, several of us were listening to a small radio when we were startled to hear about the tragic attack on Pearl Harbor by the Japanese. As World War II was declared, we knew that all of our lives would be changed.

I received my navy orders to report to the Oak Knoll Naval Hospital at Oakland, California, by May 10, 1944. I reported to the office at Oak Knoll Naval Hospital. I was now officially a navy ensign.

As I remember back over fifty years, within a day or two I was in uniform, taking care of patients in the burn ward while I also learned the navy's way of doing things. Every week or so we were alerted that a convoy of ships from the fighting in the Pacific would soon arrive, bringing new patients.

Many of our patients were undergoing a series of reconstructive plastic surgeries to repair damage done earlier. Ambulatory patients helped us take care of bed patients and admit new patients. Their friendly joking and assistance soon made new patients feel welcome. Some wanted to talk about their experiences, like the barely eighteen-year-old sailor whose oil tanker had gone down with burning oil engulfing everyone trying to escape. The young sailor was severely disfigured by burns on his face, head, arms, and body. Talking about it seemed to be his way of trying to accept the fact that he really was scarred and that nothing would ever again be normal for him. Another patient had only moderate burns, but he had been told that he would never see again. While he was despondent and wanted to be left alone, occasionally other patients quietly made brief visits to his bedside, gradually making him feel one of the group. He was still depressed, but he did not feel alone, as the other patients gave him moral support and understanding.

Another patient had been confined to bed for some weeks. As he began to feel better, he wanted to get up and walk around, but his orders as a bed patient remained. Finally one day, with nearby patients as lookouts, he sneaked into the bathroom and was almost back to his bed when he was seen by a corpsman. When the doctor was told of this adventure, he laughed. When patients are determined enough to sneak out of bed, he explained, they are well on their way to recovery. This improved the morale of the whole ward.

Some of our patients, between operations, were encouraged to get passes and take the bus to Oakland to get used to being among civilians again. Some who had gone once refused to go again. They said that some children and many adults would stare at their scars, crutches, or bandages and whisper, point, and laugh at them. Since they were in uniform, it was obvious that their wounds were a result of the war, but many people reacted in a cruel, unthinking way, ridiculing anyone who looked different in any way.

Once when I was working a late shift, all but one of our patients who had been out on passes were back in bed. Suddenly, the door to our ward was jerked open, and in walked our marine patient. He was tall, strong, good-looking, and a little unsteady on his feet. He was angry and mumbling something I couldn't understand. As he stood in the hall, he suddenly punched a hole in the plasterboard wall. This was entirely out of character, as he was a friendly, good-natured person whom I had never seen angry before. I quickly called the corpsmen, who, with the help of another patient, soon had our marine sleeping peacefully in bed.

In the morning he was embarrassed to see the hole he had made in the wall and explained that he had been out with a buddy who had noticeable scars. They were enjoying a fine evening until several civilians began making crude, ridiculing jokes about them. Since getting into a fight could have caused serious medical problems, especially for his buddy, they controlled their anger and walked away quietly. However, the anger and frustration remained. All of us in the ward understood, and the wall was soon mended without comment.

Many of our patients preferred to remain in the ward or on the base among others in uniform, where they were accepted without question. It was a sanctuary where they felt safe. Planning on moving back into civilian life was traumatic for many, especially for those with extensive scars that could not be corrected, even with skilled plastic surgery. Some of the luckiest patients had families who would occasionally visit them and plan for their homecoming with joy and acceptance, but others just had to hope that their families and friends would not desert them.

I will never forget how the patients on 74 A Burn Ward developed close friendships and acted with compassion and good cheer, even when they felt sad and worried inside. It was a happy ward where I had many friends, and I was content to work. Once I was transferred to a medical ward, but within a few weeks I managed to get transferred back to my favorite ward, 74 A.

During my months at Oak Knoll, I remember that we did have a few drill sessions and even marched in one dress parade on the base.

We also had to pass a swimming test, which was easy for me because I enjoyed swimming. Navy life included lighthearted times too. Being stationed fairly close to San Francisco was an experience most of us enjoyed. When we were off duty, a few of us nurses would put on our dress uniforms and take the local bus to Oakland and then the "A" train to San Francisco. There we would happily spend all day sightseeing, eating at favorite restaurants, shopping, or maybe seeing a movie before starting the long journey back to the base.

We heard that the military needed nurses to sign up for sea duty on a navy hospital ship that would soon be commissioned. As much as I liked working on the Burns and Plastic Surgery Ward, the opportunity to go to sea on a hospital ship seemed irresistible. Very soon my official application was on file in the office, and I was notified that I was accepted and I would receive transfer orders within a few weeks. Many friends, both patients and coworkers, were disappointed that I would be leaving.

One interview that touched me the most was when our top surgeon called me into his office and tried to talk me into changing my mind. He knew that I liked working on the ward, and he sincerely believed that I would be unwise to go into a situation where I might find problems I didn't expect. He had been in the navy for many years and said that women in areas closer to the war were assumed to have loose morals, and he was convinced that I might get a bad reputation, whether or not it was deserved. He assured me that if I had been his daughter, that is the advice he would give me. But I had the self-confidence of youth that I would get along all right. The promise of new adventures was too great to resist, so the surgeon reluctantly agreed to my transfer.

At the airport I was disappointed when someone with a higher priority got the last seat on the last plane departing that day for the East Coast. Since I was suffering from chills and fever, the kind people at the airport arranged for me to stay all night in the stewardesses' overnight room at the airport. How grateful I was to crawl into bed and have a good night's sleep.

The next morning I felt much better and was soon on a plane flying east. Not long after we were airborne, the stewardess began handing out small gifts to all of the passengers. We were delighted to hear that the war in Europe had just ended, and the airline company provided key chains for all with a small medallion inscribed with "V-E Day, May 8, 1945" and a wish that we would always remember our flight that historic day.

When I finally reached Norfolk, Virginia, and reported aboard my ship, the USS *Consolation*, I was assigned to share a small inside stateroom with another ensign—a tall, blonde, cheerful young nurse. We became good friends, and I felt very lucky to be aboard. Our small stateroom did not have a porthole, so we found a stick-on picture of a porthole and soon felt right at home.

On May 22, 1945, the entire new crew assigned to serve on the USS *Consolation* was aboard for the official commissioning ceremony. We also went on a shakedown cruise in Chesapeake Bay and returned to the shipyard in Norfolk. Since modifications on the ship would require more than a month, we were encouraged to request official leave, so I did.

My sister Ruth was on the faculty of the University of Michigan in Ann Arbor, so we had time for a pleasant visit. One event I recall was a delicious steak dinner she had prepared for us in her apartment. When I casually mentioned that I liked the meal and that we had steak dinner fairly often in officers' mess, Ruth seemed rather shocked and explained to me that steak was a rare treat for civilians. She had been saving up her ration coupons for quite a while so she could prepare something really special. It made me realize how fortunate I was to be a navy officer. I hadn't realized how much civilian life had changed, with so many regulations, shortages, and frustrations of all kinds.

When I returned to the ship, it wasn't long until we made final preparations for going to sea, at last. After we got under way leaving Norfolk on July 14, 1945, we soon settled into a daily routine of assignments. The ship's crew was busy with the mechanics of running the ship. Since we were equipped to serve as a floating hospital but had no patients aboard, it must have been challenging to keep all the hospital personnel busy, including doctors, thirty nurses, hospital corpsmen, and two women Red Cross aides who were quartered with the nurses.

Because I was the nurse with the lowest seniority, I didn't question my assignment to be in charge of the linen room, supervising several corpsmen.

There was an old-fashioned treadle sewing machine in the linen room. When I said I knew how to use it, the medical officer in charge of the x-ray department asked me to make a dust cover for the irregular, boxlike x-ray machine. I was pleased to have a useful project to work on. Making a rough sketch of the machine, I took measurements for a guide. One of the corpsmen got some muslin from the ship supplies, and we started cutting. Sewing pieces together was simple, but when we first tried the cover on the machine, we found where angles had to be modified. Before long, the x-ray machine had its cover.

A few days after we left Pearl Harbor, we sailed west in the Pacific. On August 17, 1945, we crossed the international date line, and since we had no patients aboard, the hospital staff happily joined in a Davy Jones's Locker celebration. A carefree evening of games, special events, and movies temporarily made the war seem far away.

When we reached port, mail call was an eagerly awaited event. Even getting an advertisement was better than getting nothing. Some people were very popular, receiving a handful of letters, some even perfumed, according to the sailor handing out the mail. It was sad to see that some never seemed to get any mail, and they would usually avoid mail call. One learns to travel light in the navy, so I only saved a few of the letters I received.

When we were first ordered to the Pacific, we were supposed to be a stationary hospital convenient to the fighting wounded, but our orders changed as we proceeded. On August 28, 1945, we anchored in Buckner Bay, Okinawa. For the next few days, the nurses were allowed ashore, a few at a time. We visited the informal headquarters and were driven by jeep on a brief sightseeing tour, but we were required to have an armed guard along at all times. We were told that even though the island was considered secure, it was impossible to predict when a Japanese sniper might appear, since they were experts at hiding out for long periods of time. As I recall, some of the nurses decided not to go ashore, but I will always remember that jeep ride along the narrow road on what became a historic island.

The war finally ended on September 2, 1945. On V-J Day, we were still in Buckner Bay but with new orders. On September 9 we sailed toward Wakayama, Japan, where we helped in the evacuation of newly released prisoners of war. We departed on September 18, arriving at Hagushi, Okinawa, where many of the patients were taken ashore on September 22 and 23 to be flown to their home countries as quickly as transportation could be arranged.

We remained in the western Pacific for several more weeks. On October 26, 1945, we were in Nagoya, Japan, where we were given new orders. Our "magic carpet" orders had us soon making many trips, transporting military dependents from Honolulu to San Francisco. The new orders also included a transfer of most of the hospital staff to shore duty. Only seven of us remained from the original thirty nurses. A few doctors and corpsmen also remained on board to help care for patients and passengers.

On February 14, 1946, we finally left San Francisco, heading south. Two days later we went through the Panama Canal again, going from the Pacific back to the Atlantic Ocean. On March 3 we arrived back in Norfolk, Virginia, where we remained for several weeks. In the following months, the USS *Consolation* was assigned to stay with a navy fleet in the Caribbean.

Finally, we returned to New York City on May 24, 1946. Although I had requested permission to stay on board, I was told that all of the nurses were to be transferred to land bases. Without sea duty, I decided that the navy no longer needed me. I had more than enough points to be released from active duty, so I was officially released from active duty in the navy on August 7, 1946.

One day we had a patient transferred by stretcher from another ship to our hospital following a storm. He was in a coma and was taken directly to surgery. Apparently, he had been working on the deck of his ship when an oil drum broke loose and smashed him in the head.

After some hours in surgery, he was placed in one of our private rooms and I was assigned to monitor his condition and notify the doctor when he regained consciousness. Since the intercranial pressure had been quite severe, the doctors weren't sure how much permanent damage had been done.

Several hours later he showed signs of consciousness, so the corpsmen hurried to call the doctor. The patient groaned and asked where he was, since everything was unfamiliar. By the time the doctors came, he was fully conscious and cooperative. A few simple reflex tests indicated that he was not able to move his right arm, but his condition was much better than might have been expected.

Three of us nurses were assigned to special-duty care for our injured patient, in eight-hour shifts. I was happy to have the busier day shift. Soon our patient was well enough to be up in a wheelchair for several hours each day. Since he was right-handed, I soon began encouraging him to try to eat using his left hand, but he said it felt too awkward and that he spilled food too much.

Luckily he had a good sense of humor when I spread towels to catch any spills, and each day I insisted that he feed himself a little more of his meal before I wheeled him out on deck, where he enjoyed the sunshine and the change of scenery.

During this time I regularly massaged his right arm, with his doctor's permission. I also had him frequently squeezing an orange to try to strengthen the muscles in his hand and arm. After about a week of this, he excitedly showed me that he did have some voluntary movement in his hand and arm. When the doctor came to see him later, he had a big grin as he showed how much movement he had regained. Everyone was delighted, and the patient gradually regained full use of his arm.

I grew up in a caring family that had the sensible religious beliefs of The Church of Jesus Christ of Latter-day Saints, often called the Mormons. So when I was in the navy, I naturally declined to drink alcohol at any time. One time a friend coaxed me to go to the officers' club with her, but I soon felt out of place since drinking seemed to be the main source of entertainment. Leaving was easy.

Later, on board my ship, it soon became apparent that I was the only nurse who never drank alcohol. This solved a problem, because when nurses were invited to attend captain's dinner aboard another ship or a party on land somewhere, I always volunteered to stay on board in case of an emergency.

One time, in Honolulu, an officers' party was planned on a large private plantation. As usual I did not get an invitation, but I planned to go ashore since no one was needed to stay aboard in port. But one of my best friends, the assistant chief nurse, said she was required to put in an appearance at the party. She promised that if I would only go with her, we could soon leave, so I finally agreed.

We enjoyed the colorful scenery and admired the large swimming pool. About the time we arrived, someone playfully pushed one of the officers into the pool, fully clothed. Obviously the party was well under way. My friend and I promptly changed into our bathing suits and jumped into the pool, where we swam alone for a while. I was glad to avoid those who were acting foolishly; apparently, my friend and I were the only ones who were sober. Soon my friend's recently sunburned back began to hurt, so we climbed out of the pool. I was given some soothing lotion to rub on her reddened back, which gave her some relief. Back in uniform again, we were urged to eat. We had some delicious sandwiches, but I politely declined anything to drink, no matter how harmless it seemed. My roommate had already explained how some people liked to spike innocent-looking drinks to make people involuntarily drunk. Since I was so strong-minded, I'm sure I made many "happy" people feel uncomfortable, especially when they were behaving foolishly. Anyway, when my friend and I said we wished to return to the ship, we were happily told good-bye.

An important element of fighting a war is the need to provide effective medical care as soon as possible to the fighting forces. Medics and corpsmen travel with military units. MASH units and front-line hospitals care for the men as close to the fighting as possible. Hospital ships are another means of bringing effective up-to-date medical care within a short distance of the wounded. Such military platforms saw service in World War II, Korea, Vietnam, and again in the Persian Gulf conflict (Operation Desert Storm). Alice's ship, the USS Consolation, *was one of the first U.S. Navy hospital ships.*

Virginia Scherbel Armstrong

Virginia Scherbel Armstrong

I entered the Army Nurse Corps in April 1941 before World War II at the request of the Red Cross Nurse Association. I was assigned to Barnes General Hospital in Vancouver, Washington. When I arrived the hospital consisted of hastily constructed wooden buildings with ramps between them and a firewall running through the center. There were no patients or equipment. An administration group and army corpsmen who had been transferred from Fitzsimmons General Hospital in Denver, Colorado, were already there. These corpsmen were our technicians for the lab and x-ray, served as wardmen and cooks, worked in the motor pool, and performed many other duties. The doctors arrived at a later date.

Our first activities (with the help of the corpsmen, who had been trained in army hospitals) involved ordering equipment and supplies for the wards including chairs, cots, bedding, pajamas, robes, and other items, as well as dressings, bandages, and surgical instruments. Everything smelled of mothballs and had to be aired out and cleaned. Our first surgical instruments were all caked in wax and had to be cleaned of the wax before they were usable. We were told that all this equipment had been stored since World War I. Some instruments were familiar and similar to those we had used in our previous work, but some were completely different than any we had ever used.

Once the hospital was in some kind of order, we started receiving patients. Our patients were mostly transfers from post hospitals, like Fort Lewis in Washington and Fort Stevens in Oregon. Consequently, patients usually arrived in groups from a few to as many as seventy-five at a time. They were sent through the admissions area and then assigned to the type of ward they needed, such as ENT, urological, medical, or psychiatric. It was only a short time before the hospital was completely filled with patients suffering from a variety of illnesses.

I was the nurse in charge of an open psychiatric ward at the time of the bombing of Pearl Harbor. Patients who were out of bed went to the mess hall for their meals. My patients had gone for their meal but rushed back to the ward to tell me that Pearl Harbor was being bombed. I thought at first that they were kidding me as they always did, but when we turned on the radio, we heard the news of the bombing and later of the president, Franklin Delano Roosevelt, declaring war, December 7, 1941. Most of my patients wanted to be sent right back to service, and most of them were. However, the hospital was kept filled with patients from the posts, as it was filled even before war was declared. The hospital went on full alert and was soon painted camouflage, and our activities away from the hospital or post became restricted as to distance and type of activity.

I received my honorable discharge from the service in July 1942, so you see my army activity was limited. I did return to work at LDS Hospital in the nursery during the war years, which was plenty busy. I was also attending the University of Utah during that time.

Estelle Morrison Burton

I was a cadet nurse during World War II, and I went to Mary Hitchcock Memorial Hospital at Dartmouth College School of Nursing in Hanover, New Hampshire. We were privileged to be able to take some of our nursing classes at Dartmouth College itself, which made it especially nice. I graduated at the top of my class and received a scholarship to Simmons College in Boston.

I went into the navy hoping to become a flight nurse. The war was just over, and we were in what they call a "state of war." My first assignment was at Jacksonville Naval Air Station. Because of some supervisory experience and my scholastic record, they put me right into head nursing and evening supervisory situations and threw the book at me. It was very challenging and very enjoyable—challenging because I did a lot of problem solving.

Back in those days nurses did not start intravenous lines. One day I was the head nurse on the orthopedic ward and they brought a black sailor back from the OR, which was three buildings away. He was in severe shock. I called a commander who was in charge of the unit and told him the situation. He said to give him so much Esgotin (I think it was called at the time) intravenously, stat [immediately]. I had never given an intravenous shot in my life. Medical residents and interns always started intravenous lines in those days. The patient was a very dark-skinned black man. All of the corpsmen gathered around the head nurse, and I thought, "I am going to lose face if I don't hit this vein, and this man is going to die." Thank goodness he had big veins. I felt boom, and in it went. It shook me up pretty good, but I didn't let on. Esgotin was an adrenaline-type solution, and it brought his blood pressure right back up. I didn't lose face in front of all of my subordinates. When the doctor told me to administer the shot, I said, "I don't do that." He said, "You do it. I'll be right behind you." I said, "Sure you will—three buildings away." He laughed. He was a full commander and I was an ensign. He told me to do it, and I did it.

One day when I was still head nurse on the orthopedic floor, the phone rang, and it was the chief nurse, who said, "Miss Morrison, would you please give your narcotic keys to the nurse in the next building and come to the administration building. Is your narcotic count balanced?" I said, "Yes, of course." She said, "All right, well, we'd like you to come over to the administration building please, after you give your keys to the nurse on the next floor." I said "All right." I turned around and right by my side was a hospital chief corpsman standing there. He said, "I'll walk over with you." Little did I know I was under arrest—nobody told me. So we walked across the lawn over to the administration building. They took me around the corner and there was a master at arms swinging his club, and he had a gun on and three men sitting in chairs outside of the administration building. They said, "You can sit right here." I said, "Well, if I have to wait, I'll go get paid," and I went around the corner. He looked at me and he looked at them, and I guess he decided I was the best bet of the group to come back. I didn't have any idea I was under arrest, so I went around, got my paycheck, and came back. The master at arms looked quite relieved when I came back.

They invited me into this room wherein sat naval intelligence. They are very important, and they were the only ones who were nice to me. The Florida Narcotics Bureau and the Jacksonville police were also there. They sat me in a chair and their opening statement was, "We understand you are addicted to morphine." I said, "No, I'm not." They said, "Well, roll up your sleeves so we can see the tracks on your arms" (navy nurses wore long sleeves). I said, "No, I'm not going to roll up my sleeves for you, but the chief of medicine has an office right across the hall, and if you want me to go over there and roll up my sleeves for him, I will be happy to." I just didn't like their attitude. They were flippant and almost rude, when I hadn't done anything. So I went across the hall, and the chief of medicine looked at them and came back and told them, "No, there are no scars or tracks or anything on her arms." They said, "Tell us every time you have had morphine since you were born." I said, "At the very beginning?" "Yes." So I decided I might just as well be deceitful as they were, so I said, "When I was five, I had my tonsils out, and I had a little pain and they gave me something, but I don't know what it was." I was just being obnoxious, because they were pushing my buttons the wrong way. I took them all the way through to an appendectomy at age twelve. Then they said, "We understand that you sold eight grains of morphine for $35 on the corner in Jacksonville, Florida, last night." I said, "Number one, I wasn't off the base last night; number two, I have never been on that street in Jacksonville; and number three, if I would have sold that morphine, I would have gotten a lot more than $35 for it." I was a complete bust to them; they didn't get anywhere. All I could think of was people who had been charged with something they didn't do.

The naval intelligence officer had very little to say, and he was the only one who was extremely polite and courteous to me. The others were rude and crude and really annoyed me. But then they let me go. I didn't know that day what the result was, but I found out the next day that they had caught three veterans' administration patients who had come in from Cuba and had come across the fence into the Naval Air Station. They were the ones that had sold the morphine, but they had accused the nurse on the ward, and that was me. They were my outpatients.

In the navy you are sick until you are fit for duty. We had a ward with fifty-two patients. I actually had two wards; I had an orthopedic ward and a dirty surgery ward, and each had fifty-two patients in it. I also had one or two wards, it varied from time to time, of outpatients who would come in the morning for their medication. They lived in another ward; they weren't well enough to go back to active duty, but they didn't have to be on the sick ward. They were supervised by a navy chief. They probably didn't have enough navy nurses to watch over them.

I was in Jacksonville from January 1948 to December 1948, and then my father became quite ill, so I had a hardship transfer to Massachusetts, and I was transferred to Chelsea Naval Hospital.

Leona Berg Campbell

Leona's daughter tells her mother's story.

Leona Berg Campbell, my mother, graduated from the Grove LDS Hospital Nursing School in 1923. She was a supervisor after graduation and for most of my childhood did private duty nursing.

In 1943 she and my father worked at the Topaz Japanese Relocation Camp about twenty miles outside of Delta, Utah. My father was the placement officer there, and Mom nursed in the hospital.

The hospital was a very modern facility with the most up-to-date equipment for that time. There were two Japanese doctors in the hospital, and my mom considered them tops in their fields. For example, after surgery they had their patients up and moving around shortly after their operations. This was a new innovation for Mom.

Those days in the hospital at Topaz were very happy ones for her. She told how clean and virtually scrubbed the mothers-to-be were when they came to the hospital for their deliveries and how she enjoyed taking the beautiful new babies to their mothers.

When she left the hospital after her 3:00 to 11:00 shift, it was a thrill for her to walk home and look up at the sky—the stars seemed so close to her out there on the desert.

Ruth Udy Dare

It was September 1943, and the war was raging in Europe and in the Pacific. LaRue and I went to see the movie *So Proudly We Hail*—a film about army nurses. That made our decision final to join the Army Nurse Corps. So we went up to Fort Douglas, Utah, and signed up and told them we would be available for assignment January 1944. We requested that we would be stationed together.

Our army life of twenty-four wonderful months began. The change in temperature from Utah to the Sacramento area was surprising to me. We took a late evening train to Medford. A bus took us to Camp White, which was five miles away.

We filled out papers of all kinds, learned our army numbers, and were given shots. We had our teeth checked, our eyes checked, and were issued two pairs of glasses as well as corrective lenses in our gas masks. We were put in a barracks with lots of other new army nurses.

We went to parties at the officers' club, where LaRue and I were always the only ones not drinking and smoking. Sometimes it was fun, sometimes boring. I was thankful we had each other. One day I was summoned to the chief nurse's office. I couldn't imagine why. I was reprimanded for coming in late—drunk. This time I was innocent, a case of mistaken identity. It wasn't easy convincing her of my innocence. I was pretty shaken by that experience.

For an extra week we worked eight hours daily in the hospital. We had six weeks to learn what the army was all about and received our orders to report to Sawtelle Station Hospital in west Los Angeles, California. The hospital was set up in domiciliary buildings used for World War I veterans, within walking distance of Westwood Village and near Santa Monica.

It was an exciting life for us. We went to church at Wilshire Ward when our work schedule would permit. We also went to Hollywood Ward a few times. I felt the Tabernacle Choir broadcasts were my link with the Church at that time. LaRue and I were good for each other and helped each other live the gospel even though we could not attend church regularly.

In March I was called home to take care of my sister Vivian, who had given birth to her eighth child at home without a doctor in attendance. She had developed a postpartum infection. It was my first plane ride and I was alone, worried, airsick, and scared. Family met me in Salt Lake City and took me to Cottage Hospital in Burley, Idaho, where Vivian was hospitalized. Penicillin, which would have cured her, was not available for civilian use. There were no antibiotics. She did seem to be getting better, so after two weeks I came back to California. She was still in the hospital, but my leave was up. The ironic thing is that I had been giving penicillin shots every four hours to soldiers with venereal diseases in the G.U. ward but couldn't get any for my sister who needed it so desperately. She left eight children when she died about a week after I returned to Los Angeles. This was a very difficult time for my parents. They had now buried their firstborn child and had taken her baby—also named Vivian—to raise. Now they were worrying about my chances of being sent overseas. When I joined the army I assured them there was no chance that I would receive an overseas assignment because of my myopic condition and because they said I was underweight (116 pounds).

I was transferred to Birmingham Hospital when Sawtelle was closed. Birmingham was an extremely large complex, like a small city, located on Victory and Balboa Boulevards. After the war ended it became a VA Hospital and then a high school.

We were working very hard now, receiving convoys of patients from the China-Burma-Indonesia area—lots of psychiatric patients. Nurses were being sent overseas from Birmingham every week or so, and LaRue and I became worried one of us might go without the other. So we went and talked with the chief nurse and told her we would very much like to stay together—even on an overseas assignment. Our orders came in September to join the 81st Field Hospital. We were elated that we could be together.

On November 20, we were assigned to the 81st Field Hospital assembling at Camp Lee, Virginia. It was a long train ride. Camp Lee was about twenty miles from Richmond. It was a staging area where units were made up. The personnel for the 81st were from many different banks from San Diego. The chief nurse was Captain Eileen Donnelly from Massachusetts. We had 18 nurses, 22 officers, and 186 enlisted men. LaRue and I were the two youngest nurses.

On Sunday we found an LDS service in the camp. There were very few there, but we had the sacrament and a Bible study class—friends even though we were strangers.

We worked in the hospital while we were there and enjoyed the city of Richmond and the beautiful countryside. This was my first experience in the South, and I didn't like what I saw—blacks in the back of buses, separate entrances, and so forth. This was all new to me, and I found it very distasteful.

On December 16, 1944, the 81st Field Hospital personnel boarded a train, and on December 24, 1944, we were taken to the New York Harbor. There we boarded the *Vollendam*, a former Dutch luxury liner, now a troopship. The crew was British. There were at least two thousand infantrymen on board. Christmas Day was spent on board ship in the New York Harbor. On December 26, 1944, at 5:00 a.m., we moved out. When we awoke we were out at sea. We were with a big convoy of ships, including tankers and destroyers. We were headed for the European theater of operations.

The North Atlantic in midwinter can be very rough. We zigzagged across, trying to avoid enemy submarines. Many times we would be aware of depth charges being dropped, indicating the presence of the enemy. That was nerve-racking but I felt an inner peace that all would be well. Some of our nurses were basket cases. We also encountered another enemy—the storms that blew up forty-foot waves, making it impossible to go out on deck. Many were seasick, including me. I felt a great deal of sympathy for the enlisted men in the hold of the ship in hammocks. Our food wasn't that great. We ate lots of Nabisco sugar wafers, which we could buy at the ship store. We were onboard ship for nineteen days.

On January 7, 1945, we arrived at Southampton, England. Here we received orders to cross the English Channel to the French port of Le Havre. This port had been completely destroyed. It looked burned and was still smoldering. We docked long enough for the two thousand infantrymen to climb aboard the LST boats, their destination—the front lines. I thought how young those boys looked and wondered how many of them would return home. We headed back again across the channel to Southampton after playing cat and mouse with U-Boats. We finally made it around the west coast of England, ducking in at Milford Haven, Wales, to avoid submarines, and then running—or steaming—as fast as we could through the Irish Sea. Docking in Gourock, Scotland, on January 13 at 3:30 p.m., we finally felt earth under our feet. After twenty-one days the 81st was in Scotland.

The next leg of our journey was a troop train to Beeston Castle, England, and then a bus to Oulton Park three miles away, near the city of Chester. It was very cold. We were dressed in fatigues—full regalia—and were carrying sleeping bags. Our luggage consisted of a bed roll, in which we had stashed everything we thought we would need for a year. Oulton Park was a series of Quonset huts. Each had a small stove in the center where we burned compressed coal dust. The washroom and toilets were in another Quonset hut. We preferred using our helmets and washing up around the stove in our hut.

We slept on double-decker cots with inflatable rubber mattresses, and the sleeping bags and warm cotton blankets we had brought from Richmond saved our lives. We stacked black woolen blankets on top of that. We wore more clothes at night than during the day. I always put a fancy nightgown over the other layers as a morale booster. We were lucky—our cot was close to the stove. We took turns getting up to keep the fire going during the night. We had lots of mail and packages from home waiting for us here.

On January 18 we went to London on a three-day pass. Westminster Abbey was badly bombed and damaged, and sandbags were everywhere to protect it. Each night air-raid sirens wailed, indicating German U2 rockets were being sent across the channel to bombard south England. The Red Cross served waffles and ice cream cones—a taste of home. I was so happy to be there and see all the places I had heard about.

When we returned to Oulton Park we found the latrine frozen up. It was the coldest winter in England in eighty-two years. Our stovepipe plugged up. We couldn't get our fire to burn, so we went to bed to get warm. Finally some of our boys came and cleaned it out for us. There were soot and ashes everywhere, but we were warm again.

Our hospital [unit] had been divided into three platoons. Each platoon had six nurses, seven officers, and sixty-two enlisted men. LaRue and I were in A Platoon. Each platoon could function on its own if necessary. On January 24, A Platoon nurses were assigned to the 109th General Hospital near Liverpool. We stayed there until March 11. We were working ten hours a day. Our uniforms were brown and white striped seersucker with field shoes and olive drab wool socks. We didn't look very glamorous, but the boys didn't seem to care. They were great patients and helped us a lot if they were able to be up and about. We were taking care of some boys who were left off our ship at Le Havre. They had been up to the front and were wounded. Seven hundred of those boys who were on the *Vollendam* were killed in a train wreck the same night they got off our ship. We loved taking care of the soldiers. We had been in the army fourteen months and had enjoyed every bit of it.

On March 11 our whole unit moved back to Oulton Park. On March 21 our hospital unit left Oulton Park, traveled by train for eight hours to Salisbury, then went by truck to a staging area called C-5. This was an area for units shipping to the continent. This time it was for real. We were headed for the real war—the combat zone. On March 25 we left Southampton on board a ship called the *Dobrieske*. It was a Polish steamer with a U.S. Navy crew—a ritzy ship with deluxe cabins and wonderful food. It was an overnight ride across the channel to Le Havre, France. From there we took an overnight train ride to Paris. We spent the whole day in the Paris train station. We were in combat dress including helmets and were not allowed to leave the station. We ate K-rations for all our meals that day. K-rations were dry foods packed in a box about the size of a Cracker Jack box. There was one for breakfast, one for lunch, and one for dinner.

We left Paris by train on March 27 in the evening, traveling to Luneville, which is near the city of Nancy. It was 2:00 a.m. on March 28, and our unit was headed for Mannheim, Germany. We traveled in eighteen 2½-ton trucks. It was a seventeen-hour ride never to be forgotten. There were no bathrooms along the way; we had to make our own. We used four army blankets held up by eight nurses to make four walls between two trucks right in the middle of the road. It made a private bathroom for us. We rode in the back of a truck sitting nine on each side. Canvas covered the top and sides of the truck, and the back flap could be opened or closed depending upon the weather. As we began to drive through Germany we had to be very cautious; there was danger of land mines exploding. The German people in the villages were mostly old men, women, and children. They looked at us with hostility as we drove through, which was very understandable.

We were near the Rhine River as dusk approached. At Ludwigshafen we seemed to be obstructing the passage of an armored tank division. Their commander asked our Captain Corley, in charge of our unit at the time, what we were doing there. Captain Corley explained we were on our way to Mannheim. The tank commander replied in disgust, "You'd better wait until we capture it." Some of our nurses stuck their heads out at this time, and the commander looked at us and said, "Wouldn't you know, a bunch of women."

We didn't care for his reaction, but chances are he saved our lives. Our orders had been misinterpreted. We were to go to Marnheim, *not* Mannheim. The tank commander told us to go about twenty miles northwest. We had no map. We were driving in blackout. The bridges had been bombed. The Germans had turned road signs around so the allies would have a difficult time getting to their destinations. We were driving in circles. At 11:00 p.m. we were in Golheim. We went across fields, through streams and barnyards with cows, chickens, and pigs. At 1:00 a.m. we were back in Golheim again. We got into areas where we couldn't turn around and had to back all the trucks out to where we could move forward.

Ted, a member of our company, had a compass and offered to try to get us to Marnheim. It was a moonlit night—he would walk into a town and see what was ahead and then come back and move the convoy. He finally found a station hospital set up in tents. They gave him a map. He got us to Marnheim about 3:00 a.m. It was now pouring rain, and we waded in mud up to our knees. We slept the rest of the night in an old building on cots with two dirty army blankets, near the 27th evacuation hospital.

The next day, March 29, in Marnheim—that elusive city—our own tents were set up and we were cozy with our sleeping bags and air mattresses. Candles were our lights. In two more days we had electricity from our own generators and stoves in our tents—even violets growing on our floor. We heated water in buckets and were allowed a helmetful for a bath at night. Our unit was attached to the 7th Army here, and we were waiting for orders. On April 5, we moved to Dieburg, about forty-five miles from Marnheim. We crossed the Rhine River on a pontoon bridge at the city of Worms. This city had no buildings standing—just rubble, dust, and dirt. We witnessed total devastation of homes and countryside as we traveled over bomb-pocked roads in the backs of ambulances. German people pushing little carts containing their only salvageable possessions were everywhere. In Dieburg we set up our hospital in tents; our living quarters were also tents. An expression of the enlisted men, whose job it was to set up, was "pitch, ditch, and b——."

LaRue and I were assigned to the tuberculosis ward. We set up isolation techniques as much as was possible. We were constantly washing our hands in creosol solution. Our patients were displaced persons. They had been in German concentration camps and had been freed as our soldiers liberated the areas. They were Russian, French, Italian, and so forth. We spoke none of these languages. Most of them had been in Germany long enough to know German. So with the few basic German words we knew, and lots of hand waving, we were able to work with them fairly well. It wasn't easy. We found the patients in our ward spitting on the floor of the tent (ground), which we couldn't allow. It was difficult to make them understand they must use sputum cups. (Is it any wonder I developed tuberculosis later on?) Another big problem was teaching them to use the latrine. These patients were suffering grossly from malnutrition and had been so badly treated. They would hoard any scraps of food they could find.

We had received no mail for two months, but we were working such long hours we hardly had time to think about it. Our work went smoothly, except for the interruptions by "Bed-Check Charlie." The first night we heard his plane fly over, a few of us nurses came out to see how close he was. All of a sudden we heard him strafing the highway very close to us. You could feel the heat and the pressure as the bullets hit the road. We all hit the ground automatically. After that memorable night, "Bed-Check Charlie" made his nightly visits but never strafed so close again. His target was a radar station nearby—not the big red crosses painted on all our tents.

Our hospital in Dieburg was in operation for nine days. We worked long hours, very hard. We handled eight hundred patients during that time. Thank goodness our water situation was good. We were able to shower every day and wash our hair.

On April 18 our hospital received orders to split into three platoons. Each platoon was being assigned to a different area. A platoon was made up of five nurses, six officers, and about sixty enlisted men. LaRue and I were assigned to A Platoon and went to Weinsburg to set up a hospital. Weinsburg was one hundred miles south of Dieburg. Our living quarters were German homes—one for nurses, one for officers, and three for enlisted men. We set up our hospital in three buildings nearby. These buildings had been part of a German prison camp for allied officers. They had been moved out only a few days before we arrived.

Our house was lovely—three stories and very well furnished. We had running water for the first time since our arrival in Germany. It was a luxury even though it wasn't warm. The beds all had down coverlets and pillows. The wine cellar was filled with bottles and barrels of booze. The basement was well stocked with bottled fruit, jams, and jellies. We tasted them all. They were delicious. In the backyard were blooming apple trees; strawberry plants; currant, raspberry, and gooseberry bushes; and a garden. The house was on a corner. I remember the beautiful blooming wisteria vine growing over the entryway. We found German officers' uniforms, medals, flags, arm bands, and lots of papers upstairs. This house probably had been occupied by German officers who had been in charge of the concentration camp next door.

The people whom they had moved out for us were an elderly man and two girls. They would come back to feed the chickens and to water the garden. They came one day and wanted to go down in the basement and get some potatoes. We didn't let them in but went and got the potatoes for them. We felt sad that they had to move out of their homes for us. At the time they were our enemies and couldn't be trusted.

I had an eerie feeling while we were there and now have a guilty conscience that I participated in what we called "liberating" some of their property. Rationalizing at the time that what we were doing was okay—even though I knew it wasn't—I came home with a down pillow, binoculars, and a green and silver tea set. At the time I thought if I don't take it, someone else who stays here next will. It didn't belong to me, and no amount of rationalization made it the right thing to do.

Our hospital capacity was one hundred beds. We received patients from three evacuation hospitals and the displaced persons center. LaRue was assigned to night duty. I was on days. She was the only nurse on at night but had ward boys in each barrack. She would walk from one building to another making rounds and said it was very scary. We had a variety of patients. There were four babies: one with measles, one with pneumonia, and premature twins with impetigo. In the seven days we were in operation there at Weinsburg, ninety patients passed through. We sent our last thirty-three patients to

Heilbronn, five miles away, where unit C was working.

We were at rest for three days. Weinsburg had terraced hillsides—lots of grapes growing there. Artillery fire would shake the area often, as the front line was not far away. I had an allergic reaction, which we blamed on the creosol antiseptic solution we had been using. My hands, feet, and eyes swelled beyond recognition. After lots of Benadryl and finally an adrenalin injection, I recovered and was happy to be well again.

There were all kinds of rumors now about the war with Germany coming to an end. We received the great news on May 9—V-E Day—victory in Europe had finally occurred. Now that the war in Europe was over, our unit was not needed as a fourth platoon with the 54th Field Hospital. On May 12 unit A moved from Garmisch to Heilbronn to join unit C.

It was a twelve-hour ride in a convoy of trucks to this city. We were returning to the area where we had been eight days before. The only building remaining in Heilbronn was the hospital, and it was located on one side of the city. The story we heard was that in twenty minutes of bombing, the city was leveled and twenty thousand people were buried in the debris—we believed it. As we walked down the streets the stench of death was very evident. A high wall surrounded the hospital. We had army guards at the gates. The gardens around the hospital were beautiful and there was a nice swimming pool. The Neckar River was nearby. We lived in the hospital building, and LaRue and I had a nice room. We unpacked our clothes for the first time since we left the United States of America. Our clothes were actually put on hangers in a clothes closet and in drawers. We had all the comforts again—hot and cold water, electric lights, and so on.

The equipment we used in the hospital was mainly German. The operating rooms were beautiful. Our patients were liberated prisoners of war: Russians, Poles, French, Italians, and so forth. Many had been brought here to work for the Germans. LaRue and I had a large surgical ward. We had to work really hard. We were admitting and discharging patients each day, and numerous surgical operations were performed. Most of the patients in our hospital were men, but we had five women and two babies at one time. Another time we had fourteen kids with measles in the nursery. The oldest was four years old. Our daily census was usually two hundred. We worked twenty-eight days at this hospital. After the first week, it seemed like almost a normal life. We worked hard. Language was a barrier, but we used German with most patients. We enjoyed the Russians a lot. They were appreciative and cooperative.

While we were at Heilbronn, we were made first lieutenants. I could change to Silver Bars now and get a few more dollars each month. Most of my money was going home to the bank. I needed very little there.

On June 7 our unit A turned the hospital over to a German medical staff. Unit C had left a few days before, and unit B was in Goggingen. On June 8 all units of the 81st Field Hospital met in Schwetzingen. We had orders to report to the CBI (China, Burma, India theater of war).

Schwetzingen is near Heidelburg. We had seen this historic city when we moved from Dieberg to Weisburg. It was not touched by the war. It is a picturesque city with the castle on the hillside and the Neckar River winding through. On the banks of the river lilacs were blooming. In Schwetzingen, one section of town was inhabited by the army. In the barracks where we were assigned, LaRue slept right under a window. When she would rise in the morning, she would be greeted by a chorus of "good morning lieutenant" from the boys across the street. We'd go out in the strawberry patch nearby and pick berries for breakfast. We really hated to leave Germany. It was such a beautiful country. The people who still had homes kept their homes and yards so clean. Their woodpiles were stacked perfectly. On June 11 we left by train for Marseille, France.

On June 23 we had an exciting event happen. We had a wedding in our unit. Ann Salvadore, RN, married John Toren, an engineer she had met when we were in England. It was a lovely wedding with the reception in the Carlton Hotel in Marseille. We went in one Sunday. There were about thirty-five people attending. We met people from Salt Lake, and it was good to be with those who thought and felt as we did.

On Sunday, August 5, LaRue and I went into Marseille to Sunday School. It was a conference. President Hugh B. Brown from the British Mission was there. There were about two hundred people in attendance—all military. It was a thrilling experience to be in the presence of one of our Church leaders and listen to his message for us. There were three nurses there—including us. It was a great day for us and reminded me again how grateful I was for having been born in the Church and for having parents who taught me so much, and grateful too for having had LaRue's companionship through this army experience.

We were preparing for a new adventure; we would soon be leaving the European theater of operations and be on our way to the Philippines, and we were busy getting ready to go. We had heard that an atomic bomb had been dropped on Hiroshima, but war still raged in the Pacific.

On August 9 our unit, the 81st , boarded the U.S. Navy transport *General George O. Squire*, bound for Manila via the Panama Canal—to the China, Burma, India theater of war. For five days we enjoyed a beautiful trip—the water was smooth as glass—quite a contrast to our North Atlantic crossing nine months earlier. We spent all our time out on deck, then we began hearing rumors that Japan had surrendered and the war was over.

On August 15 we were told officially that the war was indeed over. The Japanese had surrendered. This was V-J Day with celebrations taking place at home in cities and small towns all over the USA. As we watched the bow of our ship, we could see the course change from the Panama Canal to Norfolk, Virginia—USA. We were headed for home! There was great jubilation aboard ship—my feelings were mixed. I was glad the war was over, of course, but I had enjoyed being in the Army Nurse Corps and doing the work we had done. It was hard to think of separating from people we had lived and worked with so closely for so long.

We all spent the next five days talking with one another about future plans. We wondered what would happen to the 81st. I celebrated my 24th birthday on the high seas. On August 20 our ship docked at Norfolk, Virginia. We went by train to Camp Patrick Henry, arriving there about noon. This was a receiving center for many units. From there we were sent to various reception stations with orders to reassemble as a unit at Camp Sibert, Alabama, after a thirty-day leave.

On September 2 LaRue and I flew to Salt Lake City. LaRue took a train to Denver, and Orville and Mother picked me up at the airport. I spent until October 13 at home in Malta. There was a lot of time to contemplate the future. On October 14 LaRue and I reported at Camp Beale, California, then later took another transcontinental train ride to Camp Sibert, Alabama, where we reported on October 23. It was good to see all the personnel of the 81st again.

LaRue and I decided to be discharged from the army. We both had enough points to qualify for discharge. During this time I received a phone call from home telling me my father had died on October 25. My discharge was processed immediately, and I began finding the fastest way to get home. I could get an air force flight out of Atlanta to Denver. It was a nightmare for me to go home to this unexpected sadness. This was my first experience hitching a ride on a military plane. It was cold and uncomfortable. In Denver I found another plane going to Hill Field in Ogden. Dad had had a stroke and, fortunately, only lived a few hours. His funeral was on the 30th of October. I felt sad that I hadn't gotten to know my dad better. I know he loved me and was proud of me.

I met LaRue in Salt Lake after she was discharged, and we went to LDS Hospital to talk with

Maria Johnson—the director of nurses who had been such a tyrant. Now she welcomed us with open arms and offered us jobs to start the first day of the year. LaRue was going to work in urology and I was to work in orthopedics.

After my separation from the army there was a time of great adjustment in my life—from a life filled with excitement to going back to Malta to stay with Mother. She needed help to adjust to her new way of life as a widow. It was a period of change for both of us. I had had a letter from Maria Johnson, superintendent of nurses at LDS Hospital, offering me a job as head nurse in the operating room. When the new year arrived—1946—we packed up and moved to Salt Lake City. We rented an apartment on the Avenues, and I started working in the operating room at LDS Hospital. I felt excited. LaRue was with us also.

LaRue was marrying Ted Elliott, the army officer from the 81st Field Hospital, and I was marrying Doug Dare, a patient I had met and dated at Sawtelle and Birmingham Hospitals. Our courtship had been mainly by correspondence (writing and phoning). We were both marrying men who were not members of the Church. We had strong testimonies of the truthfulness of the gospel, and we were willing to gamble that both Ted and Doug would accept the gospel eventually (they both became stalwart members).

I was very fortunate to have LaRue Haynie Elliott with me. She was a devout member, and we helped each other. We were the only Church members in the 81st Field Hospital with one exception—an MD who didn't really want to admit his membership. I married a nonmember patient I had met in California. He became a very active member, and we served a mission in Western Australia and a mission at the Mesa Family History Center.

Idonna L. Davis Doerig

At the beginning of my adult life, I served two years in the United States Marine Corps Womens' Reserve on active duty in World War II. After discharge I applied for and was accepted at the Dr. W. H. Groves LDS Hospital School of Nursing, attending under the GI Bill. I started school in 1946 and graduated in 1949, passing my nursing state boards after graduating in 1949.

I then worked as an office nurse for Drs. Thomas and Bowen from 1949 to 1953 in Provo, Utah. Enjoying my military experience, I applied for and was accepted into the United States Air Force Nurse Corps in 1953 as a first lieutenant. First I was stationed in Arizona, where I met and married my husband. We were transferred to Alaska when it was still a territory. I was a medical nurse on a medical ward and then became the nurse in charge of the outpatient department for the remainder of my tour of duty. We then were transferred from Alaska to Hamilton Air Force Base in California. I was assigned to the obstetrics clinic, later becoming the nurse in charge of the clinic. I was released from active duty in 1959.

I then became a medical reservist as a clinic nurse. While there, I became the charge nurse of the flight. On my two-week tours of duty and weekend duty, I was assigned to Travis AFB as a reserve nurse. This was also in the ob-gyn clinic. I also went with medical nurses and technicians to meet air evacuation planes from Vietnam. It was quite an experience to see military patients on these aircraft, some with IVs going and other treatments needed. Some of the patients had come straight from the war zone. It was good to see them doing so well and getting back to good medical care. It makes one realize how tragic war is. I retired as a lieutenant colonel from the USAF Reserve Program after serving twenty-two and a half years.

LaRue Haynie Elliott

For almost a year, my roommate, Ruth Udy, and I had debated what we would do when we finished our nurses' training at the Dr. W. H. Groves LDS Hospital School of Nursing in Salt Lake City, Utah. We had graduated from training in May 1943 but would not finish until we took and passed state boards at the end of August.

We had pretty well decided we would go into the service, but we wanted to stay together. We didn't know how much the army would do to get us assigned to the same hospital or to the same outfit overseas, so we kept putting off making a final decision.

In November I received my patriarchal blessing. My grandmother thought it would help me make up my mind on what I should do. In my blessing one of the things it said was that with my training in these trying times, I would be able to serve many people.

Ruth and I talked of this and about the opportunity we would have to use our knowledge and skills in serving in the armed forces. We went to see the movie *So Proudly We Hail*, a story of nurses in the South Pacific. We decided right then to join the army.

The first week in December we made an appointment for a physical at Fort Douglas and to fill out papers. After the physicals we were told to report back on January 3, 1944. We quit work at the hospital and went to our homes for Christmas, knowing it might be a long time before we'd be home again. By the end of December we were back in Salt Lake.

On January 3, 1944, Ruth and I joined the army. We took the oath at Fort Douglas, Salt Lake City, Utah. We were commissioned second lieutenants in the Army Nurse Corps by Colonel Alma T. Skoog. She was so nice to us. Ruth and I told her we had been together for three years and wanted to be assigned to the same places. She said she would do the best she could. It went on our records that we wanted to be together.

During our four weeks of basic training at Camp White, Medford, Oregon, we were issued gas masks and practiced gas mask drills a number of times. Tear gas was used in the gas chamber. We really learned how well a gas mask could protect. That tear gas really made us cry until the mask went on.

On February 7 we all left for our assigned stations. Ruth and I headed for the Sawtelle Station Hospital in Los Angeles, California. The hospital was located in Westwood Hills west of Los Angeles toward Santa Monica. I was assigned to the orthopedic ward. We were asked about signing up for overseas assignments. Ruth and I both wanted to go. The orders would come from Colonel Skoog in Salt Lake.

We received a shipment of boys from the Hawaiian Islands who were put in the psychiatric ward while I was on nights. I worked there from 11:00 p.m. until 2:00 a.m. for a few nights. It was sad to see those young men so disturbed. Some tried to talk and couldn't; others would stumble over simple words, leave words out, and break down and cry. They had been through some very bad war experiences.

I was assigned to the medical ward where I was head nurse. We were very busy now. The patients from another medical ward had been moved into ours, so we were jammed, the reason being that we had received word that Sawtelle Station Hospital would be closing in June. All our patients would be moved to Birmingham General Hospital (BGH) out in Van Nuys in the San Fernando Valley. We didn't know where our personnel would go—maybe overseas or maybe to Birmingham General. The colonel came and inspected our ward and gave us a "very good" rating. Captain Kane, our medical doctor, said, "Well he'd better; we can't have even the colonel telling our red-headed nurse off."

On June 25, 1944, we began evacuating patients to Birmingham General. Our nurses were being sent to different places. Again Ruth and I were hoping we'd stay together. By the end of June all patients had been sent to Birmingham General, and Ruth and I were assigned there too, along with a few other nurses. BGH was a large hospital, like a city. It had everything we needed right there. Hollywood was ten miles away, Van Nuys was eight. There was a large psychiatric ward in the hospital, and many movie stars came to entertain the patients. I worked in the tuberculosis area, wearing a gown and mask all day. Outside the temperature was 105 degrees. It was hot work.

Near the end of September, we were hearing all kinds of overseas rumors. In October we were alerted for overseas duty. Ruth and I talked to the chief nurse, Major Gallagher, about staying together. She promised to talk to Colonel Skoog. We were very busy on the wards with malaria cases. They had such violent attacks of very high fever. I'd hear them scream, "Lieutenant Haynie," from their rooms, and I'd go running. They would shake so bad that the whole bed would shake. I would just hold them. Their bedding and pajamas would be soaked with sweat. We spent a lot of time changing bed linen. I was so glad to be taking care of them.

On the morning of November 20, I was called to Major Gallagher's office. I picked up orders for Ruth, Ann Salvadore, Mary Hunt, and myself. We had been assigned to the 81st Field Hospital stationed at Camp Lee, Virginia. Colonel Skoog had kept her word. Ruth and I were together. Major Gallagher shook my hand and said, "Lieutenant Haynie, stay as sweet as you are." I always felt this was a high compliment from her. Ruth, Mary, and I left Los Angeles on a train headed for Virginia. We traveled four days and nights, finally arriving in Petersburg, which was three and a half miles from the camp.

Camp Lee was about twenty miles from Richmond. It was a staging area where units were made up. Personnel in the 81st Field Hospital were pulled from many different areas of the States and brought to this camp. Our commanding officer was Major Gerald Banks from California. The chief nurse was Captain Eileen Donnelly from Massachusetts. We had 18 nurses, 22 officers, and 186 enlisted men in our unit. Ruth and I were the two youngest nurses. On Sunday we found some LDS services in the camp. There were very few there, but we had the sacrament and a bible study class. It felt good to be among close friends even though we were strangers.

On December 16, 1944, the 81st Field Hospital left Camp Lee for Camp Kilmer, New Jersey. We boarded a train in the evening. For the next week we waited at Camp Kilmer for our orders. It was cold and snowy, but we marched in the mornings and played basketball.

On December 24, 1944, our hospital personnel were taken from Camp Kilmer to the New York City harbor. At four o'clock in the afternoon, we boarded a ship named the *Vollendam*. It was a Dutch ship run by an English crew. There were at least two thousand infantry men on our ship. Their quarters were down on the lower deck. They slept in the lower hold. Somehow my name was put on a list to be in charge of some of the men in the hold. The persons who made out the orders thought Lieutenant LaRue Haynie was a male officer. When they found out I was not, they quickly changed the orders. Christmas Day was spent on board ship sitting in the New York Harbor. On December 26, 1944, at five o'clock in the morning, we moved out. We were with a large convoy of ships including tankers and destroyers. We were headed for the European theater of war.

We were onboard ship for nineteen days. We had lots of experiences during that time. I was seasick a few times but not like some. Captain Donnelly was on her bunk most of the time. Our food wasn't very good, but we were hungry and we ate to keep our stomachs full. We had fifteen girls in our stateroom using triple-decker beds. I was on the top. It took some doing to climb up to it. There was no room to walk because our luggage covered the floor, so we just crawled around. We were living out of cloth bags.

We knew there were enemy submarines around us because we'd hear the depth charges explode. We didn't think about being afraid. As I stood on deck looking at the vast expanse of sea, I thought of all I was leaving and wondered what the future would be.

It was a long ride, and the sea was rough. On January 7, 1945, we arrived at Southampton, England. Here we received orders to cross the English Channel to the French port of Le Havre.

This port had been completely destroyed. It looked all burned and was still smoldering. We docked here to let off about two thousand soldiers on to LST boats. There were large flatboats used to move men and equipment from the ship to the shore. This was the time of the Battle of the Bulge, so these young boys were headed for the front lines. As I watched them leave, I thought how young they looked and wondered how many would die before the war would end.

We headed back across the Channel to Southampton. After playing cat and mouse with U-boats, we finally made it around the west coast of England, ducking in at Milford Haven, Wales, to avoid the submarines. Then, running as fast as we could through the Irish Sea, we docked at Gourock, Scotland, on the 13th of January. At 3:30 p.m. we felt land under our feet. We rode a troop train to Beeston Castle, England, and then took a bus to Oulton Park three miles away. We arrived there in the wee hours of the morning. It was cold with just a little snow on the ground.

The nurses moved into a hut with a coal stove in the middle. We had double-decker beds. I was on the top, Ruth on the bottom. We were lucky because we were close to the stove. We had hot and cold running water for showers some of the time. We washed clothes in a bucket or in our helmets. We were happy even though we were shoveling coal to keep warm. We'd take turns getting up in the night to tend the fire. We really slept in solid comfort with sleeping bags and air mattresses. We all had lots of mail and packages from home waiting for us there.

Our stovepipe plugged up. We couldn't get it unplugged, so we went to bed to keep warm. Finally some of the boys came over and cleaned it out for us. There were soot and ashes all over, but we were warm again and happy to be where we were even with the mess. About this same time, in the very cold weather, our latrine froze up. What a time we had with that. It was the coldest winter in England in eighty-two years.

At ten o'clock that morning, March 28, our unit headed for Mannheim, Germany. We traveled in eighteen 2½ ton trucks. It was a seventeen-hour ride never to be forgotten. There were no bathrooms along the way. We had to make our own. We'd use four army blankets being held up by eight nurses to make four walls between two trucks right in the middle of the road. It made a private bathroom for us.

We rode in the back of a truck sitting nine on each side. We had a covering of canvas over the top and down on the sides with a flap in the back that could be open or closed depending on the weather. As we began to drive through Germany, we couldn't step off the road when we stopped to rest a few minutes. There was danger of mines exploding. The German people in the villages were mostly old men, women, and children. They looked at us with hostility as we drove through, but why not, we were their enemy. Our soldiers had captured their villages only a few days before.

As it began to grow dark, we were about to cross the Rhine River at Ludwigshafen. An armored tank division was there, too. We seemed to be in their way. The tank commander asked Captain Corley, who was in charge of our unit at that time, what we were doing there. Captain Corley explained we were on our way to Mannheim. The commander in disgust replied, "You had better wait until we capture it." We nurses stuck our heads out of our truck about that time. The commander looked at us with contempt and said, "Wouldn't you know, a bunch of d—— women." We didn't like him very much right then, but he probably saved our lives. Our orders had been misinterpreted. We were to go to Marnheim, not Mannheim. The tank commander told us to go about twenty miles northwest.

We had no map. We were driving in blackout. The bridges had been bombed, and the roads were little village roads. The Germans had turned the road signs around so the Americans would have a hard time getting to the right places. With all this, we were driving in circles. At eleven o'clock we were in Goldheim. We went across fields and streams and through barnyards with cows, chickens, and pigs. At one o'clock in the morning we were back at Goldheim again. There were places we got into and couldn't turn around, so we had to back all eighteen trucks out to where we could move forward again in another direction.

Lieutenant Ted Elliott, an officer with our group, had a compass and offered to try to get us to Marnheim. It was a moonlit night. He'd go into the towns to see what was ahead, then come back to move us. He was alone walking through those streets. By the time he'd get back to us, all the drivers would be asleep. He'd go along waking them up. When he would get to the eighteenth truck and give the order to move, the number one driver would be asleep again. He finally found a station hospital set up in tents. They gave him a map. He got us to Marnheim about three o'clock in the morning. It was pouring rain, and we waded in mud up to our ankles. We slept the rest of the night in an old building on cots with two dirty army blankets. We were near the 27th Evacuation Hospital.

The next day, March 29, in Marnheim, our own tents were set up. We were cozy in our sleeping bags and air mattresses using candles for light. In two more days we had electricity and stoves in our tents and violets growing on our floor. Our water supply was better. We'd heat it in buckets and were allowed one helmetful for a bath at night. Our unit was attached to the 7th Army, and we were waiting for orders.

On April 5 we moved to Dieburg, about forty-five miles from Marnheim. We crossed the Rhine River on a pontoon bridge at the city of Worms. This city had no buildings standing, just rubble, dust, and dirt. So many of the German towns and cities were in ruins. In Dieburg we set up our hospital in tents and were living in tents. Our water situation was good here. We were able to shower everyday and wash our hair. Ruth and I were assigned to the tuberculosis ward. We set up isolation techniques as much as possible. We were washing our hands in creosol constantly. Our patients were called displaced persons. They were people who had been in German concentration camps and prisoner-of-war camps and had been freed as our soldiers liberated the areas.

They were of many nationalities: Russian, Polish, Italian, British, French Colonials, and others. We spoke none of these languages, but most of them had learned some German, so we tried to converse in German. With the few words we knew and using our hands and acting ability, we were able to work together fairly well, but it wasn't easy. We found the patients in our ward spitting on the floor, which was the ground, and we couldn't allow that. It was hard to get them to understand they must use a cup. Another big problem was teaching them to use the latrines. Most of them were nothing but skin and bones from malnutrition.

We had no mail for two months, but we were working such long hours we hardly had time to think about it. Our work went smoothly except for the interruptions made by "Bed-Check Charlie." The first night we heard his plane fly over, a few of us nurses came out of our tent to see how close he was. All of a sudden we heard him strafing the highway very close to us. You could feel the heat and the pressure as the bullets hit the road. I was standing looking up in the sky when suddenly Ted (Lieutenant Elliott) appeared out of nowhere. Next thing I knew I was in the mud and he was on top of me in a flash. The rest of the girls hit the ground automatically. After that night Bed-Check Charlie made his nightly visit, but never strafed so close again. His target was a radar station some distance away.

Our hospital at Dieburg was in operation nine days. We worked long hours and very hard. We handled eight hundred patients during those nine days. One night some of us nurses went to a party in a nearby town given by officers who were patrolling the town. They were living in a German mansion. They served chicken and champagne for those who drank. On April 18 our hospital was ordered to break up into three platoons with each platoon being assigned to a different area. Ruth and I were in A platoon along with four other nurses, six officers, and about sixty enlisted men. We were assigned to set up a hospital at Weinsburg, Germany. This was one hundred miles south of Dieburg. Our living quarters were private homes: one for nurses, one for officers, and three for enlisted men. We set up our hospital in three buildings nearby that had been part of a German prison camp for Allied officers. They had been moved out only a few days before we arrived.

Our house was a lovely German home, three stories, and very well furnished. We had running water for the first time in a long time. It was a luxury even though it wasn't warm. The beds all had feather mattresses. The wine cellar was full of barrels and bottles of wine. The basement was stocked with lots of bottled fruit, jams, and jellies. We tasted them all. They were delicious. In the backyard were blossoming apple trees, and there were also strawberry plants, currant, raspberry, and gooseberry bushes, and a garden planted. The house was on a corner, so it had a big lot.

We found German officers' uniforms, medals, flags, armbands, and lots of papers upstairs. It probably had housed German officers who were in charge of the concentration camps nearby. The people who moved out for us were an old man and two girls. They would come back to water the garden and feed the chickens. They came and asked to go down and get some potatoes from the cellar one day. We wouldn't let them. We got the potatoes for them. It was sad to think of people having to move out of their own homes for us, but we couldn't afford to feel bad. They were our enemy, and we couldn't trust any of them.

In the seven days we were in operation there, ninety patients passed through our unit A hospital at Weinsburg. We sent our last thirty-three patients to Heilbronn, five miles away, where unit C was working. We were at rest for three days. Ruth got real sick at this time. Her hands, arms, and face all swelled up. It was a reaction to the creosol, which poisoned her blood. Ted had to cut her ring off with bone cutters. She was better in a few days.

On April 30 two of our officers from unit A left to make contact with the 54th Field Hospital, to which our unit A was to be attached as a fourth platoon to go into combat in support of the 101st Airborne Division. Ted left in search of trucks to move our hospital equipment and personnel. He traveled fifteen hundred miles looking for transportation for us. The problem was the front line was moving so rapidly; therefore, the field hospitals were moving, too. The unit with the greatest priority received the trucks. Finally, on May 5 some of us was able to move. We traveled by truck two hundred miles to Garmisch Partenkirchen to await orders. The country we saw on this ride was beautiful.

Garmisch Partenkirchen, Germany, is in the Bavarian Alps. The Olympic Games were held there in 1936. The homes were big and beautiful, furnished with antique furniture. Ruth and I had a room with windows that looked straight up at the mountains. There was lots of snow on them, but down in the valley it was hot. There was a big lake, a swimming pool, and many tennis courts.

The rest of unit A arrived the next day, and the boys took us for a ride to Oberammergau, three miles away. There we explored the Passion Theater, where the Passion play is produced every ten years. There were no electric lights, just skylights in the ceiling. We went through all the dressing rooms of the players. Each room had costumes ready to be worn, three thousand costumes in all, made from material from the Orient. There was Herod's gold throne and the huge cross used for Christ. In one room was nothing but many pairs of sandals. As I looked at all this, my mind turned back to my teenage years, when Louise and I had spent time with the Day family. Mrs. Day had often spoken of her trip abroad and time spent in Oberammergau attending the Passion play. She had said the play lasted eight hours.

There were all kinds of rumors now about the war with Germany nearing the end. On May 9, 1945, the war with Germany was over. We had a parade down the streets of Garmisch. With the war over, our unit was not needed as a Fourth

Platoon with the 54th Field Hospital. On May 12, unit A moved from Garmisch Partenkirchen to join unit C at Heilbronn. It was a twelve-hour ride in a convoy of trucks to this city. We were going back almost to where we'd come from eight days before.

The city of Heilbronn had many buildings destroyed. A very large German military hospital was located on one side of the city, which was probably why it was not hit by the bombing. This is where we joined unit C. The story of Heilbronn was that it took only twenty minutes to bomb it to pieces, and twenty thousand people were buried underneath all the debris. We believed it, too. As we walked down the streets, the smell was so bad that we'd have to hold our breath in so many areas.

On June 7 our unit A turned the hospital over to a German medical staff. Unit C had left a few days before, and unit B was in Goggingen. On June 8 all units of the 81st Field Hospital met at Schwetzingen, Germany.

The city of Schwetzingen is near Heidelburg. We had seen Heidelburg when we moved from Dieburg to Weinsburg. It is a beautiful city with a river winding through it. On the banks were lilacs and other flowers. In Schwetzengen one whole section of the town was inhabited by the army. In the barracks where we were assigned, I slept right under a window. I'd rise up in the morning and be greeted by a chorus of "Good morning, Lieutenant" from the boys across the street. We'd go out in the strawberry patch nearby and pick berries for breakfast. We really hated to leave Germany. It was a pretty country. The people kept their houses and yards so clean.

For the past six months the 81st Field Hospital had spent time in England, France, and Germany. We'd followed the 7th army into Germany and participated in the battles of Central Europe and the Rhineland. We had been awarded the European-African medal and Eastern Theater Campaign medal with two Bronze Stars. Now we had orders to be sent to the China-Burma-India theater of war.

On June 11 we left by train for Marseille, France. We traveled three days and four nights, arriving at our staging area at four o'clock in the morning. Ted, having gone ahead of our unit, was there to meet us. He took the nurses to the 235th General Hospital, where we were billeted during our stay in Marseille. We were in barracks, and there was a dining hall. The officers and enlisted men of our unit were stationed at Saint Victoret, France, about fifteen miles from us. This was a staging area for many units. They all lived in tents and had to stand up to eat. It was a hot, dirty, windy area.

Our living quarters were very good. We were having classes but not working. Ruth and I saw lots of nurses from Birmingham General who had come over after we left. They had been stationed in general hospitals in France since they came. It was good to see them. With so many units in it, this area was crowded, and we stood in line for everything. We'd get up at six o'clock to take a shower.

Ruth and I found out there was a Mormon church in Marseille. We went in one Sunday. There were about thirty-five people attending. We met people from Salt Lake. It seemed good to be with those who thought and felt the way we did.

I was brown and freckled from the sun. My hair was more like blonde than red. I was badly in need of a permanent, so I experienced the fun of a French one. It was different because the perm was given before the hair was shampooed. It was fun and a lot of laughs. I had real curly hair when finished.

About July 14, our commanding officer, Colonel Gerald Banks, was accidentally shot. He was sitting in his tent when a bullet from a gun two tents away went off and struck him in the head. He was taken to the 43rd General Hospital, where surgery was done. His condition was serious. Our head nurse, Captain Eileen Donnelly, asked Ruth and me to take special care of him. Ruth had the day shift and I had the night. The colonel was not liked very much. He was strictly military and unfriendly. As I spent time with him getting to know him better, I found him to be a quiet man but very friendly, and I liked him. He recovered but was released of his command and sent home within two weeks. Major John B. Moring assumed command of the 81st Field Hospital at that time.

On Sunday, August 5, Ruth and I went into Marseille for Sunday School. It was conference and President Hugh B. Brown from the British Mission was there. There were about two hundred people in attendance—all soldiers. It was thrilling to see so many boys there, knowing that most of them were Mormons. There were three nurses counting us. I was reminded again how grateful I was to have been born in the Church, and to have parents who taught me so many good things. I talked to Ted often about the Church. We read a lot from my two little books, *Principles of the Gospel* and the Book of Mormon. He was genuinely interested, and I was so thankful I could share with him some things about my beliefs.

It was so close to our shipping-out date, my mind was on going to the Philippines, and we were busy getting ready. This was an entirely different venture we were about to undertake. We'd heard that an atomic bomb had been dropped on Hiroshima.

On August 9, 1945, the 81st Field Hospital boarded the transport *General George Squire*, bound for Manila, Philippine Islands, in the China-Burma-India theater of war. For five days we enjoyed a beautiful boat ride. The water was smooth, and we spent our time out on deck. Then we began to hear rumors that Japan had surrendered and that the war was over. It was on August 15 we were told officially that the war was over and that this was V-J Day with celebrations taking place at home in cities and small towns all over the country. As we looked at the bow of our ship, we saw it change course from the Panama Canal to Norfolk, Virginia, United States of America, and we headed home.

There was great jubilation aboard ship. My feelings were mixed. I was glad the war was over, but I loved being in the army and doing the work we'd done. What would happen to the 81st Field Hospital? It was hard to think of separating from people we'd lived and worked with for so long. We all spent the next five days talking with one another about future plans. We wondered what would happen to our unit. Ruth's birthday came and went. Ted gave me a friendship ring. It was one he'd been wearing, and I had admired it.

On August 20 our ship docked at Norfolk. We took a train to Camp Patrick Henry in Virginia, arriving at noon. This was a receiving center for many units. From here our personnel was sent to various reception stations with orders to reassemble as a unit at Camp Seibert, Alabama, after a thirty-day leave. Ruth and I went to Camp Beale, California, as soon as we could get a train out. It took us four days to travel from Virginia to Camp Beale. On August 27 we took at train from Camp Beale to Los Angeles, arriving the next morning.

We stayed in Los Angeles another couple of days. On September 2 Ruth and I flew to Salt Lake City. I took a train to Denver. She went to Idaho. Mother, Dad, Louise, and Frances were in Denver to meet me. We drove home to Alamosa.

I went to Salt Lake to meet Ruth so we could go to Camp Seibert together, but as soon as I arrived in Utah there was a telegram saying our unit had been given an extra fifteen-day leave. I stayed in Salt Lake, spending time with my Aunt Myrtle and my Grandmother Haynie and visiting friends at the hospital where I'd graduated. On October 14 Ruth and I reported to Camp Beale and then later took a train to Camp Seibert, where we reported on October 23. It was good to see all the personnel of our unit again.

She and I had decided to be discharged. We were working on this when she received a phone call from her family saying her father had died. The quickest way for her to get home was to fly out of Atlanta. Captain Donnelly gave me permission to go with Ted to drive Ruth there. We drove there, got her on a plane, and drove back to camp. We arrived back about four o'clock in the morning. While I was going through the process of being discharged, Ted and I had a few days to talk and think and plan. I was going back to Salt Lake to arrange work at the hospital for a while. He would go to his home and start his practice of optometry again. He would plan to come to Alamosa for Christmas to meet my parents.

After I was given terminal leave on October 30, 1945, I left for Salt Lake. My final discharge from the army was dated December 22, 1945. Ruth met me in Salt Lake. We both got jobs as head nurses in the operating room in the LDS Hospital to begin the first of the year. She was in orthopedics and I was in urinary. We found an apartment near the hospital where we would live with her mother and her two-year-old niece, Vivian Ottley. Then we went to our homes.

Ted came for Christmas. He stayed about seven days. We went to Manassa. He met a lot of my relatives there. He wasn't used to such big families. He had only a few cousins, but I had many. He told Mother and Dad that he liked the Mormon Church and that he'd like to be a Mormon someday. He told me he loved me and wanted to marry me. I couldn't say for sure how I felt. I knew him very well. The months overseas working closely together in all sorts of situations had taught us a lot about each other. My big concern was marrying out of the Church. When he left Alamosa the last of December, we knew we'd continue to write letters everyday, and by Valentine's Day I would have an answer for him.

My army story would not be complete unless I told you that yes, I was married to Ted Elliott. We were married in a double wedding with Ruth on June 7, 1946, in my home in Alamosa, Colorado, by the ward bishop. It was a lovely wedding with family members present. We spent three days together on our honeymoon and then we parted. Ruth and Doug went to Texas and then to California, and Ted and I went to New York. We had been well aware that this would be a separation for us after more than five years together, and it was a tearful one.

Ted's little daughter, Nancy, came to live with us in February 1947, and our son, Robert Frederick, was born two years later. Shortly after our thirtieth wedding anniversary, Ted joined the Church. He was baptized in the baptismal font in the Salt Lake Tabernacle by our son, and one year later we were sealed in the Salt Lake Temple with our children as an eternal family.

I am thankful today, as I was at the time of my army life, for my heritage and for the values I learned as a young person, especially to know and appreciate the gospel of Jesus Christ—a great and wonderful gift.

Dove Chandler Fife

My first station was Fort George Wright, Spokane, Washington, where I spent about six weeks learning nursing in a military hospital. My classmate, Zelta Walker [Hendricks], was also stationed there, which was a great help to me. We were the only LDS nurses there. In October 1943 we were both transferred to Fairmont Army Air Force Base, near Fairmont, Nebraska, located in the midst of huge cornfields. It was a B-29 base, where airmen, most of whom had flown missions in B-17s and B-24s over Africa and Europe, were retrained to fly B-29s, the biggest of all the bombers.

The Base Hospital served the base personnel and their families. We had a maternity ward that was full much of the time. Much of my time was spent working with these women and their babies. There were nine wards, as I remember, as well as surgery, a delivery room, a laboratory, and a kitchen for each ward to which food, prepared in the main kitchen, was brought each meal. There were medical, surgical, maternity, and psychiatric wards. Our chief nurse was Captain Erma J. Rabou, and Lieutenant Colonel Crouch was chief of the Medical Corps. We had twelve, maybe fifteen nurses, as I remember, and a nurse anesthesiologist, who all lived in the nurses' barracks.

When I volunteered for the Army Nurse Corps, three of my brothers were already in the service. A younger brother, James J. Chandler, had joined the navy in 1942 to attend the music school in Washington, DC. He served throughout the duration of the war aboard the aircraft carrier USS *Ranger* in both the Atlantic and the Pacific war zones. An older brother, Samuel C. Chandler, had served his mission, had graduated from Ricks College, and had planned to teach school when he was drafted. He served in the Signal Corps in England. When the youngest brother who served in this war turned eighteen, he was permitted to graduate from high school then was taken into infantry and served at Fort Lewis in Washington and then in Okinawa.

I had graduated from nurses' training at Idaho Falls Hospital School of Nursing in September 1942; I volunteered and joined the Army-Air Force Nurse Corps in August 1943. In June 1943 I became engaged to be married to Leland J. Fife, who had graduated from University of Idaho and had volunteered shortly after Pearl Harbor for the navy. He was accepted for officer's training school and was assigned to the school at Columbia University. After his graduation there, he was assigned to the carrier escort USS *Nehenta Bay*, serving in the Pacific. Early in the morning of February 28, 1944, he called me from San Diego, saying that his ship was being serviced, and he had a week off and wanted me to come home and get married.

I managed to do this, with some difficulty. On the evening of February 29, I received my temple recommend, and on Thursday we traveled to Salt Lake. We were married on Friday, March 3, 1944, at 9:30 p.m. in the Salt Lake Temple. We spent two wonderful days there, and early Monday morning he left on the train to go back to sea. In the next two years we spent less than thirty days together. He arrived home to stay on Christmas Eve 1945. We are still together, fifty-seven years later. It has been a good marriage. We have raised seven beautiful children, and we have thirty grandchildren and fourteen great-grandchildren. All of my brothers, two brothers-in-law, and my husband and I returned home unhurt. What a wonderful blessing!

I was very blessed and happy to have my good friend Zelta Walker Hendricks as a companion for the entire time I served. We were the only Church members in the nurses' barracks or the hospital personnel at Fairmont Army Air Force Base. We did belong to the LDS servicemen's group on the base. We had at least fifteen people, and we met every Monday evening, as I remember. We sang hymns, prayed, had the sacrament, and took turns giving a lesson. It was a big help to all of us.

Zelta and I tried to go to Lincoln, Nebraska, to attend Church with the branch there as often as we could. To do so, one of us had to have the day off with the other just coming off night duty that morning. We took a bus from the base to York, where we caught a train to Lincoln, about fifty miles away. We would attend Church and then spend the rest of the day with the family of the branch president, Brother Allen, and take the train back to York and a bus back to the base that evening, getting there late and tired but spiritually fed.

My ward in Idaho Falls was very supportive. I was given a set of small servicemen's scriptures and also often received little brochures with messages from one of the Presidency of the Church or the Quorum of the Twelve. My bishop, Delbert Groberg, wrote to me a number of times. My mother wrote to me every week without fail, and all of my family was very supportive.

My testimony remained strong and was a great strength to me, as was my temple marriage. I never doubted but that Leland would be all right and come back to me. He did, for which I thank my Heavenly Father daily. I know my Savior lives and watches over us. I know that Joseph Smith was a prophet of God, as is Gordon B. Hinckley today. I am most grateful for my membership in the Church.

There was one time when I did not hear from my husband for more than ten weeks. During this time another nurse, who was married shortly before her husband was called to duty overseas, was sent word that he had been killed in action over in Germany. We all sympathized with her, and they were all very kind to me. It was quite a difficult time for me, but through my prayers and faith that Leland would be all right, I was able to keep a positive attitude. Then one day the mailman delivered a large packet of letters, for which I was most grateful. The same thing happened to him very often. Because I was married, I was released before others, in September 1945.

My most warlike experience as a nurse, other than caring for sick soldiers, happened when our nurse anesthetist was killed in a plane accident on the base. She had gone for a joy ride in a Piper Cub plane with her boyfriend, who was a successful combat pilot. They evidently flew too low and somehow crashed. The plane burned. He was killed instantly, and she had third-degree burns over her entire body. She was wrapped completely with vaseline bandages, with space only for breathing and a straw through which she could be given liquids and an opening for waste elimination. I was assigned to be her special nurse. It was hard not to be able to do much to relieve her suffering. She was conscious but lived only a few hours. I'm sure that there were many in the war zones with equally or more traumatic incidents. My experience was just a taste of what it was like for others.

Lillie Jacobs Fitzsimmons

Lillie Jacobs Fitzsimmons

"To . . . comfort those that stand in need of comfort"
(Mosiah 18:9)

I earned my nursing degree at LDS Hospital in Idaho Falls, Idaho. After graduation, I worked at the new Utah Valley Hospital in Provo, Utah. I was living in Provo when the war broke out. Among my associates there was a lot of talk about the war. Several of my friends enlisted or were drafted into the military. The demand for nurses was high, and I decided that I wasn't going to sit on the sidelines for the whole war. Returning to my home in Idaho, I volunteered as an army nurse and was immediately called into the military, commissioned a second lieutenant, and sent to San Luis Obispo, California. A few months later I was transferred to Palm Springs, California, and from there I was assigned for overseas duty.

In January 1943 we shipped out of San Francisco in a converted cruise ship bound for Brisbane, Australia. Brisbane was a staging area for medical personnel. From there I was sent to Lae, New Guinea, with about twenty-five other nurses. New Guinea was an active war zone, and Lae had been pried from Japanese control only a short time before we arrived.

The situation in New Guinea was demanding. We worked twelve-hour shifts, sometimes longer, toiling until we completed our task, and it was hard work. Besides nurses there were corpsmen and about ten doctors. I can't say enough good about the corpsmen. I don't know how they knew so much—and they worked very hard.

Coming as I did from Sugar City, Idaho, where nearly everyone in our community was LDS, the military environment in New Guinea was new to me. During my eighteen months on New Guinea, I went to church only one time. Most of this was due to our heavy work schedule. Somehow three members of the Church found out that I was LDS and contacted me, picked me up at my barracks, and took me to a sacrament meeting. At that meeting there were only those three men and myself.

One day I noticed a young soldier reading a Bible. Some of his buddies began to give him a hard time. As they were all enlisted men and I was an officer, I called them together and suggested that if we all spent more time reading the scriptures we'd be better off.

I was constantly amazed at the attitude of the soldiers who were injured as they came into the hospital. It was remarkable. I don't know how they held up; the jungles were miserable places, and, coming from the continental United States, none of us knew anything about a jungle. They were so thick you couldn't see five feet in front of you. A group of Australian soldiers who were out on a training exercise fired bullets right through our hospital. They couldn't see us and didn't know we were there.

The most common maladies treated in our hospital were skin problems, followed by mosquito-borne diseases: malaria and dengue fever. We rarely saw men who had battle wounds—most of those were treated in field hospitals and in shipboard hospitals and were then sent back to the States. We spent most of our efforts treating diseases. There were a lot of skin diseases and other illnesses not seen in America. We tried one thing, and if that didn't work, we would try another, then another—none of us knew what these diseases were: we were "practicing" medicine. A lot of good came out of war. Doctors found out a lot about the body and about tropical diseases. Medicine makes great advances during wartime.

We also had to learn to deal with the tropics, especially the rain. You could hear the rain coming through the jungle a long time before you could see it. The sound of the rain hitting the heavy foliage would come closer and closer to us, the rivers and creeks would turn into raging torrents, and the streams would start changing their courses. Following one especially heavy storm, our quarters were almost destroyed and had to be rebuilt. The civil engineers had to keep pushing jungle growth away from the hospital.

I really enjoyed the work and the people on New Guinea. It taught me how the human spirit can overcome any disagreeable thing you have to live through, no matter where you are put. If you believe your experiences are miserable, then that's the way it will be. You make the choice in your own mind. The nurses I worked with were from many places; we were kind of a motley group thrown together. And we learned to pull together.

We also had to learn to deal with the snakes and insects that came into our quarters. The quarters we first lived in had a thatched roof. Termites got into it and had a feast. Every morning the top of the mosquito netting around our beds was covered with saw dust. Mildew got into the leather in our shoes, and they quickly disintegrated.

And the food! The food was terrible. We picked weevils out of the bread, which we sliced thin so that we could see the dark spots. Nurses are fussy people. The cooks would tell us that it was protein, and since the bread was cooked it wouldn't hurt us. All the canned fruit was taken out into the jungle to make "happy juice"—white lightning. Our mutton and pork came from Australia and was so heavily salted that I couldn't eat it. The butter looked and tasted like axle grease colored yellow. So whenever we received an invitation for dinner aboard a navy ship, where we thought we would get a good meal, we always accepted. There we ate like royalty, and we never got enough. The Australians invited us to dinner once and told us that we would be having fresh corn on the cob. But the cook, never having prepared corn on the cob, deep fried it. It was awful. We didn't go there for dinner anymore.

Everywhere we went while in New Guinea, we went under armed guard—even to the latrine at night. If we went out on a date, the officer had to carry a sidearm. And there was an armed guard in the hospital at all times.

We were used to doing our nursing in white uniforms and starched hats, but we soon found out how impractical that was. We learned that we could be good nurses in suntan pants and boots. We also became inventive. If we didn't have a piece of equipment we needed, we found a way to improvise.

We had two operating rooms, an x-ray room, a dental clinic, lab facilities, and two hundred and fifty beds in our hospital. And just twenty-five nurses. When any of us got sick, that put an extra strain on the rest. There were no replacements. These beds were generally filled all the time.

As medical practitioners, we were not immune to infection or disease. I think the first mosquito that bit me following my arrival in New Guinea gave me dengue fever. Dengue fever causes the temperature to spike to 105 for a day, then return to normal for a day or two, then shoot up again. When the fever passes, you're left feeling weak and depressed. After going back to work, I didn't have the strength I previously had. I had to go back to work because there was no one to take my place. The others just had to work more hours.

To prevent our getting malaria, we were on Atabrine. Atabrine took the place of quinine, which had been used in the Far East for many years to control malaria. It only controlled the symptoms of the disease; there was no cure. That's what we did for a lot of things—just took care of the symptoms. The Atabrine colored our skin and our eyes, so I looked like I had a wonderful suntan. After I got home it took several months until this was cleared out of my system and my natural coloring returned. We sure could have used penicillin, but that didn't come along until we got to the Philippines.

One night a sergeant walked into the hospital. I can still envision this man walking on the sidewalk between the different units. When he came in, he said to me, "I need help." He had been stringing electric wires and was electrocuted. When the doctors got to him, he was in such a state of shock that he didn't realize he had been burned. We kept him in our hospital for some time and then sent him to a general hospital in the States where there was a burn unit.

After my discharge from the army, I was on the train traveling between Salt Lake City and my home in Sugar City, Idaho. There were a lot of ex-servicemen on this train returning to their homes. One of them approached me and said, "You're Lieutenant Jacobs; you saved my life." It was the man who had walked into the hospital in New Guinea so severely burned. I believe he was from Idaho Falls.

After eighteen months in New Guinea, our unit was sent to the Philippines. We arrived there about the first of August 1944. We were assigned to be part of the invasion force and scheduled to enter Japan five days after the initial landing. As there was a desperate need for nurses, I was immediately put to work in a general hospital located at the University of Santo Tomas. The Japanese had used this facility as a POW camp. When Manila was liberated, our forces freed the internees and made it a hospital.

I fell in love with the Filipino people. They are absolutely wonderful, sweet, and thoughtful people. And they were so happy to see us. A few of us were invited out to their homes, and we got to go into the nipa huts, which stood on stilts, where I watched men carving wood. The Filipinos took care of us, did our laundry, cooked our meals, and helped with the care of patients in the hospital. When I injured my back and became a patient, two small Filipino men, who were corpsmen, came with a stretcher to carry me downstairs to the x-ray unit. I wasn't sure they could get me there, but they did fine.

Manila was a staging area for more than a million personnel brought in to prepare for the invasion of the Japanese homeland. The hospital facility at Santo Tomas was established to treat those who became sick or were injured among these forces. We mostly dealt with the same kinds of sicknesses and skin problems we saw in New Guinea.

We didn't see any of the Allied prisoners of war who were repatriated—they were all taken care of at Clark Field. We took care of Japanese captives who were incarcerated at the Bilibid prison in Manila. Our living conditions in the Philippines were wonderful compared to New Guinea. For a while we lived in a resort hotel in San Fernando, then in quarters at the University of Santo Tomas.

It was an enormous relief when the atomic bomb was dropped. After the experience of fighting the Japanese armies all through the Pacific theater, we knew that if we had to fight them on their home islands, the war would go on and on. They simply never gave up; they would have to be burned out of their hiding places as we did on Iwo Jima and Okinawa. All my life I have been taught to be kind to other people, to care for them—the thought of burning them out was terrible. But I hated what was going on around me; the cruelty inflicted by the enemy on our soldiers had to be stopped.

While in New Guinea, I toured some of the caves where the Japanese held out. These went back into the mountain for some distance. We also heard stories about how our soldiers had been tortured by the enemy. Hearing these things has an effect on you. But you can't dwell on it and you can't allow yourself to be filled with hate, because hate doesn't affect those you hate—it only destroys you. Not having to go through the nightmare of fighting through Japan was a great relief. It would have been a bloodbath. None of us in the Pacific theater thought dropping the bomb was a bad idea.

During my tour in the Philippines, I did not meet any other Mormons or have the opportunity to attend LDS Church services. The people I worked with knew what religion I was, and sometimes we got into long conversations about The Church of Jesus Christ of Latter-day Saints.

Following the Japanese surrender, I had the choice to go to Japan with the occupation forces or to go home. Suddenly I was homesick, and I chose to go home. The ship I came home on took thirty days to get from Manila to San Francisco. All of the female personnel lived in the ship's infirmary. Those of us who were nurses took care of those who became sick while en route.

I never worried about being in a war zone; I never expected anything other than that I would come back. I had a feeling inside that I would return home safely. This feeling stayed with me all the way home. After leaving the Philippines, our ship lost one of its propellers. This slowed our trip dramatically.

We skirted a typhoon all the way across the Pacific, and though we weren't in the center of the storm, we felt its wrath. Huge waves fell over the vessel as it tipped into the swells; our lifeboats hit the water and were torn off the ship. As the storm rolled us into one giant swell, we spotted a floating mine at the top of a wave, coming directly at us. Somehow it missed us. All this time I felt the calm assurance that we would arrive safely. We did—on December 24, 1945.

During the two and one-half years I was in the army, I served in eight different hospital units. My military experience taught me tolerance and taught me that there are good people everywhere. I learned that I could get along with people of different religions and ideals without having to accept their lifestyle or their beliefs.

Erma Louise Hirschi Gantenbein

I was born in Montpelier, Idaho, on May 10, 1921. I graduated from nurses training at LDS Hospital, Idaho Falls, Idaho, in September 1942. On June 1, 1943, I joined the Army Nurse Corps as a second lieutenant. I reported to the hospital at Fort Ord, California. At that hospital, I was assigned to the postoperative ward. I gave medications, changed dressings, and so forth on surgical patients. I was then assigned to the 22nd General Hospital in Beaumont, California.

March 28, 1944, our hospital unit left California for overseas training in Camp Kilmer, New Jersey. May 10, 1944, we left the United States of America via New York City. Our entire hospital unit left on the HMS *Andes* for England. May 19, 1944, we arrived in Liverpool, England. Our hospital unit was sent to Blandford, England. We had to set up our hospital from empty barracks. That included everything—twelve hundred beds, all the wards including surgery, autoclaves, central supply, nurses' stations, and so forth. June 6, 1944, was D-Day; that evening, wounded solders were admitted by ambulances. I was assigned to the postoperative ward. My duties were to clean wounds, change dressings, send patients to shower, and then check them for further wounds. That meant seventy-two hours of straight duty that night and the next couple of days until we were exhausted. We worked twelve-hour shifts steady from that time on until toward the end of the war. On May 8, 1945, General Eisenhower signed the Victory European Papers.

September 2, 1945, was V-J Day (Victory Japan). On September 19, 1945, we were joined to the 227th General Hospital. We were prepared to go to the South Pacific, assigned to the army of occupation. They had us pack our gear three times, and we even loaded it on the ship one time, to go where—we were never told. Finally, on December 12, 1945, we were reassigned to the 220th General Hospital in preparation to return to the USA. On January 7, 1946, I was discharged at Fort Des Moines, Iowa.

Lina Jane Stratton Garret

When I heard the call for nurses to serve in the military, I couldn't wait to enlist. For someone who had never stepped outside of her hometown of Memphis, Tennessee, the thought of representing my country and being able to travel to overseas locations was very exciting. When I was young, the glamour and excitement of the unknown mesmerized me. Over the next four years, my travels would be a study of contrasts. My parents supported my decision, even though I know they were worried about my safety. I now realize the depth of their love and how difficult it must have been for them to say goodbye to me since my brother had died very young, leaving me their only child.

In 1941, I entered the Army Nurse Corps in Memphis, Tennessee, and became Second Lieutenant Lina J. Stratton. I got my orders to Bringhurst, Louisiana.

I arrived in Louisiana at a newly constructed camp with the nursing quarters still being completed. It was called Camp Claiborne. I was one of seven nurses who arrived about the same time. Later on the group of nurses grew quite a bit. For two years I was at Camp Claiborne, where I received extensive operating room training. Then, in February 1943 I received my orders to go overseas. Of course it was a time of great excitement for all of us because we had been expecting it for a while.

In March 1943 our overseas journey began. Ironically, this trip would begin on a British luxury liner that had been converted to a troop ship. The swimming pools, which were once enjoyed by the upper-class passengers, were now filled with supplies, barrage balloons, depth charges for submarines, and all sorts of other equipment. Daily life on the liner included lifeboat drills.

The luxury liner was a very fast ship that could even outrun a submarine. Because our ship was so fast, we traveled alone instead of in a convoy. We first headed south to Bermuda along the East Coast, then up the coast of Africa to Casablanca. It was there in the harbor that we saw our first piece of the war, which was a sunken French ship turned on its side. When we arrived ashore, we were housed in a hotel. Later on we were lodged in a boarding school for girls that had apparently been closed for the duration of the war.

From there we went on to Rabat, the capital of French Morocco, where we began what I call my two-and-a-half-year camping trip. We slept in tents for the first time, which would have been memorable enough itself, except they were erected on the sultan's racetrack! From Rabat, we went on board a train that was sort of primitive. It was rough and very uncomfortable riding.

Oran was the main seaport of the Mediterranean and our staging area prior to being shipped to Italy. When we got to Oran, we called our staging area "Goat Hill." However, there was only one little goat on that hill, and I couldn't see how he survived since there was such a small amount of vegetation on the hill. We stayed in Oran for quite a while in preparation for going to Italy. Over time, the pilots of a nearby airbase began flying over the nursing area where the showers were. When people found out what they were doing, those pilots received immediate orders to stop. After our time in Oran, we headed to Italy.

It's funny how you can have two different views of the same event. At night, from the safe distance of our area, the red tracer bullets that were part of the air raids on the harbor reminded me of a spectacular Fourth of July fireworks show. But in the daytime, as we made our travels on the Mediterranean into Salerno, Italy, the memory of the beautiful night skies were replaced by the devastation the artillery fire and fighting had done to the landscape, completely shredding the trees.

Since the army didn't like to have ships in the harbor because of all the air raids, we had to travel in a small boat out to the Mediterranean where our big boat was. Once again it was a British ship named the *Durban Castle*. We were on that boat several days before landing in Salerno. When we went ashore, we only brought with us the bare essentials, a canteen of water and K-rations, which were much better than sea rations. There the ten of us were put into one area and told not to leave. We waited a pretty good length of time. Darkness came, but still no one had come for us. We found a quartermasters' company across the road, so each of us went over there and borrowed some blankets. We ended up sleeping in a plowed field that night. Sometime the next day, someone finally came and got us.

Late 1943 found us stationed at a field hospital in Monte Cessina, where the Allies were stopped and where we operated on the most serious casualties. My surgical team was attached to the 11th Field Hospital, which was made up of three separate units. When the fighting was going on and as the front line advanced to the rear unit, the hospital would leapfrog the other two and the surgical team would go with the very first unit of the hospital. Our hospital in Cessina was set up in a place we called Horseshoe Bend. We would be on call at night just like we would be in a regular hospital. Since there were usually four surgical teams attached to a field hospital, it was sometimes necessary for us to all be working at the same time.

Once in Cessina, we were stopped for so long that we operated on the casualties as they came in. My team got the most serious cases. I guess the only patients we did not operate on were those who had head injuries. Those patients were sent to an evacuation area or a general hospital in the rear.

Now others may think of pasta when they think of Italy, but I think of mud. And, of course, they always picked a muddy place to set up the hospital. We had lots of mud in Cessina, and unfortunately our tent was pitched over a mudhole that was not properly ditched in. Water would pour through our tent, ensuring that we always had mud along with our other creature comforts—an electric light and a pot-bellied stove. Each of us in my tent would take turns getting up in the morning to start the stove's fire with wood that we found in the area. The flooding in our tent was so bad that we ended up taking hold of several little blocks that came in the ends of the big shell-case boxes to stick in the mud so that we would have something to step on. One night when it was raining, I was awakened by these clicking noises. When I took out my flashlight to see what was making the clicking noise, I discovered it was from pieces of floating wood that were hitting each other.

At one time, our tent was on a slight slope where behind us was the American artillery with the big guns and on the side of us was the German artillery. Every morning and every evening the big guns would go off over our heads from both sides. At first it was frightening. The first morning when it happened, I felt like the guns were sticking up on the top of our tent, but of course they weren't. As the saying goes, you never hear the one that gets you. I would be asleep when all of that racket would go off and awaken me, so I would pull my sleeping bag off and move onto the ground to sleep. It was only a matter of two feet, but I was more comfortable on the ground than in bed.

While stationed at Cessina, Mount Vesuvius erupted. Although frightened because I had never seen anything like this before, I thought the dark clouds of ash hanging over the mountain were stunningly majestic.

After Cessina, we went to Naples, traveling by boat up the Anzio beachhead, where there was some of the heaviest fighting of the war. Anzio was a small, ten-mile-square area with many hospitals and fighting units. The hospital was in a large foxhole covered with a tent and sandbagged for protection. The cots were dug out on the inside and sandbagged as well, so we were very well protected. In the daytime, I could look up and see thousands of tiny holes where shrapnel had passed through our tent. As far as supplies, I ran the team and made sure we had all of the essential supplies that we needed to operate. We had two sets of surgical instruments that we rotated. While one was being used, the other was being sterilized for the next case. All the instruments that we carried with us were sterilized and ready to go. This meant that as soon as we got to our location of operation, all we had to do was unpack and get the patient on the operating table, and then we'd be ready to go.

At times, we would set up a hospital in a school or some other building that had been abandoned. I don't remember a whole lot about Anzio, except we kept on working one day after another since our guys started to fight for the breakthrough out of the beachhead. The work was relentless, and once my team worked for thirty-six straight hours. I don't remember stopping to eat or sit down, although I know I must have. At one point, Major Madding said, "We'll do one more case and then stop." I was so exhausted when he said this that I began to cry uncontrollably. Understanding my exhaustion, Major Madding ordered me to bed, where I slept for sixteen hours. One time a German soldier was injured and needed blood. One of the officers, who was Jewish, told him we were giving him Jewish blood. We actually always used plasma.

Unfortunately, one of our nurses, Laverne Farquah from Texas, was killed at Anzio. She went to visit a friend who was sick and was sitting on the side of a cot when a shell went through her tent and killed her.

France in the winter of 1944 was very cold with a lot of snow on the ground. Once again, my surgical team was attached to a British hospital. We didn't have all the comforts of home there like we had with our army hospitals. We were in a tent where the only thing of any comfort was the abundance of blankets. In the evening, I would go over to the operating tent where it was more comfortable and stay there as long as possible before having to go to bed. I ended up "borrowing" a hot water bottle from the British hospital that I used to keep me warm, although it seemed like it took forever to do so. I ended up keeping the hot water bottle and bringing it home with me.

A bit later, our hospital was relocated to a place so close to the German lines that it was possible for our hospital to be run over. It was also possible for the Germans to break through the line and attack us. We were ordered to quickly pick up what we could carry and move to a rear area until the threat was over. When we went back to the hospital, not a thing had been touched. We were glad because we had left quite a bit of equipment there.

In October 1944, Germany was invaded, and the personnel at the hospital that I was with crossed the Rhine River at Worms over a bridge that the engineers had put up. The fighting was still going on by the time December came around, but another nurse and I got a leave to go to Paris. We were there for one week during the time that the Battle of the Bulge was going on. The Battle of the Bulge was the last major fighting that Germany did, and as far as that goes, it was also the last major fighting that we did. There in Germany I was awarded the Bronze Star for my work and my ability as a surgical nurse.

In the winter of 1944, as Germany began to retreat, I became sick and was transported to a hospital in Paris. After spending two weeks recuperating, I was devastated to learn that I would not be returning to my surgical team but would finish the war with another unit. Fate intervened by way of a young captain with whom I had been corresponding throughout the war. One day he appeared at my hospital door and said, "Let's get you back to your unit!" I knew I would be considered AWOL, and although scared, I trusted him and left. We slipped out of the hospital unnoticed. He then put me on a plane that was heading toward my unit. Major Madding was shocked to see me but heartily welcomed me back and made the necessary calls so I could stay.

There wasn't a whole lot of fighting going on by May 1945, so when Germany surrendered to the Allies, it was time for us to go back to Italy where our main headquarters had been. Then in July, we began being sent home to the United States.

Since the war with Japan wasn't over, people were sent home according to the points system. I don't remember how those points were figured out, but the more points you had, the better chance you stood of being shipped back to the States. I had over one hundred points, so I was sent home quickly. The other nurses were sent to Japan to help with the war effort there. I went back to Naples, this time flying, and stayed in a hotel for a few days. Then with several other nurses, I boarded a U.S. Navy ship and landed in Norfolk, Virginia, nine days later. It was great to be back on American soil and talk to my family again.

Those four years of service broadened my nursing skills and taught me strength, compassion, and endurance. It also taught me to look for beauty in everything and everyone that surrounds me. I saw the horrible things war could do, often while in places that are considered to be the most beautiful and luxurious sites one could want to visit—Morocco, Naples, Paris, and the Swiss Alps. How fitting that my travels ended upon my return to Memphis on August 15, 1945—the same day that Japan surrendered!

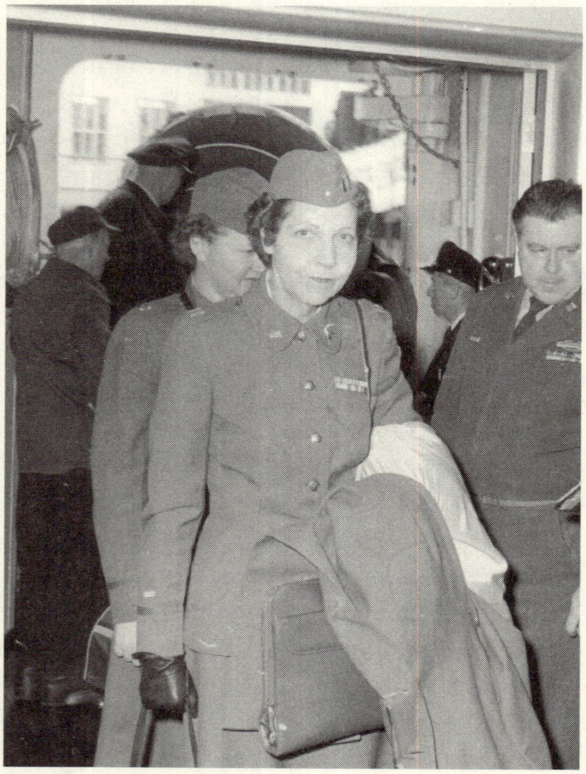

Emma Bailey Gunnell

Emma Bailey Gunnell

Emma B. Gunnell was in the U.S. Army Nurse Corps from 1943 to 1963. She served as a registered nurse, training in the United States and in England. She worked in field hospitals in Europe, also serving in the Philippines after liberation. She returned to the United States, where she served in many army hospitals. She returned to serve in a hospital in Hawaii during the Korean conflict. She retired in 1963 with the rank of major.

She was born August 3, 1903, in Wellsville, Utah, the daughter of William Jeffs Gunnell and Mary Bailey. She trained at LDS Hospital in Salt Lake City and graduated as a registered nurse in 1925. In 1927 she worked as a night supervisor at the Idaho Falls LDS Hospital. In the 1930s she moved to the Beverly Hills area of California, doing private nursing duty. In 1943 she entered the Army Nurse Corps, just before her fortieth birthday, and was stationed at Bushnell Hospital at Brigham City, Utah, for a short time. In 1944 she was serving in England during the bombings and was there during D-Day, June 6, 1944, for the invasion of France. Later in 1944 she was stationed in the Philippines and returned to the States where she was stationed at Camp Breckenridge, Kentucky, and later at Fort Huachuca, Arizona. She also served in Hawaii at Tripler General Hospital. In 1963 she was discharged from the service with the rank of major, having completed twenty years of honorable service in the military. She worked at the Letterman Hospital in San Francisco. She passed away at the age of ninety on November 26, 1993.

Rosmary Clara Harms

Rosmary Clara Harms participated in World War II as a German nurse on the Russian front.

The push of people that came to the United States after the war was because there was nothing left there. Germany was a country in ashes—a country of hungry people, no jobs, no laws, no anything. Some of them went back after the European countries started building up again and had the idea that there still is life to come. So many places in the world never continued to grow.

I served in the Red Cross Nursing Corps during the Second World War. I was born on October 6, 1923, in Essen, Germany—what we know as the "Little Pittsburgh of Germany." My parents were Emma and Ulysses Klatt. My husband's name was George Harms, and we were married in August 1947. I was living in Germany, and my father was a dentist. When I was in the seventh grade, he said that he thought it would be a good idea if I were an apprentice with him. That way I could have basic skills that I could use for the rest of my life.

Transportation was streetcars. I had a week's ticket, and I walked probably fifteen to twenty minutes to get to the stop, climbed on a streetcar, and went to school or wherever my friends went. My dad had me taking classes at the university. We got about five or ten minutes on the streetcar, and the conductor said, "This is as far as we are going." I said, "I have a ticket that takes me to the end of the street." "Not with me you haven't," he said. "So how am I going to get there?" "Walk," he said.

We were probably on the outskirts of town. It was like everything was dead. It was the morning after the Crystal Night. All the stores, glass, and anything that belonged to the Jews were all destroyed. The main street had light poles on both sides of the streets, and each pole had a Jew hanging there by his feet. I cannot cry about it. I cannot tell you what I felt like. I couldn't explain it, what was going on. My brother found me and got me by the neck and said, "Turn around, Sissy. Let's go home." But I remember that was the end of Germany right there. There was no pity, no sorrow for anyone. I didn't love anyone. I loved me. I was still alive, and that was most important to me. If you mention the Crystal Night to any German, they stop dead in their tracks and look at you and they say, "What do you know about that?" The stores were all destroyed and put on fire, and everything was burned down.

I started working with the Red Cross in 1940–41; in 1942 I was in Russia in a field hospital there. We had an operating room that was like a double-wide trailer that pushed out and then in again when we were traveling. It was self-sustained; it was loaded with batteries, and we had a cycle technique. A cycle technique looked like you were sitting on a bicycle and peddling like crazy in order to create friction. It provided enough electricity to speak on a field phone or produce a little electricity for light in the batteries that we were carrying. The whole arrangement was just enough to survive, nothing else.

I worked just with the Red Cross, nothing with the army. It was a lie because the Red Cross is Swiss-oriented nursing—neutral. The German army would have nothing to do with that, but it was a good cover-up. I got training as a medical assistant from my father then went to a nursing school in Germany for about eight months because the government told us we got points. That was mostly good for grocery coupons; if you were hungry enough, you went into just about any kind of deal. I only went to nursing school for eight months, and then I went to Essen, where I lived and grew up, because the factories were there that made bombs, and if you volunteered to work there, you could stay at home.

I took a class once or twice a week for terminology on recognizing instruments and things like that. I was surprised it wasn't all that hard; I thought it would be much harder if you didn't have enough know-how. But I qualified when not many others did. Then I was assigned to the Red Cross Nursing Unit, and we went to Russia in an area called Lupiz Lofleen. It was a middle area of the three countries: Germany, Poland, and Russia. I was drafted into the service. I did not volunteer.

It was wintertime, and we had summer clothing. There was no heat. The cold was tremendous; it was unbelievable, below zero, even in the operating rooms, or what we called the pits. It was so cold that we wore sheepskin gloves to keep warm. We looked at the Russian women, and we mentioned to each other, "Good Lord, look at the size of shoes that woman wears," but they were all wearing two pairs of shoes. They had a pair of felt shoes in the inside of another pair of boots. We learned quickly that was the only way to keep your feet warm. We had nothing warm to wear unless we undressed somebody that was dead and kept the clothing for ourselves. We still had nothing to eat.

There was a field on the outside of town. As far as your eyes could see, there was nothing there except a dead cow. One day we decided to go and see what was going on, and that dead cow had been cleaned out very nicely, and there were snipers inside the cow who were picking us off like flies.

Nobody was assigned to anything. When the wounded were coming in, you worked. If you needed sleep, you would leave and take three hours of sleep and then be back again to work. I often questioned whether the doctor was really a doctor. The knowledge the man had was noticeably zero. That scared a person. He would say for instance, "I can't go on, I just can't go on." At first we all just stepped back and let bygones be bygones. But then I took on enough nerve and said, "Well then, step aside and give me room." I got to a point where I got pretty good at things.

We took care of whatever soldiers came to our hospital. We were wondering why we had so many soldiers who came who couldn't talk, and it took a while for us to catch on to what was going on. We found that they took the uniforms off the German soldiers and put them onto the Russian soldiers so that we would take care of them. It took a long time for us to catch on. We didn't mean to or want to take care of the Russian soldiers; that was not what we were there for.

The whole situation was terribly cold. There was no way that anyone could survive. Once a tank crawled into one of the smaller towns where we were. There were probably seventeen men, no more than that, who came outside and sat on the tank. It was so cold that they froze to the tank. We couldn't get them off. Most of the time their whole buttocks came off too.

The medicine was gone. There was nothing left anymore. We took care of frostbite you wouldn't believe. One toe, all the toes—none of them were saved up to the knee. As a matter of fact, I had a brother that lost both legs due to frostbite. You would think that they would welcome the help and comfort that you gave them. They looked almost good at the end of a couple days, like they were healing. The soldiers didn't want to heal; they would trick us and put cat hair in their wounds so that infections came along just like crazy overnight, because they didn't want to go back. We had a good supply of medication at first; we had morphine and xylocaine, which was very acceptable. I don't think that any of the soldiers really, truly had a deep sleep when they had an amputation of the arm or the leg.

We took care of frostbite, gunshot wounds, and pretty much everything that came around. The death rate was probably eight out of ten. The only antibiotic we had was neosporin in powder form. Once someone had it, it did not mean they would get better, because some would not keep their wounds clean and they picked at them. It was blamed on the poor education of the people who didn't heal. I have memories of young boys saying, "Cut it off, please cut it off, so I can't pick it no more."

We did not have a commanding nurse; we were all responsible to the doctor. We got mail maybe once a month when it was in a drop zone out of an airplane. That was how the supplies came too until at last there were no more. The get-along attitude amongst those of us that were supposed to work well together was failing more and more. We were three girls, and we tried to walk just to get out in the air and a little exercise, and the doctor said, "You don't have to go that way, I went there already yesterday, and there is no way out." So I said to my lady friend that I was walking with, "He thinks that we are going to take off." He kind of watched us. We were searching for something to do, to get out from the area, but how can you? There was no way that you could run. The frost would have gotten you. The Russian women would always wear five or six layers of clothing, and when it was time to wear clean clothing, they just took the bottom layer off and kept peeling off each layer. It works. It is one way of keeping warm.

Our relationship with the Russian people was that they were afraid of us. There was no question about it. One morning, someone said, "Look out, company coming." I went out to talk to her. She kept pointing to the other direction, and inside they were overhearing what was being said, and they were already investigating what she was trying to tell me. She said to me, "Paninka," which is a young woman. I said yes, I was a paninka. "Matuska," she said. I said, "No, I am not a mother." She said she was a mother. I asked her if she had milk, and I imitated how to milk a cow. "No," she said. Three days later she came with a half of a bucket of milk. Where did she get that? There was nothing as far as your eyes could see. We could only figure out that there was something underground someplace, where some of the people were hiding and had a cow. We never heard anything, not even the cow mooing. It was absolutely not real. You couldn't see a footstep the next morning, and we tried to find where that woman had gone, because we thought that where there was a half a bucket of milk, there was probably a bucketful. She carried a little broom with branches of a willow tree, and as she was walking she was wiping away her footsteps. We didn't drink the milk because we were afraid it was going to be poisoned. There were some of the wounded that volunteered to drink it, they were so hungry. We were at the point that we said, "Fine, if you want to try it, try it." We were sorry that we didn't help them.

The cold was unreal—you don't know what it is like to be cold. We started out with IV fluids as well, but it didn't last and we had nothing. We felt bad putting the wounded in little red hay wagons. The horses were cold too. We couldn't make them do anything because they were hungry and not fed. The route back was to the Ukraine and Poland, most of the time into Austria. Most of the time there was the hate of the people who were left behind and saw us fleeing with half-dying people. We got thrown out. We were totally ignored. Some of the natives attacked the wounded soldiers, and we tried to do the best we knew how. By that time I had my hair cut off because I discovered that I had lice and I couldn't take care of it, so I had my head shaved. I found myself an ace bandage, so I looked like a boy. I would probably say that we got 250 miles into Russia off of the Polish border, going towards Moscow. The people there were Greek Orthodox. They only took care of their own and nobody else.

I was a prisoner of war for just about two weeks, and that was when I met my husband. He came and inspected me, and he spoke fluent German; he was of German background. His great-grandparents came from Germany before the First World War. They left to escape the draft; they didn't want to be soldiers.

I was kept as a prisoner of war because I had no hair when I was found and I was not recognized as a girl. When they found out that I was, I was out of there quicker than a bullet. I would have had no special favors if it hadn't been for my husband, who would get me a warm meal every once in a while and go into a PX and buy me a warm sweater or something like that. I don't think I could have made it if it weren't for him. I would have run. I know I would have given an honest try. I would have run.

After I was a prisoner of war, I was told to go home. I could go home, but I did not want to go. The home in which I grew up with my mother and father (I am the youngest of five children) was no longer there. The only one that had a roof over his head was my brother William. He took my parents in, and he said that he was going to go out and see if he could find me, and he did find me.

I never would have imagined that while I was on the Russian front, my life would have taken me where it has. I thought I was definitely going to die. I had given up. There was really nothing whatsoever left for me. It changed as time went on, and people say I am a strong person and I should compliment myself for this, and that helps. If I was right, I didn't back down, and it made the difference.

Everything burned in Germany. The country was in ashes by the time that everything was over and done with. There are people there with severe burns from those forceful bombs who don't look like people anymore because they were hurt so badly.

Why could not anyone see where we were headed? The fanatics of the "Heil Hitler"—I often wondered if they really meant it or if it was just a show to save their lives, their attitudes, and what they stood for. The hate amongst the people themselves was unbelievable. You no longer said, "Live on; you are my brother or my sister."

I made the best choice of my whole life when I joined the Church. I have never had so many friends. I have a quick temper, and I am able to control my temper.

The greatest lesson that I learned from the war years is to not trust anybody; you might be digging your own grave. It is not always so, but I have never forgotten how to give love and care to those who need it. I don't believe that I ever will deny anybody any help if I can help that person. I think probably that as I get older I get softer, but I have a strong will. You will be able to do a lot for yourself if you know how.

Ora Mae Sorensen Hyatt

When the United States declared war on Japan, December 7, 1941, I was in my first year of nurses' training at Salt Lake General Hospital. Two years later, in 1943, the Cadet Nurse Corps was organized as a means of encouraging more young women to fill the great need for nurses in our country's war effort. We who were already in training were offered the opportunity to join the program, which had decided benefits for those who did. We received sixty dollars a month during our last year of training, if we signed a contract to continue working as nurses after graduation. It could be a civilian hospital or in the military service, but we agreed to work for the duration of the war.

I was filled with patriotism. I wanted to be a part of our country's military forces to win the war. As a cadet nurse, I volunteered to spend my last three months of training at Bushnell Army Hospital in Brigham City, Utah. I was assigned to surgical and penicillin wards.

After our three years were completed and we graduated as registered nurses, my classmate Elaine Spry and I volunteered for active duty in the U.S. Army Nurse Corps. We were sworn in as 2nd lieutenants at Fort Douglas. Our pictures were in the *Salt Lake Tribune* and in a magazine called *Army Life*, because we were the first two cadet nurses in the Ninth Corps area (eight western states) to be commissioned as lieutenants in the Army Nurse Corps.

Our first orders sent us to Fort Lewis, Washington, for four weeks of basic training followed by a six-month hospital assignment in the Ninth Service Command. Then we could be sent overseas, if we were willing. Elaine and I readily agreed to go overseas, as long as we could stay together. This request was granted and we were never separated in our assignments.

At Fort Lewis, we learned the ways of the army—its uniforms, military terms, and hospital procedures. We even had a sergeant who drilled us in marching, saluting, and so forth. We went on an overnight bivouac and slept on the ground in a sleeping bag. Elaine and I were so cold we kept all our clothes on and both crawled into one bag.

Fort Lewis, Washington
October 30, 1944
Dearest Mother,

Thanks for sending my letter of appointment and if you have sent some hangers and towels, that takes care of everything. We were given our clothing issue:

2 brown and white seersucker dresses
2 caps to go with these duty uniforms
1 dark green skirt and jacket
2 tan shirts and a tie
1 pair brown oxfords
1 woolen scarf
1 brown purse
1 pair brown leather gloves (really nice)
1 dark green cap with the big gold army insignia on the front
1 long sleeved woolen sweater (tan colored buttons down front)
1 dark green cape
1 rain coat with parka hood

We pay for this out of our $250.00 allotment and if we want anything else we buy it ourselves. We're also given two fatigue suits but we give them back when we leave Fort Lewis.

Spry and I went to Seattle Saturday and bought some gold bars for our uniforms. They are only gold plated and they were $1.25 a pair.

We found out they held an LDS meeting on Sunday evenings so we weathered the storm and looked up the chapel. I guess there were 12 or 15 people present but, Oh! It was just perfect! We sang those old familiar songs and prayed just like they do in the good old Center Ward.

Love,
Ora Mae

Fort Lewis, Washington
20 November 1944
8:00 a.m.
Dearest Mom,

I'm all excited and happy. I've got a date with a Mormon lieutenant. Remember I told you about this boy I met in church who was from Illinois? He always takes charge of the Sunday night meetings. He's the only lieutenant besides Dr. Malouf who comes to church. The others are all enlisted men. We usually go to Malouf's afterwards for a "fireside."

Please write soon, lots of love,
Ora Mae

Our first Sunday at Fort Lewis, Elaine and I checked the bulletin board at the Post Chapel to find when and where LDS services were held. They were in a basement room at 7:00 p.m. We received a warm welcome from the Mormon servicemen the evening that we arrived. It was a rare event to have females in attendance. The officer in charge of the meeting was Lieutenant Preston Hyatt. Following sacrament meeting, a fireside or social hour was held at the home of Dr. and Mrs. Malouf. It was a chance to get better acquainted than we could during church.

Ora Mae Sorensen Hyatt

Our time at Fort Lewis was coming to an end. The Mutual (YW and YMMIA) of the Tacoma Ward held a Saturday night dance, to which all servicemen from Fort Lewis were invited. LaVerne Richardson (another nurse from Salt Lake) and I were on our way back to the post after a day in Seattle. She suggested we drop in at the dance. Lieutenant Hyatt asked me to dance and then cut in repeatedly when I danced with someone else. He asked me for a date the following Sunday, and we were together almost every night of the week I remained at Fort Lewis.

Basic training was over. Elaine and I were assigned to DeWitt Army Hospital in Auburn, California. Nursing in an army hospital was different from a civilian hospital because our patients were all young men. We had corpsmen, comparable to nurse's aides, to assist us. We gave medications—mostly penicillin shots (the latest miracle drug)—changed dressings, and did the charting. We didn't have the recent battle casualties, but some had been shipped home with long-term recoveries ahead, such as the loss of an arm or a leg.

Lieutenant Hyatt went home to Joliet, Illinois, on his last leave before going overseas. He returned to Fort Lewis by way of Auburn, California, so he could give me an engagement ring. Then in his first letter after he rejoined his unit, he wrote of a plan to get married *before* he went overseas. We each obtained permission from our commanding officers for an emergency leave.

We traveled separately to meet in Salt Lake and were married in the temple. I wore my mother's wedding dress. My parents met their new son-in-law, and I met his mother. Then we returned to our separate military assignments.

Back at DeWitt General Hospital, it was just one week before Elaine and I received overseas orders. We went first to Fort Sill, Oklahoma, by train, to join the 376th Station Hospital. There we were issued new uniforms and equipment and were given additional overseas training for our new assignment. We learned to go over the side of a ship (three stories high) on a rope ladder. We also practiced crawling on our stomachs under ropes a foot off the ground. We were taught that if and when we were captured by the enemy, the only information we could give was our name, rank, and serial number (N785226).

There was an airfield across the street from the nurses' quarters, and Elaine and I made friends with some "flying sergeants." During our free time, we went flying every chance we could. Pilots who needed to get more hours of flying time would practice in small planes called L-4s and L-5s. These were built with an extra seat behind the pilot. These student pilots seemed happy to take us along. We were always required to strap on a parachute but never had to use it. These young pilots enjoyed giving us a thrill with an occasional loop-the-loop and dipping their wings from side to side.

Fort Sill, Oklahoma
19 April 1945
Dearest Folks at Home,

> Tomorrow I will have been in the army exactly 6 months. Imagine that! Guess where I went this afternoon? To Dallas, Texas, and back in a C–45. That's quite a large twin-motored plane, used mainly for chauffeuring high-ranking officials around to different Posts. It has room for five passengers and two pilots. We were at the hanger when they were getting ready to leave and they asked us if we'd like to go along.

Our port of embarkation was Seattle. Our destination was "top secret," but everyone in our unit guessed we were headed for the South Pacific theater of the war. We sailed on May 7, 1945, on a large transport named the USS *Admiral Capps*. There were 5,500 service troops on board. Elaine and I were bunked in the ship's hospital area along with two other nurses from our unit. We were fortunate to have such spacious quarters and portholes to see outside.

We spent two weeks in the harbor of Eniwetok, May 20 to June 5. We were allowed to go ashore three times. We stopped again on June 8 at the island of Asor in the Ulithi Atoll of the Caroline Islands. During the next twenty days we went ashore only once. The hospital personnel started taking atabrine, one a day with our evening meal, to prevent malaria. Rumors were that the Allied Forces had not yet been successful in securing the area that was our destination. And because our ship was filled with only service troops, our arrival had to be delayed.

It seemed we traveled very slowly, and so did time, as we zigzagged on our course across the Pacific. Everyone on our ship was friendly enough, but the officers were not to mingle with the enlisted personnel. An exception to this was in our small group of LDS Church members. When we held our meeting each Sunday, there was a spiritual bond in that room that transcended all military rank or station.

There was one incident on our voyage that stands out in my memory. It was late one Sunday afternoon, and the ship was moving peacefully through the ocean. The stillness on board was broken by the shrill whistle that always preceded, "Now hear this!" Then, "The smoking lamp is out." That meant all portholes were covered and complete silence was observed. It was eerie! Minutes passed, and the next command was, "Man your battle stations!" We had practiced these drills before. Those who were not part of the ship's crew had preassigned places on the deck to assemble in small groups to keep out of the way of those manning the ship's firearms. The next thing we heard was really frightening. It was, "Prepare to abandon ship!" We knew this was not a practice drill. We quickly put on our life jackets, and again we waited. In the silence, I thought, "I am not a good swimmer." We hadn't been in sight of land for weeks. I was so far from home; no one would ever find my body or know what happened to me. I didn't want my life to end this way. My heart was pounding as I prayed silently for Heavenly Father's help.

After what seemed like an eternity, another announcement came over the loudspeaker that informed us the danger had passed. We were free to move about the ship and "the smoking lamp was lit." There was no official announcement as to what had happened, but we heard that an enemy submarine had been sighted following us. Or perhaps the ship's captain arranged that exercise to see if we were prepared well enough for an attack.

A convoy accompanied us as the USS *Admiral Capps* left Ulithi on June 28. Four days later, we arrived in the harbor of Okinawa after fifty-seven days onboard ship. My one worthwhile accomplishment during that time was to read the Book of Mormon cover to cover.

We came into the harbor in the black of night. The nurses were all wearing fatigues, combat boots, and helmets, and they carried our musette bags. We went down over the side of the ship on a rope ladder (as we had practiced) into a landing barge below. Open trucks waited for us on the beach. We drove without headlights over rough dirt roads. We could see fires here and there in the distance and hear gunfire. We traveled about ten miles inland from the beach to a bivouac area—a large tent filled with army cots. We walked from the tent up a dirt path, still in complete darkness, to fill our helmets with water from a limited supply. I had joked about taking a bath in a helmet, but this was for real. The water in our helmets was for bathing and washing clothes. We filled our canteens for drinking and brushing our teeth from a canvas bag hung over the limb of a tree. We got to bed at 2300, under mosquito bar. We were instructed to grab our helmets at the sound of an air-raid alert and to run to a nearby ravine, which was our bomb shelter.

During this first week or so, our meals were the regular dehydrated food issued to all GIs, and we ate standing up or sitting on our cots. I really appreciated Elaine's sense of humor and her wit. We could laugh about our inconveniences and help each other over the rough spots.

Elaine and I were anxious to get to work so we, with LaVerne and Mary Anne Tonne, volunteered for detached service with the 27th Field Hospital while waiting for our own unit to get in operation. The 27th was set up in tents, with the nurses' stockade a short distance away. An armed guard took us to and from the hospital tents. Each nurse was accompanied by a guard on night duty as she made her rounds because of the Japanese snipers in the area. We worked twelve-hour shifts, 7:00 to 7:00, each nurse in charge of two or three tents full of wounded men.

One night, a sniper was surprised in the act of stealing food from the mess tent. The guards joined in the chase to capture him as he darted between the tents of the hospital. However, he had a grenade, and he pulled the pin and blew himself to pieces rather than be taken alive.

We worked as part of a surgical team closer to the front lines than the 376th Hospital. We were very busy—long hours of care, readying the injured for transportation away from the battle zone. The wounded had to be evacuated in case the Japanese recaptured the area. I also worked on a neuropsychiatric ward. These patients were unable to continue in the daily battle to survive, and they seemed to live in a dream world of their own. This continued for about two months before things smoothed out and the four of us returned to our own hospital unit.

We found the 376th had been attached to a larger hospital, the 233rd General, located in a former schoolhouse.

Okinawa
20 August 1945
Dearest Folks at Home,

Ten months ago today Elaine and I joined the Army Nurse Corps. I hope by the time we've been in a year we are back in the States or at least headed that way. I keep saying we'll be home by Thanksgiving, but I honestly don't believe that myself.

We are now working at the 233rd General Hospital. Spry and I were lucky to get in a tent that has been built up—that is, it has a floor, wooden framework, and a screen door. Many of them are still living on the ground. It's up to the individual to get their own building done. You have to make contacts with some Seabees, quartermaster outfit, or Enges and get your "friends" to work for you. The two girls who had this one built have only been in the army four months. They flew over from Hawaii about two weeks ago. We're sleeping on army cots again, and the first night I really missed the mattress and springs we had at the 27th. You get used to things in a hurry.

I was thinking yesterday about my patriarchal blessing. I just realized that another part of it is being fulfilled. As I remember, it said I would have the chance to spread the word of the gospel both at home and abroad. When I first read that I thought that meant I was to go on a mission, and I didn't think that would ever happen. I've never had the desire to go on a mission but I don't mind talking about my religion and explaining it to nonmembers. So many of my patients have asked me about Mormonism, and

> although I will never make any converts I can tell them enough so if they're really interested they can follow it up when they leave the hospital. One of our roommates at the 27th was very interested in our beliefs. She asked to read some of the *Church News*—those small-size overseas editions. Also some other pamphlets called *Youth Speaks*. The subject always seems to come up when I'm with new people and refuse their offer of cigarettes, coffee, beer, etc. Will you send me a copy of my blessing?
>
> Your letters always breathe of home and I love them so.
>
> Lots of love,
> Ora Mae

We lived in an enclosure surrounded by barbed wire. Armed soldiers still patrolled our compound to protect us from Japanese snipers.

There was a PX (post exchange) as part of the hospital facilities, and usually we could obtain toiletries there, but one time I was out of shampoo and the PX was out of it also. I thought shaving cream might work—they had a good supply of that—so I lathered up my hair with shaving cream. That was not a good choice. When I poured water over it to make some suds, they disappeared and my hair was a gummy mess. One more lesson in the life of a nurse overseas.

Our chief nurse invited Elaine and me to go with her to the Yontan Airfield to put another nurse on a plane to the United States. While Captain Burley was filling out the necessary papers, Elaine and I walked a short distance down the road. I went off into the tall grass where I could see some unusual flowers. I noticed a convoy of open army vehicles going by, and I waved. The driver of the first truck was amazed to see an American girl just a few feet away. He turned to look in my direction and didn't realize he slowed down. The driver in the next truck was also looking at me, and he ran into the truck in front of him. The third and fourth trucks did the same, and there was a chain reaction of collisions because the drivers were distracted—and I was the cause of it. Oh me!

Our mail delivery was irregular, but when it came we usually got a stack of about twenty letters. Mail was one of the important things we looked forward to from day to day.

Elaine and I made contact with some Latter-day Saint servicemen on Okinawa and located the time and place for meetings. There were four nurses and one sergeant in our hospital unit who were Latter-day Saints. Whenever we were off duty on a Sunday, our friends would send a jeep to take us to church. It was held in a large tent at 10th Army Headquarters and other times at the 11th Bomb Wing, which were both some distance from our hospital. We really enjoyed that association with members of the Church. We felt like true brothers and sisters—the next best thing to being with family.

Sometime in August we heard that General Doolittle was bombing Japan and then that President Truman authorized the dropping of atomic bombs on Nagasaki and Hiroshima. Our patients were guessing the end of the war was near. Then one evening, while we were watching an outdoor movie, the sky suddenly became alive with rockets and flares. Ships in the harbor were sounding their horns. There was shouting and shooting all around us. The movie stopped, pandemonium broke out and GIs were yelling, "The war is over!" We hugged one another and laughed and cried in excitement. Our first thought was, now we can go home! It was disappointing to wake up in the morning and realize the truth; it might take months before we'd actually get there.

Released POWs from the Bataan Death March in the Philippines were sent to Okinawa to receive necessary medical care. They also needed to be fed and nourished until they were strong enough for the long flight home. They looked like skeletons. Their physical condition was deplorable, and many were too weak to eat by themselves. Some would cry silently as we fed them as if they were babies. It was heartbreaking to see the results of their cruel captivity.

On September 16, a typhoon struck Okinawa with winds of ninety miles per hour along with torrential rains, which caused a lot of damage. It's hard to describe the force of that storm. Fifteen seaplanes were dashed upon the beach. Hospital wards were blown down. Some patients were placed under their beds for safety. The nurses and medical staff braced against the tent poles to keep them erect and to keep ourselves and the tents from blowing away. We stayed on duty for twenty-four hours straight, wading in mud six to twelve inches deep. The nurses' quarters were soaking wet but were still upright.

One of the after effects of that destruction was that our food was in short supply, and we were rationed to two meals a day. We were fortunate to have some friends in the Seabees who invited us to their mess one evening for a dinner of steaks, ice cream, and fruit. This was a rare treat after eating powdered eggs and powdered milk, canned hash, and beans for the past few weeks.

Next we received news that our 376th Hospital Unit was being sent to Japan as part of the occupation forces. On October 5, we boarded an LST (landing ship tank). It had a flat front that could be lowered to allow tanks and trucks to drive out of the ship onto the beach. It was not a very large ship—its capacity was only about 387. A second typhoon hit the area as we were on our way to Japan. This was of even greater severity than the one we endured on Okinawa. The ship was tossed from side to side and up and down by a wind of over one hundred miles per hour. I got firsthand knowledge of seasickness as we were thrown about by the mountainous waves. Our LST was blown off course, and our three-day trip to Japan took seven days.

After the winds and rain subsided, we reached the Yokohama harbor safely—no casualties. A huge destroyer and a U.S. Naval Hospital ship, the *Marigold*, were anchored next to us. Our nurses were temporarily transferred to the hospital ship.

We saw the war's devastation on the city. The U.S. Army Engineers went to work on a bombed-out Japanese hospital at the Tachikawa Airfield (between Yokohama and Tokyo). They rebuilt it enough for the 376th to set up operations there, and we went to work once more.

Our patients were again the prisoners of war from the American and Allied Forces. They were so appreciative of everything we did for them! I remember especially the look in their eyes when meals were brought to their beds. They cleaned up every crumb—practically licked the trays. One evening while on duty I found some sugar, canned milk, and cocoa in our nurses' station. I used the electric hot-plate and made a batch of fudge for all the patients. They loved the unexpected treat!

The nurses lived in bamboo barracks with no heat of any kind. It was early winter (October) in Japan, and we had just come from tropical Okinawa, which made a huge difference in the temperature. We were cold all the time. We went to bed with all our clothes on, trying to keep warm. The toilets were nothing but a trench in the floor with a handrail to hold as one squatted. These toilets were first on the list of changes to be made (for upright replacements).

The hospital doctors and staff were helpful in making improvements and procurement for the nurses. They also made transportation available to us so we could see the surrounding area of Japan. The cities lay in ruins from repeated bombings, and the people had fled to the hills and rural areas. They took with them everything of value that they could carry. The few Japanese remaining in the cities looked at us suspiciously. We had been their enemy a few weeks ago, and, not being able to speak a common language, we could only stare at each other.

I had worked at the Tachikawa hospital for only a few weeks when orders came that I was to return to the United States to be discharged. Married nurses were given priority to go home. I was happy about going back to the States, but my husband Pres wouldn't be there. He was still in India, with too few points to be discharged. I felt like a traitor leaving Elaine in Tachikawa, but parting was inevitable, and we said a tearful good-bye.

I came home on military transport planes in four days. We made stops to refuel and to change planes at Guam, Kwajalein, Johnson Island, and Honolulu, and then we made our final landing at Hamilton Field, near San Francisco. It was dark as our plane approached California. Along the coastline were the words (spelled out in lights), "Welcome home—well done." When I saw those words and realized I was really home, I couldn't stop the tears rolling down my cheeks. As long as I live, I'll never forget the joy of landing in the United States of America and the pride I felt in the country to which I belonged!

All the returning military servicemen and women were given access to free phone calls anywhere in the country to let their family know they were home. I called my folks in Manti, Utah, and after many tries the Manti operator said, "No one is home at Sorensens'. I think they're at the show." (Small towns keep track of everyone.) I kept trying and finally reached them after the movie was over. It was heart-warming to hear the voices of my mother and father! It was also pure heaven to have fresh milk once more, and what luxury to use American plumbing, heating, and electrical appliances! I never before appreciated these things like I did at this time. Just to turn on the faucet and get clear drinking water, or a hot shower, seemed absolutely wonderful.

I traveled by train to Fort Sheridan, Illinois (north of Chicago), where I was to receive my discharge. My home address had changed from Utah to that of my husband when I was married. We were traveling as a group of military personnel, so I agreed to what the majority wanted.

I completed my discharge routine at Fort Sheridan, which was effective December 15, 1945. I worked as night supervisor at my alma mater, the Salt Lake General Hospital, for several months, until Pres wrote that he was coming home.

Mary Jane Neville Johns

Mary Jane Neville Johns

This past Christmas (2000) I received Tom Brokaw's *The Greatest Generation Speaks* from my eighteen-year-old grandson. He had inscribed it, "Dear Grandma, Thank you so much for all you do. I don't say or show my love and appreciation to you enough. You truly are from the greatest generation. Love, Nick." After reading the book, I realized I had never told him of my involvement in World War II.

I was a navy nurse by choice. The war started when Japan bombed Pearl Harbor while I was a student nurse. We hurriedly put blackout drapes on all the windows. We continued our senior year at Mercy College of Nursing in San Diego, California—the home of numerous military bases of all the branches of the armed forces. After graduation I worked in the Washington DC area at the national Red Cross Headquarters. I knew the military needed nurses, so I signed up for the

Navy Nurse Corps. My choice was based not only on the appearance of the NNC uniform, but also because I would always have a clean bed and good food wherever I was stationed. In December 1943, I reported to the Long Beach Naval Hospital for duty.

Military wards consisted of two private rooms and a ward housing eighty beds. The nurses were in charge of the entire ward, the assigned enlisted personnel, and the total care of the patients. The actual work was performed by corpsmen and WAVES (Women Accepted for Volunteer Emergency Service). The orthopedic ward housed battle-wounded men, many of whom had contracted osteomyelitis because miracle drugs had yet to be invented to protect them. The cardiac ward housed many young seamen who had drunk all sorts of poisonous liquids (torpedo juice, one hundred proof alcohol, and so forth) to escape the horror of the death and injury they were seeing all around them. Other wards contained mental patients and patients with infectious diseases and various other ailments and problems. At night a lone corpsman was in charge of one ward and a supervising nurse took care of ten wards with eight hundred patients!

I was eventually transferred to the United States Naval Hospital (USNH) at Norman, Oklahoma. Here we met our first American POW patients, most of whom had been captured on Corregidor, who suffered terrible hardships as the Japanese marched them to POW camps—starving, beating, and killing them at will. Those who survived the agony ended up as slaves in the coal or salt mines in Japan, working in unbearable conditions. The coal dust and salt permeated their lungs, and almost constant coughing continued throughout their lives. We treated their wounds, but their minds had seen so much terror that it was hard for them to cope with life and families and love. Smiles were nearly nonexistent despite our best efforts.

I am always somewhat reluctant to say that the war years were some of the most happy and fun years of my life when so many citizens suffered horror, pain, and death.

La Rue Tucker Johnson

I applied to the Salt Lake General Hospital and was accepted, but I hadn't had chemistry or geometry, so they told me I had to do that. I went to West High to get those classes. You had to have those classes in high school. Then I applied for the nursing program at the hospital and I got into that in 1939 or so. There were thirty-two nursing students who all lived together in a boarding house. Three later dropped out. Our teacher was excellent. Her name was Miss Bilger.

I was a senior when the war started, and that's when the Red Cross came around recruiting nurses for the army. I signed a paper that I would go into the army after I passed my test and graduated. I wasn't part of the Cadet Corps, which was part of a separate recruitment. I told them I didn't want to go in until after Christmas. I graduated in August 1942. I told them that and they agreed to it.

La Rue Tucker Johnson

I didn't enter the army until January 1943. I worked at the Richfield Hospital until January.

I was inducted at Fort Douglas. Then they sent me to Boulder City, Nevada. There was a military hospital in Boulder City. I went to this unit and they put me in surgery because I was the newest one out of school. I don't know why, but the surgery unit was very small and not used much. In fact, they did tonsillectomies and a lot of little things. They also did circumcisions. The boys that worked there thought it would be a real kick if they got me in, so they scheduled me to help with a circumcision. I did one circumcision on an adult, but it was all right. They just laughed about it. We didn't have any men nurses; they were orderlies. Some of them were even younger than I was. I was there for six months.

I worked in surgery there at the hospital for only six months. Then we joined the unit that was going overseas. I wanted to go overseas because things were so dull. They sent me and my friend to Camp Stoneman in California. There we learned to march. We went through a thing called an obstacle course. We had to crawl through a barbed wire thing, so that was our training.

Stoneman was up the river from Oakland. We were sent down the river on a ship and got onto a big liner. These were borrowed Norwegian ships. They were huge and fancy. Then we went overseas. Our unit was called a hospital ship platoon. There were two doctors, one dentist, twenty-one enlisted men, and five nurses. When we got on the ships, they would put the nurses up with the officers. We nurses went in as second lieutenants. I think I got paid two hundred dollars a month. I remember my folks were having financial problems. My father had been injured at the coal mine, so he wasn't able to do a lot of work. So I could apply for extra help for my family. I don't remember how that worked, except that I did that and was able to send them some money.

We went to New Caledonia. It's a thousand miles off New Zealand and Australia. It had been a French penal colony, but it was mostly natives and some French people. When we got there, we got off the ship and they put us to work in a field hospital with tents. It was on the beach. The reason they had hospitals there was that there were no mosquitoes. They didn't have to worry about things like malaria. The main hospital was quite large, and it was an army hospital. They would send all the wounded from the islands where they were fighting down to this area. We were assigned to a little hospital. It was called the 27th Field Hospital. There were just beds and tents standing in the grass and the sand.

They would bring us patients by ships. A lot of them were ambulatory. Then they would send us back to the States to take care of these ill patients on the ship. So I made three trips over from San Francisco to New Caledonia. We would take the wounded from New Caledonia home and then come back on another ship. All the ships were ocean liners because they'd have sick bays. Sometimes there weren't too many who were really ill. One time I was on one of the ships, and they had a whole group of patients with casts on. Of course they called us on deck when we first got on the ship and said, "Now if anything happens, don't try to save these people with casts on because you would just sink." Nothing happened, fortunately, but we worried about the possibility of torpedo boats.

On one trip that we made, we were going over to the island and Artie Shaw and his band came to entertain the troops on the islands. That was the only time we went convoy. One ship carried supplies, one carried personnel, and one was a mine sweep. We were in line but still zigzagging. One day we went to breakfast, and we were sitting with the officers. Artie Shaw was on the ship, and he was oh so excited. He sat down and said, "Did you know that we were chased by a submarine last night?" And we had noticed. The ship just took off at an angle. But he was really impressed and excited about this thing. We had had to take off across the ocean and go away from the convoy. Fortunately, nothing happened to us, but the mine-sweep ship was sunk that night.

When I first went on those big ocean liners, I thought, "Well, I've never been on an ocean. Oh dear, how deep is it?" Then I thought, "There's nothing I can do about it. I might as well enjoy the ride." So I did. There were five nurses, and we were stationed at the very top deck with the officers. We would sleep in the same area. The ships had Indonesian servants. One night, one of the girls woke up and she said there was an Indonesian servant man standing there with a great big machete. He didn't do anything, but they took him and put him in the brig. I don't know what happened to him. He was just in the doorway with this great big knife. After that, they assigned us a male MP stationed outside our door. But because of situations like that, the ships wanted to get rid of the women. Finally, after the third trip, they stopped sending women. That was the time we went to New Zealand for three weeks and worked in the hospital there. Then they took us out and left us in the islands, and I was there for fourteen months. The navy guys didn't want us on their ships interrupting things anymore. New Caledonia was a beautiful island.

I was sent to the States for surgery for an ovarian cyst. After I got home from my surgery, they let me choose a place to go, and I said, "I'd like to see New York since I've never been there." They assigned me to Staten Island. They had a big group of buildings that had been orphanages and the army had taken them over for hospitals. That's where I was assigned. I went in January and was there until May, and it was horribly cold and nasty weather in New York. I thought, "I don't want to stay here anymore." So I asked for the hospital ship, which was an army ship.

When my friend and I signed up to go on this ship, they wanted nurses to go to the Philippines and bring patients back. After they assigned us, the ship broke down and they sent us to Charleston, North Carolina. They were trying to fix the ship. Finally they sent us to New Orleans. I returned to my group on the ship and went to New Orleans and then to Panama. The ship broke down again on the way to Panama, so we stayed in Panama for three weeks. Then they fixed the ship and we got to go through the Panama Canal. We were still in Panama when the war with Germany ended. Then they didn't really want all these nurses, so they sent us to Los Angeles. From there we were discharged.

There was one guy who had a great, huge decubitis ulcer (bedsore). I spent most of my time massaging that, because you can cure one of those if you massage it. It took the whole trip, but he got better. One time, when I was over in the islands, we had a lot of black soldiers. One day I heard this great argument going on in the back, so I went down there and here was this large black man with a knife. I said, "You put that down." These were big men. Anyway, he obeyed me. I went back up and said, "My heavens. How did I do that?" People had more respect for officers back then.

Another patient I had wouldn't eat. The food was bad, I grant you. One day I got real angry said to him, "Now you eat what they bring you!" I guess he did. I was really mad.

Back in New York, I was assigned to a psychiatric ward, and that was really sad. These soldiers came back from the Battle of the Bulge, and half their brains would be gone from being shot at. Some of them couldn't even move. It was so sad.

In the islands, one of the doctors was a Latter-day Saint and so we had a little church. Mainly I remember that it was more of a study group. Occasionally we would have sacrament on Sundays, but not very often. This doctor would get us together. There were never any conferences near us.

When I got out of the service, I continued nursing. I got a job at Salt Lake Clinic. Because I had graduated from the Salt Lake General Hospital, I did go down there for a few weeks and worked in a pediatric ward.

My father was a bishop. I think that I always had a testimony. Of course, my folks were born of pioneer parents and lived in Fairview. I've always been a member, but I've learned to appreciate that now. I guess I never used to think of it much. But because of that I guess I left the alcohol and tobacco alone, which I'm very thankful for now.

Olive Eloise Crouse Kauffroth

It was April of 1944. World War II was raging in Europe and the Far East. I was a senior student nurse at the LDS Hospital School of Nursing in Salt Lake City, Utah. Our school, along with seven other schools in the Intermountain West, was asked to recruit nursing students who were in the last six months of their training. The students selected would be sent to a military hospital to complete their training, and they would be encouraged to join the Army or Navy Nurse Corps for the duration of the war.

I was one of the seven students from our school who elected to join the Nurse Cadet Corps. We were issued gray dress uniforms to be worn with a gray beret. Impressed with these new uniforms and with the fact that we would get $60 a month over the six-month period, we thought our new life had much to offer. I even remember how I spent my first $60: I bought two dresses for $7.95 apiece, bought a war bond for $18.75, sent $10 to my mother, paid my tithing, and had $9 left for pocket money.

It must be said that I was twenty-one years old and as innocent to the ways of the world as could be. My life to this point had been spent with my mother and brother and extended family, with my teen years in Heber City and then in Salt Lake. My younger brother had joined the navy at seventeen and was already stationed in the Solomon Islands in the South Pacific. Little did I know that with this new uniform and responsibility I too would gain a new view of the world and experiences around the globe.

So it was that the seven of us nurses, dressed in our good-looking uniforms, were sent by bus to Bushnell Army Hospital near Brigham City, Utah. Bushnell might well have been a million miles away from Salt Lake City. The hospital was a four hundred bed amputee/psychiatric center. Most of the patients were soldiers who had been wounded in combat. We were faced with the reality of the war and the reality of good people coming in

Olive Eloise Crouse Kauffroth

with life-changing wounds. Our lives, as well as theirs, would be changed.

We were scheduled six hours of nursing care on the wards plus two to three hours of classroom study each weekday. I was assigned to an amputee ward. As we made rounds to be introduced to the patients, I thought I would not be able to take care of the terrible wounds we saw; however, the doctors, the nurses, and the patients themselves patiently taught us how to care for all their wounds. We became skilled in evaluating, cleaning, medicating, and bandaging these awful amputations.

As we worked and studied, we developed an understanding of many things that would help the young wounded soldiers. We learned that it was important to develop a positive attitude to help them cope with their injuries and go on with their lives. One of our greatest tools in helping them was humor, as we always urged them to see that life still held joy and promise.

As the patients learned these lessons in healing, so did I. These lessons would help me cope with problems later in my own life. We learned of perseverance and positive attitude, and of humor and always looking for happiness. We came to understand that there were emotional tools to use to help them get well physically.

In the middle of our time at Bushnell, we traveled home for graduation exercises for the LDS Hospital School of Nursing. The graduation exercises were held in Kingsbury Hall of the University of Utah. We graduates were dressed in our white duty uniforms and nursing school caps, plus we wore our blue capes with the identifying LDSH in gold on the collar. We each carried a bouquet of a dozen roses. Elder Harold B. Lee, then an Apostle of the Church, was our graduation speaker. After the ceremony, Elder Lee asked to speak to the nurses who had volunteered to spend time in a military hospital. He spoke to us as a group and told us that we did not have to work in the military to fulfill our obligation as cadet nurses, all we had to do was to work in a hospital, even here at home. He then spoke to each of us individually and shook our hands. When he came to me, he told me, "You understand you can stay home." I replied that I did understand, but that I had decided to become an army nurse because of my profound experiences at Bushnell. I then asked him if he had ever been there. He said he had not. And I said, "Perhaps if you go there, it might change your mind." He replied, "I want to ask you to always remember that you are a Latter-day Saint woman." Though my statement to him might seem rather impertinent, I believed strongly in the work we were trained to do and in helping the people who would need our help in the war effort. I have never regretted my decision.

On June 20, 1944, the first casualties from the Battle of Normandy began to arrive at Bushnell. We had returned from graduation to full schedules. Now, there were literally hundreds of new patients within a few days. In this era, this was a near miraculous movement of wounded; they went from the foreign battlefield to a treatment hospital in the United States in ten days or so. To get them home so quickly meant better treatment of their wounds and more lives saved. I witnessed bravery during that time that I simply have not experienced since.

It was those experiences at Bushnell that made me want to serve in the Army Nurse Corps. After we completed that six-month assignment, we went home to take our state board exams. I was sworn in as Second Lieutenant Olive Eloise Crouse, ANC, at Fort Douglas in Salt Lake City, Utah, on November 2, 1944. The day was memorable both for its significance as a monumental day in my life and also because during the ceremony, the officer swearing me in looked down to see that my galoshes were on the wrong feet. His laughter, my embarrassment, and his comment, "Young lady, I hope you pay more attention to details in your army career," made this one of life's funny and embarrassing moments that I've never forgotten.

In the next few days after my swearing in, I was sent by train to Fort Lewis in Washington State for two weeks of introduction to the details of army life. We then were taken to Torney General Hospital in Palm Springs, California. Torney was another new experience for me in a long line of new places.

After two days of orientation, I started the traditional night duty: twelve-hour shifts (from 7 p.m. to 7 a.m.) thirty nights in a row. After the thirty-day stint, a nurse had two days off and then began another schedule of thirty more nights on duty. In the short time I was there, I worked sixty-seven nights and felt like I had been born working nights!

The patients at Torney were very different than those I cared for at Bushnell. Almost none had wounds. Instead, they had diseases from the South Pacific. Many patients had what is known as "jungle rot," and it truly was that horrific. The condition made them lose body hair and patches of skin, and this made them miserable most of the time. The only cure was various lotions, medications, and ointments that were supposed to help, but the medications helped only for a brief time. In spite of this, in the short period I was there, only a few patients died from that disease.

Although caring for patients was the critical task, we also had fun. Movie stars from Hollywood often came to Palm Springs, and almost all of them wanted to come and visit the patients. Of all the many stars I met, my favorite by far was Frank Sinatra. He gave me and three other nurses a thirty-minute personal preview of songs that he was going to sing as a guest on the *Bob Hope Radio Show* that evening. It was exciting and a dream for all of us. He even got our names and was going to dedicate his songs to us that night, but the rule was that the names of army personnel could not be publicized. So the wonderful Mr. Sinatra said, "OK, you'll know who you are." That night he dedicated his performance to "four lovely nurses." I never forgot how handsome and how charming he was to us that night.

Duty came in the form of different ways to use our nursing skills. The chief nurse at Torney took note that two of us were from Salt Lake City and would assign us alternately as escort officers to return patients to the psychiatric center at Bushnell in Brigham City. I did this duty twice. The first time I traveled by train with about twenty "section eight" patients, plus six MPs with a sergeant in charge. The second time I went was as the escort for a nurse lieutenant who had been serving in New Guinea. Her roommate there was raped by six enlisted men, who were court-martialed and hung for the offense. The nurse lieutenant who was raped committed suicide, and her roommate was determined she was going to come home no matter what. Somehow she got herself transferred to Torney Hospital as a psychiatric patient and was referred to Bushnell. I was locked in the train compartment with her all the way to Bushnell, during which time she assured me she was not dangerous. I believed her, but it didn't do a lot to relieve my mind. I felt sorry for her and spent a sleepless night. I've often wondered what happened to her later in life.

Escorting these people to Bushnell gave me an opportunity for a brief visit home to the Salt Lake area after each trip. Because I knew I would be sent overseas soon, I was grateful to get to visit my mother and aunts whenever I could.

Then the orders came. In April I received word to proceed to Camp Beale, California (near Sacramento), which was a large staging area for army personnel who were being sent overseas. When I got there, the whole camp was in chaos because instead of sending five thousand to the camp, by some mistake in orders, ten thousand were sent there. They didn't have anything ready for us. I asked a sergeant I met at the gate where I should go to check in, and he said, "I don't know, but let me give you some advice: if you see a line, get in it, because sooner or later you'll be in it anyway."

After a few days, things did get straightened out. I was assigned to a group that included fifty nurses, twenty-five doctors, and two hundred medical enlisted men. We were told that we would be going overseas by ship but were not told the destination, and we were told that there would be five thousand army personnel on board. We trained for three weeks at Camp Beale then were taken to the port of Los Angeles. There we boarded our ship, the USS *Collins*.

When we embarked, our destination was still unknown, although we speculated that we might be bound for Europe. When we were about twelve days out to sea, we saw another huge ship out our porthole. The navy captain informed us over the ship intercom that this British destroyer would be our escort to our destination. He also told us that he had opened secret orders that informed him we were to proceed to the port of Calcutta, India. The entire trip was scheduled to take about forty days.

Three or four days later they gave a few of the army officer personnel permission to hear the radio broadcast of Tokyo Rose. She would transmit messages such as, "Good afternoon, USS *Collins* and USS *Patrick*; we know your location. Don't you wish you were home in Nebraska?" or "It won't be long and we're sorry, but we are going to sink your ship." It was frightening and seemed so foreign to our way of life.

Soon after that, one Sunday morning at nondenominational church services, we were on deck with all army officers and were singing the navy hymn. At that moment, we heard the loud sirens from all three ships and the call, "General quarters, man your battle stations. The no-smoking light is lit. All army personnel are to return to your quarters below decks." We already had tears in our eyes from the navy hymn, as it beautifully asks for protection from peril for those at sea. This general call to quarters scared us profoundly, and it was then we truly realized we were in real danger. We felt we were in peril, as the words of the hymn had suggested. The navy officers later told us they could see Japanese airplanes off in the distance, but they didn't have to fire the big guns of either the troop or battleship.

We sailed on without incident to the port of Calcutta, India. The port was at the mouth of the shallow Hooghly River. Docking was impossible, so slowly we were taken by smaller boats to port, about one hundred people at a time. We noticed the people dressed in very colorful clothing. We could see people bathing in the water, washing their clothes, dumping garbage, and collecting water in containers to take home. Along the riverside there were burning ghats: funeral pyres made of sandalwood where the Hindu people burned the dead. But most of all we smelled something we had never smelled before or since: the terrible odor of Calcutta—six million people without much sanitation. Those sights and sounds were a far cry from the innocence and familiarity of the lives we had left in the United States.

We were taken to the U.S. Army hospital in Calcutta. After several days of orientation, we were told we would be going into China by air. But a few days later, our orders were changed and the nurses were told we would be assigned as replacements for nurses in the CBI (China-Burma-India) theater of operations. I was happy that two other nurses I had met aboard ship who were from Salt Lake were assigned to the same hospital: the 181st General Hospital near Karachi, India, in the Sind Desert, which is now Pakistan. The two nurses from Salt Lake were from the St. Mark's School of Nursing, and we were happy to be together.

Our Catholic chaplain was concerned about everyone, both personnel and patients at the hospital. I was the only Mormon of record, and it showed by the "M" for "Mormon" on my dogtags. The chaplain located three LDS men at the U.S. air base about forty miles from us. He arranged for transportation so I could attend a group service with them. One of them was a returned missionary, but mostly they were just very homesick and only wanted to talk about going home.

On August 7, peace was declared, and we all knew that we would be sent home soon. In order to clear the theater of war, it was planned to send half of the Americans home via Karachi and half via Calcutta. The soldiers and personnel in Burma and Assam were sent across the Indian continent by local trains. It took about ten days for them to travel cross continent, and when they arrived at the 181st Hospital they were infected with many diseases: dengue fever, malaria, and any other infectious disease you can think of.

About this time, the army chaplain asked if my roommate and I would be interested in helping with two projects. One was a leprosarium with about thirty to forty patients but no medical supplies or medicines, and the second was an orphanage of twenty-five children who needed clothing and food. The children were Eurasians, with Indian mothers and British or American fathers, who had been abandoned by all. The needs of these people were very great, so about ten nurses, five doctors, and the chaplain put about twenty dollars each into a fund, which raised about three hundred dollars. With this money we bought army surplus clothing, food, and medical supplies. These supplies were taken from supplies that were declared surplus and were scheduled to be destroyed when the Americans left, so we got a great deal for the money we raised. The leprosarium had been using old, bloody, and used rags, which they rinsed out and used over and over again for bandages. We were able to supply them with new bandages, medicine, food, and some clothing, for which they were very grateful. The nuns at the orphanage were so happy to receive a large supply of food and clothing for the children, and we did this as long as we stayed there. The children were beautiful, and we were touched by their predicament. Most of them could speak some English to us. We always wondered what would happen to the people who so needed help after we left.

In January 1946, all female personnel were to be sent home ASAP because of the rioting of the Indians against the British. About this time, all Indian political prisoners were released by the British, including their leaders: Gandhi, Nehru, and Jinnah. It was a fascinating time to watch history taking place.

It took us twenty-one days to fly home. We made stops in Teheran, Cairo, Casablanca, and the Azores. We stopped in St. Johns, Newfoundland, and flew to Fort Totten, Long Island, New York. There we received orders to travel by train to Camp Beale, California—exactly where we had started from ten months before. We received our discharges, and I went home to Salt Lake to work part time at the LDS Hospital and attend school at the University of Utah. In June 1948 I received my degree in nursing and a secondary teaching certificate. Soon after graduation, I went on a vacation to California. While there, I applied for a license to practice nursing in California. When I picked up my license to practice in California, I was asked if I would be interested in working in San Francisco. There were several jobs open, and I thought, "Why don't I just go for the job interview for practice?" I got the job—in the French Hospital School of Nursing. I taught medical/surgical nursing, audited the doctors' lectures, and supervised their nursing practice.

It was spring of 1951, and I had been there about three years when I received a letter recalling me to active duty in the army. The letter was addressed to "Captain" Olive Crouse. It went on to tell me that my assignment would be as an instructor in one of the advanced army medical technician schools that the army was about to open.

A few weeks later in early January 1952, I was told the Advanced Technician's School was ready to be activated. I was sent to Walter Reed Army Hospital in Washington DC for even further orientation. There were to be four schools activated; one at Walter Reed, one at Fitzsimmons, one at the Presidio, and one at Tripler in Hawaii. I was assigned to the school to be set up at Fitzsimmons. Each school would operate at the hospital assigned, but their orders and supervision would come directly from Washington DC. The faculty for each school was four RN instructors who would teach nursing, monitor courses, and supervise nursing practice. Each school would have one hundred regular army enlisted personnel selected to be students. These students were the kind a teacher dreams of: eager, smart, and highly motivated to do their very best. At the completion of one year of study, the students could take a test to become advanced technicians. The students hoped this would help them to eventually be promoted to warrant officers, but that hope was never realized.

By January 1953, the first class had graduated and the second class was in place and doing well. It was in that January 1953 I was introduced to a major, an air force pilot and air traffic control specialist who had recently returned from duty in Korea and was now stationed at Lowery Field, Denver. He would later become my husband.

In May 1953 an interesting moment occurred, once again admonishing me to remember my Latter-day Saint background. I was home on leave. My mother had asked me to have my picture taken in full uniform, captain bars and all. After we had completed that, we went to ZCMI department store. We were on the second story and waiting for the elevator when some people around us whispered that President and Sister David O. McKay were in the building near us. We stood there with a group of ten to fifteen and the elevator opened. There stood President and Sister McKay. Everyone said "Welcome!" and they were smiling and shaking hands. He saw me in uniform and came to shake my hand. I'll always remember how piercing blue his eyes were as he looked directly into mine. He asked me where I was from and where I was stationed and, still holding my hand, he asked if I was a member of the Church.

"Then, my dear," he told me gently, "always remember that you are a Latter-day Saint woman." It was yet another time I would be reminded of the importance of the Church in my life.

In June 1953, the air force major and I were married, and my husband had to decide whether to stay on active duty or to return to the air traffic control position he had in New Orleans, Louisiana. I could stay in the army as a married woman, but if I became pregnant or had children I would be automatically discharged. As often happens in life, in August 1953 I found I was pregnant; this ended my career quickly and abruptly. My husband left for New Orleans, and we made plans for the future. However, I was not discharged until November, and it was a very hectic time.

In sitting down to remember and record all the chapters of my army life, I've enjoyed recalling the people I met and friends I made during these times. I truly loved what I was doing; to be an army nurse during World War II was such a challenge. When we remember these times of our youth, it is always with the warm glow of hope and such promise for our lives. For me, the times were exciting and full of important lessons. But even more important was to be in those hospitals helping the people who had been far away from home serving their country was an honor. I still feel that every young man and woman should have this opportunity to spend time in service to their country. At the time of this writing, I've just celebrated my eightieth birthday. I've been blessed with many good memories from all the years. Certainly the ones recounted here have a special place in my heart.

Lola Prestwich Lamoreaux

World War II was declared while I was still on probation in nurses' training at the Dr. W. H. Grove LDS Hospital School of Nursing in Salt Lake City, Utah. In 1944, during my senior year of training, the U.S. Army Cadet Nurse Corps was organized to help alleviate the nursing shortage brought on by the war. As seniors we were invited to be participants. From that first class of cadet nurses at Bushnell General Hospital, five of us from the LDS Hospital School joined: Thelma Larkin, LaVerne Richardson, Evelyn Gunderson Skinner, Eloise Crouse, and Lola Prestwich.

We were issued a gray woolen uniform suit for off-duty wear. It had red epaulets on the shoulders and an arm emblem on the left sleeve. It was an attractive outfit with the gray shoulder bag and gray cap with the cadet insignia on it. Mother sent me a newspaper clipping of us five in our cadet uniforms that was published in a Salt Lake newspaper prior to our departure for Bushnell General Hospital. I was excited and felt like a celebrity. On duty we wore our school's student uniform.

Bushnell General Hospital was a typical military base in appearance. It was located where there had previously been a fruit orchard in Brigham City, Utah. There were still a few trees about. Bushnell was mostly an amputee, plastic surgery, and neuropsychiatric center.

We were encouraged by our leaders and each other to attend church, which I did occasionally at the chapel on base. The times I attended, there were not many present. The were no LDS services. Most of the LDS military personnel probably went into Brigham City to attend church. I did not. I was a member of a large Mormon family and was raised in a Mormon community. Having the opportunity to work with those of different faiths helped me realize that most people are kind, tolerant, and understanding.

It was a sad awakening for me to meet all the young boys missing a leg or an arm, moving about in the hospital corridors forever changed by the horror and waste of war.

Our three months at Bushnell gave each of us a glimpse of and feel for military life and nursing. After our three months were up we went back to the school of nursing we came from to complete our full three years of training, take state board nursing examinations, and attend commencement exercises for the class of 1944. Our commencement exercises were inspirational, colorful, and a spectator's thrill as well. With our long-sleeved uniforms, black stripe on our caps, blue capes, and red roses, we were *it* for the evening. When we marched in with the remainder of the school, the student nurses in white following, it was a delightful honor.

After graduation I worked in surgery for three months at LDS Hospital. I took night call frequently. Life became humdrum. I decided to change my life. World War II was still being fought both in Europe and in the South Pacific. Helping the war effort seemed the right move for me to make, so I enlisted in the U.S. Army Nurse Corps. I was given a temporary appointment and commissioned a second lieutenant in the army of the United States and assigned to the Army Nurse Corps.

I was alone when I went to enlist. I took the oath of office on the first day of December 1944 at Fort Douglas, Utah. On the third day of December, I left Salt Lake City for Madigan General Hospital at Fort Lewis, Washington, for basic training. I traveled by train. This was the first time out of the state of Utah for me and I was anxious, but to my delight I met on the train traveling to the same destination for the same purpose a college friend, Cecil Josephine Burns. We had both entered nursing schools in Salt Lake City: she attended the Holy Cross Hospital School of Nursing, and I attended the LDS Hospital School of Nursing. Cecil was not a member of the Church, but she was a very good person.

Basic training at Fort Lewis lasted one month. First Lieutenant Rex P. Rutter threw the book at us. He tried to teach us the military way of doing things. He drilled us on military ethics, procedures, and conduct. We learned of chemical warfare and venereal disease. He saw that we could march, take cover, pitch a pup tent, dig trenches, and endure a bivouac in the rain. Our drill sergeant would put a rock in the hand of any nurse that turned the wrong way when marching orders were called. That sergeant must have thought we were a group of ninnies. We were photographed for an ID card; given metal ID tags to wear around our necks; issued anklets, panties, field shoes, and vests; and given $250 for uniforms. Tetanus, typhoid, and smallpox immunizations were updated, and our blood was typed. We were introduced to patient wards but did not actually get involved in patient care.

With basic training over, many of us newly commissioned second lieutenant nurses left for our assigned post on January 8, 1945. Most of us left by troop train heading south. This was a unique experience. Each town we passed through, a crowd was cheering. I was assigned to Torney General Hospital, located in Palm Springs, California. I arrived there on the 11th. Palm Springs is situated in the desert with mountains to the east. It was a resort community for the rich and famous. Part of Torney General Hospital was once the El Mirador Hotel. Extending out from the hotel buildings were many wood barracks. There were patient wards and housing for personnel. I was assigned to a barracks close to the women's ward. My first roommate was not a member of the Church, and she smoked. She thought I was very unworldly, but regardless we got along okay. There was nothing that could entice me to smoke, drink alcohol, or flirt. The one thing that was irritating about living in this barracks was the ants that invaded our clothing if we did not seal it up.

My first nursing assignment was to the dermatology section. Most of the patients were diagnosed with a skin problem that was called jungle rot, an atopic dermatitis prevalent in the South Pacific Islands. All these patients were treated the same way. We gave them oatmeal baths, then spread ichthammol ointment over the infected skin areas and bound the areas in gauze dressings. Some of the boys looked like mummies after treatment.

Tec-3 Lawrence W. Lilley was Major Hookey's main assistant. Sometimes, I thought, he rather resented us young commissioned female nurses. Lilley was a registered nurse with much experience in universities and hospitals in New England. He really deserved a commission.

When I was on the afternoon shift, some of the patients would come into the office and tell me their problems and experiences on the front line of war. I listened. That is all they needed. Even the corpsmen needed a listening ear. One evening I was in the nurses' station doing some charting when one of the corpsmen stopped by the desk and started visiting. He told me that before he entered the army he had killed a man for raping his sister. I was shocked and without words. Finally I told him that he did not need to confess to me but to God and ask His forgiveness. The patients were up and about, and their need was family, home, and peace.

Throughout army general hospitals the NP (neuropsychiatric) sections were experiencing as great an influx of patients as the other sections. The purpose of beginning an NP school for nurses was to send the boys home or back to service as mentally and physically well as possible. To do this, trained personnel were needed. The neuropsychiatric school at Bushnell was the first in the Ninth Service Command. There were twenty-six army nurses and one cadet nurse in this first class. Lieutenant Colonel Olin B. Chamberlain was the chief of the NP section. Captain M. K. McGee, ANC, was the director of the school. We were privileged to have such an opportunity.

The most disturbed patients were behind locked doors. We were advised not to visit the wards without an attendant. On one of the wards there were German POWs doing janitorial work. This was unexpected. They appeared very young. There was a guard with them.

Some of the treatment was difficult for me to accept. I was observing and helping in an insulin shock therapy clinic when a patient died suddenly. The therapy was frightening and risky. I did not administer insulin but observed the reaction the patients experienced. Some of the patients had severe convulsions before the nurse could get 50 percent IV glucose administered. Agitated patients were given a continuous therapeutic bath. The temperature of the water was maintained at around one hundred degrees Fahrenheit. We covered the tub and patient with canvas restraints. Barbiturates were used for sedation.

Our graduation ceremony was held in the Bushnell post chapel. We were awarded certificates, and a class photo was taken. There was a party held in the post officers' club.

I returned to Torney General Hospital July 1. It was summer and very hot in Palm Springs. I was not assigned back to the dermatology section. I was assigned to the women's ward and nursery. In this section there were nurses who had been POWs of the Japanese and there were also the labor and postpartum patients. I was in the nursery most of the time. The head nurse thought that was a good place for me. The delivery room was just a door away from the nursery; therefore, I helped out when things got urgent.

I remember one of the nurses that had been a POW on the ward. She was a sad young nurse. While in prison she developed leukemia and was very ill at times. She had a record player next to her bed, and she played "Clair de Lune" over and over. Her name has gone from my memory, but her image returns when I hear that melody.

One night there were a couple of labor patients in my care. One was an Egyptian war bride. She didn't speak English. I couldn't make her understand that screaming didn't help. Another labor patient was in the room and had to endure the shrills with me. At that time relatives were not allowed to remain with labor patients.

As there was no LDS church in Palm Springs, the only time we LDS nurses attended a service was when an LDS priesthood holder stationed at the post brought us together. It was on one of these occasions that I first bore my testimony of the truthfulness of the gospel of Jesus Christ, our Savior.

After the atomic bombs were dropped on Hiroshima and Nagasaki and the Japanese surrendered in August, Torney General Hospital started preparing for closure by transferring and discharging patients. Personnel were being transferred to other general hospitals. I was transferred to Dibble General Hospital in Menlo Park, California. My orders were to report to Dibble on November 15, 1945.

Dibble General Hospital was located in a choice area. It was built on 127 acres of the old Timothy Hopkins estate, one mile north of Palo Alto. In September 1945 it was annexed to the city of Menlo Park. This site was selected because of its proximity to San Francisco, where many of the wounded men arrived from the South Pacific.

Dibble was a large, efficiently run facility. I was assigned to the neuropsychiatric section. In the NP section there were six wards. Two wards were locked wards. The nursing staff spent most of their working hours behind the locked doors. One of the locked wards was for psychiatric general prisoners. In the other locked ward were patients needing constant surveillance. Nurses were cautioned to be accompanied by a ward attendant when visiting patients in rooms or in the ward and when leaving our stations (office). The nurses' station had a divided door so a patient could communicate with the nurse while she and medications remained protected. All doors throughout the section were knobless. The windows had bars over them. The entire section was fenced with high chain link and barbed wire. The more ill patients were unpredictable and capable of sudden violence. Kindliness and friendliness were often misinterpreted.

Several cases I remember because they were unusual. Corporal B's case was the most unique. Corporal B was admitted to our section with a patch on his right eye. He was confused, agitated, and probably in pain. As the history of his eye injury was revealed, the staff learned why he was so disturbed. He had been involved in many of the South Pacific campaigns and had received a medal of honor. On the ship returning to the United States of America after many months in the jungles he studied the Bible. In Matthew 5:28–29 he read: "But I say unto you, That whosoever looketh on a woman to lust after her hath committed adultery with her already in his heart. And if thy right eye offend thee, pluck it out, and cast it from thee: for it is profitable for thee that one of the members should perish, and not that thy whole body should be cast into hell."

Corporal B followed instructions. His right eye was gone. Before his discharge from the section, he captured our hearts. He became the staff's favorite patient. He recovered psychologically, but he was still wearing a patch on his right eye when I last saw him.

A patient with a diagnosis of schizophrenia called me a dumb idiot because I could not read his scribblings on the wall of his room. His wall was covered with just groups of letters. He had his own personal language. His behavior was most bizarre. He would laugh, shout, and become aggressive, and he seemed to be hallucinating. I was relieved that I didn't have to enter that room without backup personnel. When a patient became combative, he was given an intramuscular injection of paraldehyde.

At Christmastime the Red Cross and USO gave the NP patients a party in the section. I went with the patients who attended—most of them did. The party went well. At the end of my shift, I left the section without much thought of checking the prisoners because there was an attendant with them. They were not allowed to go to the party. The next morning I was called to a hearing. I had no idea why. When I got there, it seemed all the commanding officers on the post were seated around a table. My anxiety level escalated. Soon I learned that some of our psychiatric patients had escaped during or after the party. They had robbed and committed other crimes. I had to admit I was completely unaware of such. The high-ranking panel of inquisitors treated me okay, but I felt like I had not conducted myself as an officer. After that episode I went to the principle chief nurse, Major Margaret Hessions, and asked for a transfer to another service. No transfer. Talking to her did help me patch my shattered self-esteem a little. The affair was hushed, so I never heard how the prisoners escaped.

I had my trials as an NP nurse. This was one. One of our prisoners was from the Philippines. As I was making rounds with an attendant, he handed me a letter. I read it, then gave it to then Chief MC. It was a love letter. I didn't give it much thought until the next time I stepped into the ward: that guy picked up a mop to attack me. The ward men apprehended him. I had never spoken to the guy. He was angry because I hadn't answered his letter. With the whole ward watching the episode, I was embarrassed.

There was tragedy too. One patient, after being transferred to an open ward, hung himself from a basketball hoop. Open ward patients could go anywhere in the hospital and were encouraged to become involved in all the services available and attend the recreational programs brought to Dibble.

Before my tour of duty was completed at Dibble, general electroconvulsive (electric shock) therapy was given to most patients not responding to other measures. This therapy was not used at Bushnell General Hospital during our training, and I had never observed or assisted in the treatments. Before the electrodes were placed, the patient was given an intramuscular muscle relaxant and strapped to a gurney. Two to four attendants bodily restrained him, a soft bite block was placed in his mouth, and his mouth was held closed. This was to prevent fractures from occurring during the convulsions. A medical officer held the electrodes and delivered the voltage. The patients lined up in the hall, sitting on the floor until they were called for their treatment. The convulsions would begin immediately after the electrical stimulation to the head. Afterward the patients were returned to their beds unconscious. The therapy helped most of the patients, but they didn't like it. After waking they were confused. They did gain weight and associate more with each other. Most boys were given ten or more treatments. The war was over, and the hospital was preparing to close. The goal was to have the patients ready to be discharged to their own care or to the care of a relative and not to a VA hospital as wards of the government.

When we could, we Latter-day Saint nurses went to San Mateo to church. There we became acquainted with navy servicemen. Crawford Gates, the LDS composer, was among them. We were invited to other Church functions and to the homes of some members. Nellie Falconer, Goldwyn Wimmer, and I were Church members stationed at Dibble at the same time. The nurses I worked with showed no religious tendencies that I was aware of. The opportunity to discuss my faith with them was never present, nor was I mature enough in LDS gospel doctrine to introduce anyone convincingly to Mormonism; however, I was sure they knew I was a Mormon.

On May 31, 1946, special orders were issued to many of the staff at Dibble General Hospital relieving us of duty and reassigning us to Letterman General Hospital, located at Presidio in San Francisco. I went home on a short leave before reporting at Letterman.

I arrived at Letterman General Hospital on June 13, 1946. The war was over, but still there were war victims receiving treatment. Letterman was located in probably one of the most beautiful areas in the United States.

There were a fair number of LDS personnel and patients at Letterman. We were drawn to each other, and there was usually someone available to go places with.

My first assignment in the hospital was on an officers' surgical orthopedic ward. It was here that I first administered penicillin to patients. Nearly every patient on the ward was given an intramuscular injection of penicillin every three to four hours. It took one nurse's complete time on duty to administer this penicillin. There were no disposable syringes then, so the medication nurse had to care for the syringes and needles too. She also had to mix the penicillin. I remember one patient, a major, was always cheering me on. He had a family, and he recognized a shy young nurse in a ward full of men.

I went home in the middle of August on leave. My little brothers wanted their picture taken with me in my uniform. They dressed in their

Boy Scout uniforms for the photo. This is a choice snapshot of mine. While I was home on leave, Dad wanted me to wear my uniform to church so he could show me off to the town folks. I would not. The war was over, and I thought the uniform out of date and out of place for church. I have regretted letting Dad down when he was so proud of my service in the Army Nurse Corps. My teenage obstinance had surfaced. There were two service stars displayed in the front window at home, and Dad was never hesitant in mentioning that one was his daughter, Lola.

When I returned after my leave, I was assigned to surgery. I had requested this. I soon learned that I was no match for these army surgeons. They were not happy in their work and especially not happy with a green scrub nurse. It took time for me to adjust to the army's way of running operating rooms. There were a couple of great surgical nurses there that could stand up to those unhappy physicians. Ruth Wise took me under her wing and attempted to teach me how to handle these male "wonders." Regardless, I never became a superior surgical nurse.

The nurse was the instrument assistant. She selected all the instruments needed for her assigned operating room, for a full day's schedule of cases, the afternoon before. She placed them in trays and autoclaved them. The nurse on the night shift set up all the operating rooms with all the instruments the scrub nurses selected for all their cases. The night nurse worked from 7 p.m. to 7 a.m. If an emergency came in she had to assist with that as well. She had a surgical technician working with her. The technicians were the circulating assistants. The nurses draped the patients while the surgeons watched. Ruth was very good at draping. It was a good experience. Most cases were reconstructive or orthopedic.

Thanksgiving 1946 one of the long-time regular army technicians invited the OR nurses to a Thanksgiving dinner at his home. He cooked us a traditional Thanksgiving dinner with turkey, dressing, pumpkin pie, and so forth. His compassion was touching.

Church members at Letterman would take a streetcar and then a bus to an LDS church across the city when we were free to do so. Among the group were Second Lieutenant Ruth Tuckfield, Maud Redd (Red Cross), Blanch Davis (civilian worker), and several enlisted men whose names I have forgotten. This was good. We became good friends. For a few years we were in touch, but there have been decades of silence since.

After two years in the Army Nurse Corps, I knew I did not want to be a career military nurse. My enlisted time was up, and I opted to return home to Utah. I left Letterman General Hospital on December 6, 1946. I was given thirty-five days of terminal leave and official discharge January 10, 1947.

Blanche Whiting Love

In 1941 I had been working at Fort Douglas, Utah, in a small station hospital. I was being paid by funds from the CCC program that President Roosevelt started to assist the unemployed following the Depression.

I was the only nurse, and my main duty was the operating room. Also, I helped with patient care and supplies, and I taught the enlisted soldiers hospital work and patient care. Equipment was not thrown away but reused, and instruments were boiled just prior to surgery. Syringes and IV sets were all washed, packed, wrapped, and autoclaved. We also made our own 2x2 and 4x4 bandages. We cut the gauze from a large roll, folded them, and packed them to be sterilized. I was on call twenty-four hours a day. I worked eight-hour days. If I went anywhere I had to let the officer on call know where I would be.

I enjoyed my work, so I enlisted in the army in 1941. In the beginning I was assigned to Fort Douglas. At that time the 38th Infantry was stationed there. Then the air force army nurses were sent, and we lived in one of these beautiful homes in officer's row, which surrounded the parade grounds. Later, barracks were built and we lived in them.

Later we were assigned to a large general hospital at Camp White near Medford, Oregon. This was a training center for army and hospital personnel to prepare them for overseas duty. Nurses worked in twelve-hour shifts. It was a training center and we had more casualties, so the operating rooms were very busy. We also had basic training, which included the obstacle course.

There was lots of activity at Camp White—units were coming and going. A few of us were sent to Camp Lockett. It was an R&R (rest and relaxation) hospital. Camp Lockett was east of San Diego on the Mexican border. A unit of POWs (prisoners of war) were also there. We did not have a chief nurse, so I was the acting chief nurse with the rank of captain.

There were churches at Camp White, and some soldiers from northern Utah held LDS services. There was also a small LDS branch in Medford, Oregon, which was held in a private home. Camp White was about thirty miles from Medford, and I was without transportation.

We worked very hard. My army experience was a learning and a very enjoyable experience. For those who were sent to foreign duty it must have been very stressful duty. Two excellent nurses who were with me at Camp White were sent to foreign duty and had to have psychiatric care after the war. I was discharged in 1945 at my own request. I am proud to have served my country as an army nurse.

Gladys Madsen

Gladys Madsen

I was born on May 26, 1920, in the area of Bountiful, Utah. I enrolled in nursing school at the Salt Lake City General Hospital on Twenty-first South and State Street in Salt Lake City. I attended nursing school from 1940 to 1943.

I decided to join the navy. The war was on, and it was a matter of being patriotic and being needed. I was commissioned an ensign in the United States Navy Reserve Nurse Corps on November 5, 1943, and I reported for active duty at Naval Hospital, Mare Island, California. This hospital was a center for amputees and people with other related injuries. This tour of duty was followed by a tour in 1945 at San Leandro Naval Hospital in California, which was a center for battle fatigue patients. In 1946 I was assigned to Bethesda Naval Hospital in Bethesda, Maryland, and served there until July 1946, when, as an LTJG, I received my release from active duty and joined a navy reserve unit in Salt Lake City, Utah.

Following my discharge I attended the University of Utah College of Nursing, where I received a bachelor of science degree in nursing in August 1949. I took a position as charge nurse on a medical floor at the Salt Lake City Veterans Administration Hospital, where I worked until July 1954. I only worked with registered nursing staff and male hospital attendants during my time at the VA. The concept of licensed practical nurses had not come about yet. We also had no intensive care units at that time. The registered nurses simply cared for everyone on the regular nursing unit.

In July 1954 I received a letter from the navy inviting me to return to active duty or resign my commission. I decided to return to active duty and was assigned to Oakland Naval Hospital, Oakland, California. In 1955 I was assigned to the Naval Ammunitions Depot Station Hospital in Hawthorn, Nevada. In 1956 I was assigned to

Naval Hospital Guam in the Mariana Islands. I was promoted to lieutenant while I was in Guam. I worked in the operating room and as a general duty nurse for one year and then received orders to Yokosuka, Japan. This was very interesting duty with many interesting places to see.

From Japan, I received orders in May 1958 to Hospital Corps School in San Diego, California. During this tour I augmented, or changed status, from reserve to regular Navy Nurse Corps in November 1958. I made the decision to do this based on the counsel from my superiors that being regular navy would make promotion easier and my position in the navy more stable. I served in San Diego from November 22, 1958, until 1963. Those five years were most challenging and rewarding and were good duty.

In 1963 I was transferred to Naval Hospital Camp LeJeune, North Carolina. This was a marine base, and my duties were staff education, corpsmen detail, and supervision. While at Camp Lejeune, I was promoted to lieutenant commander. In 1966 I received orders to return to Naval Hospital Oakland. During this tour at Oakland I served as the nursing service education coordinator. I was instrumental in establishing a ward clerkship program. I also served as the first infection surveillance nurse and as a supervisor on the orthopedic ward. Oakland was a center for amputees. I was promoted to commander in July 1968.

In June 1971 I reported as the chief nurse at Base Dispensary, Marine Corps Base, Twenty-Nine Palms, California. I was active in nursing education programs at this command and as a Bureau of Medicine and Surgery sponsored lecturer at other commands.

After thirty years of service in the United States Navy Nurse Corps, I retired on November 3, 1973. Retirement services were held on February 1, 1974, with full Review of Troops and Marine Corps Band. During my thirty years of service I had been awarded the following medals: Navy and Marine Corps Meritorious Unit Commendation, Navy Reserve Medal, American Campaign Medal, World War II Victory Medal, and National Defense Service Medal with Bronze Star.

A career in the U.S. Navy Nurse Corps gives a nurse many opportunities for further education and interesting travel, but most of all, many long-lasting friendships. The navy is a good career for a nurse. It has been good to me, and I have never regretted a minute of it.

Elizabeth Anna Gleason Mayland

This represents a record of the letters which I wrote to my family when I was sent overseas as a nurse during World War II. My mother saved the letters. This group covers the time from when we boarded the ship *Kungsholm* until we got to Germany. I was assigned to the 85th Station Hospital, which served in several rear areas for short periods of time until after the European phase of the war was over. Our unit was then disbanded, and the personnel were transferred to other units for service in the Far East. On June 26, we flew from Trier, Germany, to Marseille, France, where we staged for our new duties. Combat in Germany ended the middle of May, when our unit was set up in a former school overlooking the Rhine River at Bensberg, not far from Cologne. We had crossed the Rhine River on a pontoon bridge. After being set up we then treated the prisoners who had been released from the German prison camps.

In early August we prepared for our next assignment in the China-Burma-India theater. It was about the eighth of August when we boarded the ship. The news was encouraging for the end of the war with Japan. We learned that the atom bombs had been dropped and that Japan had surrendered. The instructions to the ship's captain had been changed—we were United States bound! We arrived at Newport News, Virginia, on September 2. All telephone lines were busy as we all sought to alert loved ones that we were once more stateside. We were sent to the military facility nearest to our homes. I went to Fort Dix, New Jersey. Then we were given a thirty-day leave.

15 January 1945. At sea—Atlantic.
Dear Mother and family,

It is almost a week that we have been at sea—really it hasn't seemed long—mostly, I suppose, because it has been filled with new experiences. I have enjoyed every day of it and knowing you would too, I'll try and tell you about it as much as possible.

From the time we started (and until we reach our destination) we have taken routine precautions against any emergency. Even though we travel in convoy and danger is comparatively small, we are prepared for any event that might occur. At night "blackout" is rigidly enforced, but is no actual hardship for we do have lights in our staterooms, or wherever we have to go.

Today it is absolutely gorgeous. There is usually a strong wind felt especially when standing forward on the promenade. I like the sensation there—wind in the face, salt spray blowing up, the feel of the boat as it rises up on the waves and surges forward so majestically. You are so aware of the Supreme Power who controls all—I can understand the call of the sea; it is a release from the small things in life which are sometimes irksome. It is great, magnificent, beautiful, and faith inspiring in its vastness and turbulence. I like to fly better, because of the swiftness, but the sea is to some what the air is to others, and the land is to a few.

There is joy in living—being aware that you are very much alive, and that you hold power over inanimate things—that all is for our appreciation—each new days brings that realization to me, and perhaps that is why I haven't even had time to be seasick—I might miss something if I were.

We get up about eight o'clock; most of the hours are at our own disposal with just enough scheduled to make the day pass quickly. The boat is crowded, but everything is efficiently arranged so that one is hardly aware of that fact. The officers eat in a large dining room in three groups; we are in the last one. We have two meals a day with "coffee hour" for a luncheon at which time they serve coffee, tea (one order of lemonade or hot chocolate for me), and cookies. The nurses have breakfast at ten o'clock and dinner at seven fifteen.

The dining room is beautiful; when I first entered I thought it was a dream. When the boat was taken over for military purposes, it was not changed—neither was the cook—and better food I have never eaten! We have assigned tables for the trip; from two to six at each one. I am at a table for two and by some unknown chance have the chief nurse as my dinner companion, which could not be more pleasant. Our meals are served in courses—we have a waiter to each table except in cases like ours in which the waiter serves two. We order from a menu. The food cannot be equaled. About every other evening we have an orchestra composed of boys on the transport playing for us during the dinner hour. You can readily believe that at times this journey to me seems like a luxury cruise.

There are five of us in a stateroom which necessitates double bunks. I sleep on a top one very comfortably. At night after being out in the air many hours and participating in the day's activities, only a few rocking motions before I am safe in dreamland. Our clothes are always near at hand, likewise a life preserver—we can't leave our room unless we have it with us. Every afternoon we have "abandon ship" drill so that the procedures will be familiar. We are the only group of nurses on board, in fact.

With Love, Elizabeth

27 January 1945. Somewhere in France.
Dearest Mother and family,

While there is left a few minutes of daylight, I'll try and get this letter started. Writing by the light of a dim lantern is rather difficult. At least now we have a fire going in the little stove in our tent so that it is warm enough to think of something else aside from the necessity for heat for comfort. By now we are fairly well settled in these humble living conditions, but we are thankful that it will not always be this way.

Now there are fourteen of us living in one tent. We sleep on cots; at least for the past two nights we have been warm. Compared to everyone else we are fortunate—referring to those at the front. Here we live the same as the boys. We should be moving on in several weeks.

I do understand why letters are not written more often. Circumstances are not conducive. People are amazingly kind and unselfish under these circumstances. It must be difficult for everyone under these circumstances.

Love, Elizabeth

V-MAIL Lieutenant Elizabeth Gleason, 0789101 85th Evacuation Hospital, APO 18085 5 PM, NY, NY.

Dear Mother and family,

I decided with one air mail and one V-mail a week some sort of delivery should reach you regularly and let you know how I am faring.

Gradually conditions have forced us to become accustomed to them; they haven't changed any though—we still bathe, shampoo, launder, and live from a helmet. Our greatest amount of energy goes to keeping the fire burning. Our unit has its own mess so that the food situation is much better—have to walk quite a distance though. By visiting other units in this area we are able to supplement our meager supplies and conditions. Tonight I write by the aid of an electric light and at the same time listen to a radio—a real luxury—a result of visiting an ordinance battalion tent. One of the girls is ironing a shirt. Some of the officers came for us in a truck. As I said, people can be kind; we never go anywhere alone, so you need not worry.

Love, Elizabeth

4 February 1945. Somewhere in France.
Dear Mother, Daddy, and family,

We really have gotten accustomed to the hardships, and now have met enough people, old friends and new ones, to make it a pleasant memory.

Everyone waits anxiously for the daily newspaper to see what progress is being made. All of us are wondering what the future may have in store for us—here and in the other theater perhaps. We want to do our part of service, but we also want to return to that promised land. When I see the conditions of this country, I know God has been good to us for preserving us from such similar circumstances.

Even here we do feel the effects of war by the explosions of land mines, booby traps, and other accidents of that nature. Last night I was visiting this ordinance group I mentioned previously. We were quietly listening to their radio; about ten o'clock we heard a nearby shell and investigated to find that two officers had been injured. Really made use of my profession sooner than I expected. War is hell—the thoughts brought to my mind were quite depressing and rebellious—that such things must be! Yet when I see some things and hear others, I wonder how deserving are we as a people, or peoples of peace?

Love, Elizabeth

12 February 1945. France.
Dear Mother and Daddy,

I just wondered how you were receiving my mail. Since we have moved again from a tent to a chateau some fifty miles from where we were and away from the rest of the unit, our mail has suffered another delay. It is about a week at least since we received our last batch of letters. Nevertheless, I hope from day to day we will hear from those we love best.

This building must have been an old Catholic school or monastery. It is similar to a castle in the center building, having a wide entrance with rounded tower structures on each side. The stairs are all dark and wind steeply up to the third floor, where we live beneath the eaves. Our quarters consists of one long room about twenty feet wide in which over fifty of us live. We sleep on cots as before, but have more space in which to hang our "junk." Toward the one extremity are two latrines and twelve wash bowls, which we all use; I am located most advantageously, being about three steps from each. Being a stone building of old design, it is damp, poorly lighted, ill-ventilated; it is heated by a small woodburning stove, about one-third as large as the one in our living room. Needless to say, to really benefit from the stoves, one practically sits on them. Cold running water is all that is available, and it cannot be used for drinking or brushing teeth; so we have to carry drinking water and heat water. We continue to wear the same clothes as on board ship and at the other camp—they are very adequate, only much dirtier than before.

Our day's schedule consists of calisthenics, road marches, lectures, inspections, and eating. We enjoy the road marches, because it is about the only time we get to see beyond the gates.

4 April 1945. Germany.
Dearest family,

Your daughter has gotten many places now that she never dreamed she would and seen many things that I never expected to—even a month ago. Certainly this last year has been an eventful one—not exactly as I would have desired, but since circumstances have not permitted what I want most, I shall make the best of what I do have. They have certainly been eventful, as I said before.

We came here by ambulance. It was a long, weary journey in dismal weather. There is not much in Germany that remains inhabitable. There is scarce a house undamaged—most of the city of Aachen is in ruins; your imagination can't picture the desolation. Discarded tanks, trucks, and even ambulances are along the roadside. We are not setting up as a unit hospital yet at our present site but will be moving on in the near future. At night we hear the big guns thundering in the distance. We are fairly free from danger here, so you need not worry. When we do begin to work, I rather think it will be on the other side of the big river—we are with the 15th Army.

Bye for now—don't worry—I'm safe. Love to all, Elizabeth

The war in Europe ended in May. The unit to which I was assigned was disbanded. I was transferred to the 35th Station Hospital, and we were flown to Marseille on the 26th of June for staging for the CBI theater. We were billeted in what had been a French cavalry post outside the city. The first Sunday there, I attended a meeting of Latter-day Saint service personnel. After climbing steep steps to the meeting place, as I was about to take one giant step, I heard a voice saying, "Can I give you a helping hand, Lieutenant Gleason?" as a young man reached down to my hand and helped me up the step. It was Roy Olson, whom I had met when he was in Officers' Candidate School at Carlisle and attended church services at the Harrisburg Branch. It was great seeing him, for we had a pleasant, friendly relationship. Through him I met other members of the Church, who made very positive impressions on me and influenced my decision to be baptized.

We were staged there for about six weeks and then boarded a ship for the CBI; however, the war with Japan ended, the ship captain's orders were changed, and we returned to the States, landing at Newport News, Virginia, on the 2nd of September 1945.

Alexander M. Morris

I began working in the medical field in 1939. As a boy I was a patient for the lecturers in the Red Cross. They used me to demonstrate bandages and things like that. I was about seventeen years old when I went into the Red Cross as a worker. The war had not started then; I was just helping with emergencies around my home in Hexam, England. As volunteers with the ambulance in my hometown, when there was an accident they'd pick us up. It was sort of like how you folks do it here with paramedics, but you actually pay them to work. We didn't get paid.

As soon as the war started, a little hospital was built in my little hometown. It was controlled by the local doctors. Each area had a poor law institution where indigent people were housed, and it had a little hospital attached to it. When the war was imminent they built this hospital across from the workhouse. They built a series of eight or ten hutments (huts). At the front end of the hut there was an office and utilities. The rest of the hut was just two rows of beds on both sides. We had eight of those. One of them had an operating table, and another one was for storage. All the rest were lined with beds. There were about thirty beds, fifteen down each side in each hut.

I was with the Red Cross as a volunteer, and six of us were employed to set the beds up and get ready to receive these patients. That was voluntary work. But when we got the patients, then we became employees. Just two or three of us became employees, and they brought in professional nurses from other hospitals and other places. They taught me how to take care of the patients. I was already in the Red Cross, and we had done home nursing and hygiene and sanitation. We were ready for any emergency. The closest city was New Castle on Tyne because it was on the Tyne River. Hexam was also on the Tyne.

First of all, we took care of the people off the streets—the poor. Then the Germans actually threw us out of Dunkirk. We got a trainload of wounded and filled up the whole thing with patients. Dunkirk is in France, to the south of England, but we were up in the northeast of England. They filled the trains with patients and brought them up. Some of them were walking wounded. Some of them had to be carried. Several of them died in the process of getting from the railroad station to the hospital. They were in bad shape. When the hospital was filled, the patients would go to other hospitals in other towns. These patients were in an awful state. In one night we received 375 patients. They filled up the whole hospital, and it stayed full pretty much for the rest of the war.

Alexander M. Morris

It's still there as a hospital. About two-thirds of the patients who came from Dunkirk survived.

We took care of all kinds of patients. We had several with spinal injuries and legs half gone. I don't know how many doctors we had in this hospital, but two to three of them were at the hospital all the time. As we got more and more patients, they expanded the hospital about two to three blocks. Eventually there were ten or twelve of the hutments and space for sterilizing, a little office space, and beds down the sides. There were about eight of those huts full with patients, two of them were for storage, and the other one was for administration. The one in the center had an operating table.

The first operation, during which I was fortunate to be in the operating block, I was working as a "dirty man." The doctor took this leg off that was infected with gas gangrene and gave it to me and said, "Here, get rid of this." Nobody told me what to do with it. Nobody had any idea what to do with this highly infectious stuff. The leg was infected—that's why it had to come off. At the far end of the same hutment there was a room with a furnace producing steam for sterilizing. I took the thing and threw it into the furnace and burnt it. I just got the lad to open the door, and I threw it in. I told him to turn the furnace up full. I don't remember if it produced an odor or not. I got a commendation from the Mediglovers for thoughtfulness of that. That was my first experience with real infection. We set aside one of the furnace rooms in one of the blocks to do that so we could put all of that highly infectious stuff in one spot. They set aside the room because I had been smart enough to do it the first time. After that we put any limb that had to be removed for any reason into the furnace. After that I worked in the operating room as a "clean man."

I worked in England for a couple of years before I was sent away with the army. Then they started using it for patients from the bombing of England. We had a lot of patients come that way. It was a lot of hard work. We weren't trained as nurses; we were just trained as Red Cross first-aid men.

When I had to go into the army, they sent us for army training in Clairvo, where we had a little eight-man unit. There was an area where the doctor held sick call. I was there for about six months. Then after that we moved all around England looking after the casualties in the military police. The military police had to have a medical service. The military police were defending England from the Germans. When it was my turn, only two of the men who were working with us as male nurses worked with me. First of all they drafted me into the army, but the man said, "Oh, you are a Red Cross man," so I went to a medical unit. I was in a medical unit for the rest of the war, and I was always in charge of the nursing unit because of my previous experience.

We went to Normandy, France. I wasn't there on D-day. I was aboard ship on D-day. We didn't get to Normandy Beach until the next day. My unit went in on the most northerly beach. We went to the extreme outside of the beach. There were the Germans, Canadians, and Americans. My unit was in between them. It was very scary. Not a lot of people were killed in my unit. One or two were killed, and several were injured. I was looking after patients with another fellow. He said, "Look, Sandy." (That was my nickname.) Something had come through the tent and just took his finger off right in front of him. We had some rough times. We were supposed to carry weapons, but we didn't. We hoped the others would protect us. We took care of the wounded on the beach. It was a pretty terrible experience. I can't describe it because it was just splashes of water around me. If you'd be in the middle of it, ten yards and you were gone. It was really bad for the first few hours. There's nothing great about it. It was just dirt. It was terrible. I can't find words to express how terrible it is to be there like a sitting duck. We had no protection except from the other soldiers that were round about us. It would get a little quiet, and then we would do what we called a sweep. We'd go around and try to find those who we could help and bring back. When we found people, we would bring them back to the beach, put them aboard a ship, and take them to a hospital in England. It took just hours to get from Normandy back to England because they are just across the English Channel from each other. It wasn't an easy job.

We were supporting a tank brigade. We got to Normandy, and we climbed up the ships into boats, and we came in with our medical unit and looked for a place to set up a camp. Our CO found what he thought was a great place. It was a stone quarry. There was little soil and then rock. So we were stuck there. We couldn't dig a foxhole or anything. All the protection we had was under vehicles. We got attacked there.

I was involved in the Battle of the Bulge. We were thrown back by the force of the Germans. Unfortunately the German tank brigade with all the medical units was right there in front of us in Cannes. The Americans were involved in that battle as well as the British. They kept trying to advance, but the Germans kept pushing them back towards the beach again. When I was there we took care of every kind of patient. One kid had his face taken off. We were able to save some lives. We moved them back to the beach and then took them home. We would take them to a field unit first, and then those who had to be evacuated were shipped back to England. Those who didn't survive were just stuck there. People don't realize how much devastation there was. The bodies were taken care of by another unit whose only job was to take care of the dead and body parts. Shock was the thing that killed. More people died of shock than of actual injury. We tried to get something warm into the men to try and prevent the shock. They were in shock from just being in that terrible business.

We got through the Battle of the Bulge. The next place was Falaise. That was the beginning of the end for the Germans. Wherever the tanks went, we went. Nymegan, Germany, was the farthest I followed the tanks. That was on the border between Germany and France. Nymegan is the last place I can remember on the continent before I came back to England.

At the end of the war, after Nymegan, we came back to England. They took our red hats and gave us black hats and shipped us up to Norway. Red hats represented the British unit, and the black represented an airborne British unit. We shifted from a tank support to an airborne unit. We dropped into Norway. We went on a glider into Norway. There was more than one person to a glider. We used to sit on the back of the glider with the strap around us. There was a jeep on the floor. Suddenly the floor was opened, and the jeep went down, and we were on the sides of the glider. They didn't mean to drop the jeep at the same time. The gliders were huge enough to fit men and equipment, but they had no motor—they were just pulled. There were dozens of gliders. They chose gliders instead of airplanes because airplanes had engines. Someone actually guided the gliders after they were released in order to get them to land as soft as possible. In Norway we just sat there and twiddled our thumbs with nothing to do because the Germans gave up easily at the end of the war. We took a lot of German prisoners of war. I never took care of any of them. I was always in charge of the units that had five or six beds for emergencies.

Once I was going to meet a friend of mine in France, in Falaise. While I was on my way, I felt that I should turn around and go back to my duty station. I did. Later I found out my friend had been killed and if I had been with him, as I had planned, I would have been killed too.

I don't remember where I was when the final German surrender came.

During those times in the army, I was the only Latter-day Saint I knew of. I'm sure there were many others, but not in the British Army. At that time there were only very small branches. When I lived in Hexam, there was a branch of the Church there with about eight or ten members. We met in my mother's drawing room. My mother didn't join the Church because my dad didn't. My dad would support the Church in the arguments about it that they had in the pubs there. We didn't really get lessons. The missionaries came, and my mother looked after them. Dad had a garden and grew vegetables, and the elders always left there with their arms full of vegetables and my mother's bread. Dad wouldn't join the Church, but he would support it. I think he believed in the gospel, but he liked his pint of beer and his pipe. We've done all the work for him, but whether or not he accepts it, it's up to him. But I stayed faithful my whole life, even while I was in the military.

After we got established on the continent, we were close to the Americans. We went into a little village and commandeered a school as a medical point. I had some time, and I wandered down this lane into an American camp. There was this big building with an awful lot of noise and I opened the door and there were all these American soldiers. A man, a sergeant at the far end, saw me and said, "Oh, we got an Englishman here." Then there was silence. I told them what I was doing. I was looking for some members of the LDS Church. He then named about eight members of the Church. That's where I met Glen Ogalvie. The Ogalvies later became my sponsors when I immigrated to the United States I was actually able to go to some Latter-day Saints meetings during the war.

I was president of the Hexam Branch and a district leader. I visited small villages and towns that had a few members. I did this during the war to keep these little branches alive. I came home to Hexam after the war. When we were no longer needed, we were shipped back to England, but we never got to visit home during times in between.

Mary Harris Olson

I chose to go to nursing school after I graduated from high school in Blanding, Utah. We had a county nurse who was the sweetest, nicest lady and a good friend of mine. She did so much good in the county, and that was what helped in my decision.

I went to school at the LDS Hospital School of Nursing in Salt Lake City, Utah. I graduated in

1940 before the war started. Nursing school was a great experience. When we entered, there were more nurses than they had room to house in the nurses' home. There were five cottages across the street where nurses lived too, but they were also full. There were eight extra students, and the seventh floor of the LDS Hospital had not been finished, so they put the eight of us over there. We had the time of our lives. They couldn't lock us in, so we would roam around and do the things that we wanted to do. There were some nice doctors who were good friends to us, and they let us watch autopsies and go to deliveries. We were moved into the nursing home. I eventually ended up in Cottage Three across the street. We had more freedom than some of the other students. We had lots of fun and a lot of hard work. We worked eight-hour days, and usually they were split shifts. We would often go to class in between the shifts. We took some classes at the University of Utah and some at the hospital. I didn't get a degree from the University of Utah. Very few did. Nursing school was a three-year program.

As students we had certain rotations we would have to do: medical, surgical, OB, pediatrics, and the diet kitchen. It fell to my lot to spend most of my specialized time on medical wards. That was the pits. People would come in and stay for months. Some just came to die. There were different diseases that caused their deaths, and some died of old age. Many of them were church charity cases.

I remember in nursing school that the first thing we did was remove flowers from the patients' rooms at night and water them. The next thing was making a bed without a patient in it. We went from that to making beds with the patients in them. Then came the great privilege of emptying bedpans. I went in to help one little girl, and she was gagging her head off trying to get her bedpan emptied and cleaned out.

None of us could ever imagine why our pediatric head nurse ever went into the field of pediatrics. She wouldn't let us touch the children or pick them up or do anything to comfort them.

Mary Harris Olson

If we touched anything in the room, we had to use little pieces of paper. We used them when she was looking, but I would pick up the babies when she wasn't looking or when she was off duty. What many of the children needed was love, and we weren't permitted to give them that. Many of the children were there quite a while and were dying for some love and affection. Giving them love was far more important than the other things that were done.

They did not have antibiotics when I was a student. Sulfa came in about the time I graduated. Many people died of pneumonia, which was one of the major killers. I don't remember giving penicillin when I was in the military, but I gave a million of those shots later on. I don't remember having stryker frames. There were no respirators or anything of that sort. There was none of the wonderful equipment we take for granted today. The IVs and blood transfusions were nothing like they are now. We used very primitive homemade gastric-suctioning machines. Incubators for premature babies were boxes with light bulbs in them. I remember we had a little premie, Baby Christensen, who was in one for about six months, and we all fell in love with her. She died suddenly when she was about six months old, and it broke all of our hearts.

The Red Cross urged us to join their organization when we graduated from training. They soon encouraged us to join one of the armed services. About a year after graduation, I joined the army and was sent to Camp Roberts in California. I remember exactly where I was when Pearl Harbor occurred. It was Sunday morning, and I was in a ward full of soldiers. We had a large Jewish doctor who came into his office and sat hunched over a little radio all morning long.

I spent my entire military service at Camp Roberts. It was located between Los Angeles and San Francisco. It was a training facility for infantry and artillery soldiers. Only occasionally did we have really seriously ill patients. I worked in a variety of different wards that had patients with different problems. At night we worked twelve-hour shifts for a month at a time.

My youngest brother trained at Camp Roberts in the infantry while we were there. He was killed in Okinawa. I think many were killed as they were getting off the landing boat. I was always glad that he never had to kill anyone because he was the kindest, most loving person that ever lived. He was on a mission and was drafted immediately after he came home. The day I got married he arrived in Salt Lake City and came to our wedding. I cried all through our wedding because I hadn't seen him for such a long time.

I got married in March 1941. I met my husband, Ernest L. (Roy) Olson, at church. Roy was in the Medical Administrative Corps and his barracks were right close to mine, so we'd walk to church together. He was a Mormon and he was cute, and there weren't many Mormons in that area at that time. It was during the war, and there was a major in the medical division who was a good friend. We decided that we wanted to get married in the Salt Lake Temple, but there was one hitch. They were giving very few leaves at the time. I was due to have one, but Roy was not. Major Bryan said, "If Mary gets to go, it won't do a bit of good to go home to get married if you aren't there," so he made it possible for us to go home and get married in the Salt Lake Temple.

There were only two Mormon nurses there, both from the LDS Hospital. Church was just sacrament meeting. There were no weekly activities either. No General Authorities came to visit. There were really good officers who were members of the Church, and we had a good group of members. We had a good-sized chapel. There were probably about a hundred people each Sunday. Attendance would vary because it was a training facility.

My husband went from there to Fort Lewis, Washington, and then to England and France. In France the war ended while they were waiting for a ship to be repaired that would take them to Japan, so he was sent back to America. I got pregnant and was released from the service and returned home. I was in the service from 1941 to 1944. We had a beautiful little girl who was five months old before Roy ever saw her.

I was sorry for all the suffering that the atomic bomb caused, but I was happy that they used it because in the long run it saved many lives and ended the war. I hate to think of the suffering it caused the poor, helpless Japanese people, but it helped bring the horrible war to a close.

I'm sure being in the military changed my life. You can't help being changed when you go through something like that, but I have never sat and analyzed it. I am still active in the Church and have had many satisfying experiences that have helped shape my life. I have filled many callings in the Church and at the present I am a visiting teacher supervisor and a visiting teacher. My husband has been a bishop, stake president, mission president, and temple officiator. Church has always been the center of our lives, thank goodness!

EULA LOUISE "HEDY" WELKER PETERSON

Eula Louise "Hedy" Peterson entered the navy on December 18, 1942, and received her orders to report to Mare Island by February 23, 1943.

It was at Mare Island where I learned the hospital and navy policies. While at Mare Island I spent three months on an orthopedic ward caring for patients who fought at Guadalcanal. Most of the patients had limbs missing. It made one heartsick to see all these young men who would go through life with this disability. I have pictures of several of them. I really enjoyed my three months there and hated to leave.

I was then transferred to the diet kitchen in the communicable disease department. When I was in nurse's training, I had three months of the diet kitchen, and one of those months I was the dietician for the hospital while our dietician went home to New Zealand for a month's vacation. After nurse's training I worked at the Southern Pacific Sanatarium in Tucson, Arizona, and took care of the special diets there along with my regular job. I chose to go to the diet kitchen, as very few nurses like working there and I had quite a bit of experience along that line. The only problem was that from then on in the service, most of my time was spent in the diet kitchen. Conditions were very good there. We had everything we needed to do a good job of caring for our patients. Before I left Mare Island on August 27, 1943, I was able to train my crew how to run the diet kitchen.

I arrived at Saint Margarita Ranch on September 1, 1943, and on September 3 it was officially commissioned and accepted from the contractor for the navy, and Captain Joseph L. Schwartz (MC) assumed duty as the medical doctor in command. We nurses helped wash windows and clean up the place in those three days before the hospital was opened. It took us six months to become equipped with all the things that were needed to run the hospital efficiently.

The first three weeks I helped one of the doctors set up an orthopedic ward as well as we could, and then I was transferred to the diet kitchen as I was the only nurse that had experience there. This diet kitchen had three steam vats, a stove, two refrigerators, and a counter. We had some of the best cooks and bakers there. All loved their jobs and got along so well. I really enjoyed the diet kitchen, but felt I was losing my skill at nursing. I spent most of my time there in the diet kitchen until a dietician arrived at the hospital to take my place. I worked a couple of months with her to get her in the routine as she was fresh from school.

My chief nurse, Margarite Ann Orr, wanted me to go to Washington DC and train as a dietician, but I had come into the navy to be a flight nurse, and I found out that my chief nurse did not send my name when the chance came up because she wanted me to become a dietician. I did get to spend a couple of months on wards before my orders came through. I was detached from Saint Marguerita Ranch on December 28, 1944, and ordered to report to "port in which the commander, Seventh Fleet may be and report to him for duty."

Four of us nurses went to the South Pacific on the SS *Monterey* on January 20, 1945. We were left at the U.S. Naval Base Hospital 14, which was at Finchhaven, New Guinea, on February 4, 1945. At the time of our arrival, this hospital was folding. All the seriously ill patients had left, and they were waiting for the few patients remaining to leave as soon as transportation was available. As usual I was given duty in the diet kitchen. This time my job was much harder as we had no fresh food—just powdered, canned, and dried food—and the patients did not care much for their diet. This is what we all ate. The hospital was made up of Quonset huts. We nurses had a bathroom in our Quonset. There was an officers' club we could go to on our time off. We had a swimming area blocked off in the ocean where we could swim. We were only there about a month and a half and had very few patients and they did not need much care, so it was like a vacation in the Pacific. It was there that I was made a lieutenant (JG) NC on March 1, 1945. We were told we would be going to the Philippines, but four hours before our orders arrived for the Philippines they sent us nurses to the U.S. Naval Hospital 15. We were told that Commander Halsey did not want nurses but was told he had better get them or be sent back to the United States, and we were the closest nurses available.

After a six-hour flight, sixteen of us nurses, including our chief nurse Lieutenant Elizabeth A. Walsh, arrived in Manus, in the Admiralty Islands, on March 20, 1945. The Admiralty Islands are found in the Bismark Sea just south of the equator. Manus was a supply depot for the front line, so it was a very busy base. Ships, planes, and equipment were repaired there. Seabees were stationed at Manus. Our hospital had patients who came from the Philippines. Most of them were badly hurt and would be returned to the States for further treatment and then reassigned if possible. The Seabees did a beautiful job of constructing our hospital and living quarters.

Again, everything around was Quonsets. It was built in a coconut grove. We were not allowed to leave the grounds without permission, and then only if an officer went with us. They did not know if there were Japanese snipers still on the island. The island of Manus was sixty miles long and forty miles wide at its widest. It was a jungle if you got off the beaten path. There were about twelve thousand natives on the [Melanesian] island. My nursing time in Manus was spent in an orthopedic ward and as usual in the diet kitchen. Our hospital was well equipped, and our patients ate pretty well. They still had dehydrated and canned food, but we had planes flying to Australia each week and ate better than we did at Hospital 14. As for the officers, we had fresh food all the time. Our commissary officer knew the right people in Australia. We had steak every week.

The climate was ideal. It could get cool in the evening, but about all we wore was a poncho to keep from getting wet. When it rained it was like pouring a bucket of water over you. The rainy season was just starting when I left the island and had about ended when I went to the South Pacific. When the war in the Pacific ended, I was released from active duty on my birthday, November 1, 1945. I returned to the States on the USS *New Kent* on November 18, 1945, to San Diego. I had to be detached from the navy at San Francisco and was granted a two-month leave, so officially I retired from the navy on January 31, 1946.

My family was very supportive. I never was in an area where they really had to worry much about me. I received letters from my family regularly, and since I worked mostly in the diet kitchen and had a PX handy they never had to send anything to me. My needs were few and I knew my family loved me very much.

Each base I was assigned to always had a chapel on its premises. There was also a chaplain available. I am sorry to say I never inquired if there were any members of my church on the base except for when I was on the Admiralty Islands. I heard there were a few Latter-day Saints who met when they could, but I realized I would be the only girl and, being rather shy, decided not to try and attend. We were allowed to attend church on Easter no matter what shift we were on, and I always attended. Being a nurse, I had to work on Sundays in most nursing jobs, and I had got out of the habit of going to church. I made up my mind then that I would wait until I could have a job where I would have the weekends off before I went back to church. I had been paying my tithing since I graduated from nursing school and prayed every day. I have always been very spiritual. The first roommate I had in the navy was a Latter-day Saint. She was only at Mare Island about three months when she quit to get married. She was from Salt Lake City, and her father was in insurance. Her name was Jean Vandehei. I never ran across another nurse that was a member of the Church, but they all knew I belonged to The Church of Jesus Christ of Latter-day Saints as I let them know I did not drink, smoke, or drink coffee because of my religion.

Before I was called to active duty, I received a letter from the President of the Church and three little books—the Book of Mormon, the Bible, and the *Principles of the Gospel*. I was looking though my scrapbooks I have of my navy experiences, and I found three small copies of the *Church News*. I also found a letter and a Church newsletter from my bishop, Martin Tate, so I know I did hear from him. As far as gifts and care packages, I don't remember receiving any while overseas. I had everything I needed, and working in the diet kitchen gave me access to all the food I could want, and my family and friends knew this. Instead of sending me birthday and Christmas gifts, my family would buy something for my hope chest and put it in there. I received letters from family and friends frequently while overseas.

Two things happened when I was stationed at Mare Island that I will always remember. When I worked as a nurse in a civilian hospital before I joined the navy, we kept our appendectomy patients in bed for at least seven or eight days after the operation. I had been on the ward at Mare Island about a month when one of our patients had to have an appendectomy. The doctor left orders to get the patient up that evening. We nurses were horrified. We thought we would kill the poor patient if we got him up. Well, the doctor came that evening and got the patient up himself and saw that we continued to get him up each day. We were amazed how well that patient did. He was up running around in five days. That was the beginning of getting patients out of bed as soon as possible.

The second incident that happened occurred in this same ward. We had a patient who had his right leg amputated. His artificial leg had arrived, but he refused to put it on. He was very depressed. A week went by, and no one had been able to talk him into doing anything about it. One Monday morning I talked to a couple of the corpsmen, suggesting that they hold the patient and I would put the artificial leg on him and we would make him get up and walk. It was agreed and that is what we did. He was very angry with us and I don't think he ever forgave me for doing it, but from that day on he went everywhere on his artificial leg.

Eleanor Roosevelt came to visit the patients at Mare Island. I saw her walk across the lawn near our barracks, so I dashed in and got my camera and took her picture. I always admired that lady.

I'll tell you about the time my ward burned down at Santa Margarita Ranch. The doctor on the ward hated Friday, inspection day, and would schedule patients from his ward for surgery. We used patients in the wards to help in keeping the ward clean. The last couple of weeks the doctor had done surgery on the patients in this ward, and that Friday morning he had scheduled surgery for eight patients. There was no one to clean up the ward, and my corpsmen and I had to care for these patients before and after surgery, so when the inspection crew came around I was getting a pre-op shot ready. They asked why my ward was not clean, and I told them I did not have any patients that could help and my corpsmen were needed to take care of the eight patients that were going to surgery. Well, they always did a fire drill, and of course it was my ward that could not do anything about it, so we burned, supposedly. The poor doctor was the one who was told he must never have surgery on Friday mornings but be available in the ward when there was inspection.

Virginia Kay Rawley

While I was in nurse's training at LDS Hospital in Salt Lake City the federal government came up with the idea of having a Nurse Cadet Corps. If a person joined the Cadet Corps she would complete her training at a miliary hospital and then would be eligible to join the Army Nurse Corps.

I joined the Cadet Nurse Corps while I was still in nurse's training at Salt Lake City's LDS

Virginia Kay Rawley

Hospital (1941–44). We were told we could go to an army hospital to finish our training. I was sent to Bushnell General Hospital at Brigham City, Utah. It was a huge hospital. There were many wards, but I can't remember how many patients were there.

I was assigned to an officers' ward that had many amputee patients. The chief nurse took me into the room of one the patients and introduced me, saying, "Lieutenant Rawley, this is Miss Kay. She is going to be taking care of you." Lieutenant Rawley had been a navigator on a B-24 Bomber that crashed and burned on a test flight. Lieutenant Rawley was trapped in the burning wreckage. They could not take care of him at the March Field Station Hospital in California, so they sent him to Bushnell.

Lieutenant Ed Rawley and I became acquainted. I helped take care of him. He lost both hands but soon became ambulatory, and we would take walks around the hospital area. I finished my training, graduated from LDS Hospital and started working at Bushnell. I was assigned again to take care of Lieutenant Rawley . Gradually he became ambulatory after months of surgery. We would take walks around the area at Bushnell and several times went into Brigham City.

I went up to Fort Douglas and joined the Army Nurse Corps. I was sent to Fort Lewis, Washington, for basic training. Upon completion of basic training, I was commissioned a second lieutenant and sent to duty at Palm Springs, California. After serving there for a while I was transferred back to Bushnell General Hospital, where I had served as a cadet nurse.

In the meantime Lieutenant Rawley was asked to go back to duty to travel to various hospitals in the United States to give encouragement and teach other arm amputees how to effectively use their "hooks."

He and I kept in touch, and in June 1946 we were married in the little chapel at Fort Douglas, Utah. After the wedding we went to Marysvale, California, where I was discharged from the army.

Edla Johnson Terry

I was born in Salt Lake City on October 12, 1916. I went to high school in Brigham City, Utah. I enrolled and attended nursing school for three years at the University of Utah. I also worked for a while at the Dean's Hospital in Ogden, Utah.

After finishing school, feelings of patriotic duty seemed to urge me to enlist again. A classmate, Elna Rich, and I decided to sign up together. We were accepted as second lieutenants in the Army Nurse Corps. We were to report to duty at Camp White in Medford, Oregon, on August 1, 1944, for our basic training.

The induction center had a connected hospital. There we did mostly bedside nursing. Our assigned work schedule was a twelve-hour duty in which we rotated day and night shifts. We also had drills and preparations for overseas assignments.

After two months at, Elna received orders to go to the European theater, and I received orders to go to Barnes General Hospital in Vancouver, Washington. I remained there until March 1945, when I received orders for overseas duty in the South Pacific. I left by train for Camp Stoneman, California.

On March 31, 1945, Easter Sunday, we donned our helmets and in full dress uniform boarded the SS *Monterey* in San Francisco, California. There was a certain excitement as well as apprehension and anxiety. We were assigned to quarters and found that we were about six to a small room, three bunks on each side with one bathroom available for each room. We were instructed that we would be served two meals a day in the officers' dining room. As the boat pulled out of the harbor and passed under the Golden Gate Bridge, doubts filled my mind. We had a luscious meal as we left, but it didn't stay with me very long. Many, including me, were seized with seasickness. I was sick for about two days and then seemed to overcome it.

Edla Johnson Terry

The voyage to our assignment was a month long, partly because the ship took a zigzag course. When we crossed the equator, April 9, 1945, there was a special celebration to initiate us into the "Domain of Neptunus Rex." All aboard the SS *Monterey* were found worthy to be trusty shellbacks.

As the ship went steadily on its course, the temperatures became much warmer and we found it very uncomfortable in our crowded quarters. Several of us would take a blanket and go on the deck of the ship to sleep at night. Once in a while there would be a breeze that made the climate a little more tolerable. We often felt sorry for the enlisted troops who were in the hold of the ship where it was extremely warm and uncomfortable.

We enjoyed the meals aboard the ship very much. Even though we were allowed only two meals a day, we were allowed to eat all we wanted. We often saved bread or crackers for the midday.

As we drew closer to our destination in the Philippines, there were more frequent showers. As we continued to sleep on the deck of the ship, we got wet but not really cold. At the time we docked in Manila, I was ill. Since I had a fever and cough, I was unable to disembark with the rest of the staff. They went to work at the 313rd General Hospital while several of us who were ill were taken by a small craft to shore. We were then taken directly to another hospital, the 120th General Hospital, which was located in the former Santo Tomas University. This hospital was recently built in preparation for the invasion of Japan.

There were many patients in the 120th General Hospital who appeared to be very ill. The two most prevalent diseases were infections: hepatitis and malaria. My illness was diagnosed as a viral pneumonia with no special treatment except bed rest and a good diet. I was not confined strictly to bed but had to remain at the hospital for about three weeks, from May 1 to May 24, 1945. I did have visits from several nurses from our outfit, which helped with being in such a strange new place.

When I returned to my unit, the 313rd General Hospital had moved to its permanent location, which was about twenty miles east of Manila near the Pasig River and the small community of Pasig. Several other hospitals were in that general location, and it was our understanding that these hospital units were set up for serving casualties (as fighting continued in areas surrounding the Philippines) as well as for the possible invasion of Japan. The commanding officer of the 313rd was Aubrey Carter, a lieutenant colonel in the U.S. Medical Corps. He commanded respect from all the personnel in the hospital because of the high quality of his administration as well as his fairness and kindness to all of the personnel. Our chief nurse was Major Irene Klemp. She was an excellent nurse and a very fine person. She demanded that nurses assigned to the hospital give the best nursing care to our patients.

In the beginning it was almost like camping out. The ward units were large army tents staked down around a cement floor, and the hospital beds were army cots. These facilities for patients were satisfactory in good weather, but when the rainy season came things were different. The rain would beat underneath the tents and easily get the patients wet.

We nurses lived in several long, barrack-like buildings made of corrugated tin. We each had a small area, which included an army cot, our foot locker, and a place to hang our uniforms. Because of the danger of malaria, we slept under mosquito netting each night. There was a shortage of water, so we were only allowed a canteen and helmet full of water each day to use for drinking, personal cleaning, and washing our clothes. Our toilet area was an outdoor latrine made of a canvas material and located a good distance from our quarters. We made certain that we took someone with us when we went to the latrine after dark because occasionally a stray [enemy] Japanese would be found roaming around the area.

The mess tent, or eating area, was part of the hospital unit. We had been issued a mess kit earlier, and this was our eating utensils during our stay there. We all sat around long wooden tables. After finishing our meal, we would scrape the uneaten food into the garbage can, immerse our utensils in boiling soapy water, and use a stiff brush to clean the mess kit. It was then rinsed in clean boiling water. It was very important that such technique be used to ensure that we would not become ill from eating off of dirty dishes. There were frequent complaints about army food, which at times was not the most appetizing. The eggs were reconstituted dry eggs. We did not have fresh milk, vegetables, or fruit. Most things were canned in large quantities. We often had a drink that we called battery acid, a citric acid powder provided to supply vitamin C. The packages of food that occasionally came from home provided the basis for a party. As we got together, we would talk about the things that we liked or disliked. All we could hope for was better times.

The nursing duty at the hospital was interesting and rewarding. We rotated through services and alternated shifts. We did work in an eight-hour shift with one day off a month. Many of our patients were wounded men from battle areas other than the Philippines, for at the time the island had been retaken. Some patients were victims of diseases such as infectious hepatitis (which was very common), malaria, and tapeworms. Occasionally we would care for the Filipino national soldiers.

As time progressed and we became settled in at the 313th, we established routines and developed friendships. Our physical surroundings became more habitable and comfortable. The hospital wards were built on a more permanent base, which made it easier to give nursing care. Boardwalks were built between buildings, which really were a help, especially during the rainy season. A recreation hall was also built for the nurses. We were all proud of that facility. Bamboo and other materials typical of the Philippines were incorporated into the decor. Showers and inside toilets were built. It was pure luxury to be able to have a daily shower.

I remember one time when new nurses came to our unit. They came at a time when the water had been shut off. A nurse approached me and asked what they could do to brush their teeth since the water was shut off. I replied, "Use your canteen and spit on the ground like we did." Not a very kind reply, I suppose, but I guess I wanted her to know what we had been through.

In our hospital unit there was another Latter-day Saint member, Dale Callister. We were able to attend special Church meetings away from the base. Our commanding officer gave us special permission to do this and even provided a jeep and a driver for our use. We were grateful for this consideration. We were able to attend three different LDS servicemen's conferences in Manila. The first one was held on May 13, 1945, at the Central Church of Christ chapel near Santo Tomas University. A total of 271 people attended this conference. Elder Wayne B. Garff presided and conducted. It was thought that this conference was the first known LDS conference to be held in Manila. Several servicemen spoke, and, since the day happened to be Mother's Day, tributes were given to mothers. The sacrament was blessed and passed to the large congregation. Attending this conference were four other LDS servicewomen who were WAC members and American Red Cross workers.

A second conference was held on August 12, 1945, which 474 people attended. We were in the shell-scarred auditorium of the Manila Normal School. Elder J. Morris Richards of Phoenix, Arizona, presided at the meeting. A third conference was held on November 11, 1945, in the Ellinwood church in Manila. In addition to these conferences, Dale and I were able to attend some special LDS activities of the MIA, including a Christmas party. It was really a wonderful opportunity to be able to attend these Church functions and to associate with other LDS men and women. It really lifted my spirit and helped me to carry through the time I was in the Philippines.

In August 1945, at the time of the surrender of Japan, prisoners of war who had been held in other islands surrounding the Philippines were repatriated. Some were received in our hospital, along with both Dutch and English prisoners. We never saw any patients who were women. While some were in fairly good physical condition, there were many who were suffering the effects of prolonged starvation. Many had vitamin deficiency diseases such as scurvy and beriberi. I remember especially one English soldier who was so emaciated that he weighed only eighty pounds. Although food was given to him, he seemed unable to tolerate it, and he continued to have diarrhea and other gastrointestinal symptoms. Many of the Dutch patients had contracted tuberculosis and were of necessity isolated from other patients. Adequate isolation was hard to maintain, as often the water for hand washing was limited. However, we did the best we could under the circumstances.

Eventually, we heard through the army newspaper about the United States bombing Japan. After the atomic bomb was dropped on Nagasaki, the whole complexion of the war changed. However, I don't recall really being personally affected by the event. I don't think it changed my life in a major way, although I did feel sad for all of those lives lost. After the Japanese surrendered and the armistice was signed, personnel from our unit began to talk about going home.

The nurses from our unit began to be discharged or transferred to stateside hospitals. If personnel were discharged, it was determined by their length of time in the service, their age, and the overseas ribbons they had been awarded. As the time came for my discharge, I was excited about going home, but I realized that the end to an interesting and challenging experience was near.

When I was discharged, I bid adieu to those in my unit and I was taken to a debarking area to await assignment for a ship to return home. I was with a group that boarded the SS *Brazil* on December 13, 1945. We arrived in the United States on December 29, 1945, and were taken directly to Camp Beale, California. The crossing was uneventful, although Christmas was spent aboard ship. I received the rank of first lieutenant just before I was officially discharged from the Army Nurse Corps on February 1, 1946.

Being in the service changed my life by giving me a broader outlook of the world and contributing to my nursing skills. I value my experience in the service, especially in the Philippines. I wouldn't mind going back there someday. When missionaries go to the Philippines, it brings back a lot of memories for me. I even have a grandson, or perhaps a great-grandson, serving his mission there.

Henrietta Oberlander Thomas

I did enjoy my two-year experience in the Army Nurse Corps during World War II, and I feel that maybe some of the young people should know about what we nurses went through serving our country. I served in the Army Nurse Corps from December 26, 1944, to January 7, 1947.

I entered nurse's training at the St. Joseph's Hospital School of Nursing in Kansas City, Missouri, on September 1, 1941. At the time we entered the war I made up my mind that I would join the Army Nurse Corps when I finished training. At the start of my junior year in training, the U.S. Cadet Nurse Corps was organized and I joined it. When you joined the Cadet Nurse Corps, you signed an affidavit that upon completion of your nurse's training you would either join the Army or the Navy Nurse Corps or remain in general duty nursing for the duration of the war. Since I had already made up my mind to join the Army Nurse Corps, I joined the Cadet Nurse Corps. One of the main reasons I chose to do so was because of the stipend that they offered us, because at that time my folks were having a hard time making ends meet.

As far as I know, I never had any contact with any LDS nurses during my tour of duty in the army. I believe that there were two reasons for that. The first reason is that I don't think there were too many LDS nurses in the services during the war. At that point in time, throughout the entire United States, the general opinion of the majority of the people were that women should not serve in the military in any capacity. My mother really was not all that happy that I chose to join the army, and neither were the parents of many of the nurses I served with. Joining any of the military services was something that "nice women" did not do. Because of the family orientation that the LDS Church stresses, I believe that many parents discouraged their daughters from joining the service in any capacity. The second reason is that I never saw service in a predominantly LDS community.

During the war, the military had divided up the United States into service areas for convenience. There were so many states in each service area. Missouri was in the 7th Service Command, and the States in that command were Missouri, Iowa, Minnesota, Michigan, Wisconsin, Nebraska, Kansas, Colorado, and Wyoming. The nurses from those states had their basic training at Camp Carson (Colorado Springs), Colorado, and upon completion of the training we were assigned to army hospitals in those states.

On Saturday, February 3, our training ended. We were all very happy that our training was over with. Upon completion of training, I was assigned to the 7th Regional Hospital located at Fort Warren (Cheyenne, Wyoming).

On February 6, 1945, six other nurses and I reported to Fort Warren for duty. Two months later, on April 6, five of us nurses stationed there, who were from the same basic training class, were directed to report to the office of Major Fox, who was the chief nurse of the hospital. She told us that orders had just been received for the five of us to go overseas to the Pacific theater of operations.

At that moment we were relieved of our nursing duties and orders were cut for us to take a ten-day leave home before we were shipped out. We were to leave as soon as we had made travel reservations and had our suitcases packed. The ten-day leave passed all too quickly, and we returned to Fort Warren.

The next morning after we returned from our leave, we had a meeting with Major Fox, and she gave us our instructions for going overseas. She could not tell us our overseas destination because the orders only stated that we were going to the Pacific theater of operations. On April 26 we would go by train to the replacement depot at Camp Beale, California. We could expect to spend from three to five days there before we boarded the ship to take us overseas. We would spend anywhere from ten days to three weeks on the ship.

It took us about twenty hours to travel to Camp Beale. There were many other army nurses traveling on that train also, and we found out that they were all headed to Camp Beale. There were about three hundred army nurses in the group that I was in that were assembled at Camp Beale. We were being shipped overseas to replace those nurses who had been serving in that area since the war had started. They came from all over the United States.

V-E Day was celebrated on June 8, and we were still at Camp Beale. While the war was over in Europe, it was still going on in the Pacific theater, and islands were still being invaded. The chances were very good that we would be assigned to a hospital unit that would accompany one. Medics went in with the troops, but the hospital unit did not land until the island was secured. Since the ports and docks would be demolished in the invasion, we would have to go in like the troops did: climb down landing nets into boats to be ferried ashore. Then we would have to help set up the hospital, and that might include digging foxholes and slit trenches.

When we left Camp Beale, we traveled across country by train and boarded the ship *St. Olaf* at the Brooklyn Army Base. The *St. Olaf* was a Liberty ship. When the war started, there were not too many ships for transporting supplies and troops, so the Liberty ships were hurriedly built to do so. They were not built for speed. The top speed was eleven knots, which was very slow, and we would be going through the Panama Canal to the Pacific theater of operations (PTO).

The *St. Olaf* had an overall length of 441 feet and a breadth of 57 feet. The hull of the ship was painted white and had a wide green band painted all around the side of the ship. Breaking up the green bands, midship on each side, was a sixteen-foot-tall red cross. Two twelve-foot red crosses were painted on the upper deck as well as on each side of the ship's smokestack. According to the rules of the Geneva Convention of the Red Cross, all hospital ships were to be considered neutral by the enemy because they were on missions of mercy. They carried no armaments at all, and they were to be illuminated from sunset to sunrise. The enemy was also to be notified twice a day of the exact location of the hospital ships.

The ship was manned by a crew of merchant marines, and there was a small detachment of marines aboard the ship for "peace-keeping duties." The medical complement consisted of fifty-six medical department officers including eighteen doctors, thirty-seven army nurses, one dietician, one WAAC reconditioning officer, one Red Cross worker, and 151 enlisted corpsmen. It had thirty-six wards designed to handle from 2 to 108 beds. The operating rooms, laboratory, x-ray department, and dressing station room had all of the latest in hospital equipment.

We did not associate with the nurses who were permanently assigned to the ship. Rumor had it that their chief nurse had forbidden them to associate with us. It seems that when she found out that nurses would be transported on the ship, she felt that because she was the chief nurse, she should be in charge of our group. The captains would not relinquish their command of us, and it ticked her off. She ordered her nurses not to have contact with us, and our captains honored her request. Our group was referred to as "the passenger nurses" by the ship's crew. We understood that those who were permanently assigned to the ship referred to us as "the cargo" and we referred to them as "the snobs." Later, after we landed on Saipan, we met some of the nurses socially, and they all said that they felt sorry for us but that we should be glad that their chief nurse did not have control of us. She was an old time army nurse, and she was very strict in all that she did.

During the trip through the Panama Canal, we were allowed to be topside for the entire journey. It was interesting going through the locks, with the ship being raised and lowered. Sailing through Gatan Lake was also interesting. There were dense jungles on both sides of the lake, and we could hear the chattering of monkeys and the singing of birds and could occasionally catch glimpses of them. It was very hot and humid during the time that we were in the Canal Zone. Our ship docked in Balboa, the western terminus of the Panama Canal. We spent the night there, and we were given a five-hour shore leave in Balboa.

On the Fourth of July, the ship's captain put on a very impressive fireworks display for us. An announcement came over the loudspeaker in the afternoon that there would be fireworks that night. The movies were canceled and the passenger nurses' time on the deck was also canceled. About 9 p.m. the lifeboat drill would sound, and we were to report to our lifeboat stations. When the alarm sounded, we reported to our lifeboat stations. The captain welcomed us, and the chaplain gave a prayer. The captain announced that all of the lights aboard the ship would be extinguished, and during that time we were not to move from our position until they came on again. When the lights were out, a very eerie feeling came over all of us because of the complete darkness and also because we realized that we were sitting in the middle of a big ocean, far from any land. There was only a crescent moon, so the sky was a very dark blue with a few wisps of clouds, and the ocean was almost black and still, with an occasional ripple of a wave.

The captain told us that we were in the Southern Hemisphere of the earth and that until we returned to the Northern Hemisphere we would not be able to see the familiar constellations, the Big and Little Dippers. He pointed out the Southern Cross and the position of the North Star and listed the other main ones in that area. He told us that the early sailors depended upon the stars for navigation and that even with all of the modern navigational aids, the sailors still relied on the stars.

He gave us a patriotic talk about how our forefathers came to America for freedom and that we should be thankful to them for the foresight that they had to establish the American government. He told us that we should be proud to be defending our country and even to die for it if that was necessary. Then he asked to sing the first verse of "America the Beautiful" and follow that with our national anthem. As we started singing, the first two flares were launched, and as soon as they died down others were launched, two at a time. Then on the last verse of the anthem, six flares went off. The first flares really lit up the area, but the last ones blinded us. The chaplain gave a closing prayer, the lights came back on, and we stumbled back to our rooms because our eyes were not focusing too well. We crawled into our beds and went to sleep without the usual banter and chatter that went on at bedtime.

Another very special and memorable day was July 18, when we crossed the international date line. It was customary among sailors who had never crossed the line to have their heads shaved and to be initiated into the Ancient Order of the Deep, the Domain of Neptunus Rex. Those who had not been initiated into it were called polliwogs, and those who had been initiated into it were called shellbacks. When the sailors were initiated into the order, part of the ceremony was shaving the hair off their heads. On the 17th, messages were piped into our rooms that we should be prepared for the next day, and so forth.

All sorts of messages were given, such as the one that told us that we would have our hair cut off. We nurses did not think that they would do that, but then we were not too sure about that. We hardly got any sleep that night, not because we were worried about our hair, but because we were kept awake all night long. About every hour, dreadful sounds were piped into our rooms, such as yells, screams, clinking of chains, dragging of heavy items, and so forth.

We had been instructed to wear our fatigues the next day. When we emerged from the stairs to the deck, we were immediately squirted with seawater from the ship's big hoses, and that continued off and on throughout the whole ceremony. The shellbacks had formed a paddle line, which we had to crawl through on our hands and knees. We went through a paddle line three different times during the entire initiation. We climbed up a ladder to a platform, where our faces were painted, then down and up another ladder to a platform and had a concoction of flour, water, and broken eggs, including the shells, poured down the back of our shirts. We climbed down from that and formed two lines behind chairs. One line was for the sailors, and the other was for us nurses. The sailors had their heads shaved, and we women had mixture of flour, water, cooking oil, molasses, and sugar thoroughly massaged into our hair. To end the initiation, we climbed up another ladder and slid down a slide into a child's swimming pool that was filled with water. Shellbacks helped us out of the pool and officially declared us "trusty shellbacks." The ceremony was finished off by having a nice picnic-type lunch served to us on the deck. All parts of our bodies were covered with black and blue bruises. We had to shampoo our hair several times to get all of the gunk out of it.

It took us seven days to reach the Canal Zone and a complete day to traverse it. The day after we sailed from Balboa, we were informed that our destination was Saipan, which was located in the Mariana Islands. We were happy to find out where we were headed, even though we had no idea of where it was located. Even though the voyage was a long one, forty-one days, it was a nice one. We had smooth sailing all the way since there were no storms. Not having to travel under blackout conditions was also nice.

After we sailed from the port of Balboa, we saw no land or other ships until the day before we arrived at Saipan. On that day a freighter passed us traveling in the opposite direction. We were all very aware that the ship we were traveling on was sailing all by itself in a big ocean and that the Japanese were notified twice daily of our exact location. We felt that we were sitting ducks for a Japanese submarine to torpedo the ship, and if they did there were no ships in the vicinity to rescue us.

It was very ironic that even though our group had been assigned to the shipment on April 27, and we had been en route since then, and the Japanese were notified of our location daily after we sailed from New York, "the powers that be" on Saipan had not been notified of our date or time of arrival there.

The ship arrived at Saipan early on the morning of July 27. Since they had not been notified of our date of arrival, they had to contact headquarters in Washington DC to receive permission for us to sail into the harbor.

We were met at the pier by army trucks that transported us to the hospitals where we would be billeted. There were three army hospitals on Saipan—the 148th General and two field hospitals. I was in the group that was billeted at the 148th General. When we departed the trucks in front of the nurses' compound, we were surprised to see that our quarters were surrounded by an eight-foot-high chain-link fence, which had strands of barbed wire on the top of it. There was only one gate into the compound, and an MP was standing by it. He directed us to the captain's quarters, where we presented our orders and were processed in and given the number of our quarters. Then we were directed to go to the next room where we were given a pillow, a pillowcase, two sheets, a blanket, a bath towel, and a washcloth and were directed to our quarters. We were also told that there would be an orientation meeting scheduled at 7 p.m. It would be held in the officers' club, which was located across the road from our quarters.

In the meeting we were informed that we should not do too much unpacking because in three days, orders would be cut for our permanent assignment and many of us would be transported to other islands in the area. There was a midnight curfew for all nurses and other females on the island. At that time the gate to the compound would be padlocked. If we were late, we would have to go to the headquarters building to get in, and we would be given demerits for being late. The reason for this precaution was that there were still Japanese soldiers hiding out in the hills. At the time the United States captured Saipan, many of the Japanese soldiers did not surrender. Instead they fled into the hills, where there were many caves for them to live in. That was the reason for all the restrictions that we nurses were living under. The nurses' compound was patrolled during the day by two armed MPs and at night by three armed MPs.

We were not to leave the hospital area to wander about the island at all. When we left the hospital area, each nurse had to be accompanied by two male escorts, each wearing sidearms (holster and gun). We had to sign out, and our escorts also had to sign where they were taking us. When they signed out they not only had to give their name but also their rank, serial number, and the organization that they were assigned to. The roster was checked at midnight, and if we had not signed in and were not in our quarters at that time, the MPs were notified and a full-blown search was started for the missing nurse and her escort. If our escorts did not have us back at the compound by midnight, the infraction went on their record.

We were informed that our quarters had just been completed about three weeks earlier and the nurses who were on the island had moved into them from their tents at that time. The quarters had electric lights run by a generator that failed often, especially at night, so we had to keep our flashlight and extra batteries handy at all times. Our showers only had cold water since no hot-water heater had been installed in the quarters. There were no flush toilets in our quarters, but there was one eight-holer at the end of the compound for us to use. When we needed to use it in the middle of the night, we had to get one or two other people to go with us. Another suggestion was that we should hang our mosquito nets over our beds to keep the rats, mice, and little lizards that ran around the rafters from jumping or falling on us while we were in bed. We did not have to worry about mosquitos or other insects because our quarters were sprayed monthly with DDT and the entire island was also sprayed monthly by air.

There was a quartermaster warehouse on the island, so we could replace our uniforms if necessary, but outside of about three post exchanges there were no other stores on the island. The post exchanges carried only the necessities of life: toothpaste and brushes, shaving cream, deodorants, bath powder, shoe laces, shoe polish, and so forth—no clothes, candy, or other merchandise. If we needed other items, we were to write home to our parents and have them buy those items, wrap them, and send them to us by ship. Our mail was delivered by air, but no packages could be shipped there by air mail. When we ordered something from home, we planned on not receiving those items for two to three months. A supply ship docked on the island about every four to six weeks.

There was not too much in the way of recreation on the island. Most of the outfits had an outdoor theater set up, and there were movies nightly. There was one beach on the island that we could use, and transportation to and from the hospital was available several times during the day. However, it was off-limits to all military members from 6 p.m. to 9 a.m. During the time that it was off-limits, MPs patrolled it. If anyone was found using it during that time, they would face a court-martial. Just three weeks before we arrived, three couples had been murdered on the beach.

The Mariana Islands had been invaded by the United States in July and August a year earlier. The islands were fairly close to Japan, so they were selected by the United States to be the staging base for the invasion of Japan. Saipan was selected to be the main island for the event, so the 148th General Hospital was selected to be the main hospital that the wounded would be evacuated to after receiving their initial medical care.

The new hospital had been completed about six weeks before we arrived on the island, and the patients had been moved there from the tent hospital. It was built to accommodate up to three thousand bed patients, and it was equipped with all of the latest hospital equipment. It was not in a big building; instead, it was made up of row upon row of Quonset and prefab huts, all joined together by a boardwalk. Each ward had accommodations for thirty bed patients, and the wards were wide enough to put another row of fifteen beds in if they were needed. Like the nurses' quarters, they were set up on cinder blocks. There was an old-fashioned screen door at each end of the ward. The windows were much smaller than the ones in our quarters, and they only had screens on them, no panes of glass.

The nurses' station was at the front end of the ward. It was a cubicle, as the rooms in our quarters were. The nurses' desk was made from a very large shipping crate, and a chart rack was fashioned from a smaller one. The medications were kept in one of the big white metal medicine cabinets with a lock on it. The telephones were field-type ones in a big leather case, and you had to crank them when you used them. The hospital was equipped with backup generators for electricity. There were two or three private rooms on each ward, which were made of the partitions.

The beds were army cots that had a metal head and foot rail. Neither the head nor the foot could be elevated. There were some bedside tables, but most of them were small shipping crates that sat on their ends. There were some folding chairs, but here again many sat on upended shipping crates. There was a shower room, another room that had a bathtub in it, a restroom with commodes, a bedpan room, a storage room, and a nurses' restroom. Since the plumbing often plugged up, those patients who were ambulatory were encouraged to use the light and airy latrines that were located just outside of the ward. The hospital had both hot and cold running water. The surgery, laboratory, and x-ray and other departments had the latest in medical equipment.

The two field hospitals were much smaller and were set up with mostly portable machines because they were mobile hospitals. They were both slated to accompany troops on the invasion.

The first week of August, the two atom bombs were dropped on Japan, and on August 14 Japan surrendered and the war was over. By the end of September, Saipan became a ghost island, so to speak. All of the B-29s and the fighter planes left to return to the United States, and their airfields were shut down. The airfield that the transport places used was kept open since Saipan was an important stop for the trip to Japan. The transport planes continued to bring in supplies and personnel. Only two seaplanes were left in the bay. All of the ships departed as did most of the troops. They either went to Japan in the army of occupation or back to the States for reassignment or discharge.

The majority of the other units that had been stationed there were closed. There was a replacement depot opened on the island for those military personnel who had been stationed on the various islands in the Pacific. They stayed there for a few days until transport by either ship or plane back to the United States became available. Saipan was placed on what the military called "a housekeeping basis," which meant that the buildings could be reopened on short notice if they were needed.

When we nurses joined the Army Nurse Corps, we signed an affidavit that we would serve for the duration of the war plus six months. While the other military were dismissed early when they were no longer needed, we nurses were required to complete that tour of duty.

With most of the troops returning home, I doubt if there were more than a thousand military left on Saipan, so the hospital closed down most of the wards. The only wards that were kept open were a medical ward, a surgical ward, an orthopaedic ward (one end of it had a small prison ward for members of the military who had run afoul of the law), and a female ward. If a ward had six patients, it was considered a busy ward. With so many nurses and not many patients to care for, the twelve-hour day shift was shortened to three- to four-hour shifts, and we worked a shift about every two days. This was to keep our nursing skills sharpened and to help us pass the time. The night shift was still a twelve-hour shift and was a two-week stint of duty. I was assigned to the orthopaedic ward, and it seemed to have a few more patients, since many accidents would result in broken bones.

The water in our quarters was very hard and highly chlorinated, so when we needed to wash our hair, we would put on our bathing suits and keep our shampoo handy. When a rainstorm or shower came we grabbed the shampoo and rushed out into the rain and hoped that it would last long enough for us to get our hair shampooed. There were no hair dryers, so it had to dry naturally. If you put it up in curlers or pin curls, you could not leave them in too long. Due to the high humidity and moisture in the air, it just would not dry. It really was easier to keep our hair up if it was cut short or was worn in a bun or a braid around our head. Since there were no beauty or barber shops, we cut each other's hair and gave each other home permanents that our folks sent us from the United States. It would have been nice if the pony tail hairdo had been in vogue at that time. Many times when we went on dates, our hairdo did not last because of the rain.

Since Saipan was located in the tropics, the weather was very hot and muggy with frequent rain showers. Some of them were heavy and some were light. Sometimes they were accompanied by thunder and lightning. When we left the area, we always carried our raincoat or poncho with us because we never knew when we would need them. It was a constant battle to keep mold and mildew off of our clothes. Our means of transportation was open jeeps, and we frequently arrived at our destination with wet uniforms and hair. Because of the rain, another irritant was getting the mud off our shoes. It was a very thick and gooey type of mud. We had two or three pairs of shoes that we rotated so that we could always have a pair clean and ready to wear. Our windows were only screens, so we frequently had to cope with wet floors in our quarters and on the wards.

About the end of November, a hurricane hit the area of Okinawa. Saipan was on the receiving end of it, so we had an excessive amount of wind and rain, and we were wading around in ankle-deep water on the wards and in our quarters for a day or two. The hurricane leveled the island of Okinawa, so the hospital patients and many of the personnel were evacuated to Saipan.

Because of the heat and humidity, we perspired very heavily and it was hard to keep our bodies fresh and sweet-smelling. We used a lot of deodorant and took frequent showers. Also because of the heavy perspiration, our bodies lost a lot of water. Bottles of salt tablets were kept on the tables in the mess hall for us to take as we needed them. We became very weak and shaky when we lost a lot of body fluids.

I spent Christmas of 1945 on Saipan, and it was the saddest and sorriest one that I ever spent. There was just not any Christmas spirit at all. The weather was very hot and muggy—there was no evidence of snow anywhere and no brightly decorated stores to shop in. We had no radios, so we did not have the usual Christmas songs. Maybe it was for the best, since when we heard the popular Christmas songs it made us very blue and homesick. During the church services, the songs that were sung were Christmas carols. If we felt like singing in our quarters, we sang the Christmas carols and not the popular songs.

Each of the wards did have a tree to decorate, but we had no decorations for them. Some corpsmen had been given the assignment to cut down a tree for each ward. However, there were no trees on Saipan that remotely resembled Christmas trees. The ones that they brought were very spindly and not very bushy. There were no ornaments of any kind and no craft or other stores to buy them at. We made do with the items and objects that were available to us for decorating.

One of the pilots said that he could get us all of the aluminum chafe that we needed to make ornaments from. Aluminum chafe was slivers of aluminum that were carried by the bomber crews and were thrown out of the aircraft as they approached their bomb runs. The purpose of doing that was that it fouled up the enemies' radar. They gave us a box of that, and we got a corrugated carton and cut out a star for each tree and some round circles for other decorations. However, there was not glue or paste of any kind available. The hospital had a supply of collodion, which was sometimes used as a cover for wounds instead of a bandage. It was a sticky liquid that dried very hard when it was exposed to the air. Someone came up with the idea of using it as glue, and it worked, so each tree had a star on top, but we did not have enough of it to make any more decorations.

The mess hall popped up a lot of popcorn and sent it to the wards so that it could be strung and hung on the trees. The men used small, curved suture needles and suture string to string the popcorn on. Some of the men wanted to make paper chains like we made from construction paper when we went to grade school. However, there was no construction paper available, so they cut the strips from the covers of magazines. There were no staples available to connect the circles together nor any more collodion, so we made old-fashioned paste from water and flour to use.

Other items used to decorate the trees were nail files, nail clippers, small scissors, and small surgical instruments that we hung on the trees. We punched holes into the corners of Christmas cards and snapshots of loved ones and hung them on the tree with strips of yarn. When the trees were decorated, they did look very festive and Christmassy. Since the ship had not yet arrived with our presents from our folks at home, there were no presents to put under the trees.

That night, after all of the patients went to bed, the rats and mice had a wonderful party. When the patients awoke the next morning, they found that during the night the rodents had eaten all of the popcorn strings, including the suture string, and they also had eaten the paper chains where they were fastened with the flour paste, leaving the rest of the paper lying on the floor.

The chaplains on the island decided to put on the Christmas play, the *Messiah,* and they enlisted the aid of those men and women stationed on Saipan who had musical and acting abilities to participate in the production.

On Christmas Eve, when the nurse chief officer in charge (NCOIC) and I made the 7 p.m. round, we did not hurry back to our station. Instead, we spent some time on the wards and joined in the activities on the wards. The mess hall had sent over bottles of Coke and 7-Up and big bowls of popcorn to each ward. They had tried to make fudge, but it did not set up, but they sent it to the ward anyway and we used spoons to eat it. The activities that the men were enjoying were talking about home and Christmases past and singing carols and other Christmas songs. On one ward they had a copy of Dickens's *A Christmas Carol* and were taking turns reading it out loud. Some were reading the Christmas Story from the Bible.

After getting off duty, I went to breakfast and then hit the sack until about 4 p.m., when I took a shower and got dressed for duty and went to the mess hall for dinner. They served the traditional Christmas dinner—minus salads—and gelatin desserts. In addition to the apples and oranges that we could take to our rooms, there were sacks of unshelled nuts and a sack of hardtack Christmas candy. We used rocks to crack open the nuts, and crochet hooks made excellent nut picks. The ship that brought us our Christmas presents from our family and friends in the United States did not arrive on Saipan until the middle of January 1946, just before I left Saipan.

On November 28, 1945, I was promoted to the rank of first lieutenant. At that time I was offered the chance to extend my tour of duty with the Army Nurse Corps, and I did so along with several others.

On January 10, nine other nurses from the 148th and I received orders to proceed to the two hospitals in Honolulu, Hawaii: Tripler General and the Schofield Barracks Hospital. We had been instructed to be packed and ready to leave in two days. On January 17, we were awakened about 6:30 a.m. and told that we were to be ready to fly out at 8:30 a.m. Our first stop was Guam, where we were able to have a three-hour layover. Upon landing on Guam, a bus took our group to an officers' club to spend that time, and they would not let us take our suitcase with us. About 5 p.m. we were informed that we would not be leaving Guam until the next morning. They would not take us to the airfield to pick up our suitcases; instead, they took us to the post exchange so that we could purchase a towel, washcloth, soap, toothbrush, and toothpaste.

It was paradise to be back in civilization again. It was nice to ride in a car instead of a jeep, to be able to soak in a bathtub and have lavatories instead of helmets to wash up in, and to have both hot and cold water to use. We were free to wander where we wanted to and not have to be accompanied by armed escorts. We welcomed the laundries and dry cleaners and the beauty shops and stores to shop in. It was nice to see children and people dressed in civilian clothes. It was nice to have an indoor movie to attend and the popcorn and candy that they had for us to enjoy and the restaurants and cafes to eat in. It was like heaven to crawl into bed between fresh-smelling white sheets instead of the "tattle-gray sheets" that smelled of mold and mildew that we had on Saipan. But probably the best thing was to have fresh milk to drink and fresh fruits and vegetables, salads, and ice cream. For the first two weeks I ate mostly salads, fresh fruit, and ice cream.

When I arrived at Tripler, among the items mentioned in our orientation meeting was that there was a military rest and recreation camp, Kilauea, that was located on the Big Island, Hawaii. Twice a year we could request to spend five days there. I immediately submitted my request to go there. In the middle of March my request was honored, as well as the request of three other nurses.

The army had a point system for those who served on overseas duty. You were given so many points for each month that you spent overseas. When you had the required number of points, you were rotated back to the United States for reassignment. I don't remember how many points you needed, but on the 20th of August I had enough points to be rotated back to the United States.

I was happy to be home, but I felt like a duck out of water. The war had been over for a year, and when I went into town there was no one else, male or female, wearing a uniform. I got the feeling that everyone was looking down on me. The army had lifted the restriction that you had to wear your uniform at all times, whether on duty or not, so I purchased some new civilian clothes to wear so that I would not feel too out of place when I went out.

My new orders arrived, assigning me to the Army Navy General Hospital located at Hot Springs, Arkansas. I reported for duty there on October 15, 1946. I was discharged from the Army Nurse Corps on January 7, 1947. Since I had twenty-seven days of leave time left, I was able to spend Christmas with my family.

My decorations and citations are the Asiatic-Pacific Theater Medal with one Bronze Battle Star, the American Theater Medal, the Meritorious Unit Award, and the World War II Victory Medal.

I am proud that I volunteered to serve my country when it needed me. It was a very exciting and interesting time for me. I traveled extensively and had many varied and interesting experiences that I will remember for the rest of my life. The most important event was meeting my husband-to-be, Thayne L. Thomas.

Karla LaVore Paul Tripp

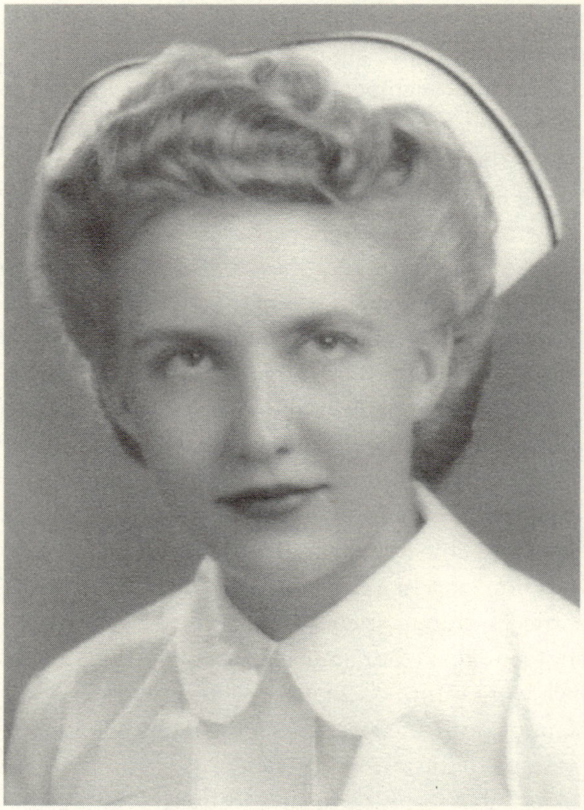

Karla LaVore Paul Tripp

I started nurses' training in August 1940 at LDS Hospital School of Nursing and graduated September 1943 as a registered nurse. I was working night duty in nurses' training when Pearl Harbor was bombed. I woke up and went out into the hallway. It was so quiet, and everyone was huddled around the radio. It was just a really scary and sad thing.

Up until Pearl Harbor, none of the nurses could give IVs—all the doctors started IVs. We were short on interns and residents, so nurses could start giving IVs. Sometimes I started them before that because some of the interns couldn't hit the veins.

I think I wanted to join the service because my mother and father always taught me to be patriotic. My father had been in the navy. He served in World War I.

I received orders to Mare Island, California. I was so scared. I did not know where Mare Island was, and I did not know how to get there. You could bring one suitcase to put your things in, and I had one big suitcase—the biggest suitcase they made at that time. My dad took me down to the train station in Ogden. I got on the train and wondered how I was going to find Mare Island. As I was riding on the train, I talked to a lady who was getting off at Berkeley about how I did not know how to get to Mare Island.

There was a little man across the aisle who had apparently been listening. Just before the train arrived in Oakland, he introduced himself and said, "I heard what you were talking about. I am a nice man, and if you don't mind, I'd like to help you." He was only about five-feet four-inches tall. He had a briefcase, and I had this big suitcase. He said, "You carry my briefcase, and I'll carry your suitcase," (which was only about an inch off the floor, the poor man). He bought my ticket on the ferry from Oakland to San Francisco. When we got off the ferry in San Francisco, he took me to the bus station and put me on the bus. He said, "When you get to Vallejo, there will be a car called a Jitney. It is a big car with about three rows of seats. Tell them you want to go to Mare Island. It will cost you ten cents."

That was how I found Mare Island; it was an answer to my prayers because I had been praying for someone to help me find it. I know that prayers are answered. I will never forget that little man. His last name was Paul, and he was a little Jewish man. He owned a pawnshop in Salt Lake City. I had never seen him before and I have never seen him since, but I will never forget him.

It was really interesting to see how the boys helped each other. If one had his legs missing, he would help someone who had his arms missing. The ones with legs figured out a way to push the ones without legs in the wheelchairs. They helped one another, teased one another, and they were just great kids, great young men.

I worked on ward fifteen and had some great corpsmen on fifteen. Tom was one of the best. He wanted to be a doctor when he got out of the navy, and I hope he did because he would have made a good doctor. I had another corpsman. In the navy you had white-glove inspections on your wards, where they would run their white gloves under the screens, on top of the doors, around the rails, or anyplace they think you haven't dusted or cleaned. We had to hurry and get ward fifteen ready for inspection. This corpsman was assigned to clean the head. The other corpsman said, "Ensign Paul, he's not cleaning the head." So I said, "Okay, you tell all the patients and everybody else to stay out of the head because I am going in there." He said, "You're not." And I said, "Yes, I am. He has a job to do, and he'd better get it done or he's going on report." The corpsmen's mouths fell open and the patients' eyes went wide; I went ahead and got him out—he was really dumbfounded to think that I would go in there. I had a corpsman hold the door open and stand there while I went in and told him to come out. When he came out I said, "You have so much time that this has to be done, and either you do it or you are going on report, and if you don't do it, I'll come and get you again." After that, when I told him to do something, he did it.

Fifteen was an amputee ward. Some of those men were rascals. They would wear two pairs of pants, go over to Vallejo, put bottles of whisky in their inside pant, and tie the bottom of it so it wouldn't look like they had anything but the amputation. They would be checked by the guard as they came back on base, and they would bring this alcohol on the base. We would have to confiscate it when we found out it was there. We also had to lock up the thiamine hydrochloride. They would come and take it so that they wouldn't have hangovers. Most of those young men would help one another, and there were very few of them who had bad attitudes. They would say, "Uncle Sam got me into this, and now he'd better take care of me for the rest of my life."

There were some that were so happy to see their wives, but there were some of them who were just little stinkers. One man, in particular, had lost a leg and some of his fingers. His wife came and was so glad that he was alive, but he wouldn't even talk to her. When he knew that she was coming to visit, he would invite girls over from Vallejo to come visit. He would kiss them and love them, and she would stand there and just cry. He thought that she wouldn't care for him and that she was just being nice because she was his wife. That was one that the nurses and the doctors called a stinker—his thinking was all mixed-up. He could accomplish most things he wanted to do if he just put his mind to it.

It was interesting working there, as it was an amputee hospital. There was a lot of plastic surgery and reconstructive surgery done there. You'd see a young man walking along with skin attached from the bottom of his chin to the top of his chest. It would have a column of skin growing. They would transplant it so that it would grow. The beginning of plastic and reconstructive surgery and the use of prosthetics were started in World War II. Penicillin also came into use during that time. They had sulfa (antibiotic) during nurses' training, and we thought that was wonderful. It did help with the wounds in World War II to have this sulfa, and they would just spread it in the wounds. It was mainly just a powder then.

When we were working on ward fifteen, there was a smallpox outbreak in the shipyard. I was vaccinated for smallpox before I went, so I got a booster. The first time I didn't have a reaction to it, but when I received the second one, I had them give it in my leg in case my arm got sore. I really had a reaction to it. It got sore, and once when I was working, I heard some of the patients snickering. When I turned around, one of the patients was walking behind me holding his pant leg out because I would hold my uniform away from my leg as I tried to walk. They really liked to tease, and if you blushed, you were in for it.

I worked with one young man who stepped on a land mine. He had shrapnel all over his face and on his arms and hands. He still had a thumb and little finger on one hand. He was missing one leg, and the doctors didn't know if they were going to be able to save the other leg or not—it had so much damage to it. He was the nicest person, and his wife came and stayed there with him. He never complained, yet he had all of these things wrong with him. He said he was just happy to be alive, and he said, "I would do it over again." Most of them said that they would be happy to serve their country again.

One thing you had to be very careful about was not to walk up behind any of these patients without them knowing you were coming. One time, because I walk very quietly, I was right behind a couple of officers as they were walking down the hall. They must have sensed I was there. They both turned around real fast with their hands up like they were going to knock me over. They told me never, never to walk up behind them without them knowing I was there or else I would be hit.

While I was working in sick officers' quarters, it was interesting to see how they would cope with their disabilities. There was one six-foot-four-inch marine officer who had lost one leg and the other leg wasn't working too well, and he had injured his back, so he had to lie on his bed. He was knitting this scarf. It was about a foot wide, and he just kept right on knitting it. It went down the length of his bed, over the end of the bed, and down onto the floor. I asked him why didn't he make a couple of them instead of this big long one. He said, "No, I want to see how long I can make it."

Some would say, "Won't you please wear perfume?" (We weren't supposed to wear perfume.) They would say, "We miss girls and their perfume." So the head nurse said I could as long as it was a light one. So I bought some White Shoulders. They said, "Oh, that is wonderful. Just walk by every so often so I can smell the perfume."

There was one marine who was a lawyer. There weren't very many of the First Division Marines that lived. Most of them were killed over in the islands. The ones at Mare Island had been in the Pacific. He had been a lawyer and was engaged to his secretary. He was paralyzed from below the shoulders. She would come everyday and put him in his wheelchair and take him for a ride. At night he would say, "Won't you please give me a back rub?" We could give back rubs at this time. I had been taught the Swedish massage. He would say it was the only thing that would help him to sleep. Every night he would say, "Please give me a back rub." Some of them I did do back rubs for.

One time I came into the room and I couldn't see the patient in his room. I could hear this noise in the bathroom. He had fallen over into the bathtub and was having a seizure. I sent corpsmen to get help so we could get him up and call the doctor. They said the damage was from when he had a concussion from the shelling of the ship.

I had one patient who didn't want to live. He wouldn't try to do anything to help himself. The doctor said, "You'll have to make him angry so he'll want to get out of bed." I had to do the taunting! The corpsmen had to take care of him, so it wouldn't be right for them to be the bad guy. He became so angry that he said, "If I could get out of here, I'd kill you!" It worked! Later he thanked me for what I had done.

Dr. Parker was a patient on SOQ (sick officers' quarters). He lost his hand about to the middle of his arm. He had this stump and was learning to use a hook and everything. He wanted to be a surgeon. He would go around and take histories on all of the patients for the doctors. He wore his stethoscope, he learned to play golf with one hand, and he tied his shoes with one hand. He really wanted to do what he wanted to do, and he did it. Years later I was watching TV and it was showing this renowned eye surgeon doing this surgery, and it was Dr. Parker. He had a prosthesis that was holding his instruments, and he was working with his other hand. So that was Dr. Parker, renowned eye surgeon.

Night duty on family section included lock ward. It was really weird because I'd go over there and these corpsmen would ask me if I wanted a cup of coffee and I'd say, "No, I don't drink coffee." They'd say, "You don't drink coffee!" And I would say, "No, I don't believe in drinking coffee; it is against what I believe in." They would say, "I can't believe someone does not drink coffee."

The obstetrical section was part of family section, as were pediatrics and medical and surgeries for dependents. You had a WAVE on family section; you had corpsmen on sick officers' quarters and male wards. The WAVES were trained like the corpsmen. They would help care for patients. I would have to do the report and see that the count for admittance and discharge was correct for the family section. Working on family section was the first time I'd seen a pseudocyst. This little gal whose husband was about to be shipped out looked like she was six months pregnant. She thought she was. They ran the tests on her, and she wasn't. And the day she came in to find out and they told her she wasn't pregnant, it was just a false pregnancy, she cried and just wanted to be pregnant so bad. We also had a little baby who was hydrocephalic, and its head was bigger than its body was long. That was so sad to watch. The mother would come and stay with that little thing, and it took that baby a long time to pass away. I always felt bad about that.

I almost got killed in the family section. A little eighteen-month-old boy who was big for his age—his little hands were about an inch and half wide—was crying, so I picked him up. He grabbed my throat. He was holding so tight that I couldn't breathe. I thought, "Now, this is really going to be neat that my parents get word that I was killed in action by an eighteen-month-old boy." I finally got his fingers off and got him down so I could hold him. I was seeing stars by that time, and I thought I was going to pass out. It was freaky.

We had one little girl whose dad was an officer. He was one of the LDS officers who held firesides on the base. His name was Lieutenant Brown. He and Rex Price, who was not an officer, would hold these LDS meetings, and we would go to them whenever we could. Sometimes we would go over to Vallejo to their meetings if we could on Sundays.

There were a few prisoners of war from the Pacific who were liberated by our troops. They were sent to Mare Island. The looked like walking skin over bone. They were so happy to be clean, clothed, and eating food and to be on U.S. soil. Milk was one of the things they wanted. We had to give it to them one-quarter of a cup at a time because their bodies would have rejected it otherwise.

Then I went to the Presidio (an army base) in San Francisco for my discharge physical to be released from the navy after fourteen months of service.

Christmas was weird. I had been away from home on Christmas before because all three years I was in nurses' training I could never go home for Christmas. We were supposed to alternate, but I never got to. I had to stay there and work. I was trying to call my folks, but the lines were always busy. It was 5:30 in the morning before I got through to my parents, and my sisters and my brothers-in-law were all there and I got to talk to them. Then I asked the operator how much I owed, and she said, "Nothing. Merry Christmas." It was so neat that she would do that.

I knew from my teachings in the gospel that there was life after death, I knew that Jesus atoned for us, and I knew the gospel was true. There were a lot of people who thought that this life was it, and that was all they lived for was for today. You treat other people the way you want to be treated and be kind and thoughtful to others. I learned in nurses' training you never ask someone how they were; you always told them how they were. When you walked into a room, and there was this sad-looking person and you knew they didn't feel good, you'd say something like, "Oh, you have some pretty hairdo today," and they would laugh and say, "Yeah sure," but it would get them so they would start to feel good. You'd say, "My, you have a pretty smile," or tickle the bottom of their feet or something like that to get their mind off their problems and help them have a positive attitude. But you would listen; you didn't empathize with them where it would put them down; you always wanted to pick them up. That is what I've tried to do throughout my life.

We, as members of the Church, know that this is a choice land, and we want to keep it a choice land. We know that the government was formed through inspiration. When you are asked to do something to protect your country or help somebody else, you do it because we are all children of our Father in Heaven. It has been really hard for both Boyd (my husband) and me after being in the military to go to the parades, especially in the 60s on into the 90s. We would see people stand and talk when the flag went by, and they were so disrespectful. I said to Boyd one day, "I wonder what would happen if we had another war, if people would even go to war, if people would stand up and be counted." And then September 11, 2001, happened. People stood up. There has been patriotism and more prayer.

Zelta Walker Hendricks

It was really hard to think that you couldn't say prayers in school, because we grew up having prayers in school. I said my prayers all the time when I was in the military. I didn't always say it so other people knew I was doing it, but I always said my prayers before I went to bed. I always prayed for our country and our boys, and I still do.

Zelta Walker Hendricks

I left the Idaho Falls, Idaho, bus depot on August 16, 1943, on my birthday. I was ranked second lieutenant in the Army Air Corps (AAC). I felt an urgency to serve in the Army Air Corps. I have been a person who loves being where the action is and being involved.

I first arrived at Fort George Wright in Spokane, Washington. My nursing duties were to supervise and be in charge of forty beds, with corpsmen to assist.

At the time I entered the medical corps, women officers were wearing the blue uniforms, which were a blue jacket, cap, white blouse, maroon skirt, and black oxfords. While on duty we wore a white starched regulation uniform and a white cap. In May 1944 the official dress was changed to an olive drab color, but for summer we wore a beige suite or a dress. On duty we wore a brown and white seersucker one-piece wraparound dress with a cap to match. I starched this uniform, but most of the nurses did not. This uniform, along with the slacks and shirt, served the nurses overseas or on field duty. They said it was so much easier to launder and keep up. My olive drab nurse's uniform is now at the Rigby Museum.

On August 26, 1943, my friend Dove Chandler and I arrived on the base. We had gone through three years of nursing school together and would now spend the next two years together.

In October 1943 a transfer came for both of us to go to Fairmont Army Air Base in Geneva, Nebraska. The base there was the last stop for bomber crews and fighter pilots before going to the war zone. It was rumored at the time that German and Japanese U-boats were on both the Atlantic and Pacific coasts. Therefore, our base was inland for protection. The land was flat and sought after by military planners.

There were five thousand working at this base. There were B-17, B-24, and B-29 bombers there. Bruneau had the Spitfire fighter pilots. The hospital cared for patients from all the bases in Nebraska. The twelve to fourteen nurses at the base cared for the critically ill, supervised the ward, and trained the corpsmen. Registered nurses were the only personnel who had permission to give the medications. The doctor started and administered all intravenous injections. If a patient was ambulatory, he came to the desk for the medication; otherwise, the RN took it to the bedside.

Charlotte Sherwood Wiehrdt

A new program to train military nurses in air evacuation was just beginning. I was accepted and went through the training at Bowman Field, Kentucky, and was one of the first flight nurses, graduating December 1943. I received secret orders to join the 807th Medical Air Evacuation Squadron in Catania (Sicily) a week later. I was one of the replacements for thirteen girls who were missing on a plane that crash-landed in Albania.

Our planes landed on newly laid runways near the front lines, picking up wounded men and taking them to the nearest hospitals, at that time in Algiers, North Africa. Leonard arrived four months later and was assigned as commander of the 522nd Squadron, 27th Fighter Bomber group. We both were in the 12th Air Force and were able to meet occasionally.

I have vivid memories of the 1940s. On one flight in Italy, I was on a plane filled with men with serious head injuries. When they lost an engine, the pilot said to place parachutes on the wounded, preparing for a crash. The medical sergeant and I went to the rear of the plane to get the parachutes. Someone had removed the nylon from the parachutes, substituting GI blankets. Although the medical sergeant and I were concerned that the injured men would not have survived the parachute fall, it was a great relief when the plane landed safely.

My most vivid memories are of the men themselves. I never saw any self-pity or "Why me?" Two soldiers on one of my many air evac flights were talking to each other about which corner in their hometowns they were going to sell pencils. I looked at the two courageous young men lying before me, each with one leg missing. I had to turn away so they wouldn't see my tears.

I am thankful I was able to assist the wounded who were under my care. It was also gratifying to be part of the great American effort during World War II.

Letter from Charlotte Wiehrdt, Italy, November 5, 1944

Dear Mamma and Daddy,

I am still on Ds but should be with the squad in another couple of days. They are holding conference on December the fifth for all of us in Italy that can attend. Do hope I am down this way again about that time.

For a long time I have heard of air pockets, but a few days ago I saw, felt, and heard one that beat all. We hit one, and after all being suspended in air (even the walking patients that I had safety straps on) we came back down to the floor. The beds on the sides were in the middle, and I was holding a 200-pound colored boy on the top one. Boy, what a jolt—will give the boys something to talk about for a while—and no one was hurt except me with a bruised finger.

It is really getting chilly over this way and along with the dampness is uncomfortable. Yes, it is still raining in sunny Italy. Have to get ready for supper so will stop and wash up and mail this on the way to the mess.

Love to all of you,
Charlotte and Leonard

Althea Rawlins Woodland

Althea Rawlins Woodland

I entered the service on the first day of April 1943. My first assignment was at Letterman General Hospital at Presidio in San Francisco. I stayed there nine months and worked on the medical-surgical and the OB floors. Some of our patients came from the Pacific area. We had officers who lived on the base, and they too were patients in the hospital at times. I remember one burn case we got from the Pacific with third-degree burns on both arms and some of his face, which required skin grafts. When we would have to change his dressings, we would have to give him a shot of morphine to ease the pain so that he could tolerate the dressing change. He would not say anything, but he would lie there and just switch his hips back and forth, and we knew he hurt a lot.

While I was stationed at Letterman, I was assigned with another nurse, two doctors, and several corpsmen to transfer patients to Tuscaloosa, Alabama. Then I was also sent on a train transfer to Longview, Texas. I did get to sacrament meetings a few times while I was in San Francisco. I didn't get to go to church very often, and there was no Latter-day Saint chaplain on our base.

On February 27, 1944, a group of us were prepared for overseas duty. Our hospital was the 83rd General—it was a neurosurgical center, and I served on medical wards and also on the neurosurgical ward. Captain Lippscomb was in charge of the neurosurgical unit. Our patients were paraplegics and head injuries mostly. They were transferred to us from the evacuation hospitals after being stabilized. One of our objectives was to return them to the States in as good a condition as possible. There were also a few who had nerve injuries who were ambulatory, and they too would be returning home.

It took us two weeks to cross the Atlantic on the ship *Britannica* in a convoy. We never did know how many ships were in the convoy. We zigzagged across the Atlantic, and no one was allowed on deck after dark. We wore our life vests always. Ours had a light so if we went overboard we could be located, because they wanted to be sure they got us there. We docked at Liverpool and then were taken to Llandudno, North Wales, where we were billeted in private homes. This was a resort town that was close to England.

Our paraplegic patients were unable to do much of anything for themselves. Someone had to feed them. We read their letters to them, and we routinely turned them every two hours. Most of the time there were four of us to do this—usually one nurse and three corpsmen.

We used a lot of penicillin for infection, and this was when the penicillin was in a yellow liquid form that we gave hypodermically intramuscularly. They were big shots, and they hurt. I remember one night as I was giving one of these injections, I woke the patient, or at least I thought

I had woken him to give him the shot. I thought he was awake—he talked to me and even turned over—but when I gave the shot, he came up fighting. I was a little scared, but I did get the needle out and everything turned out all right.

The morale was high on this ward. These soldiers knew they were going home, but they didn't know the extent of their injuries, particularly the paraplegics. Many of them would be permanently paralyzed. There were some who would be able to get feeling in their legs again. Many of them had no feeling beyond their shoulders, some of them down a little further, but most couldn't use their hands. Whenever there was any entertainment brought to our unit, they always put on the show for these men who couldn't leave the ward. There were many times that we had movies, and I would go over with some of the other nurses and watch the movies with the patients. When the patients were brought in from the evacuation hospitals, we really were busy trying to make room for them and helping them to settle and doing all the extra things that needed to be done to get them situated on our wards.

After the war in Europe was over and they closed our hospital, we again were on board a ship and traveled to France. We docked in Normandy and then were taken by trucks to our new facility. It was about forty miles from Reims. We were housed in a cement building, and our hospital was not too big, but we did have some patients there. They were getting us ready to go to the Pacific, but the war was over too soon for them to send us there. So most of our time, except for the little bit of work we had to do with the patients who were still around, we were just waiting to come home. While we were there another nurse, Mary Armstrong, and I would go into Reims to sacrament meeting and MIA.

We didn't have our own transportation, so we would stand by the MPs and they would flag a jeep or another vehicle for us. We would come back to base on the army truck at night. MIA was held in a bakery. The fellow who was in charge of the meeting worked there. We played games and ping-pong and had meetings. There weren't very many times that we could go, but we did go when we could. One day when we were waiting for our ride, an ambulance came along and the MPs asked if we would like to ride in it. We said that was all right. When they opened the back of the jeep, it was half full of black soldiers. They asked us if we still wanted to go, and we said sure we would go. It wasn't a very comfortable ride. They didn't speak and we didn't either, except to say thank you for taking us.

We did have church services on the base. A Protestant chaplain took care of it. When it was getting close to Christmastime, a group of us formed a choir, and one of the enlisted men was the director. We learned Christmas carols and some other songs, and then we sang to the patients over the hospital speaker system.

My parents lived in Lewiston, Utah, and when I joined the army they were very concerned. In fact, they would rather I hadn't joined, but they supported me, and I received letters and articles and *Church News* sometimes. I even had a few letters from other people in the ward, and even the bishop sent me a letter. I felt the Lord blessed me more than I probably deserved because I had the servicemen's scriptures, but I didn't do as much reading as I should have. However, I did say my prayers, and I know my family was saying their prayers at home.

After I went overseas, I made arrangements with my mother for her to pay my tithing. I arranged for a certain amount of my monthly check to go into my local bank at home, and then she would take my tithing out of that. I know she said that I was one of the higher-paying tithepayers in our ward.

—Cadet Nurse Corps—

HISTORICAL BACKGROUND

The United States Cadet Nurse Corps was the largest and youngest group of uniformed women to serve their country during the war and postwar era of World War II. Though the original goals of the cadet program included inducing inactive nurses to return to practice and training voluntary nurses aides, the largest focus of the program was the recruitment of new students into nursing schools and the improvement of nursing education. At the beginning of World War II in 1941, a Public Health Service inventory showed there were 289,286 registered nurses in the United States. Of those, only 173,055 were active. The predicted national need for nurses at the time was 97,000. Existing nursing education institutions, about 1,300, could not stretch enough to accommodate that number. A secondary goal was set for 65,000, and 47,000 were recruited in 1942. The corps recruited nurses from July 1, 1943, to October 15, 1945. During that period of time 179,000 women, beginning at age seventeen, joined the corps. Of that number, 124,000 women graduated as nurses from 1,125 participating schools of nursing before 1948, when the corps was discontinued. Those who joined the corps received tuition, books, a stipend, and a uniform. In return, they contracted to serve as nurses in either military or civilian hospitals or in Indian Health Service or Public Health Services facilities for the duration of the war.

During the war years there was a shortage of nurses for several reasons. The direct need for nurses to care for military personnel was the most visible reason. Another reason was the growing defense industry, which contributed to a more prosperous economy. The civilian medical community was also disrupted by the fact that physicians were also called to support the military, leaving a larger portion of medical care to the nurses left in the civilian sector. The American Red Cross and the United States Public Health Service initially assisted by assigning thousands of volunteers to help with hospital care, but these organizations could not keep up with the demand.

Though the Cadet Nurse Corps only existed for about seven years, its contribution has been long lasting. Eight percent of the nursing care provided in civilian hospitals during World War II was provided by Cadet Nurse Corps students (Robinson, 2002, xi). This allowed hospitals to stay open to serve civilian populations that may have had to close otherwise because of insufficient nursing staff.

Ruth L. Johnson, a consultant with the Cadet Nurse Corps, described the improvement to nursing education produced by the institution of the corps. She noted that every school that wished to participate was reviewed. They needed to meet certain requirements for faculty and for curriculum content. Those schools that did not meet this criteria were closed. This elevated the level of nursing education. Schools were also required to have budgets independent of the facility with which they were associated. This began the process of making schools of nursing independent of hospitals and medical staffs (Robinson, 2002, chapter 2).

Finally, the nurses who were educated by the corps have become leaders in the profession, educators for current nursing programs, and care providers for millions of Americans.

Rayola Hodgkinson Andersen

War was raging. Nurses were desperately needed. The government started the United States Cadet Nurse Corps. If you joined, your tuition and housing were paid. That was good, since I came off the farm in Vernal, Utah, and had no way of paying for my education.

When we started nursing school in 1945, we were issued summer uniforms and winter uniforms. We only wore them when we had to appear for inspection and when we went to the movies. If we wore them to the movies, we got to go in for free. We started nursing school by living at Carlson Hall, which was University of Utah housing, for six months. We took all of the preliminary classes in anatomy and physiology and the nursing arts. We transferred to LDS Hospital after about six months and lived in housing on State Street and First Avenue. It was a two-story building. We had a housemother. We had to be home every night at 9:00 p.m. and were locked in. It seems like it was 10:00 on Fridays and 11:00 on Saturday night. After our first year we moved to the LDS Hospital Nurses' Home on Ninth Avenue. However, we were still locked in after 9:00 p.m. We had classes in the afternoon. It was so hot, and of course, there was no air conditioning. After a couple of months we started working on the medical-surgical floors in the hospital.

While we lived there we had classes at the LDS Hospital. We had to get up and catch the Ninth Avenue bus by about 5:30 in the morning so we could have breakfast and get to class. We had class from 8:00 am until noon. We learned about all the diseases. It was after these fundamental nursing classes that we began to be checked off on our nursing skills at the hospital. I remember that the nurses—really our nursing instructors—were not particularly kind or understanding. We had bedside stands. The bedpans were supposed to be on the bottom, and the bath basins were on top of the bedpans and other paraphernalia in the drawers. When one of my instructors was checking one of the patients that I had, some other nurse had come along and given the patient their bedpan, but she didn't put it under the basin. The instructor really scolded me about that. You didn't ever say anything. You just stood there and let them yell at you. The instructors would check to see if you made the bed right with square corners. She would run her fingers across the windowsills and across the top of the clothing closet to make sure you had done everything exactly right.

It was such a scary thing to be with the instructors. They scolded us often. The floors in the work area in the utility rooms had little octagon tiles on the floor. As I was getting scolded I used to count them to see how many I could count before they stopped getting after me. They'd say, "Miss Hodgkinson, what have you done wrong now?" I often thought that if I had known what I had done wrong, I wouldn't have done it. So I wasn't even sure what it was they were getting after me for part of the time. During this time of instruction and class work we had to go to choir. Archibald Bennett was the choir director. He happened to end up being a senator in the United States Senate back in Washington DC for many, many years. However, he always loved the choir we had at the nursing school. Even if you couldn't sing, you still had to get up at 6:00 a.m. every morning and go to choir.

As soon as we finished basic training, we worked at the hospital from 7:00 until 11:00. Then we would eat and go to class. We would then work from 4:00 until 10:00. That was our day's activity and we really had to work hard. After the first year, we started working with other nurses until we could work the night shift ourselves. I remember the first night I worked, I was on a medical floor with Evelyn Plewe Jorgensen. She was a year ahead of me. I was so scared that someone would die because we had a lot of people who did die. I would take a flashlight and creep into the room and see if the patients were alive. I couldn't even tell if some of them were breathing. I asked Evelyn what I should do. She is a character. She said, "I guess you better wake them up." It was really scary because we had a lot of deaths.

At that time, a hospital was not a place to get better. It was a place to die. Anyone who broke their hip died, anyone who got pneumonia died, anyone who got cancer died, anyone with a ruptured appendix died. Premature babies rarely, if ever, lived, and little kids with whooping cough or croup often ended up dying. One of the most feared diseases in little kids or adults was polio. I remember that Mrs. Lake, who was paralyzed, was in the hospital for over a year. In 1952, after I graduated from nursing school and had been on an LDS mission to Norway, the old county hospital had iron lungs everywhere for people with bulbar polio. It was the most dreaded disease of its time. The Salk polio vaccine came out in 1954, and everybody took the shots to begin with. Later the vaccine was given in drops. It was interesting that since the development of the Salk vaccine, I have only seen one case of polio. It was a little eight-year-old child, and it was very mild. That disease has been eradicated in our country.

We had a lot of little kids with rheumatic fever in my early days of nursing. It was so prevalent: little kids with swollen joints all wrapped up in cotton and having a lot of pain.

One of the things everyone worried so much about at that time was a patient getting a red streak up the arm or leg from an infection. If someone got one of those, everybody got busy and hot-packed the infected area, and the patient got put on bed rest.

I remember we had a lot of drunken people who came in hallucinating and having DTs (delirium tremens). We would give them a huge 5-cc injection of paraldehyde in their hip. The way it dissipated was through their breath, so their breath smelled like paraldehyde for a couple of days.

After a year and a half we would start working as the charge nurse on afternoons and nights by ourselves. We worked forty-eight-hour weeks and stayed late after our shift most of the time. We always did everything we could not to get the supervisor involved. Mrs. Reed was very nice, but Miss Clara Wall wasn't all that nice. I remember so well that if anybody couldn't sleep, we had to rub their back and give them a glass of hot milk, and usually it helped.

During those years of our hospital work, we didn't have many drugs. We had morphine and Dilaudid for pain, Nembutal and Seconal for sleep, and phenobarbital for calming people down. Of course, there was always codeine and we had paregoric, which we used a lot. I think penicillin and sulfa were just discovered and began to be used during the war. I remember my very first penicillin shot. We had our own little 3-cc luerlock syringes, and the barrel and the plunger had numbers on them, and they had to match. We had our own needles, and we had a little pumice stone that we sharpened our needles on. We had to boil the syringes and the needles three minutes between shots. The penicillin was given every three hours around the clock. I remember the gentleman that I gave my very first penicillin shot to. It was an IM injection. He was paralyzed. His name was Tommy Shields. His spine had been crushed while working on the railroad, and instead of taking a cash settlement, he decided to live on the railroad ward for the rest of his life. He was really a prankster, which I didn't know at the time. I boiled my syringe and pulled up the penicillin, and I went shaking, scared to death to give this shot. I didn't notice that he was watching me and when I touched him with the needle he started screaming loudly. I just stuck the needle in. I forgot all about pulling back the plunger to see if there was any blood in it. I just pushed in the medicine and fled into the hall, scared and shaking. Then I heard him start laughing. It dawned on me that he was paralyzed and couldn't even feel the shot.

We made rounds with the doctors too. One of the surgeons, a Dr. Richards, would come on. We would go with him to see the patients. The protocol was that he went first, the resident went next, then the intern, then the medical students, and then the nurse would tag along last. The doctor would change the dressing and then he would turn to me, the nurse, and say, "I want a piece of tape eight inches long." I could span exactly eight inches, so I would tear him a piece of tape. I would give it to the intern, he would give it to the resident, and he would give it to the surgeon. Dr. Richards would wad it up and throw it in the wastebasket. Then, he would say, "I want an eight-inch piece of tape." The resident would cut him a piece of tape, and he would put it on the dressing. It didn't matter how long the piece was. The doctor would tape it on. It was really an interesting relationship with the doctors. I remember in surgery when one of the clamps wouldn't clamp, the doctor would throw it across the room and hit the wall. I remember one of my classmates who was a very tender, sweet girl. She got a clamp that didn't work, so she just threw it across the room. She didn't realize that only the doctors got to do that. It was a very stressful time, and my roommate packed up to go home a couple of times, but I would talk her out of it. I was going to leave once. It was just too much stress and too hard a work. It was awful. But my roommate talked me out of leaving too.

We had a lot of camaraderie and a lot of fun. It was during the war, and things were rationed. One night we made some fudge up on the seventh floor. We didn't even think you could smell it throughout the whole hospital. It was the middle of the night. We had it all finished and the supervisor, Miss Wall, came up and scolded us, but not too bad. We gave her a piece and she said, "Well, don't do it again." Those were wonderful times. We bonded with each other as nurses and to this day are still very good friends. Some of the doctors were really nice. One of them was Dr. White. We had a basketball team, and after every game he would take us over to Snelgrove's Ice Cream Parlor, and we could buy anything we wanted. I always had a strawberry parfait. It had pecans in it. It was such a luxury for me in those days.

One can never think about the nurses' training in those days without thinking of all of the thermometers we had. We had to shake them all down by hand. We got smart and would put them in a little hand towel and shake them. Once in a while, if we didn't hold them tight, some of them would slip out and break. We always had to pay for anything we broke like that. All of the catheters had to be boiled and used again. Sometimes they would boil dry and everybody would know when we had made that mistake by the smell of burnt rubber all over the hospital. The doctors always had to do the blood transfusions. In the very early days of my training, the interns had to stay with the patients, if they had an IV, the whole time it was running. I remember we had a nurse by the name of Miss Ingersoll who gave the first blood transfusion by a nurse. We didn't have filters, but they did have some kind of a little chamber that they filled with sterile cotton and the blood dropped through the cotton into the patient.

At the Cottonwood Maternity Hospital, sometimes they would have a really ill baby that they didn't expect to live because it had low blood. Since I was so young and energetic and had a lot of meanness I guess, they would sometimes ask if they could take 10 cc of blood to give the baby. They never typed or crossmatched blood in those days and to my knowledge never even typed the baby. They would give the baby this 10 cc of blood. I never minded or had any objection to that. About twenty years later I was out in my garden and this beautiful eighteen-year-old and her mother came to the back of my garden and said, "Are you Rayola Andersen?" I said, "Yes, I am." The mother started crying and said, "I want you to meet my daughter. You are the one who saved her life." I said "My gosh, what was that all about?" She said "When she was a baby they never expected her to live so they gave her some blood that you had given. I have kept track of you in the newspaper because you were on a basketball team, and the one time you saved that man's life, and that was in the newspaper. I have always been grateful and I have always wanted to come and tell you thank you." I thought that was a beautiful thing, even though I really hadn't done anything to get credit. I think nursing is a wonderful profession.

One of the things that had to do with the war quite directly was that there were soldiers who lived out in the barracks at Kearns, Utah. Of course most of us nursing students were young and naïve and came from country towns around Utah, and those fellows came to date us since we were in the nurse corps. We thought they were quite strange and they thought we were quite strange. But we had a lot of fun dating them, and it helped them to not be so lonely being so far from home.

Perhaps the most memorable nursing situations that I had were during my rotation onto the pediatric ward. I still remember the names of many of those little patients. There was an eighteen-month-old boy with blue eyes and blond curly hair who was admitted with a severe case of croup. We had no particular medicine for croup. We used a humidifier when we should have been using something cold. He went into severe laryngeal spasm. I held him in my arms while the clerk tried to hunt the intern by phone. We had no other way to communicate except by phone. The baby started to turn blue. I tried to put my fingers between his teeth to try and let air in because I didn't know anything else that I could do. It took about ten to fifteen minutes to find the intern, but the little fellow died before the doctor got there, and that was really a traumatic thing.

Another experience that demonstrates the nursing care of that time was a six-year-old named Johnny. At his birthday party they were having a weenie roast. He got a pair of cowboy chaps for his birthday, and they were highly flammable. One of the little boy guests picked up a burning stick and threw it at him and hit him in the leg, catching the chaps on fire. Before his mother could smother the flames, he had second-degree burns and in some spots third-degree burns. They brought him into the hospital to die. We smeared Silvadeen salve all over his burns and wrapped him in gauze bandages from his waist to his feet and gave him morphine for the pain and just expected and waited for him to die. We didn't have any screens on the windows, and flies just flew in and out of the hospital rooms. Johnny didn't die. After about a week the doctor decided we had to change the dressings. We put him in a tub of warm water to soak them off. After about ten minutes, the water was totally covered with maggots. In spite of how gross and nauseating it was, the maggots had actually eaten all of the dead tissue, and little Johnny started healing. He was able to leave the hospital in about three months walking, even though it was stiff-legged. Actually, after that they began to implant maggots into wounds because they didn't do any harm to the body; they only ate up the necrotic tissue. An interesting side light to that story happened thirty-two years later. I have a couple of rental houses. A rental couple had bought a house of their own and had moved, so I was running a rental ad. A gentleman called and came to see the house. After the tour and discussion of the rental agreement he smiled broadly and said, "You don't know who I am, do you?" I apologized and explained that I was a nurse and met many people and because of that I didn't really know who he was. He grinned and said, "Yes, I know you are a nurse because many years ago, I was badly burned from the waist down and you were one of my nurses." I really couldn't believe it, but I said, "You're Johnny." We hugged and discussed what his life had been like.

While I was a student, one of the students came to work with her engagement ring on. Her supervisor saw it and told her to take it off because we were never allowed to wear any kind of jewelry. The student said, "No, it is my engagement ring and I don't want to take it off." She was told she would either take it off or she wouldn't be a nurse. She said, "Well, I am not going to take it off." She actually had to leave nursing over that engagement ring. After that we got smarter. One of my good friends got married, but nobody ever knew it. We were always trading shifts or doing anything we could so she could go out with this boyfriend we thought she had. In reality she had gotten married. She kept it hidden until we finished our program.

One type of case that was very difficult for patients and families and for us was a patient that had cancer with a fistula to the outside. The odor was terrible and almost unbearable. We would put some pine stuff in water and use a fan to move the air around to try to make it smell better. But I don't think it helped much because it was just dead body tissue from growths that didn't have enough blood to supply the tissue, so it died. I think of people saying how terrible cancer is nowadays, but we never have smells like that anymore. Fifty percent of all the people who get diagnosed with cancer are walking around on the streets or are in remission under treatment. We have all kinds of treatments and palliative care and are making great strides in curing many kinds of cancers.

We had many patients who had large goiters, some bigger than large grapefruits, and the only treatment was surgery. All of the patients had waited until it was pressing on the trachea and they could hardly breath. The typical visual sign was exophthalmic (bulging) eyes. I remember that occasionally the patient would have what was called "thyroid storm." These patients would become delirious and had high fevers, abnormal heart rhythms, and extreme sweating. They became very shocky. We had to cool them rapidly and give large doses of adrenal corticoid hormones. I was fortunate; I never saw a patient die from this.

Another interesting thing we saw then that we never see anymore was patients with renal failure, called uremia. We didn't have dialysis, so they had severe ascites. The treatment was to do a paracentesis when their breathing was compromised. These patients would develop sandlike granules around their nose, armpits, and wherever they perspired a lot. It was their bodies' way of getting rid of the uric acid that their kidneys could not.

Patients with liver disease always ended up dying. My most memorable patient was an American lady about thirty years old who had been working in Japan and was taken as a prisoner of war at the beginning of World War II. She said she pulled a little plow during the day in the rice paddies and was strapped down for the Japanese soldiers' pleasure at night. She had liver failure from the lack of protein in her diet; and suffered from severe ascites. We did a paracentesis every second or third day, which was the only treatment, when it caused her problems with her breathing. However, the procedure only encouraged the accumulation of more fluid in her abdomen and the continuation of her ascites.

Another thing we used during wartime—and I have never seen it used since—was sawdust in bed frames. People who had terrible decubitus ulcers that were draining would lie on the bed, and all the drainage would go into the sawdust. It had some real beneficial effects except that it was so uncomfortable for the patients. I think that is why they discontinued its use and found better ways of taking care of the problem. Another thing that we used to do was use Wangenstein drainage systems. You would put water up in the top, and the pressure of it would go down and take out the drainage from the stomach or whatever it was that was draining. It was a very happy day to see all of those disappear. During the war there were two cure-alls. If you ever got a cold, you got a mustard plaster. All it ever did was burn your skin. I guess it felt so good to get it off that you didn't complain anymore. Another thing was that everyone was obsessed with bowels in those days. If anyone ever complained about anything to do with their bowels, the first thing we did was give them an enema. To prevent that, almost every night all the patients would get a black and white toddy made of cascara and milk of magnesia. The patients hated that, but they never ever got constipated.

Many injured servicemen ended up at Bushnell Hospital in Brigham City, Utah. These patients had lost arms or legs or were badly burned or had other major injuries. Some of us students would hitchhike to Brigham City. We didn't have cars or money for bus or train rides, and hitchhiking was a safe way to travel at that time. We would go to Bushnell and date these soldiers. It was interesting to see what difficulties they had in trying to cope with their injuries. They liked to have us come because we kidded and joked around, and they felt so comfortable with us. One of the soldiers was a big guy from Texas. He had lost both legs. He asked why I would be interested in coming up there to see him. I told him, "Well I feel pretty safe with you. I know you can't catch me."

I was in Norway in 1950, just after the war. When I saw the tragedies of war, I thought then that it is the most awful evil that can ever come into the world. When I saw the kind of care that those people got compared to the kind of care that we had, even in those days, it was a blessing. In the state of Utah—I admit all of my biases right now—we have the most up-to-date healthcare of any place in the United States.

I have always loved nursing. I am still involved in nursing and am able to contribute to the wonderful profession and provide care to those who are so much less fortunate than I am.

In 2005, Rayola Andersen was the only member of their nursing class actively working in the profession.

Beth Smith Edvalson

"Why don't you become a nurse?" my older brother asked. My response was "Hmm." If I make a snap decision, it is usually wrong. I decided to think about it. I was already working six hours in the evenings, two or three days a week, at the local hospital. It was in a volunteer capacity, but I liked helping people and associating with nurses.

The war had started. My brother had enlisted and was flying a bomber. Most people's lives were anything but stable. My mother had died a few years previously, and my father and I lived in my stepmother's house.

I don't remember how I heard about the Cadet Nurse Corps, but it sounded like a marvelous plan for me. Now I can see the hand of the Lord in my life. My father was a farmer and had little money. I had a brain and a strong body, so why not put those attributes to good use helping others? My father was against nursing as a profession because "it was not a respectable occupation for a woman." Other than offering his opinion, he didn't protest my decision.

In June 1943 I entered the University of Utah with about ninety-nine other young women and spent two days taking entrance exams for nurses. I think we were part of the second group in the Cadet Nurse Corps.

Where could you find a better offer for an education? Three years equivalent to college credit, a gray dress uniform, three nursing uniforms, housing and food all furnished, plus $21 a month. It seemed like a sweet deal to me.

At this time I learned that my brother, my childhood companion, was missing in action over the Himalaya Mountain while on a bombing mission into China. I mourned deeply, but I remembered his admonitions: "You have been taught the right way to live. It is your fault if you do not learn. Always ask questions if you don't understand something."

After six months on campus, our group was divided and sent to our chosen hospital. Some went to Holy Cross, some to Salt Lake City General, and some to St. Marks. I went to Dr. W. H. Groves LDS Hospital. Some of my group who went to LDS Hospital were housed in the Beehive House in the city and had to ride the bus up to the hospital for classes and to work. I lived in the "cottages" across the street from the nurses' home behind the hospital. There were eight girls in each cottage and about four cottages. They had been private homes but were converted to house student nurses. We ate our meals in the basement of the nurses' home where the older student nurses lived.

We finally were issued our white uniforms. They were laundered in the hospital laundry and were starched so that they could almost stand alone. Still no cap, but we really liked our uniforms. The white stockings and shoes we furnished ourselves. Nylons were hard to come by. In order to get them, we had to put our name on a waiting list at the stores. When we could get them they wore like cast iron. Most of us soon discovered better shoes than the regulation Red Cross style.

We learned all the patient care procedures like the art of making a bed with a patient in or out of it. At one point I was the patient and the instructor lectured on and on. I could hear her as well with my eyes closed as with them open. I heard her say, "Well, our patient, Miss Smith, has gone to sleep!" My eyes flew open, everyone was laughing, and I was so embarrassed. Miss Shelton, a stern-faced woman with a twinkle in her eye, just looked at me.

For those first six months at the hospital, we worked when we were not in class. The day we received our caps was a proud day! The thin black ribbon would come at the end of the second year. We had been in the program a year when we received our cap, and it was time we earned our keep.

After we were worked into the system, I really liked it better. I didn't mind doing all the grungy work because it was part of the job. We gave enemas, bathed men, catheterized women, and dug impacted stools out of the elderly. One time a very old woman needed to give us a sterile specimen, and she fought us as we tried to catheterize her. The resident doctor that had ordered the specimen walked regally in the room, put his hand on her bare thigh, and in his bass voice said, "Now look here, Mrs. —— ." She let out a scream and grabbed the sheets and curled up in a ball. Needless to say we never did get a specimen, and she left the hospital the next day.

One time a three-month-old baby was admitted to the isolation ward on my floor. She didn't look very ill, but I placed her on the bed elevated on pillows and sent for oxygen. Her temperature was 100 degrees, and she was pale. I turned my back to get something, and when I looked at her again she was dead. I wanted to shout and say "Hey, wait a minute, we haven't done anything for you yet!" That was my first experience with death and being first on the scene. It was so final! We had not been taught first aid yet because they were afraid that we would use it on our patients. All I could do was run for help.

The hospital was big and drafty, and on winter nights the wind would howl and moan down the elevator shafts and through some of the doors that led to the sun rooms. The morgue was in the drafty basement, which also housed the diet kitchen, the laundry, and so forth. Late at night it was a super scary place to be.

If we made a mistake in our charting we had to recopy the whole page, including everyone else's notes, and they had to initial them. We had a narcotic count on every shift. We had to sign for each pill or dose of narcotic we used and if we dropped it or had an accident with it, we had to fill out a form in triplicate and have them all notarized. All narcotics were in pill form, and one night I took one of those tiny little white pills and dropped it. I searched that white tiled floor on my hands and knees with no results. I prayed because I couldn't think of anything else to do, then I got up off my grimy white knees and glanced into the ice chest. There on the very edge was my little white pill. I was so grateful for that help.

Seldom did anything come dose-packaged. We had to mix most things such as penicillin. One time I was going to help a resident administer some medicine to a young man in his spine. The patient was already paralyzed, but he had an infection. The doctor told me how to mix the medicine, but I read the bottle, and he had me mix it too strong. I didn't know what to do, and there was no one to ask because I was the charge nurse and he was the doctor I might have consulted. I mixed it as he said, but I have always wondered about it. The patient died in spite of us.

We were not allowed to draw blood or start intravenous fluids. We had to call a supervisor or an intern. Most of us senior nurses could do a better job than the interns, but we had to let them try. Starting an IV is a matter of feel, and some people just never got the hang of it. Most nurses carried three pieces of equipment in their pocket: bandage scissors, a kelly clamp, and a pen. One time a resident was starting an IV, assisted by one of our perfectionist nurses—the "not a hair out of place" kind—and she was a good nurse, which made it worse. The doctor got the needle in the vein and called for the clamp. As I walked into the room I saw Nurse Perfect whip out her kelly clamp, which turned out to be her scissors, and cut the tubing. Wow, what a mess! The sticky glucose fluid was running all over the floor and Nurse Perfect was paralyzed. I whipped out my kelly, I looked at it first, and clamped off the tubing. I don't remember whether the doctor had to start over from scratch or not.

I liked surgery; even counting all the sponges and instruments afterward was all right. We had to wash and pack the instruments and put them in the autoclave after each surgery. It was the night nurses' duty to sterilize them all. Every so many days we would have to wash the operating room walls and floors down with an antiseptic of some kind. That was one of those things that went with the job. I didn't like brain surgery; the instrument sounds were weird and there was always tension in the room.

My favorite floor was obstetrics. Everything was happy there, usually. I delivered babies a time or two because the doctor didn't arrive in time. Quite often as I was shaving a woman, I would realize that I was about to give the baby its first hair cut.

When we had been in the hospital two and one half years, we were divided into groups for our final six months. One third went to the navy, one third went to the army, and one third of us stayed at the resident hospital.

We were not allowed to get married until we graduated. Some of the older girls broke that rule and lived with their husbands in an apartment on the sly. They would sneak out the window of the nurses' home and make it back to work the next morning. I did ask for permission to get married and was greatly surprised that I was granted permission. Of course, my fiance was going overseas right after the ceremony, so the decision was easy.

We set the date for July 5, and the ceremony was to take place at my brother's apartment. Sugar was rationed, and I had collected all the sugar stamps I could find for my wedding cake. I had spent $90 for my wedding dress and had my picture taken in it, with the bottom swirling around my feet.

My intended came home on furlough. On July 3 he received a telegram that his furlough was canceled and that he was to report to Seattle, Washington, on the morning of July 7. We were married on the 4th of July, canceled all the invitations for the wedding, ate our fill of cake, and gave the rest away.

I was in Salt Lake City when the war was over, and the streets were full of people. We were cheering and jumping up and down and kissing everybody. (Well not everybody, but there were a lot of soldiers in the streets.) I have enjoyed and benefitted from being a graduate registered nurse. It was one of the best opportunities I could have had.

LaRee Williams Fullmer

When I attended Granite High School, mathematics was my best subject. I thought seriously of going into some field where I could use mathematics. However, at that time my teacher discouraged me because he thought that it was not for women. I had always thought about becoming a nurse, so I decided to take that as my second choice. I graduated from high school in May 1942 and began the course to become an RN two weeks later.

The first two quarters of our course, we students attended the University of Utah. The classes included chemistry, english, physiology, bacteriology, and others. After the Christmas holidays those of our class who didn't flunk out moved into quarters at the LDS Hospital where we lived and worked for the next two and one-half years. I lived in Cottage Three with seven other girls. It was an old house with four bedrooms and only one bathroom, which had no shower—just an old-fashioned tub, basin, and toilet. We had to adjust to living without very much privacy as sometimes there would be one of us using the basin, one on the pot, and one or two of us in the tub. There wasn't much hot water either. We weren't allowed to cook, but we did sneak in a hot plate that we used occasionally. One of the specialties was taffy that tasted like the cold cream that we used to pull it because we didn't have any butter or margarine.

In the basement of the main nurses' home there was a dining room where all of us had our meals. The food was not the best. In fact, most of the time it was mediocre. The one thing that was served was good homemade bread. I learned to eat lots of sugar sandwiches; we would spread the bread with margarine (there was no butter) and sprinkle sugar on top. There was always endive for the salads instead of lettuce. It seemed that every Sunday was fried rabbit. I never ate it. I thought some good LDS person must have had a rabbit farm.

I remember that during the war we did not have some of the things that we were used to having. The margarine was white for awhile and then it came with a little color packet to make it yellow and eventually it came as it is now. Most of my dates during the war did not have cars, and if they did there was gas rationing. We usually walked to town or took the bus. There were no nylon hosiery. We wore cotton hose to work.

Our nursing instructor, Miss Sheldon, was excellent. From the beginning we learned and worked in the wards, giving routine bedside care until we were checked out on giving medications and treatments. We usually had at least six patients assigned to us for care. The students were a great help in the hospital because there were very few RNs at that time. At this time new mothers stayed in the hospital at least seven days after delivery, and most of that time was spent in bed. As a result most of these patients were constipated. So the night shift nurse on the maternity ward would start about 4 a.m. to get all of the enemas finished and the rectal tubes boiled before she went off shift.

Usually when we worked nights in the operating room, there was not much going on after we had taken care of the supplies. One night when I was on duty with another nurse, I drifted off to sleep in the wee hours of the morning. The night supervisor just happened along at that time and caught me. She gave me a note and told me to report to the nursing office the next morning. I ripped up the note and went to bed. I was called early that morning and had to get dressed and report to the nursing office. I don't remember what I had to do—probably write a paper on why I shouldn't sleep on duty. But it was embarrassing to meet with Maria Johnson, our director of nursing, and her assistant.

Nurses appeared different back in those days. Everything we wore on duty had to be white. If we didn't look right we were sent to change our clothes. If we forgot to do anything that was expected of us, such as leaving a patient's room untidy, we were called back on duty, dressed in our uniforms, to finish the task. Our director of nursing, Maria Johnson, always appeared very professional in her uniform. We used to say that she went to her quarters at noon and pressed her uniform, as it always looked as if she never sat down while wearing it. All of our supervisors were always dressed very professionally in their uniforms.

I think that most nights at the hospital the supervisor was the only licensed person on duty. The patient floors were staffed mostly by students. At night if a patient needed a narcotic, the nurse had to call the supervisor to get permission to give it. We were young students on at night, so we needed supervision. Miss Clara Wall, a supervisor, would ask every time we called for a pain medication, "Have you given the patient some warm milk and washed his or her face with warm water?" I thought, "Lady, I hope that when you get sick and in pain I'm here to bring you a wash cloth and warm milk." We students would become smart enough to call her and tell her that we had washed the patient's face, rubbed his back, and offered him some warm milk, but the patient was still in pain, so could we give a medication.

At the time I was in training, the hospital nursery had a census of between seventy and ninety babies because the mothers stayed in the hospital about seven days. We would take the babies in racks that held six bassinets out to their mothers every three to four hours. In between feedings we would diaper all of the babies and give them supplemental feedings if needed. There were many dirty diapers. One of the duties of the night nurses was to clean off the diapers that were used so that they could be sent to the laundry. It was a very stinky job in a small, stinky room.

We also had our turn in the formula lab. We had to make and bottle the formula. The rubber caps that were used on the bottles would make our fingers very sore because they were so hard to pull on the bottles and then take off when the nipples were put on. We did have fun working in the nursery. One RN, as she diapered the babies, would sing her song, "Don't circumcise me if I don't need it." There were about twenty-one verses to the song.

My friend Marilyn Thompson and I were not twenty-one when we graduated and took the state boards, so we decided to stay at the hospital and work in the nursery until we could get our licenses. As RNs we could do more things, such as give the babies medications and gavage them. One of the fun things we did was to give the mothers a demonstration on bathing and taking care of a newborn. We'd choose the cutest baby to use for our demonstration. It was funny because we young girls who had never had a baby would sometimes be demonstrating to mothers who had several children. Another fun event was when we had a Jewish circumcision. The sun porch would be set up for a party. The rabbi would come and do the little surgery, and then there would be a party with lots of people and good refreshments.

About the time I graduated, the war was over, so there was no need to go into the service. I can remember when it ended. I was working on 7A—the top floor of the hospital. Looking down towards town I could hear the celebration going on. I spent the last few weeks of my training on 7A. It was the most expensive and nicest patient unit in the hospital. All the rooms were private and cost $10.00 per day. Most of the General Authorities were admitted to this floor when they were ill.

Edith Maurine Edwards Garrard

I was born July 4, 1924, in Salt Lake City, Utah, to David Samuel and Bertha Pearson Edwards. I was the eighth of nine children in the family, seven brothers and one sister. I lived all my life at the family home at 467 Eleventh Avenue until I was married. Of course, as a student nurse, I stayed at the LDS Hospital Nurses' Home on Ninth Avenue and C Street during the three years I was in training. Those were three great years of knowing and working with exemplary people.

I was a cadet nurse who joined the Cadet Nurse Corps in December 1943 and graduated from the Groves LDS Hospital three-year diploma program in December 1946. I earned my bachelor of science degree in nursing from the University of Utah in June 1947. My graduation occurred after the cessation of World War II, so I did not join the active forces. Because I had attended the U of U prior to entering the nursing program, I discovered that I could earn my BS by June 1947 if I carried twenty-one hours in one quarter plus worked weekends to earn substance money. Several of my classmates did the same.

Although my father had initially opposed my becoming a nurse, the Cadet Nurse program provided an independent means of accomplishing this goal. There was no prouder father in attendance at the nursing graduation ceremonies than my father, who had acquired an entirely new perspective of nurses and the wonderful women who were my classmates.

Although my efforts did not qualify me for actively serving as a nurse during WWII, the Cadet Nurse program did provide me with the means to become a registered nurse, which had been a goal in my life. Shortly after graduation, I married an intern I met during training. He subsequently served two more years in the military.

Four of my brothers served in the military during World War II. The eldest was a West Point graduate who became a career officer and retired as a brigadier general. After the start of the war, the second brother joined the U.S. Air Force, became a pilot, and was later based in England and flew missions over Germany. The third brother joined the Utah National Guard at the beginning of the war and served for five years, assigned to multiple posts in the Pacific area as an artilleryman. The fourth brother was an eighteen-year-old young man drafted into the infantry who served and fought in the Battle of the Bulge. So you can see that my parents were deeply concerned when I decided to join the Cadet Nurse Corps. Had the war not ended when it did, there would have been five stars in the window. Fortunately, all of the military members of the Edwards family returned home safely. All were LDS Church members.

There was no central supply when I was a student. All nurses were expected to own a syringe and a variety of needles, which we carried in a container in our uniform pockets. The needles and syringes were carefully sterilized on a gas burner in a pan of distilled water. We were taught exacting sterilization techniques. I do not recall any injection site infections. Mrs. Mason, RN, diligently taught us isolation and sterilization technique. I do not recall many of us breaching these rules. I also do not recall nosocomial infections. The supervisors were diligent in requiring students to do things correctly and according to protocol. We students paid great honor and respect to our superiors. They were giants in our eyes. After graduation, when we all scattered to different locations, we all felt that our training had been excellent. Many of the graduates of the three-year diploma program went on with their careers and achieved much professional success.

Most of the students at the LDS Hospital then were members of the Church of Jesus Christ of Latter-day Saints. The LDS Hospital was across the street from the original Ensign Ward on Ninth Avenue and D Street. The students could not regularly attend weekly meetings because of the requirement to work many weekends and shift work. Most of us attended church when possible.

As nurses, we were taught to hold doctors in high esteem. We were taught to always show great respect in their presence. It was protocol to stand whenever a doctor entered the nurses' station and to give him our chair if an empty one was not available. While making rounds with a doctor, a nurse always carried the stack of charts and made sure that the doctor entered the patient room first. The subservient attitude has continued to affect the lives of many student nurses of this era. We were also taught that we should always be ladies.

Like most of the other student nurses at LDS Hospital at the time, I was reared in a Latter-day Saint home where church activity was the norm and expected. My parents were good examples to me of what Latter-day Saints should do and be. This motivated me to gain a testimony and be an active Church member. This Latter-day Saint philosophy and belief was reinforced during our training. This was accomplished through more of an underlying teaching rather than by being actively required.

As students, our classmates became our very dear friends. In talk fests at night, we learned to cope with the traumatic and difficult experiences we encountered in our patient care. We were offered no professional psychological support system. Students carried tremendous responsibilities, and we lived by strict rules and regulations.

I have always been grateful for the Cadet Nurse program and the enrichment it brought into my life. In addition to the training I made wonderful friends. The Cadet Nurse program was wonderful!

During the inevitable difficult and emotional times that occur in a nursing career—as well as in the rearing of a family—I have received reassurance and strength from Latter-day Saint teachings and association with good people.

Margaret Maurine Harris

I entered nursing in August 1945 with the last group under the auspices of the Cadet Nurse Corps. At that time the war was coming to an end. We had only the minor inconvenience of rationing some items like shoes and sugar. At this time there was immense loyalty to our armed services, and we were happy to do what was needed. Some of my high school classmates joined various branches of the service, and we were very proud of them. My favorite woman high school teacher joined the WAVES. This was a time of intense patriotism. We were uniformed as cadet nurses complete with cap and a flowing cape.

At that time nursing was in a transition from the diploma-type nursing to collegiate. All cadets spent the first year at the University of Utah taking basic courses. The course was planned so that after the first year at the university, we would spend the next two and one-half years at the hospital that had accepted our application (LDS, St. Marks, or Salt Lake City General), and subsequently, we could spend an additional year to complete a BS in nursing if we so chose. During the last six months of our hospital experience, some could select to spend that time in a veterans hospital. About six of our classmates chose to do that and went to Albuquerque, New Mexico.

During the time we were at the University of Utah, we were housed at Carlson Hall. We tended to group with our hospital group. Though we were congenial, we banded together against any outside threat. Apparently our house mother sensed a difference between the nursing students and the others. She was heard to say, "You can take the girl out of the country, but you can't take the country out of the girl," referring to the nursing students. Many of us were from small towns and small farming communities, and most of us would have to work to be able to pay our way through college. The Cadet Nurse Corps funded our education and gave us an allowance of fifteen dollars a month, which we thought was wonderful. That fifteen dollars gave us enough that we seldom had to ask our families for money.

Our instructors were very strict. We were on probation for the first six months, which meant that some would not make it past that point. Instruction was procedure-oriented, with each step in the procedure outlined in precise order. We used our mop bucket at home as a basin to practice bed baths. We practiced on each other, quizzed each other, cheered each other on, and listened to and consoled each other over the slightest mishap. The outside enemy—the instructors, the upper classmen, and the doctors who saw students as a curse—all caused us to band together in a tight survival mode.

The hospital could not have survived without the help of the students, as many graduate nurses who normally would be at the hospital were in the armed services. Nearly all of the graduate nurses in our hospital were the head nurses, supervisors, and teachers. That format was so standard that a graduate nurse who was just doing bedside care and not being some kind of administrator was suspected of not being up to par! Our teachers taught us the procedures, but when we were on our hospital wards we were under the direction of the RN head nurse on day shifts or an upper classman as the charge nurse on afternoon and evening shifts. The nursing care was done by the student nurses. The student charge nurses were under the direction of the supervisors, but there were only two to three supervisors for the entire hospital. When there were not enough senior students to be charge nurses for each shift, the responsibility fell to whichever students had the most experience on that ward in the hospital. Undoubtedly, it was because of the responsibility given to students early in their experience that the teachers were so strict with us, realizing better than we did what we were facing.

Because of the cohesiveness among us, we knew of the tiniest mishap. Any mishap seemed to loom large to the supervisors. Burned in my memory are such things as the time one student washed the thermometers in hot water and they had to be replaced. The philosophy seemed to be to pounce on the tiniest mistake as a means of preventing any larger ones that might be injurious to the patient. I do not recall any serious injury to patients by my classmates.

It was well understood that the patients' welfare came first. We felt we had to be near death before we would call in sick. Any time a student nurse missed a day, she reported to the assistant superintendent of nurses for a review of the cause. The prospect of that interview was enough to cause us to want to "take up our bed and walk." Any day missed because of illness had to be made up. Prior to graduation, all of the missed days were added up and had to be made up before a graduation certificate was issued.

Our service times were geared towards the needs of the patient. For some time we worked the famous split shifts working from 7:00 a.m. till noon to take care of the morning bathing and care of the patient and then returning from 7:00 p.m. to 10:00 p.m. to prepare the patient for bed, which included a back rub, straightening the bed and room, and any treatments or other care needed. For a time we worked this split shift until a rule was made (by the State Board of Nursing perhaps?) that our assigned time had to be completed twelve hours from the time we began. Hence, the change was from 7:00 a.m. till noon and 4:00 p.m. till 7:00 p.m. We thought that change was marvelous. In the afternoons we had our classes, and then our study time was after 7:00 p.m. When we worked the night shift, we slept from about 8:00 a.m. till lunch and then went to classes in the afternoon. It was often hard to stay awake for classes.

I remember this time mostly as a time of intense feelings of loyalty and pride in our country, a time that caused all of us to work together for the good of our country. The nursing program was tough. We were disciplined and learned to put our patients' needs first and to depend on each other and help each other. As a result we learned many skills that have been valuable throughout our lives. Also, we have bonded as friends, which is as much felt and alive today as it was during our times together in the Cadet Nurse program.

Mary F. Hughes

Despite the fact that I have not been actively engaged in the field of nursing for the past twenty years, I always have a feeling of excitement when I go into a hospital. It comes upon me suddenly. As I see people scurrying about I feel a sense of direction, a feeling of commitment, and oftentimes the tenseness of urgency. If I search the individual faces that are about me, I see joy, happiness, anxiety, despair, and a myriad of other emotions. I walk through the corridors and cannot help but look into the rooms with open doors, for I know that in these rooms, human drama is being played out. The closed doors, especially those forbidden to the public, hold a particular fascination for me, and I am always curious as to what might be happening behind those doors.

Nineteen forty-four was an exciting year. World War II was in full swing. The war was foremost in all our minds and lives as we heard about battles on far away shores. Our eyes would scan the evening newspapers for war casualties, fearing to find a familiar name. Everyone was doing their bit to aid the war effort, and I, eighteen years old and a new high school graduate, was preparing to enter into the United States Cadet Nurse Corps.

There were not many career options open to young women at that time, and the realistic choices boiled down to three: becoming a school teacher, a secretary, or a nurse. It was not a difficult choice for me, as the visions in my head of nursing, especially at the time of war, held the promise of great adventure. An additional benefit was the opportunity to leave home, spread my wings, and see what the world was all about. The financial help offered through the Cadet Nurses program—tuition, housing, and a fifteen dollar per month stipend—had also given me more than a gentle nudge towards the profession.

After much consideration, I chose the Salt Lake County General Hospital as my place of training. The hospital was located in Salt Lake City, Utah, some fifty miles from my home—a nice safe distance that would allow me the independence I wanted while still being close enough for a visit home when things got tough. The county hospital, as it was known, was operated primarily to provide medical care for the indigent and operated on a bare-bones budget with no frills. It was a training ground for University of Utah medical students, and the Salt Lake County General Hospital nursing program was in turn affiliated with the university. Upon my completion of the three-year prescribed course, I would receive not only my diploma but university credit for course work as well.

My first six months were spent living on campus at the University of Utah along with fellow cadet nurses from three other area hospitals. We all lived in the same dorm and took the same courses. We carried eighteen hours per quarter studying chemistry, anatomy, physiology, foods and nutrition, library science, English, and other basic subjects.

It didn't take my classmates and me long to discover the fact that eighteen hours was a hefty load to carry, but it also didn't take us long to discover the fun and antics of dorm life and the excitement of life in the big city. There were trolley rides into town and excursions to an army base nearby to dance with men stationed there. When money was scarce, which was often the case, long walks about campus and the surrounding areas filled the few hours that were left.

We were a unified group, although at the end of the six months on campus, we knew we would separate for our various hospitals to continue our training. We felt we were doing our part to aid the war effort and were eager to get on with the business of becoming a nurse. The time went by quickly, and January found us at our respective hospitals, where we were to be "probies."

Our first challenge was to get settled into the Nurses' Home. This was a big three-story building sandwiched between the various other buildings that made up the hospital complex. It was where we would sleep, eat, attend classes, study, socialize, and commiserate with each other.

We probies were assigned rooms on the top floor with the expectation of moving down to the lower floors as we gained seniority. I shared my room with two other roommates. Our particular room was tucked away in the corner of the old building and appeared to have been forgotten for some time. It was my bed that I remember most vividly. It was an old, discarded hospital bed. It seemed to be a mile high, and I soon found out I was in deep trouble because my curves matched the ruts that were worn into the mattress.

Our indoctrination into the life of a probie was not a gentle one as the many rules and regulations were laid out for us by the housemother. She informed us that we were to be accountable to her for all our comings and goings. There was nightly curfew of 9:30 p.m., which would be strictly enforced. We were, however, allowed two late passes (12:00 midnight) per week, and two overnight passes per month could be substituted for the late passes if approved by the housemother. We were advised to sign out and to sign in, and we were told that any late violations would result in giving up passes for an extended time. The housemother ruled with an iron hand, and we soon found it difficult to slip anything over on her. The doors were locked at midnight, and the worst possible scenario was to be late and to have to ring the doorbell, knowing she would answer it.

The next indoctrination was that of the dress code. We were all excited when we received our six white uniforms with a cadet nurse patch on one sleeve. White stockings and oxfords would complete the uniform until we could earn our coveted cap. The hospital laundry would wash and starch our uniforms. They certainly did a good job—our uniforms often resembled cardboard boxes as we slipped into them after they were freshly laundered. No jewelry was allowed, and the necessary watch, along with any rings, were to be pinned to the uniform. Incidentally, a few engagement rings were confiscated because this rule was not adhered to. Others followed the rule, and a few engagement rings went through the laundry still attached to uniforms. Our hair was to be neatly done and kept off our collars in a net. We were cautioned that under no circumstances were we allowed on the hospital floors unless we were in full uniform. We were also given the option to purchase a coat. We thought this ankle-length cape, made of dove-grey wool and lined with red, was a splendid addition to our uniforms and was well worth the three months' stipend it took to pay for it.

Somewhere along the line, we were also given a Cadet Nurse Corps dress uniform. It was a sharp-looking uniform made of grey wool complete with silver buttons, epaulets, and of course, the cadet nurse patch on the sleeve. A jaunty grey beret completed the ensemble. There was no definite use for the uniform, but it was fun to wear and made us feel like we were very much a part of the war effort.

Our next three months were spent on probation, a time designated to prove ourselves. Our status as probies was mighty low in the medical hierarchy. We were advised of the propriety of standing whenever a physician approached us. We were also to show respect for our instructors by arising as they entered the classroom.

Our first experience on the floor was cleaning units. This included cleaning everything used by the former patient, right down to the bed springs. From this somewhat tedious task, we progressed to the bedpan detail and then on to the finer arts of nursing.

Our pharmacology course was strictly a nononsense affair. Our instructor was a stern taskmaster, and we were drilled over and over about the importance of aseptic technique and the responsibilities of administering medications. This training has served me well. After almost fifty years, I am still an avid label reader, and any lids found on my kitchen countertops are always upside down.

Finally, most of us had endured probiehood, and we were anxious for our capping. This solemn and impressive ceremony was held in a local church with proud family and friends gathering for the occasion. It was a treasured moment for me as I marched down the aisle, holding a single red rose, and my coveted cap being placed upon my bowed head by the superintendent of the nurses.

I still have my cap tucked away among other cherished mementos of times gone by. I am still very proud of it. I worked hard to receive it, and it was a badge of honor for all to see as I entered into the weighty responsibilities of nursing.

By 1943, military service had taken many of the registered nurses, and few were available to staff the hospital. There were few auxiliary people as well. Student nurses furnished the bulk of the manpower needed to keep the hospitals functioning during those crucial years.

Nurses' aids were unheard of at that time, and there was one male orderly serving the entire hospital on each shift. Possibly half of the wards had RNs as head nurses, and senior students assumed this responsibility on the other wards. There was usually one RN house supervisor for each shift to cover the entire hospital. If one was not available, senior students substituted. The hospital consisted of a medical infirmary (extended care) building, a surgical building, and an obstetrics facility. The OB facility housed the delivery room, newborn nursery, antepartum, postpartum, and gynecological wards. In addition, across the block there was a communicable disease unit. One wing was for children, while the other was a venereal disease treatment center. There were no enclosures connecting the various buildings, and the house supervisor really had a lot of territory to cover.

My first assignment was on a surgical unit, and, with my cap proudly perched upon my head, I was inducted into the real world of nursing, and once again it was not a gentle induction! After three weeks of working days, I was assigned the night shift. We rotated shifts at the discretion of the head nurse and each rotation lasted a week. My first week of nights still holds great horror for me.

Surgery II was an eighteen-bed surgical female unit. There was one large ward with six beds up one side and six down the other. At the other end of a hall was a porch with three more beds. Three private rooms plus the nurses' station were along the hall which connected the two. I was placed on the unit alone with a full census.

The patients were varied. There were no post-op recovery rooms or intensive care units, so we were responsible for all levels of care. I had a patient who spiked a 104 degree temperature each morning around 4:00. To add to this, she had a gastric tube connected to a Wangensteen suction, which was a challenge in itself. The Wangensteen suction was a monstrosity of an apparatus made of three discarded IV bottles. These were connected together by IV tubing in such a manner as to create a gentle suction when water was drained from one bottle to another, with the third one catching the drainage. The first trick was to set it up correctly; the next trick was to keep it working by keeping the lines free and the water level right by interchanging two of the bottles. If this sounds complicated, it was—much different than plugging into the hospital suction system.

I had a ninety-year-old woman with a fractured hip. She was in a spica cast, which covered her from the waist down, and she needed frequent turning throughout the night. The other patients were in various stages of post-op recovery, with a few next-day surgeries thrown in.

About mid-week, a two-year-old child with a skull fracture was admitted to the ward during the early morning hours. His condition was critical, and the physicians didn't want to risk moving him to the pediatric ward, which was on the first floor of the medical building three-fourths of a block away. I had no training in pediatrics thus far, and I still remember how ridiculous the adult-sized blood pressure cuff looked on his small arm. Somehow, my patients and I managed to survive the week, but it was a week in my life that I will never forget!

The responsibilities of student nurses were many. In addition to patient care, we cleaned beds; folded and stacked linen; and cleaned and wrapped IV tubing, catheters, treatment trays, and whatever else was around for autoclaving. We sharpened needles, boiled syringes, and kept the treatment rooms clean. Today everything is expendable. In those days everything was in short supply and was used indefinitely.

Keeping the nurses' station tidy, as well as straightening the various shelves and drawers about the ward, was the responsibility of the night nurse. Then there was the nightly ritual of soaking the bedpans in Lysol solution. This was done by placing the bedpans in the one and only bathtub, filling it with water, and swirling some Lysol around.

While on our operating room rotation, we took turns on call. During our time on the obstetrical and gynecological floor, a combined unit, we did the same. There was never any make-up time given for the sleep we lost fulfilling these responsibilities. The student nurse in the operating room on the 3:00 p.m. to 11:00 p.m. shift was responsible for all the supplies and for autoclaving all the surgical packs for the entire hospital. In addition, she pulled the instruments for the next day and visited the surgical wards with a razor in hand to prep the patients for the next day's schedule.

During our senior year, we were given the opportunity to assume head nurse responsibilities—that is, if we were lucky enough to pull day shift, which didn't happen very often.

In the diet kitchen, we were responsible for the special diets. We planned and cooked the food, set up the trays, put them on the carts, and personally delivered the trays to the patients on the floor. We were in the kitchen by 6:00 a.m., worked until after the noon meal, had a few hours off in the afternoon, and then went back to the kitchen to prepare the evening meal.

Well, somehow I survived the rigors of being a student nurse during the World War II era. The war ended, I graduated, married, had children, and worked in the profession for twenty years in a variety of capacities.

The advances in nursing and the medical field in general have been tremendous, and I have witnessed firsthand some exciting breakthroughs. It was during my student years that penicillin was introduced, and little did anyone realize the impact this discovery would have on the world. It came to us in crystalline form, and we would dilute it with normal saline as needed. It was given to patients IM every three to four hours around the clock, often with dramatic results. One such case comes to mind.

Tucked away on the third floor of the surgical building was a small private room occupied by a dentist who had been hospitalized for treatment of osteomyelitis of the spine. The room was not a particularly pleasant one to enter. It was filled with clutter. Reading material was stacked so high on every flat surface that it was a challenge to find enough space to place a food tray. As student nurses started their rotation on the floor, they were warned of how crotchety this doctor could be. Everyone knew that he had every right to be, for he had been in this tiny room for over seven years as the disease ravaged his body. He had undergone multiple surgeries as surgeons attempted to cut away the diseased bone, but the disease and the agonizing pain continued, robbing him of his health, his livelihood, and his will to live.

The advent of penicillin brought him new hope. It was known as the miracle drug, and it was not misnamed. Within a few months after treatment was started, the doctor left his tiny cubicle and returned to his home and eventually to his practice.

My first orientation as a student to psychiatric nursing was two dark, dungeon-like rooms in the basement of the surgical building of the old county hospital. These two rooms served as a holding place for patients awaiting commitment to the State Mental Hospital. It took all the courage I could muster to take food and medications to those being held there.

In the mid-fifties, I worked the 3:00 to 11:00 shift as a charge nurse on one of Salt Lake City's first psychiatric wards in a private hospital. The thirteen-bed unit was a far cry from the two rooms in the basement of the county hospital. For the most part it was a pleasant place to be, but many patients were restrained. Although restraining patients was not a pleasant task, there often was no other way to control abusive and destructive behavior. Electric convulsive therapy (ECT) and insulin shock therapy were often the choice of treatment. Lobotomy was also a distasteful method of patient control, one which carried lifelong ramifications for the patient and family.

Midway through the three years that I worked on the unit, tranquilizing drugs made their appearance. Thorazine was the first, with resperine close behind. When I left the unit, restraints had been thrown away, insulin shock therapy was no longer used, and ECT was rapidly losing popularity as a mode of treatment. What a wonderful breakthrough!

Over the years, I myself have felt all the emotions mentioned above. I have experienced the joy of hearing the first cry of my newborn babies. I have peered through nursery windows, feeling great awe as I saw a new grandchild for the first time. I have felt the pain of surgery and have welcomed the soothing touch of a hand upon my cheek. I have waited long, lonely hours outside the operating room, for the words "all went well." I have experienced the anxiety and despair of seeing my husband and daughter hover near death, and I remember how good it felt when I wheeled them out of the hospital, knowing they had another chance at life.

Through all these experiences, I have enjoyed seeing nurses at work. Oh, how proud I am of the nursing profession today. I am amazed as I observe their skills. I thrill as I see them manipulate the high tech equipment with ease and knowledge. I applaud the fact that they are no longer seen as mere handmaidens for the physicians but are now viewed as thinking, competent individuals who have much to offer the medical field in their own right. I admire their spunk, their confidence, and their eagerness to be heard. Equally as important, I am gratified when I see and feel their love and compassion for those who need their care. Yes, I really do enjoy seeing nurses at work, and as I watch, my mind often slips back over the years to June 1944.

As I watch nurses at work today, I envy the modern conveniences and technology they have at their fingertips. I admire their fine-tuned skills and their vast reservoir of knowledge, and I am very proud of their expanding role in the medical field. And now, if I may, I would like to extend a word of advice to nurses today. Pursue your goals. Strive to expand your role and continue to command respect. However, do not get lost in the modern world of technology. Do not relinquish to others your rightful place at the bedside of the patient. Be there to extend a soothing touch to those in pain. Be there for the lonely and frightened. Be there to offer gentle words of encouragement to those in despair. Be there to listen, to understand. Be there to offer solace to the distraught and grieving. Be there to comfort and to care.

As you carve the role for future nurses, fiercely guard the unique nurse-patient relationship that is yours. Recognize its healing power, for it is one of the most powerful tools you have to enhance the healing process. Cherish this relationship. It is your heritage handed down to you from past generations. Remember it is yours to pass on to those who will follow in your footsteps.

Joyce Gottfredson Johnsen

As a little girl, I always wanted to become a nurse. My father, David B. Gottfredson (physician, surgeon, and family practitioner in Richfield, Utah), would sometimes let me go to his office to help in the morning. He and the family were in Richfield from 1928 to 1941. He was called up with the Utah National Guard for World War II, and the family became "camp followers."

Our June 1943 nurse class was the first cadet nurse class to go all three years through the program. Those already in the nursing programs of the several Salt Lake hospitals were signed up into the program for the balance of their training, as desired.

It was at County (Salt Lake County Hospital) that the University of Utah Medical School had its beginnings, giving us trainee nurses additional opportunities to observe the medical students in training and to be taught by specialists

Joyce Gottfredson Johnsen

in their medical professions. County also had special wards, or departments, for communicable diseases, the elderly, and prisoners, along with an out-patient department and clinic. The communicable diseases ward was a good learning experience. During the polio epidemic, we were involved in caring for polio patients on the several polio wards. I was also aware of a diphtheria patient and a whooping cough patient while in training. In the medical ward building, there was an old folks area, where we administered medicine as part of our service on the upstairs medical ward. (The old folks had their own attendants to help them.) Also, downstairs there was a jail ward for prisoners in locked cells. If we needed to attend to them, we would take a male orderly with us to go down there. Sometimes there would be psychiatric patients in the locked area. In the outpatient department and clinics, we had the experience to care for patients with tuberculosis and venereal diseases, as well as do well-baby, maternity, and follow-up care and nutrition counseling.

One thing I remember from my cadet nurse training days was the hard, long, marble floors down the hall from the nursing supervisor's office in the main building. There was a ward there at the end. I was caring for an elderly black man in the final stages of venereal disease. His mind had been affected and his teeth were badly deteriorating. My perception of what happened was that he chewed on his teeth, then spit the debris at people, including me.

On a surgical ward, a transient had been admitted for an emergency appendectomy in the afternoon. I was on the 3:00 to 11:00 shift alone, and in the early evening as patients were put to bed, the transient wakened from the anesthesia. He was determined to leave—to get out of "this house of ill repute"—new stitches and all. I don't remember for sure, but he somehow was getting over the edge of the bed rails. I finally was able to get some help to restrain him.

The only time I experienced sickness (nausea and queasiness) was during an amputation by Dr. Cyril A. Callister. When I was asked to hold the basket to receive the amputated leg, my stomach really began churning.

During my three-month internship (the last three months of training) when I was acting night supervisor, I received a phone call from one of the student nurses on duty on the medical 3 ward. One of the patients was having some distress. From what she described, I told her to check his blood pressure, and I would come to the ward to see him. I then phoned the doctor on call to report to him and requested that he come to see the patient. After several additional calls to the doctor and several more BP checks, the man settled down some. The doctor didn't ever come. At rounds next day, as reported to me later, this on-call doctor was read the riot act by Dr. Wintrobe, because the patient had had a heart attack.

Our class finished June 12, 1946, with seventeen graduates. Our three-class graduation was not until September 3, 1946, 8:00 p.m.—the thirtieth annual commencement exercises. It was in the old Union Building first floor hall—the building just west of Kingsbury.

Class motto: "servamus fidem"

Class colors: blue and yellow

Class flower: sego lily

Class of June 12, 1946: sixteen listed, one unable to attend (Shannon Shumway Hammond), which really made seventeen in our class

Class of September 7, 1946: fifteen listed

Class of December 12, 1946: nineteen listed

We think the reason for combining the classes, some ahead of their graduation date, was to save money and to allow the later graduates to be available for armed forces or jobs as soon as their internships/nurses training was completed.

Evelyn Plewe Jorgensen

Little did I realize when I was born at LDS Hospital on November 18, 1924, in Salt Lake City, Utah, that I would spend a significant part of my life in that same hospital becoming a registered nurse and later working and teaching there. Born premature, I was very tiny but was welcomed heartily into this world by my parents, Merrold and Annie Plewe, and both sets of grandparents.

In December 1941, Pearl Harbor was bombed, catapulting us into World War II. Needless to say, this changed everything, especially for the fellows who were the right age to be drafted into the service as soon as they graduated.

I was astonished when I graduated from West High in June 1942 and realized I wasn't prepared to go out into the world of work. All of my classes had been geared toward nursing, and at this particular time, that was not possible. My folks were not financially able to send me to college. We had not fully recovered from the effects of the Depression, and I needed to work and save some money for tuition. I took a summer course in typing and shorthand and got a job as a secretary at Utah Wholesale Grocers. Would I ever be able to obtain that RN diploma?

With the war raging on two fronts, around 250,000 nurses (approximately 20 percent of the workforce) had been sent to the front lines to care for the troops. There was a massive shortage of civilian nurses, causing clinics and some hospital wards to shut down. A true nursing crisis existed.

It was at this time that Frances Payne Bolton, a congresswoman and advocate for nursing, introduced a bill to the U.S. Congress to provide money to help pay for the education of undergraduate nursing students. That was me! Almost before I knew it, I was raising my hand and repeating the words of the Cadet Nurse Induction Pledge:

> I am solemnly aware of the obligations I assume toward my country and toward my chosen profession. I will follow faithfully the teaching of my instructors and the guidance of the physicians with whom I work; I will hold in trust the finest traditions of nursing and the Spirit of the Corps; I will keep my body strong, my mind alert, and my heart steadfast; I will be kind, tolerant, and understanding; Above all, I will dedicate myself now and forever to the triumph of life over death. As a Cadet Nurse I pledge to my country my service in essential nursing for the duration of the war.

We had committed to remain in nursing for the duration of the war and six months following its completion. As a senior, we could be sent to any army or navy hospital, and if the war had not ended after we graduated, we would have been expected to join one of the branches of the service. The creation of this program was good for the country and also for nursing. The United States Public Health System, Division of Nursing Education, administered the program, and new affiliations with universities increased academic standards and afforded students more opportunities for learning. Also, racial restrictions were lifted for entrance into nursing programs.

I remember well that first day that I reported to LDS Hospital, excited but frightened. I did not know anyone who was going into this same program, nor did I realize the very strict rules that were part of becoming an RN. We were only the second class of cadet nurse students, and because of the influx of three classes a year rather than just one class, living space was limited, and extra beds were put in rooms that had already been filled. We felt fortunate to be living on the third and top floor of the Nurses' Home, which was just in back of the hospital. We had no idea how hot our living quarters would be in the summer, and didn't even realize we would be locked in at 10:00 p.m. each night by our housemother. We also couldn't imagine there would be only one bathroom per fifteen students. My name was called, and I went with three unknown roommates to begin what was to be an amazing adventure.

The rules were very restrictive. This had not changed a great deal for the student cadet. Anyone not obeying curfew could be expelled from the program, and marriage was grounds for dismissal. It seemed that there was a hierarchal arrangement for everything. We (the "probies" on probation for three months) were at one table, the freshman at another, the juniors at another, and the seniors at the head table. We got on the elevators in that same order. When a doctor came on a division, we all stood up, as we did when the supervisors and instructors were present.

We had, during the war years, an unusually well-prepared and beloved superintendent of nurses named Maria Johnson. She had returned to her alma mater after extensive experience as a Red Cross nurse and further academic education at Columbia University in New York. She always looked immaculate in her white, starched, long-sleeved uniform and cap and with the demeanor of a director of nursing. She was alert to the current trends in nursing and was responsible for many progressive changes in the hospital and the school of nursing during her years as superintendent.

At first our days began at wake-up time—5:30 a.m. We were expected to be showered and in uniform for breakfast at 6:00 a.m. Devotional was at 6:30 and class at 7:00 a.m. Later, we had clinicals at 7:00 a.m. instead of class. Most of our classes were taught by registered nurses, some by supervisors and doctors.

As probationers, we had to become proficient in nursing care based on sound principles before we could go on the hospital divisions for our clinical experience. At the end of the three-month probation, we were tested in both our nursing skills and our academic classes, and if we passed, we could then receive our cap at special capping exercises. This was a great milestone, and at last we could move to another table to have meals.

The nursing shortage was so acute that we seldom saw a registered nurse (RN) other than our instructors or supervisors. Once we had our caps, we were ready for shifts on the various divisions. Although our clinical experience had been extremely limited, we were taught well how to care for the patient and would practice some of the skills we needed to know on each other, such as bed baths, subcutaneous and intramuscular injections, and some treatments. We were given a great deal of responsibility. We would be placed on the 3:00 to 11:00 p.m. or the 11:00 p.m. to 7:00 a.m. shift and be in charge of twenty to thirty patients, with only intermittent rounds by the afternoon or night supervisors. Sometimes we would have one aide or one orderly on a shift with us, but not always. While this was certainly not ideal for the patient or the student, it was an indication of how acute the shortage of civilian registered nurses had become.

Our long shifts did not negate our need to be to class every day from 11:00 a.m. to 2:30 p.m., which meant twelve-hour days. We caught our sleep and study time as we could and wondered later how we would survive such a schedule. Our classmates became like family, and we tried to support each other as best we could.

The poliomyelitis epidemic in the 1940s was of great consequence to nursing students. Most of these patients were taken to the Salt Lake General Hospital, where they were treated with hot "Kenny packs." The smell of wet wool was noticeable as soon as the door to the contagion building was opened. Students from LDS Hospital were rotated to the Salt Lake General Hospital for experience in caring for these patients. Iron lungs were used extensively for the bulbar polio patients. It was a frightening experience for students and patients alike. When the scope of the epidemic increased, LDS Hospital and others in the valley were forced to open divisions for more and more polio patients, despite the lack of sufficient nursing help. We were just spread a little more thinly on all divisions.

By 1944 sulfa drugs were in use, which brought improvement to the treatment and prognosis of many diseases. Morphine was the drug of choice for pain. It was time-consuming to administer medications. Although penicillin was in use, most of it was given to the soldiers and others in the war. Three doctors had to sign an authorization on a priority basis, stating it was necessary for a patient in local hospitals. It was given intramuscularly every three hours, day and night. Later, in 1945, penicillin was available to all patients and was still given every three hours intramuscularly.

Oxygen therapy was the nurses' responsibility. The tanks had to be watched carefully to make sure there was sufficient oxygen available and sufficient time given to housekeeping to replace empty ones before compromising the patient. The oxygen tents needed to have the ice chamber filled for humidification and the resulting water emptied.

The hospital ran on student power, and without the cadet corps student nurses, many of the hospitals would have had to close divisions and possibly entire hospitals. Not only did the students give almost all of the nursing care, but they were also responsible to clean the hospital rooms when the patients were discharged, to clean the utility rooms at the end of every shift, to do the autoclaving in the surgery divisions to ensure sterile instruments would be ready, to prepare meals in the diet kitchen, and to leave the divisions clean and ready for the next shift.

By mid-1944, the massive Normandy invasion had taken place, and the war was raging in Europe. In the United States, procaine penicillin and streptomycin were now more readily available and could be used in the civilian hospitals. Even though these medications were still given intramuscularly every three hours with one-and-a-half-inch needles, they were the only antibiotics available at this time, and how grateful we were for them. The procaine in the penicillin helped ease the pain of the shot somewhat for the patient.

Most hospitals were in need of repair and redecorating. However, this was not the time for such improvements. We got used to chipped paint and cracked or peeling linoleum, both where we lived and at the hospital. Wartime was not a time for unnecessary expenses. Food was rationed (especially meat), gas was rationed, and silk stockings had disappeared. How could we complain, however, when many of our upperclassmates were in military hospitals either in the United States or overseas? One of the seniors from our hospital had written from the Philippines telling us she had reached some kind of a pinnacle by being a "real army nurse" because she had just had her first bath out of her helmet, which she described as being "adequate." There were sixty-nine thousand such nurses in early 1945 in the military. We were now juniors, and we still had to sit at our specified tables and stand up for our superiors (which was everyone but the probies and freshmen).

Our long, responsibility-laden days stretched into long weeks of necessary and rewarding work. Our confidence increased as we honed our skills. The medical doctors were stretched to their limits also, with many of their colleagues in various military locations. The interns were our good friends, and everyone was concerned with getting the job done, whether it be in some outdoor makeshift emergency army hospital thousands of miles away or in our own LDS Hospital with too few doctors and nurses. The instructors were probably overwhelmed with their teaching responsibilities and so many students (approximately one hundred per year) needing to know so much so quickly. Everyone was trying their best to do their part, one way or another.

Despite long hours and being emotionally and physically drained, none of our class gave up. Nursing had always been a demanding profession, but the war had certainly impacted us in many ways. Attrition was down from what is usually was. Thirty-six of us began the program, and here in mid-1945 we were all still doing our best to meet our goals and help our colleagues meet theirs. Seeing that black stripe on our white caps was a great incentive to endure, and endure we did.

Hitler had committed suicide, so the German army was floundering. The Allied forces had made their way into Belgium and Germany. There was no accurate way of knowing how many casualties had occurred during these huge campaigns. In August, the atomic bomb was dropped first on Hiroshima and then on Nagasaki, and the Japanese surrendered. World War II had ended, and peace agreements were signed on September 2, 1945. Jubilation reigned supreme, but it would be a long time until things were stabilized and our lives returned to peaceful days and restful nights. It had been a most difficult time for our country.

Almost without noticing, we became seniors and sat at that table that had looked so ominous to us for the last two years. We had become accustomed to having rabbit every Sunday and having dry tongue sandwiches with wilted lettuce brought to us as we worked the night shift. We had also accepted that we had chosen a profession that required our best in both brains and brawn. But it had given us its best in qualified instructors, understanding doctors, loving roommates, and endearing patients.

Seniors did have a lot of status. We were regarded more as colleagues and less as slaves. Perhaps it was just our perception. The cadet corps was still in force, and the need for nurses was so acute, it would not be relieved for a few more years. We were charge nurses all of our senior year, becoming more confident and feeling our worth in the hospital setting. With the war over, we would not be required to go into the military service, but we did need to remain in nursing for the required six months.

Graduation came for us in December 1946. The cadet corps had given us the help we needed to grasp our dream and to be of some small service to our country, and we would always be grateful for that. Our graduation ceremony was held at Kingsbury Hall. It was impressive as we walked across the stage in our white, starched, long-sleeved uniforms, white cap with black stripe, and a dozen red roses. In the audience were loving parents and proud instructors.

Mildred Jane Barker Lindley

March 5, 1943: This morning high school convocation exercises were held in honor of four hundred students who will leave for the armed service.

April 1, 1943: These four hundred young men who will leave so soon are absolutely the best looking, most physically fit and intelligent group of people I have seen grouped together. The boys were attempting to look pleasant and cheerful, but all of them weren't succeeding. I was afraid to look around because my eyes were so full of tears. Ordinarily graduation takes place on a beautiful June day, and everyone looks proud and happy in their caps and gowns. Today a fierce wind was blowing fine snow that cut faces and legs like powdered glass. The bare trees were lined on one side with a film of snow, and they looked forbidding against a dark lavender sky. The music was so much like a funeral that it alone would put one in a serious mood. I couldn't help but think, "Oh, darn this old war anyway. Why did it have to happen?" Yet I know these are precisely the kind of fellows it takes to win the thing.

June 12, 1944: Monday. We arrived in Salt Lake at 5:30 a.m. I reported to the hospital at 8:15 a.m. and was assigned my room and roommate and measured for uniforms. My room is a north one upstairs in Cottage Four.

August 1, 1944: So many of the familiar things I love seem to be part of the past now. My new love is the hospital. It is terribly time consuming, but at the same time fascinating and exciting. I'm now well-established in such unmentionable procedures as enemas and have had experience on four different divisions. I have six white uniforms that make me appear angelic from the waist up and old-maidish from the waist down. (The hems had to be thirteen inches from the floor, which was fine for short girls, but not for me.) Piece by piece we are getting those much-publicized gray and red cadet uniforms. I'm printing this because our charting must all be printed.

September 9, 1944: It is 10:30 p.m. and I just got off duty. I liked tonight so I'll write about it. I took seven o'clock temps and proceeded to put people to bed, give back rubs, straighten draw sheets, and get fresh water. Two emergencies came in—a boy with a rattlesnake bite and a foreigner with his arm torn off. Dr. Bingham and Dr. Barton were both there (residents or interns). Both cases were handled so quietly and smoothly that it was a pleasure to watch.

September 11, 1944: Gardenias always mean big occasions in my life, and tonight I have some my brother Heber gave me for capping exercises. But that little white cap—oh boy, that means the world to me. Looks pretty good, too. We had an open house, and our tiny cottage had fifty people. I can't realize it is honestly me. Sometimes I wonder how I got into nursing; then again, I wonder how I'll get out. Nine months have passed out of thirty-six. One fourth of the way through.

September 21, 1944: I have two dermatitis cases and spend the entire morning fixing an oatmeal bath for one and a potassium chloride bath for the other. Then I put lotion on Kennedy and boric acid packs on Dittmar. Then it is salve on Kennedy and take Dittmar's scabs off. Next it is bandage Kennedy and paint Dittmar a deep purple with gentian violet. Then I itch the rest of the day and am afraid I might be getting dermatitis.

October 4, 1944: This morning I was assigned six patients, four of whom were going to surgery. This gal was really flying—shooting morphine and atropine, giving Nembutal, rolling guys on and off stretchers, taking pulses, and getting pretty hungry. At 11:30 (I was supposed to be off at 11:00) a tonsillectomy came back bleeding a lot with a strong ether smell. He was a wild one. He opened his eyes, threw his arms around my neck and yelled, "Darling!" Then he proceeded to swear and fight. He gave me a good one in the side of the face. I staggered for a second, sat down, and passed out.

October 23, 1944: Today I started on 4B. The patients are the poorest and sickest people I've ever seen, and the hall has two or three families waiting for someone to die. It is morbid, inconvenient, ugly, and smelly. The work is overwhelming. For a starter I had an old lady who is incontinent, unconscious, and dying. She nearly broke my back and ruined my dinner, I'm sure. Then I had a hemorrhaging gastric to clean up. If it was good clean blood I wouldn't mind, but this tarry stuff—ugh.

October 26, 1944: Tonight the little Torres boy died, and it makes me feel so utterly helpless. He had a temp of 105 all day and a pulse of 130. His heart was beating so hard it shook the bed, and he was sweating so bad he would soak a pillow in a few minutes. It was rheumatic fever, and we couldn't seem to help a bit.

(Not dated): Just as I was about to break under the strain of 4B, I was transferred to 7A, the "gold coast." This exclusively wealthy division was a pleasant change from 4B. After two weeks I was assigned back to 4B, but the adjustment was not so difficult. I felt more confident and took a pride in seeing how much I could accomplish.

August 13, 1945: The whole world is waiting and watching for the Japanese to surrender. Since the advent of the atomic bomb, things have happened fast. Most of the public seem worried about what is to become of the world if the power of this thing gets in the wrong hands. After three and a half years, it is hard to believe it is so nearly over.

August 14, 1945: This is *it*. The Japanese have surrendered. Miriam and I were down town at the Centre Theater. We came out to greet the noisiest crowd I have ever seen. Horns were blowing, whistles screaming, people shouting, and paper flying. We threw our arms around each other, and the tears streamed. Nearly everyone was crying yet smiling through tears. The town is covered with flags. Buses can't follow their regular routes because of the crowds. Stores closed. People were hugging perfect strangers. Oh, now if only somehow we can have a lasting peace. We don't want to see this ever again.

August 24, 1945: Poliomyelitis is getting into full swing. The little McLachlan girl died with it very suddenly.

November 15, 1945: Wednesday. Well, now I have eighty-one days left in pediatrics. No one ever has more than eighty-four, so you see I have three days behind me. I approached it somewhat prejudiced, but so far it has been a pleasant surprise.

Fern Maurine Gore Lowery

I went into nursing for a very different reason than most nurses. As a child growing up, I loved airplanes and always wanted to fly airplanes. At that time you had to be a registered nurse to be a stewardess on an airplane. The only way I could figure to get on an airplane was to be the stewardess. My dad and I kind of had a controversy—he didn't want me to be a nurse, and I wanted to. He didn't want me to be a nurse because he came from the old-fashioned way and said that women weren't supposed to be in the hospital taking care of men. That kind of upset him. I told my dad that I wanted to go into nursing, and he said, "No, you can't do that." I had a hard head, so I said, "Yes, I am going to do that." He finally agreed that if I would go to the LDS Hospital, then he would let me go. I said, "Okay, that is no problem. I can do that." So I joined the cadet corps. I could have gone to the County, to St. Marks, or to Holy Cross, because all four hospitals in Salt Lake City had the cadet corps.

Hospitals were desperate because registered nurses had come into the service and they were really needing somebody here at home, so the Cadet Nurse program came into effect. I could see that it was a golden opportunity because that would pay my way through nursing and give me a little stipend—we got thirty dollars a month to live on. It was barely enough, but we made it do because they furnished us room and board at the hospital.

For the last six months of our training, we had to go either into a military hospital of some sort or into community service. Norma went to California and went to a military hospital there, and I went to the county hospital and worked with polio patients.

After capping, we felt pretty important and started taking on more responsibility. It was very different from today. We had split shifts to work everyday; we'd either go to work from 7:00 until 9:00 or sometimes until 10:00 in the morning, go to class all day, and then come back and either work 4:00 to 6:00 or 7:00 to 10:00 at night. Except for the head nurses and the supervisors, the students ran the hospital. The head nurses and supervisors were the only registered nurses we ever saw. Each floor had a head nurse, and then there was a supervisor there from 7:00 to 3:00, 3:00 to 11:00, and 11:00 to 7:00. We had a lot of fun in the hospitals. I think that we were very privileged because our group really cared about each other. We did everything together.

Most of our classes were taught by the physicians, and our clinical part was taught by our instructors. We got to know the doctors quite well also. We had various places we had to be in the hospital, similar to now, but in those days we had a diet kitchen, and we all had to go through the diet kitchen to learn how to prepare the diets and take care of them. I think it was a good experience, but I don't think that it was necessary to participate in all of that to be able to learn to do it. We had to prepare the patients' food and work at the steam tables, under the direction of Ms. Bilby, who was over the diet kitchen. She was the dietician.

This was during the wartime, so things were very scary. Every person during the war had to have a ration book. It had little coupons in it that you had to use when you got anything like sugar, meat, flour, shortening, gas, or anything that was scarce. Most people had gardens to grow their own vegetables but also had the coupons too in case food got scarce. So we all had to turn our ration books in to the hospital so that they would be able to get the food to prepare for us. Nurses didn't eat in the general kitchen; we had a kitchen and dining room all to ourselves that we ate in. That was really nice; we had family-style meals. We would all sit together and have a lot of fun. I think that the patients did not have to turn in their ration books; I think that so much was allotted to the hospital or the patients that they had their meals taken care of. That part I didn't have to worry about. Our ration books would have to last a certain period of time—I think it might have been six months to a year before a new one would be issued.

During those years in the hospitals, we always started off on nights and afternoons, and after our capping in our first year, we would work with a senior student. We covered the floors and took care of all the patients. Our instructor was not there with us—especially not nights. Our instructor would be there in the afternoons if we had to pass off a certain kind of procedure. But that was what we were used to, and it had to be done by us, so we just dug in and did it. As each year passed, our education progressed and we became more and more responsible for the patients. We had to buy our own syringes, our own needles, our own scissors, our own flashlights—everything. They would sell the syringes in a little case. It would have one 5-cc syringe or 3-cc syringe and two needles, and those were usually twenty-five gauge.

When we worked in labor and delivery during the war years, we would reuse as much as we could. The sponges were washed and dried and sent up to the labor and delivery area, and we rolled and folded them. The catheters had to be washed and sterilized by steam. We did a lot of things like that. Needles were sharpened on a piece of sandpaper that we carried with us. In order to give morphine, we had to dissolve the tablet in hot, sterile water and draw it up in a syringe.

Toward the end of our training, several of the students wanted to get married because their fiances were going off to war. They went to Maria Johnson, supervisor of nurses at LDS Hospital, and told her the situation. Miss Johnson—with a great deal of hesitation—agreed to let them marry. She, of course, was concerned that they would get married and not finish their training. Miss Johnson told them that if any of them did not finish training, she would never again allow students to get married before finishing training. I was one of that group, and we all graduated with a black stripe on our cap; we were very proud of it.

Barbara Jean Bowman Mace

I always wanted to be a nurse, but my parents did not want me to be a nurse. Back in those days, nurses weren't really highly regarded like they are now, there was no prestige, and my parents just did not want me to be a nurse. I agreed to go to one year of college first. My parents said that if I still wanted to be a nurse, then they would agree. I did go to college. I won a scholarship to BAC (Branch Agricultural College), now called Southern Utah University, in Cedar City, Utah. At that time it was a branch of Utah State University.

At the end of my six months at the University of Utah, I went to LDS Hospital to finish my training. Near the end of my training, the Cadet Nurse program was initiated. When we were told about the program, I applied.

That is what started me on my way to Bushnell. I went on the train. I had never ridden a train before, and that train was something else. It was really a junky train, just a local one, from Salt Lake to Brigham City. When I arrived, there was someone to meet me. I was driven to the hospital and taken to meet the nurse in charge of the cadets and shown to my room. Another girl from LDS Hospital also went to Bushnell. We were given a room together. She made the mistake of getting married, on the sly, which was against the rules. She ended up being pregnant and was sent home. I had that room to myself for the time that I was there. The rooms there were arranged so that there was a bathroom between each two rooms. Four girls shared the bathroom.

The thing that disillusioned me so much was when the captain in charge of the cadets gave us our orientation. I really had my eyes opened. I was shocked at the military. We were not to have anything to do with the enlisted men; they were below us. I spoke up and said that my brother was an enlisted man, and she said, "Well, I am sure if your brother would come to Bushnell, you could get special permission from the colonel to see him." I just could not relate to that kind of a philosophy, because to me, these were all boys out defending our country, and they were just as good as any officer.

I started out just working in the wards, but they wanted me to go to surgery because they had had previous LDS nurses up there and they liked their surgical training. In my training I had never had any neuropsychiatric nursing, but I thought I would like to do that, so they let me. As part of our training, they had the psychiatrist come and talk to us. They would bring in these boys and tell us their case histories and everything about them. I said to my friend one day, "The only difference between me and these boys is that they made the mistake of telling their troubles to a psychiatrist." I felt like I had the same conflicts, worries, and problems that they had, and I really felt a close relationship with them from that. One day one of the boys on the ward told me he was going home. He was going to get a discharge. He said he had had his life planned for a long time. When he was over in France, he was sitting there in the cold, leaning against a stone wall with the rain beating down on him, and he thought, "Sam, you could be home having some of your mother's apple pie." So he said he went crazy. I told him that he would probably be sent to a VA hospital, and he said that he had that all figured out too.

Before I went to the psychiatric ward, I had some experiences with the patients who were brought in on the convoys. Bushnell was an amputation center. They would do amputations right on the battlefield and then put the patients in sort of a cast and ship them to the States. Some of them had maggots already in the casts. The cast would be full of pus. One man had the whole side of his skull gone, and it was all infected. Those things were really traumatic to me because my brother was in the service by this time.

It was hard for me to see all those wounded boys, but I loved working with them. It wasn't long until I knew all the names. I had to fill out night reports, and they contained the name, rank, and serial number of each man on the ward. It was fun to be there. They were big, open wards. There was a little nurses' cubbyhole and then all the beds for the men. Everyone knew what was going on with everyone else. One thing that impressed me so much was how upbeat they all were. Bushnell had a lot of ramps. The buildings were joined by long ramps. Some of them went downhill. There would be boys in wheelchairs, boys on crutches, and it would be just like a big thundering herd going down the ramps. It was really something to see how upbeat and happy they could be without arms or legs and with all the other injuries they had. To me they were special people. They were humorous as well. Above the door of the latrines on the wards, the boys had hung a sign: "Soldier, is this trip really necessary?"

One of the army nurses told me not to get too involved with these boys. She said 99 percent of them were just scum. I couldn't look at it that way. I was told that if I went into the army I would be an officer. One nurse there told me that her commanding officer told her that he would rather see her be the mistress of an officer than the sweetheart of an enlisted man.

I had received word that my brother was missing in action while I was at Bushnell. The boys could see that I had been crying. I told them my sad news. They all tried to reassure me that he would be okay. My brother was not afraid to die. He would have been afraid to meet his Heavenly Father if he had done the things that enlisted men supposedly did.

When my time at Bushnell was finished, my mother came and picked me up. We returned to Kanab. When we arrived home, my dad and his brother met us with the sad news that my brother had been killed. I returned to Salt Lake to graduate and to take the state boards.

Nina Maughan Marsh

Nina Maughan Marsh

My name is Nina Maughan Marsh, and World War II started the year I was in tenth grade in South Cache High School in Hyrum, Utah. The memory of the entire student body filing into the large auditorium to hear President Roosevelt announce that our country had been attacked by Japan at Pearl Harbor, Hawaii, and that we were at war, will be forever in my mind.

The economy of the country at that time was very poor. My dad was a school teacher, and most of his salary went to pay the medical bills. For me, the Cadet Nurse program could not have come at a better time. My previous summer jobs had been picking fruit and vegetables around Cache Valley. I was unable to save enough money for nursing school.

The work and studies were demanding. We were allowed to cover the night shifts due to the nursing shortage at the time. (Many of the nurses had joined the service.) Our work gave us the warm feeling of helping the war effort. To this day I do not know how we had the strength to work eight hours, attend and study for a full load of classes, and also go to church each Sunday.

I do know how we made it. We gave such support to each other. Being a nurse called for the kind of sacrifice that only the finest type of woman could fulfill, and we, at that age, had a long way to go.

The Office of War Information (OWI) declared in their publicity information that nurses made good wives, mothers, and community leaders, which proved to be true in my case.

After I graduated from University of Utah nursing program, I received a scholarship to the University of Michigan (U of M) School of Public Health on the condition that I would return to my rural community after graduation as their public health nurse.

Dorothy Carbis Peay

Three of the five Cadet Nurse Corps members of the class of June 1945 arrived at Bushnell General Hospital in early December 1944. We had decided to serve as army nurses, and this was the first step. Bushnell at that time was not fully staffed with Army Nurse Corps members. We were at once placed in charge of certain departments. I was in charge of a neuropsychiatric floor. What a responsibility! My assignment lasted for only four days, and it was a great relief when the Army Nurse Corps nurse arrived to take charge.

My new assignment was a surgical floor. This was my first experience with amputations. Our young men who had fought so valiantly were forever changed. My first patient had been a member of an airborne unit and now lived with stumps below the knee. This did not deter him from polishing his jump boots daily. Instead of a sad atmosphere in the ward, there were wheelchair races and improvised baskets for wheelchair basketball. There were other activities that kept all of us cheerful.

It was soon announced that we would be receiving Russian POW patients. These men had been captured in Italy and had been serving as workers for the Germans. The Russians knew it was understood that they would never be taken prisoner. They were very nervous but soon became aware that we were prepared to give them care. Other than special orders regarding medical care, they took complete charge and kept everything in good order. We were offered classes in the Russian language, but most of us didn't have time for the intense study required. The day came when we were notified that Russian officers were coming to repatriate our patients. No longer did our Mongolian man flash his gold-tipped teeth in his happy smile. We were all sad when they departed.

On April 17 we received the news that our president, Franklin D. Roosevelt, had died. It was amazing how quiet a bustling hospital could become. I will never forget the sorrow.

Dorothy Carbis Peay

As our troops were moving through Germany and rescuing our POW servicemen, we were notified that we would be receiving the men that needed our specialized services. We were totally unprepared for the terrible condition these men presented to us. They appeared to be living skeletons! One man died soon after his arrival, but his parents had a short time to be with him. One man by the name of Fenwick Cole, who was a quadriplegic, refused any food or care. He stated he wanted to die. He was so tragic, I can remember his name to this day.

My time spent at Bushnell General Hospital in Brigham City, Utah, has enhanced my entire life, and I owe it to my membership in the Cadet Nurse Corps. I would never have had the experience in neuropsychiatric and in amputee services that I had been privileged to acquire. I will be forever grateful.

Betty Jo Carter Reiser

As long as I can remember, I wanted to be a nurse. Even as a child in peaceful, pastoral Park Valley in western Box Elder County, Utah, I wanted to be a nurse. An older cousin, Delila Olague Hunt, had graduated from the LDS Hospital School of Nursing. She was my idol, my role model. I wanted to be like her. She was angelic in her crisp, white uniform, her LDS Hospital School of Nursing pin, and her neatly folded cap with the traditional black stripe. I had read the Florence Nightingale pledge on her bedroom wall and was inspired to be "the Lady with the Lamp" and to care for the sick.

In June 1943, I started nursing school at the University of Utah. I didn't know anyone in my class, and I was a bit anxious but excited finally to be starting nursing training. We were assigned roommates, and I soon made new friends. I hadn't anticipated the strict discipline, rules, and regulations. Students were put on probation or expelled if they returned after 8:00 p.m. or if they were off campus overnight without permission.

We lived at Carlson Hall, a dormitory for women students, located on the southwest corner of University Street and Fourth South. The Cadet Nurse Corps occupied the entire building. We attended our academic classes at the university and received college credit.

Congress passed the Bolton Act on June 15, 1943. There was a critical shortage of nurses in the country because so many nurses were serving in the armed forces. Our schooling was then paid by the government. We received a monthly stipend of fifteen dollars the first year, twenty dollars the second year, and thirty dollars the third year. Prior to that, my father had paid for my tuition, board, and room. The financial assistance and patriotism brought an influx of students into the nursing program.

After about six months in Carlson Hall, we moved to the Beehive Annex just north of the Beehive House on the southeast corner of South Temple and State Street. We had passes and rode the bus back and forth to LDS Hospital. Sometimes we would ride the bus several times a day back and forth from the hospital to our rooms when we had split shifts and classes. That schedule was not easy, and sometimes we felt sleep-deprived, but we supported each other as we endured the odd hours.

Miss Eva Benson was our beloved housemother at the Beehive Annex. She was a sweet, gentle lady who was a good listener and trusted and loved each one of us. At the Nurses' Home by the hospital, Mrs. Edith Lambert was the housemother and Miss Mary Jane Duke was her assistant. All our housemothers were kind, understanding, and helpful and became our friends.

We started our nursing arts classes and our clinical training as soon as we arrived at LDS Hospital. We learned to care for patients in every conceivable situation. We practiced on a life-sized dummy, "Mrs. Chase," and on each other. Each new procedure we performed was supervised by one of our nursing arts instructors: Eleanor Sheldon, Edith Erickson, and Katherine Brim. The work was hard and the discipline was strict. On our day shift, each of us were assigned four to eight patients, depending on the availability of nurses. We had to assume a great deal of responsibility early in our training because many nurses were serving in the military. I feel it helped us to become better nurses.

After nine months of training, six months at the University of Utah, and three months as "probies" at the hospital, we participated in a capping ceremony. It was a thrilling, exciting experience for all of us who had dreamed of becoming nurses. With the addition of the cap, we were officially accepted members of the profession, and we were pleased with our accomplishments. Then we rotated through the specialty services: surgery, medicine, obstetrics, and pediatrics.

Student nurses were not allowed to administer narcotics or sleeping pills unless approved by the supervisor. There was only one night supervisor for the entire hospital. We learned it was useless to summon Miss Clara Wall for approval of sleeping pills until we had washed the patient's face and given him crackers and a glass of warm milk. At the end of each shift, we had to account for all narcotics and transfer the responsibility to the charge nurse for the next shift.

We had one day off each week and two weeks' vacation each year. Soon after we were capped, we became assistants to the head nurses, who were registered nurses. On the afternoon and evening shifts, the senior student nurses were the charge nurses because of the shortage caused by World War II. Student nurses kept the hospital running. Some divisions would have been closed without the services of the Cadet Nurse Corps.

Except for our uniforms, we did our own laundry. We had short-sleeved white cotton uniforms with a detached belt and the LDS Hospital insignia on the sleeve. Each of us had a navy blue cape with the same insignia. Long white stockings, polished white shoes, and a white cap completed our uniforms. If a supervisor found our shoes were not highly polished, we were sent back to the Nurses' Home to repolish them. Luckily, I never had to return to the Nurses' Home as a result of shoe inspection.

After a year in the Beehive Annex, we moved to the Nurses' Home at LDS Hospital on the northwest corner of Ninth Avenue and C Street. There was one office telephone and one pay telephone in the entire Nurses' Home. Betty and I lived on the fourth floor. If we received a call, we had to run down four flights of stairs. There were two showers, one tub, three basins, and three toilets on each floor. The tubs were in great demand. There were fifteen students on each floor. It was hectic to have everyone showered, bathed, and on duty on time.

We had to be in the Nurses' Home by 10 p.m., and then the doors were locked even though that was against the fire code. The door-locking policy caused a few of my classmates to climb in by the fire escape if they were coming in late.

One night two policemen saw some nurses climbing up the fire escape and shined their spotlight on them. The nurses were frightened, but they explained the door was locked and they couldn't get in. The policemen shined their light to help them climb the fire escape and didn't report them. We often joked we'd all burn to death if we had a fire at night because the doors were always locked. Those who were skilled in climbing up and down the rickety old fire escape would survive a fire but would be kicked out of nurses' training because they had disobeyed the rules and knew how to use the antiquated fire escape. Those of us who hadn't learned how to use the fire escape would have died in a fire.

Most of our classmates were members of The Church of Jesus Christ of Latter-day Saints. We were involved in Church activities as much as our schedules would allow. Many boyfriends and some of our brothers were in the military service, and we spent time writing letters. However, there were still eligible young men available for dating on weekends when we were off duty. We had a lot of fun double-dating. We created interesting activities in small groups in the Nurses' Home. I have fond memories of gathering in each other's rooms, talking about our futures, our boyfriends, our romances, and our love lives.

We had a formal relationship with the attending staff doctors and the interns and residents. When any of them arrived at a nurses' station, we stood immediately when we were charting and gave them the greatest respect and deference. We were trained to assist them in any way we could. We were a bit in awe of the doctors. We had the same respect for the head nurses and nurse supervisors.

On July 1, 1945, a new group of interns arrived at the LDS Hospital. We had heard that all of the new interns were married. I was just beginning my senior year of nursing school. One evening, as the charge nurse on 4B, I needed to have an IV (intravenous fluid) started on a patient. I called the telephone operator and asked her to page an intern to start the IV. When he arrived, I looked up and saw a handsome, dark-haired intern dressed in a white shirt, white trousers, and a black tie. In my mind's eye I can see the picture even now.

I told him I would get the IV tray and join him in room 425. I stood behind him as he started the IV. I was impressed with his dark hair, his neat appearance, and his gentle, professional manner. I thought, "He's probably married and has three little dark-haired boys."

That night I told my roommate Betty Sumsion I had met the neatest, most handsome intern with coal black hair and a charming smile. I said, "He's probably married and has three little dark-haired boys." Little did I dream I would be the one happily married to him and we'd have three darling little boys. Some time later Betty reminded me I had told her about the intern with three little boys.

I had just finished taking care of little Bobby Brown, one of the favorite patients of my nursing experience. He was a beautiful child with big brown eyes. I hoped to have a handsome little boy just like him some day. He was only four years old and had to have a shot of penicillin every four hours, day and night. He never fussed or cried, as most of the children did. As I gave each shot, he would implore, "Miss Carter, please don't put it in the same hole."

My first date with Hamer was on Monday, August 20, 1945. We went to a movie with Dr. Johns and his wife, Virginia. It's interesting neither one of us can remember the theater or the movie.

I continued as a charge nurse on 4B. Periodically Hamer would appear as if by magic. At the end of my shifts, he would walk me to the Nurses' Home, which was on the same block and not even thirty yards from the rear entrance of the hospital. However, we preferred the long-way-home scenic routes via Ensign School, around the block, or along the winding paths down Memory Grove.

Later I was transferred to 7A—the "Gold Coast"—the most expensive rooms in the hospital. I never did understand why anyone thought they'd get better care or get well faster in the fanciest rooms. There I worked with Druce Betensen and Venna Jensen, who was the student charge nurse. They were two of my favorite nursing friends. Venna was in the class six months ahead of ours.

The 7A division was smaller and quieter than the other divisions in the hospital. Hamer seemed to find ways to stop by and visit. There was a small, enclosed sun porch on the south end of the floor. Hamer and I were attracted to the porch to enjoy the view, as were many others.

One night we were standing in the sun porch talking quietly and looking over the beautiful lights of the city. Suddenly we were aware of another person in the room. It was the ever-present Miss Arvilla Bauer. She was the small, quiet, aloof, and efficient night nursing supervisor. She moved so quietly we didn't hear her arrive. She appeared almost magically out of nowhere. That scenario was repeated many times. Frequently we'd find her in the hall as we rendezvoused at the end of my shift. She may have felt she was my guardian. I sensed she was pleased I was dating Hamer. Many years later she became one of Hamer's patients.

Soon the whole hospital was buzzing about the romance. On the elevator I met Dorothy Bird and Mary Christensen, two charge nurses from surgery. They told me what a wonderful person and fine doctor Hamer was and how lucky I was to be dating him. I felt the same way. They didn't have to convince me. Everyone at the hospital and at the Nurses' Home was in favor of Hamer. I was too, but I didn't let him know it immediately.

On November 20, 1945, Hamer asked me to marry him. I anticipated he might give me a ring on my birthday, December 8. He had made a date for dinner to celebrate. I was so excited. When Hamer arrived, Betty Sumsion said, "Just run down the stairs and throw your arms around him and give him a big kiss." I did run down into his arms, but I let him give me a big kiss later, far from the eyes of the audience at the Nurses' Home.

After the birthday dinner, we drove to Seventeenth South just west of Foothill Boulevard. It was a beautiful, clear, star-studded night with a spectacular view of the sparkling lights of the valley. Hamer slipped a ring on my finger and gave me a big kiss. That reconfirmed he was the one.

We wanted to be married in the Salt Lake Temple before I left on January 31, 1946, for Dibble General Army Hospital in Palo Alto, California. However, there was a major problem. The Army Cadet Nurse Corps provided the opportunity for us as student nurses to spend that last six months of our training at various army hospitals. Betty Sumsion was enthusiastic about the program and was anxious to go. She thought it would be a great adventure to travel and have new experiences. I was not so adventurous, and it took some persuasion on Betty's part to convince me to sign up. We had no control over where we would be sent, but Betty and I were assured we would be assigned together. We signed up for the program a year or more before I met Hamer. Betty was disqualified because she had a severe visual impairment in one eye.

When I wanted to be married, we tried to persuade the army to have someone else go in my place, but they wouldn't release me from the obligation. Some classmates went to places such as Bushnell General Hospital in Brigham City, Utah, some to Letterman General Hospital in San Francisco, and some to a military hospital in Seattle, Washington, and to various other places. Four classmates and I were assigned to Dibble General Hospital in Menlo Park, California.

During my training Miss Maria Johnson was the superintendent of nurses. She was an austere, authoritarian maiden lady who ruled over the student nurses with an iron hand. She had taught school for eight years before she entered the LDS Hospital School of Nursing and graduated in 1919. She worked with the Red Cross for several years and did graduate work at Columbia University in New York City. She contributed significantly to the advancement of the nursing program and helped obtain accreditation for the School of Nursing. She stayed abreast of the changes taking place in the nursing profession.

We respected and admired her for her professionalism, her training, and her expertise in nursing. Her philosophy was that if a person wanted to be a nurse, she must be willing to devote herself wholeheartedly to the program, which Miss Johnson did to a high degree. She was attractive in her immaculate white uniform and her beautiful white hair, and she was the perfect picture of what a nurse should be. However, we did not have the feelings of love for her that we had for our housemothers. We were filled with fear and trembling if we heard or read the words, "Miss Johnson wants to see you in her office."

I made an appointment with Miss Johnson to ask permission to be married. I had been to Miss Maria Johnson's office only once before. The next morning I was called to Miss Johnson's office. She was elegantly coiffed and stately in her white uniform and white cap with its black stripe. She stared at me for what seemed like hours. I tried to explain the circumstances, but she countered, "What makes you think just because you wrote for permission that I would sign it?" I explained it was a special, once-in-a-lifetime occasion. She glowered, she threatened dismissal in disgrace, and she made me feel like a criminal who had committed a major offense, hardly worthy of being forgiven. When I began to cry, she dismissed me and said, "This is a very serious offense. Don't let it happen again. You cannot go anywhere unless you have a signed permission slip."

With fear and trepidation, I made another appointment with Miss Johnson to ask for permission to be married. She called me on 4B and told me to come to her office. I asked for permission to marry Hamer. She sat in her chair and stared at me like a cigar store Indian to show me she was in control. After an interminable period, she snapped, "You know the rules as a member of the Cadet Corps. I can't give you permission to marry while you're in training." She lectured me for several minutes about obeying the rules, keeping my commitment to nursing, patriotism, loyalty, and unselfishness.

Whenever we were called to her office, she seemed to delight in making us squirm—she was in the driver's seat. One classmate said, "Whenever you visit Miss Johnson, just hurry and cry and she'll be finished with her scolding and will dismiss you." One classmate went home to visit her sick mother and didn't have a signed permission slip. When she returned, she was called to Miss Johnson's office. After a long harangue she started to cry and was dismissed. However, she was placed on probation.

After I left Miss Johnson's office, I held my composure until I returned to 4B. Peggy Ann Staub, the student charge nurse for the shift, asked how the interview had gone. I burst into tears and blurted, "Miss Johnson said, 'I can't ever give you permission to marry while you're in training.'"

Peggy Ann called Hamer and said, "We need to you come down to 4B." Hamer asked, "What do you need?" Peggy Ann answered, "You have a weepy girlfriend." Hamer came to the floor where I had retreated, teary-eyed, to the utility room. I told him what Miss Johnson had said—that we could never be married while I was in training. Hamer said he would go talk to her. She was as smooth as snake oil and sweet as honey with Hamer. She told him she did not have the authority to approve our marriage while I was in training. She said he would have to talk to Mr. Howard Jenkins, the hospital administrator, which he did.

Mr. Jenkins told Hamer he did not have the authority to approve the marriage and Hamer would have to talk to Bishop LeGrand Richards, the Presiding Bishop and chairman of the Board of Trustees of the hospital. Hamer made an appointment with Bishop Richards and presented his case.

He told Bishop Richards that we wanted to be married in the temple, but that we might not be able to be married in the temple for three years if we were away in military service. Bishop Richards listened patiently, then called Mr. Jenkins and said, "Howard? Dr. Reiser is here in my office. You know the situation. He is a good case. I think we'd better bend the rules a bit."

Bishop Richards gave permission for us to be married before I finished my training. Years later, Bishop Richards became Hamer's patient. Hamer attended him for many years until he died. At the time, Bishop Richards was the oldest of the General Authorities of The Church of Jesus Christ of Latter-day Saints.

We began to make plans to be married on January 7, the first day the Salt Lake Temple was open in 1946. We were married by Elder David O. McKay, a member of the Quorum of the Twelve Apostles. He cautioned us to keep our romance alive and not to let our romance die. He reviewed his three Cs of a successful marriage—communication, courtesy, and consideration.

We were married exactly twenty weeks after our first date. During that time our paths crossed almost daily as we performed our various professional responsibilities at the hospital. I loved Hamer and I knew he loved me. The Holy Ghost reaffirmed the marriage was right.

Even though we had received official permission to marry and were then married, one day Miss Johnson said to me icily, "If you become pregnant, you will never walk across the stage or receive your dozen red roses for graduation." Not to worry. I was not pregnant and didn't have a baby until two years later.

On January 31, 1946, I left for Dibble General Hospital in Palo Alto to finish my training. We five nurses from LDS Hospital and the four from the Salt Lake County General Hospital arrived at Dibble Army General Hospital in Palo Alto and were welcomed with open arms. They, too, needed the help of the Cadet Nurse Corps. However, we went back to being "probies" again. We had to be in our rooms by 10 p.m. with lights off at 11 p.m.

We had to record our weight every month, just as we had done at LDS Hospital. The director wanted to make sure we weren't losing or gaining too much weight. To the director, it was a measure of our health and well-being. Today such procedures would be a violation of our privacy and our civil rights and would not be tolerated.

Our classmates at home were now mighty seniors and could stay out until midnight every night and had great freedom. The only classes they had were refresher courses in preparation for state board examinations. We were concerned that we didn't have any extra help to prepare us for the tests. However, when the time came for the exams, we all passed without difficulty.

The director of nurses at Dibble was a large, tall, hardened, cigarette-smoking regular army nurse. At my first interview with her she asked me about my plans for graduation. When I had told her what Miss Johnson had said about pregnancy, she said, "Oh, I hope you are pregnant. We'll give you your own special graduation with three or four dozen roses." What a contrast to my superintendent of nurses in Salt Lake City.

Because I was married, Miss Cheney thought it would be appropriate that I spend some time in the kitchens observing food preparation. It was a fascinating experience. I spent a couple of weeks in the efficient kitchens and learned a lot about hygiene, planning menus, and preparing food for great numbers of people. I learned how important organization and efficiency are in providing large amounts of food.

There were approximately 4,500 psychiatric patients at Dibble. Most were from World War II, but some were from World War I. There was a small group of about thirty veterans from the Spanish-American War. They were elderly, gentle, sweet patients, most of them bed-ridden. We gave them back rubs and nursing care and helped make them comfortable. They were so appreciative of anything we did for them. Most of the World War I and II veterans were ambulatory, but some had severe psychiatric and emotional problems. Some catatonic patients stood all day long in the same place with their heads down. I had never seen such behavior, and I felt so sorry for them. I wished I could have done something to help them. However, there was little that could be done for them at that time. The cadet nurses were given responsibilities on all the divisions except those housing patients with violent tendencies. The most traumatic experiences I remember are of assisting electroconvulsive therapy. It haunted me.

We spent time each day assigned to interview various patients. Often it was the most effective way to obtain information regarding their mental health and their problems. We'd play games, usually card games, and ask questions. Some of us cadet nurses had never played cards and weren't very good at it. Most of the patients were very good card players. The goal was not to win games, but to gain information in the conversation that would be helpful in their therapy.

We became skilled in interviewing the patients. We didn't ask yes or no questions such as "Have you heard any voices today?" We'd phrase the question to ask, "Have you heard men's or women's voices today?" That caused them to think a bit before they answered. They would identify the gender and we'd ask, "What did they tell you?"—and on and on. Then we'd give an oral report or a written report on our interview at staff meeting. Many of the more severely ill patients thought they were Jesus or other authority figures. As Jesus, they'd tell us what we needed to do. They'd continue to remind us every time we saw them.

One day a small group of patients and two of us cadets were playing games at a large table. Suddenly and without provocation, one of the more disturbed patients doubled up his fist and knocked another patient to the floor. It was a sudden, unexpected, frightening confrontation as he threatened all of us. Someone pushed the emergency button, and two orderlies appeared quickly and restored order.

The majority of the patients were otherwise normal, wonderful young men who had broken emotionally under the stresses of war. Some were hospitalized for treatment of drug and alcohol abuse. Some had day passes and worked outside the hospital. Though the practice was forbidden, some of the regular army nurses and some of the cadets dated patients and orderlies.

We had evenings and weekends off duty. Some of that time we spent studying. I wrote to Hamer every day. We were always free to go to Sunday meetings and to MIA meetings on Tuesday. Carolyn, Vivian, and I were very faithful in our attendance.

After most MIA meetings, the ward had a dance for the servicemen. Carolyn and Vivian always wanted to stay. I didn't want to stay to the dances, but I couldn't go home alone. The regulations for cadet nurses specified we had to stay together or go two-by-two. The teacher encouraged me to dance because there were twice as many servicemen as there were girls. It presented some problems. Even though I wore my rings, several of the servicemen asked me for dates. I danced, but I soon learned to say, "My husband is also in the army. He is a medical officer."

Hamer continued to romance me and sent big and beautiful pink, white and pink, or red azalea plants. Everyone was impressed with his thoughtfulness. He sent little gifts and occasional telegrams, and letters went back and forth almost every day.

In one of Hamer's letters he wrote:

> I've thought perhaps there may be some good in our separation. For one thing it has made me know how much I love you and how important you are to me and what a great part you play in my life. It has made me appreciate you so much. You're the poet in the family and should know this: I believe it was Alexander Pope who wrote an essay or a poem which said, "Whatever is, is right." He implied there is something good in everyone and everything. In a way, perhaps our separation is one form of a blessing in disguise. It's the best we can do at present. The greatest blessing will be mine, though, when you are in my arms once more, forever. I hope I dream of you again tonight.
>
> Loving you again,
> Hamer

Meanwhile, Hamer finished his internship on March 30, 1946, and was awaiting orders to report for active duty as an officer in the U.S. Army Medical Corps. Early in April I received a telegram at the Nurses' Home at Dibble saying, "Tentatively planning meeting you Saturday. Reserve room in Palo Alto." I was so excited I could hardly sleep. The next day another telegram said, "Classmates and others have orders. Can't make trip. Smile. Love, Hamer." I was so disappointed I was in tears.

At 3:45 p.m. on Friday, May 3, 1946, I received a telegram from Hamer reading, "Arriving Army plane Letterman Hospital this evening. Meet me with weekend pass if possible." At 4 p.m. the same day I received another telegram that read, "Grounded for weather, Wait until I telephone." I was crushed. I sat by the telephone hoping it would ring.

Hamer had volunteered to accompany a young serviceman with a brain tumor to Letterman General Hospital in San Francisco. A medical corpsman was assigned to accompany Hamer. A crew of three airmen manned the old battle-scarred B-25 bomber. Hamer hoped he and I could rendezvous after he delivered the patient to Letterman. After aggravating delays due to bad weather, the flight was called off until the next day. The group left early the next morning to fly to San Francisco. Hamer called to tell me the time of arrival and said to meet him at the Greyhound Bus Station which was right on the way to Letterman.

Even though I was twenty-one, an adult in the eyes of the law and legally married for four months, I had to obtained my "letter of authorization" from my parents so that I was free to meet Hamer in San Francisco. Carolyn accompanied me to the Greyhound Bus Station. Hamer arrived shortly: I was so happy to see him that I wanted to smother him with hugs and kisses. Hamer told me to wait at the bus station while he delivered the patient to Letterman Hospital.

At that time on a weekend in San Francisco it was difficult to find a hotel room. The city was full of servicemen on leave. We couldn't find a hotel where we could spend a two-day mini-honeymoon. However, we stayed at the fancy Sir Francis Drake Hotel the first night. With the servicemen's discount we paid six dollars. I was thrilled to be with Hamer. He was so handsome in his military officer's uniform. I was full of love as I watched him as he talked on the telephone with Mom and Dad Reiser to report his safe arrival. We'd been apart for three months, and I thought, "We hardly know each other. I can't wait until we're together permanently."

Early in May we nurses received a letter from Miss Johnson informing us that commencement would be Friday, June 7, 1946. A banquet would be held June 5 and a mother's tea one day that week. State board examinations would be July 11 and 12 and would cost ten dollars. We had to complete and return the application before that time. One June 10 we could take a review and national achievement test she had given to the nurses at home to acquaint us with the type of questions used in state board examinations. The most interesting paragraph was, "The nurse shortage is still acute so we hope you will plan to return to your home school for employment. We are very pleased with our new salary schedule which pays $165 per month with one meal and laundering of uniforms." The offer was not tempting. As a medical officer, Hamer was making $175 a month plus allowances for housing and meals. I was tempted to answer, "No thanks. I'm joining my sweetheart and that's worth more than money to me."

We cadet nurses returned to Salt Lake City on United Airlines on June 3. That was my first airplane ride, and I worried I might be airsick. I talked to the stewardess who gave me a bag and said she could give me oxygen, which sometimes helped.

We had a memorable graduation program on Friday, June 7, 1946, at Kingsbury Hall on the University of Utah campus. Mother and Daddy and Mom and Dad Reiser attended. Each of us wore a long-sleeved white uniform and a cap with the coveted black velvet stripe. Some of us were tearful when we realized we would not see each other for a long time. Our close three-year association was at an end. We had been family. Now our paths would diverge. Over three years we had developed strong friendships that have lasted through the years. Neither time nor distance had diminished the love and concern we felt for our classmates.

The graduation speaker was Bishop Ralph Hardy of the Ensign Ward. Dr. Vivian P. White, president of the medical staff of LDS Hospital, gave remarks, and Wallace F. Bennett led the nurses chorus in several songs, two of which were "I'll See You Again," and "Thanks Be to God." The graduates recited the Nightingale Pledge. Maria Johnson presented the graduates and gave each of us our school pin. Presiding Bishop LeGrand Richards, chairman of the Board of Trustees, awarded us our diplomas. After three continuous years of hard work, I carried my long awaited traditional bouquet of a dozen red roses and walked joyfully across the stage.

Our class started at the University of Utah with seventy-two students. Some of them went to the Salt Lake County General Hospital for their clinical training. Others went to St. Mark's Hospital. Some failed various classes—notably chemistry in the first quarter. Some lost interest and dropped out of the program. I had planned to enter nurses' training and had taken chemistry in high school. I was well prepared and had no trouble with the classes. After three years there were thirty-nine graduates in my class.

After graduation I went to Park Valley and studied for state board examinations. I missed Hamer very much. My excitement consisted of waiting for the mailman to bring me love letters three days a week. After I passed the Utah State Board of Nursing examination, I flew to San

Antonio, Texas, to join Hamer, who was stationed at Brooke Army Medical Center.

The Church of Jesus Christ of Latter-day Saints was a stabilizing force in our lives wherever we went. When my classmates and I arrived at Dibble General Army Hospital in Palo Alto, California, we sought out the Church immediately. It became our anchor and our family. Later, in Texas, most of our social activities were with the Church members. They became another family. We made choice friendships, some of which continue today. We had opportunities to give service and develop leadership skills that have served us well. Our testimonies were strengthened by the examples of faithful members in small branches.

Finally, I had passed the Utah State Board of Nursing examination and had a Utah nursing license. I had my crisp, white uniform, my LDS Hospital School of Nursing pin, and my neatly folded cap with the traditional black stripe. I honored my Cadet Nurse Corps commitment, obtained a Texas nursing license, and worked at the Nix Memorial Hospital in downtown San Antonio.

After three years of hard work, with some interesting adventures along the way, I had accomplished my lifelong dream. Now I was a real nurse.

Ellen Poelman Warner

June 1942 was the time of our class graduation from East High School in Salt Lake City, Utah. I began classes at the University of Utah in September 1942 with the help of a small scholarship and money earned the previous summer. During those war years, the campus was confined to the lower circle and certainly was not the extended campus of today.

We walked back and forth to school much of the time but could ride the streetcar part of the way (to Ninth South) for about four cents. We had little coupon booklets.

I continued classes each fall, winter, and spring quarters of 1942 and 1943. In the fall of 1943, a friend told me about the Cadet Nurse program. When I investigated, I found that it offered a wonderful opportunity for education as well as service during wartime.

December 1943 our group began classes as cadet nurses. We stayed at the University of Utah for classes until June 1944. The Salt Lake City girls lived at home while out-of-town girls lived in Carlson Hall on campus.

Of about fifty-five to sixty girls who started in our group at the University of Utah, thirty-four graduated in December 1946; several received degrees from the University of Utah in June 1947.

College credit from the University of Utah for our hospital classes was minimal. Consequently it required sixteen quarters of classes and work for me to graduate with a BS degree in nursing education in June 1947—usually twelve quarters of a full schedule would provide a BS or BA degree during those years.

Nurses had worked twenty-four-hour shifts for many years. That, fortunately, was not our experience. A forty-eight-hour week was the norm when we graduated in 1946. Soon forty-four hour weeks became a treat to us. We earned $140 per month as staff nurses. I earned $180 per month as a head nurse with a BS degree. I am grateful for the opportunity of earning a university degree and learning skills that are very helpful in raising a family.

I am grateful the Cadet Nurse Corps was a part of my life.

— THE KOREAN WAR —

HISTORICAL BACKGROUND

At the end of World War II, Korea was divided at the 38th parallel by the United States and the Soviet Union. The USSR supported a communist government in North Korea, and the United States successfully supported the installation of a democratic government in South Korea. In the post–World War II forties and fifties there was great national concern over the spread of communism. This concern intensified into an anti-communist hysteria (Roark 1998, 1048) in June 1950 when ninety thousand North Koreans crossed the 38th parallel into South Korea. President Harry Truman's advisers felt that the communist governments of Russia or China or both had instigated the attack. Thirty years later, former Soviet leaders indicated that the Kremlin had simply acquiesced to North Korean plans. However, on June 30, 1950, Truman decided to commit ground troops in Korea. Roark states,

> Sixteen nations, including many of the NATO allies, sent troops to Korea, but the United States contributed most of the personnel and weapons. The United States deployed almost 1.8 million troops in Korea and essentially dictated military strategy. Yet Congress never declared war. Truman himself refused to call it a war. At first he said that it was simply the United States, as a member of the United Nations, "going to the relief of the Korean Republic to suppress a bandit raid." When pressed by a reporter, he agreed that it was a "police action under the United Nations," and "police action" became the official label for the war. (1050)

The "police action" seesawed from one side to the other. From June to September, North Korean troops punished United Nations troops and advanced south to Pusan, South Korea. In September, UN troops led by General Douglas MacArthur advanced toward the 38th parallel from both North and South Korea and liberated Seoul. In November, UN troops were within forty miles of the Korean-Chinese border, but one hundred fifty thousand Chinese troops came across the border over the Yalu River and drove UN troops south of the 38th parallel and recaptured Seoul. Three months later the UN troops advanced again to the 38th parallel, and President Truman decided to negotiate a peace.

The peace negotiations began in July 1951 and were not concluded until July 1953. Talks went on amid a great deal of controversy in the United States about whether the United States should push to eliminate the communist threat in Korea and Asia or settle on containment of the communist "threat" to its previous borders. The controversy cost Harry Truman his popularity and the Democratic Party the U.S. presidency. More importantly, the conflict had a high cost in lives and materials. Again Roark recounts,

> In July 1953, the two sides reached an armistice that left Korea divided as it had been three years earlier. The war took the lives of 54,000 and wounded more than 100,000 Americans. Total UN casualties included 118,515 killed, 264,591 wounded, and 92,987 captured, most of who did not return alive.
>
> Korean and civilian casualties were heavier still. More than 1.6 million North Koreans and Chinese were killed or wounded and 3 million South Koreans died of war-related causes. The nature of the war and the unpopularity of the Rhee (South Korean) government made it difficult for soldiers to distinguish between friends and enemies, since civilian populations sometimes harbored North Korea agents. Consequently, as one journalist reported, the situation "forced upon our men in the field, acts and attitudes of the utmost savagery" the blotting out of villages where the enemy might be hiding, the shooting and shelling of refugees who may *be North Koreans*. (1054)

The Korean War is sometimes referred to as the "Forgotten War." Dr. Paul Edwards (Scott, 2001) says, "It's not that the Korean War is being forgotten, it's just that Americans don't think of it . . . and the government has ignored it'" (26). The Korean War veterans did not come home to the glorious homecoming that had welcomed veterans of World War II. "They would have to return from an unresolved political conflict to an American culture no longer interested in identifying with the GI experience. Korean War veterans were the first to experience this dispiriting phenomenon that would be prevalent for years to come." (26)

Though articles and books about military nursing during the Korean War are few in number, at least two accounts summarize, in some detail, the work of navy and army nurses during that conflict. Captain (ret) Doris M. Sterner (1996) and Colonel (ret) Mary T. Sarnecky (1999) have written histories of the U.S. Navy and Army Nurse Corps, respectively. These histories provide excellent information about the status of nursing care provided to members of the military during the Korean conflict. Only a brief summary of their histories is appropriate for this account.

Health-care conditions in Korea at the end of World War II were inferior to those of Japan. Sarnecky (1999) notes that the system in Japan was "comparable to that in existence two hundred years previously in colonial America" (286). In 1947, shortly before the Korean conflict began, Ianthe Swope, first lieutenant, described the conditions at the 71st Station Hospital in Pusan, Korea. "During the biting damp cold of the winter season the wards were not warm. More than one day no baths were given because of the cold. Though we wore the brown and white striped seersucker uniform during the day, the night nurses were permitted to wear wool shirts and trousers . . . [and the] liner to [the] field jacket. As cold as it was on the wards I did on occasion return to the ward or stay around in an inconspicuous place to keep warmer than I would have if I had been in Quarters" (286).

The nurses who worked in these conditions worked twelve to sixteen hour shifts with minimal nursing staff as a result of the drawdown of military troops after World War II. They became proficient at putting up whole tent hospitals and base camp facilities in the shortest possible time in order to begin caring for patients. They took care of patients on ships such as the USS *Consolation*, *Haven*, and *Repose*; on trains; in helicopters; and in vacant schools. They took care of many times more patients than their facilities were designed to accommodate. They provided care for active duty troops, civilians, Korean POWs, and orphans. They were pioneers in the use of new medical and nursing techniques such as dialysis, vessel grafting, care of cold weather injuries, and new developments in amputee care, which accounted for saving lives and limbs, improving patient care, and increasing quality of life. They became the first to practice what would become principles of critical care. They became independent practitioners who functioned at high levels of assessment and critical thinking. They performed medical and surgical techniques to allow physicians to provide more complicated care to a greater number of patients. They took care of patients while the military was advancing, retreating, being shot at, and dying. They too were attacked, and some died. Others returned home to struggle with the memories and the horrors of war. They were an amazing group of nurses.

Bonnie Jean Hughes Hubbard

After high school my parents encouraged me to go to college. I wanted to go to Brigham Young University with some friends, but it was beyond our financial means. I could go to the University of Utah in Salt Lake City, and I could live at home.

I remember getting off the bus at the university, which seemed huge. After awhile, I found the administration building. Both my sister Elaine, a registered nurse (RN), and Mom wanted me to consider nursing. It wasn't something I had always wanted to do, but looking at the long lines and hundreds of students waiting, it suddenly sounded good when I found a very short line and a large sign that read "Nursing."

College degrees were new to the nursing field. You could be a licensed practical nurse (LPN) in a year and a diploma RN in three. Most people thought it was silly to spend four years when you could get an RN certificate in three. The year 1949 was only the second year the university had a nursing school where you could get an RN and a bachelor of science (BS) degree. We went four quarters a year for four years. They had not decided what could be left out of the nursing program or basic BS curriculum, so we got it all.

I worked sixteen hours a week as a hospital aide the first year of college, so I was very busy studying, taking classes, and working.

I moved into the County Hospital School of Nursing dormitory the summer of 1950. On June 15, 1951, "capping" exercises were performed. Most nurses do not wear caps now, but then it was a big deal. It meant you had passed your probation and someone thought you could really be a nurse!

There were fifteen in our class—all female. The next year would see four leave. In August 1953, not only were we ready to graduate from the university, but the Salt Lake County Hospital also held a "pinning" ceremony. We all took the Florence Nightingale Pledge. Eleven of us dear, dear, friends had laughed and cried, studied and played together. We spent long nights cramming together. We supported each other through giving our first enemas, inserting our first nasal gastric tubes, delivering our first babies, and experiencing our first surgeries. We tried to comfort the psychiatric patients and support the public health crisis. We dated the interns and resident physicians and essentially became a family. We even bought a car together when we got tired of riding the bus to the university.

After graduation we took the state board exam to become registered nurses. The exam was a national test. It took ten hours for two days and had six sections. It was three months before we learned the results of the test.

During that time, I worked at the county hospital as a graduate nurse, as did most of my classmates. Since nurses were very scarce, they relied on us for lots of different positions and different shifts. I worked from June to December as the head nurse of a sixty-five-bed male medical floor.

After graduation we faced the big problem of "What now?" Four of the class joined the U.S. Public Health Service and were assigned to Alaska. My roommate, Alice Coyte, met her husband there and has been there ever since. Three were married right away and started their families. Two returned to their hometown to work. Two joined the U.S. Army to see the world. Barbara Kerr and I were off for an adventure. It was during the Korean War, and not only did it seem a patriot-type thing to do, but we both really wanted to see something besides Utah. Later, when we moved to Ohio in 1957, I registered in that state.

Barbara Kerr and I left Salt Lake City on a wintry day in late February 1954. My parents were a bit reluctant to send me out into the big world, and my brothers were appalled. My brothers had all been in the services and had a low opinion of army nurses. In the end, they all sent me off with their blessings.

We were second lieutenants and were headed for Fort Sam Houston, Texas, for officers' training school. We spent two months learning how to read a map, salute, march, set up camp, survive in the wilderness, shoot a gun, purify water, control insects, build a latrine, and survive chemical and atomic warfare, just to name a few things.

After basic training, Barbara and I were assigned to Fort Hood, Texas, the army's tank center. It had been some time since we had done any nursing, so it was good to get back to a hospital. It was in the middle of nowhere, but the men outnumbered the women eight hundred to one, which made the social life good. Six nurses from basic training went with us. It was a surprise when three of us received orders to go to the Far East in less than three months. Even though the Korean War was going strong, we were told the chance of going there was slim. Everyone was sure we would be stationed in Japan, so we took a foot locker full of pretty clothes.

We landed in Japan and never left the airport before we were being fitted with boots, long underwear, and fatigues. All three of us arrived at a MASH unit on the 38th parallel in Korea, on a cold, rainy day in October, less than three days after we left hot, sunny Texas.

We lived in tents at the MASH and learned to pack up an entire medical unit in half an hour. There were constant helicopters bringing in the wounded, and we worked eighteen to twenty hours a day. We could have a shower every three days, and we were assigned to use the latrine twice a day (6:00 a.m. to 8:00 p.m.). There was only one, so since there were only three women and lots of men, certain hours were assigned.

It was a busy and sad time. Several young men died, but we were also able to save many and send them on to the evacuation hospital. It was a United Nations effort, so we had many patients from many different nations. I was especially impressed with the Turkish soldiers.

After the fighting stopped and the truce was signed, we moved to an evacuation hospital. It was a bombed-out building with no roof or running water, but it was better than the tents. We had a bathroom just for females (there were eight of us), and we could shower every other day. We lived in Quonset huts. Toilet paper was a priority. Every month Mom would send me a boxful, and I was so popular when it arrived.

The nicest thing about Seoul was the fact that I got to meet many of the Korean people. I taught English classes to Korean doctors and nurses and got to visit their villages, shrines, and homes. There also was an LDS branch in Seoul, and when I could get Sunday off I could go to church, which was something I had really missed.

In October 1955, I was promoted to first lieutenant. I also was evacuated from Korea in late December 1955 when I was infected with hepatitis B from a contaminated needle. I flew directly to Hawaii and then on to Denver, Colorado, the nearest army hospital to my family. I was in Fitzsimmons Army Hospital in Denver for nearly three months. When I was well, I was assigned to Madigan Army Hospital in Tacoma, Washington. I was there for one year, from March 1956 to March 1957, and then I was discharged from active duty with the army.

Barbara G. Toomer

I went into nursing because we were just coming out of the Depression and my family did not have much money. I just happened to run into somebody who knew about St. Joseph's College of Nursing in San Francisco. She said, "Why don't you apply?" I did. I was living in Manhattan Beach, California, at the time. That was how I wound up as a nurse. It was none of those longtime ambitions or always-wanted-to-do-it things. It was, "Here is the opportunity. Do you want to take it?" Yes, indeed, I did.

I went to El Camino Junior College and graduated from there in 1949. After that I went to San Francisco to St. Joseph's College of Nursing. My nursing program was from 1949 to 1952. It was a three-year program. At that time the four- and five-year programs were just coming into effect, but we felt as though we were good learners and that we had the hands-on ability to take care of things. That was probably to make us feel better. I know the nurses from the four- and five-year schools looked down on us. They did a lot of classroom work. I remember when I was a probie and I had been there about two days, I got my uniforms and I was on the floor at night and went to class during the day. It was scary, but we did it. After about two months, people started dropping out and I said, "No way. I have put in two weeks or two months (or whatever it was), and this is it." There were seventeen in my class who graduated, and we started out with twenty-five or twenty-six.

I graduated from St. Joseph's College of Nursing, which was associated with St. Joseph's Hospital. Our three-year program was really intensive and we learned. But on the other hand, we did not learn things we should have, that we could have, that other nurses were learning. I did not have the slightest idea how to give an IV, and I had never done a male catheterization. We were back-rubbing bedpan experts. We did basic things, including medications. We were loaded with classes in anatomy, physiology, and nutrition.

We did our pediatrics and communicable diseases in San Francisco General Hospital. In fact, most of the schools of nursing did it there because most hospitals didn't have pediatric or communicable disease areas. There was nothing in geriatrics. Nursing went from hands-on to supervision, except in places like the ICU.

I graduated in 1952 and I went back home and worked at St. John's Hospital in Santa Monica as a surgical nurse in the operating room. I wanted to be in OB-GYN, but there wasn't room. They asked if I would mind going in to OR, and I said I didn't. I did that for a while. I do not really remember how it came about that I joined the military. The Korean War was on and my father and my family were extremely patriotic. My father unfortunately had a heart murmur, so he could not join the armed services during the Second World War. He bought airplanes for the army at Lockheed. My sister had joined the air force. She had no education; she just joined as a private. It was probably in our blood.

I enlisted in the Army Nurse Corps and was sworn in by my father, a notary public in Manhattan Beach. I was sent to San Antonio to basic training. I was assigned to Fort Bragg, North Carolina, but San Antonio is where I wound up. That was a long way from home, but I had been away from home in San Francisco for three years, so I really was never homesick. I just had a wonderful time, especially in basic training.

The thing I liked best about the army that sticks with me more than anything else was the educational opportunities to learn from physicians and nurses from all over the country. You really learned different techniques and different ways of looking at things. I had not realized we were so sheltered, but we (nursing students at St. Joseph's) really were medically sheltered. I had never given an IV. I was assigned to the emergency room and it was at that point the doctor showed me how to give an IV. In training I had taken care of patients with IVs, but the nurses couldn't give them. You had to call a doctor or resident to do it. You were really leery about residents because they did not have the knowledge. It is really a pecking order in the medical profession.

In the army I had to know how to put in an IV because I was running an emergency room. We had a doctor in the ER all the time, but this was an active-duty post. We had special forces and paratroopers—young kids who were doing crazy things. These were gung ho guys who felt as though they were Superman and were surprised when they got hurt. I learned how to use a Stryker frame. I had never seen a Stryker frame and did not know anything about spinal cord injuries. These kids were diving into this lake that said "No Swimming, No Diving, Shallow Water, Off Limits!" Of course we had broken necks. We also had people from the war coming back who lived in that area or whose home residence was in the confines of North Carolina, South Carolina, and Virginia.

The hospital had at least five hundred beds. They were long dormitory-type open wards, except in certain areas like the officers' wards and the women's and dependents' areas. We took care of everything from people who had fainted all the way up to broken backs and broken bones. I was able to continue to do things that had originally been considered physicians' tasks, like starting IVs and drawing blood. In my time at Fort Bragg I was in the OR and was in charge of a couple of wards and the emergency room. I was the charge nurse on the 4:00 to 12:00 shift for six months.

I was at Fort Bragg for the full two years. I never moved. I had a two-year commitment. Just before my two-year commitment was up, I was pregnant. At that time as soon as you said you were pregnant—oops, out you go—so I did not want to let them know. When my husband was assigned to Saigon, I was assigned to Tokyo. Since I had served two years, I got out. I saw my husband off at the air force base at Travis Field in California. Then I stayed in California and had my oldest daughter.

In Fort Bragg we spent two to four weeks out in the field in a MASH field hospital. I remember this master sergeant coming in the door of the tent, strapped down with weapons, and I said, "Leave those guns at the door. I don't want to see guns in here." I don't like weapons. I certainly didn't want them in my MASH unit; that is for sure. I remember him standing there and saying, "Lieutenant, these aren't guns, they are weapons." I said, "Well then, leave those weapons outside." We ran that MASH unit for practice; it was a field exercise. We were in the field during April. I remember going from the field to church on Easter Sunday in a helicopter. They dropped me off by my barracks and I changed uniforms, went to church, came back, changed uniforms, got back into the helicopter, and went back into the field.

There was a male student in my nursing class in San Francisco. It was sort of an experimental thing. Paul was really a great kid. There was no problem with Paul, and he graduated with us and became an RN with us. The nuns thought he was wonderful—the sun rose and set around Paul. I stayed in San Francisco about six weeks preparing for my state boards. Paul and I both worked on the wards, and he earned more money than I did. I went to the sisters and I said, "This is not right, we are classmates, we are both here for only six weeks while we are studying to pass our state boards. What is the deal here?" She said, "Well, he is going to have a family someday." I didn't like that idea at all, but a little while later while I was in the army, along comes Paul with the sergeant's stripes. They wouldn't give him a commission as a nurse because he was male. I don't know when that changed, probably between 1956 and 1960, but it did change by Vietnam. I do know that he was an RN and that he was there as an RN.

Being in the military was a wonderful experience professionally and personally. I think the military changed my outlook on people as a whole.

—THE VIETNAM WAR—

HISTORICAL BACKGROUND

The military involvement of the United States in the affairs of Vietnam spanned the administration of five U.S. presidents and almost thirty years. In 1945 the Truman administration provided aid to the French who were trying to maintain their Vietnamese colony from Vietnamese rebels led by Ho Chi Minh. Eisenhower believed in the domino theory. Roarke (1998) quoted Eisenhower: "You have a row of dominoes set up. You knock over the first one, and what will happen to the last one is the certainty that it will go over very quickly" (1067). Roarke noted that Eisenhower "warned that the fall of Southeast Asia to communism could well be followed by the fall of Japan, Taiwan, and the Philippines" (1067). By 1954 the U.S. was providing 75 percent of the cost of the war to the French. However, Eisenhower stopped short of providing troops to the French. France was defeated and signed a truce in 1954. This truce created the countries of North and South Vietnam. Kennedy continued to provide support to the government of South Vietnam and ultimately supported South Vietnam in the conflict between the two nations, providing troops and materials. Johnson continued the support, making the Vietnam War "America's War." Again Roarke commented:

> The Americanization of the war increased the number of U.S. military personnel in Vietnam to 540,000 at peak strength in 1968 and to more than three million total throughout the war's duration. Yet not only did this massive intervention fail to defeat the North Vietnamese and their allies in South Vietnam, but it added a new burden to the costs of fighting the cold war—intense discord among the people at home. Believing that the war was immoral or futile, hundreds of thousands of Americans protested it. (1138)

Nixon was president of the United States when the formal accord ending the conflict in Vietnam was signed in Paris in 1973.

During the Vietnamese conflict, hundreds of thousands of U.S. military troops were being sent overseas to fight on the front. One of the most important aspects of a military conflict is the ability to care for the casualties at the front, transport the critically wounded to adequate medical facilities, and return those well enough to the battlefield. Militarily savvy people have known this since the Crimea, when the British sent Nightingale to care for the troops. They have known it since the Civil War, when most of the casualties resulted from disease and inadequate patient care. It is the reason people like Bickerdyke, Dix, and Barton were accepted at the battlefront. It was obvious in World War II, when the Cadet Nurse Corps was formed to provide nurses to care for the troops. During the Vietnamese conflict, when hundreds of thousands of U.S. troops were being sent to Indonesia, it was clear that health care providers were essential. Male physicians were drafted and sent to the front, and nurses were heavily recruited. The Nurse Corps Candidate Program was instituted, a program similar to the Cadet Nurse Corps of World War II.

Possibly more nursing literature has been written about the effects of war on veterans and nurses from the Vietnam War than any other. As noted above, it was America's War. It is the war remembered and experienced on some level by most Americans over forty years old. What happened there will impact Americans for generations. It is impossible to review in this work all the nursing literature concerning nurses serving in Vietnam. Perhaps two summaries of the conflict will provide a sense of what nurses endured. The first is from a 1995 edition of the *Nebraska Nurse,* the official publication of the Nebraska Nurses Association:

> The Vietnam War started insidiously. Although American military advisors were a presence in the area from 1945, their numbers escalated. . . . No one is exactly clear about how or why but the numbers grew steadily after that until the early 1960s, when thousands of American soldiers were involved.
>
> The first American military hospital was established in 1962 and the number of military personnel and nurses grew steadily until the war was halted in 1973. Initially female military personnel were not "in country" but soon the need for nurses outstripped the number of male nurses available.
>
> In the end, over 250,000 women had served, 11,500 of whom actually served in Vietnam, or "Nam" as it came to be known. Women worked as clerks, mapmakers, intelligence specialists, photographers, air traffic controllers, Red Cross and USO volunteers. But the largest number of women in uniform were nurses, sent to care for soldiers and civilians in hospital beds that grew in number in 11 years from zero to 5,283.
>
> Air Force, Army, and Navy nurses served on helicopter med-evac flights which lifted-off directly from the battlefield, in inflatable hospitals in tenuous settings within Vietnam, on jet med-evac missions that picked up battlefield casualties from units in Vietnam and delivered them to hospital centers in the Philippines, Japan, and Okinawa for stabilization before the long flight home.
>
> Women of the Army Nurse Corps averaged two years service in Vietnam. Many were novices—only 35% had more than two years nursing experience when they left the U.S. Army nurses were 79% female, some were married, most were not. They served a 12 month tour of duty often living in tents and quonset huts. The quarters "leaked, were bug infested, noisy, and almost always humid." Some stabilized war wounded GIs in transportable, inflated "buildings" which posed constant problems with maintaining electricity and drainage.
>
> While nurses at more permanent sites wore white duty uniforms, most others wore lightweight fatigues. Nurses worked a six day week, in twelve hour shifts, "except during emergencies when everyone worked." Hospital-based nurses were deployed to surgical ICUs, recovery and emergency rooms, and in med-surg areas.
>
> As in other wars, hospital admissions for disease outnumbered battlefield injuries. Diseases commonly treated were malaria, viral hepatitis, and diarrheal, skin, and venereal diseases. The most common diagnosis was FUO—Fever of Unknown Origin.

> The length of stay of battle-wounded soldiers was shorter than in previous wars due to the availability of whole blood, rapid aerial evacuation, and advanced medical and nursing procedures. The hospital mortality rate was 2.6% per 1,000 compared to 4.5% per 1,000 during World War II.
>
> The war that began insidiously somehow ended. It was not a popular war, many refused to serve, and those who served, nurses as well as soldiers, came home to find their service was, by and large, not appreciated. The Vietnam War is a wound slow to mend. The first sign of healing was construction and subsequent appreciation of the Vietnam War Memorial Wall, known to many veterans as "the Wall." The 10 year struggle and dedication of the Vietnam Women's Memorial is an indication that the tours of duty by women as well as men are now honored. The scar tissue of that "ugly little war", although still tender, is forming. (*Nebraska Nurse*, 1995)

The second account is that of author Elizabeth M. Norman, summarizing the gathering of the accounts of fifty nurses who had served in Vietnam:

> The nurses' professional and personal experience in Vietnam was complex. It was a year involving difficult and rewarding nursing situations and dangerous and satisfying personal situations. Their twelve month tours were divided into three periods: the first three months of adjustment, the middle six months of routine when Vietnam became familiar, and the final three months. The final three months were an ambivalent time. The women wanted to go home but they were torn by the friends they would leave behind.
>
> The stressful experiences of the nurses in Vietnam were not very different from those of nurses in other wars. The youthful age of the patients, the severity of injury seen, the lack of progress information on transferred patients, the death of friends, the unpreventable deaths, working with wounded enemy patients, and the triage system all proved difficult. Often the stress was balanced by friends, patients who recovered, and the ability to practice and be respected for their nursing skills.
>
> Two factors, the branch of military service and the year served in Vietnam were responsible for different patterns in the wartime nursing experience. Each service had a unique practice environment—shipboard, aircraft or land based—that resulted in disparate environmental and combat dangers. Those nurses who served in Vietnam early in the war, 1965–1967, worked with traditional battle injuries and enjoyed some level of support from home. Those nurses in Vietnam during the peak of fighting, 1967–1970, experienced more triage situations and enemy attacks at the same time people began to openly question the purpose and wisdom of the war. By 1970–1973, nurses worked with more self-inflicted wounds and drug overdoses. It was hard to maintain morale and be a participant in an unpopular war.
>
> More nurses returned home with a stronger commitment to the profession. They were convinced that nursing could have a direct impact on patient care. The decision to remain in critical care work, however, varied greatly. Over half of the fifty nurses decided to leave this specialty area for work in clinical areas where there would be fewer dying patients and injured young people.
>
> The level of Post-Traumatic Stress Disorder decreased from their first year home when over 30% reported high level of distress to a level of 14% at the time of the interviews. The nurses at greatest risk for PTSD included those who experienced more personal danger and professional stress in Vietnam, and those women who did not have a strong social network after the war. An examination of PTSD, however, does not provide a complete portrait of the nurses' reaction to serving in the war.
>
> Vietnam was unique in their lives. Nothing before or after compares with the stresses and the rewards of serving overseas. Because of its uniqueness, the war continues to be a focal point with which the other life experiences are compared. (Norman, 1992)

Anonymous

When I was a little girl, my grandmother was hospitalized with appendicitis. I thought her nurses were wonderful. They were very attentive to her needs and sometimes even let me help with her care. It was then that I decided to become a nurse. During high school I was a "pinky," volunteering at the hospital. Sometimes there was just a nursing student and me to take care of a whole floor of patients. I loved the work and never wavered in my decision to be a nurse.

I received my BSN from Cornell University–New York Hospital School of Nursing in 1966. I joined the Army Student Nurse program for the last two years of my education, with a commitment to serve on active duty for three years. My first duty assignment was at Walter Reed. I had married a few weeks after graduation, so my husband and I moved to Washington DC. I had been assured by my army recruiter that I would be assigned to a post where my husband would be able to accompany me. Too late I discovered that the army had no intention of keeping that promise. Walter Reed was a wonderful arena for learning the practical skills that had not been taught at Cornell. Unfortunately, seven months later, I received orders for Vietnam. I shipped out, and my civilian husband stayed behind. We grew apart during that year, and the marriage ended soon after I returned.

My first duty station was the 67th Evacuation Hospital in Qui Nhon. I arrived in September 1967 and served there for three months. Mostly I was assigned to medical wards or the POW ward. In the 67th the POWs were kept in a separate ward. We had both medical and surgical patients in the POW ward, which was challenging from a nursing perspective. However, I did learn many skills that would help me later. The care of patients with malaria, hepatitis, and multiple gunshot wounds was not stressed at Cornell. Nursing in Vietnam was definitely on-the-job training!

In December 1967, I was one of several nurses who volunteered to transfer to the 71st Evacuation Hospital in Pleiku. Pleiku is in the central highlands of Vietnam, very close to the Montagnard villages where special forces operated. Some units a few miles north of Pleiku were taking heavy casualties, and more nurses were needed to handle the large influx of patients. In Pleiku I was assigned to the post-op unit in the surgical "T." This building was designed in the shape of a T to facilitate handling multiple patients arriving at the same time. The ER/triage area was in the vertical part of the T. A hallway connected the ER/triage area to the six-bed OR located in half of the horizontal part of the T. Patients were lined up in the hallway to await their turn in the OR. From the OR patients were sent to post-op, which was located in the other half of the horizontal part of the T. Post-op was a thirty-six bed unit with eighteen beds for a recovery room and eighteen beds for surgical intensive care.

Working there was a very challenging nursing experience. We were always busy but were usually well-staffed with all the supplies and equipment we needed. The only time we had a supply problem was when a short round, aimed at one of the military installations near us, blew up our water supply. Until it was repaired, we had no clean water. We brushed our teeth and administered medications with soda, beer, or whatever clean liquid was available. The patients in post-op were the most severely wounded in the hospital. Our job was to stabilize the patients and evacuate them to hospitals in Japan or the Philippines. After that we rarely found out what happened to them. Sometimes our patients got well enough to be sent back to their units. At those times we wished we hadn't done our job quite so well. Sometimes our patients died, although not as many as one would suppose.

Medical care at the 71st was the best I have ever seen. For me, nothing in civilian life could ever equal the level of care we were able to give at the 71st. Of course, no one had a life outside the hospital to distract us from our mission. If we needed a doctor or more nurses and corpsmen, we went to their hooch and woke them up. If they weren't there, we would check the clubs or the other hooches, which were gathering places for bridge games and other fun activities. Even after exhausting twelve-hour shifts, almost everyone was willing to come back to help out when needed.

Our ward was the only one in the hospital with regular hospital beds with side rails. This was because our patients were too sick to get under their beds if an alert was sounded. We went on alert frequently because of our location, which was in the middle of a triangle made up of the Pleiku airbase, engineer hill, and artillery hill. When an alert sounded, almost always in the middle of the night, we would put on flak jackets and helmets, put tree branches across the side rails, and throw an extra mattress over the tree branches. These mattresses were to protect the patients from falling debris in the event of a direct hit on the hospital. The staff would get under the beds of the sickest patients and creep out with flashlights to render needed care. As the assistant head nurse, I was in charge from 7:00 p.m. until 7:00 a.m. The head nurse was in charge from 7:00 a.m. until 7:00 p.m.

There was one policy on the post-op ward that I never agreed with. The POWs were placed in whatever bed was available—sometimes in the bed next to a soldier wounded in the same firefight. POWs were to be given the same level of care that was given to the United States soldiers and Allied troops. I found that policy especially difficult when many wounded arrived at the same time, and all our time and skills were needed to care for our own guys. We knew that if the POWs got better, they would be turned over to an interrogation team. Nobody on staff knew exactly what happened in those interrogations, but many rumors circulated suggesting that these guys were going to end up dead anyway. It seemed like a waste of time and resources to go to extraordinary means to patch up the POWs. Of course, we did try to give them good care because that is what nurses do, regardless of the patient's politics. I always felt sorry for our soldiers, though, when they realized the guy in the next bed was one of the enemy soldiers.

Many of my experiences on the post-op ward were memorable. There are some experiences that are difficult to talk about, even thirty years later. There was a fourteen-year-old civilian Vietnamese boy who had lost a leg in a firefight in his village. The surgeons amputated his leg below the knee. He could have lived, but he didn't want to. One of our Vietnamese workers told us that he would not be able to survive in his culture with a prosthetic leg. He refused to eat or cooperate with his care in any way. He just gave up and he died about a week later.

One of our U.S. soldiers had his arm amputated above the elbow. It was very difficult for the staff to take care of him. He would throw his food and bath water at anyone who came near him. He also would shout curses and threats that were very disturbing to other patients as well as the staff. On the day we had finally had enough of his behavior, I was determined to break through his rage. My goal was just to get him to stop his verbal and physical assaults on everyone around him. I pulled a chair up next to his bed and told him I was going to remain there until he was ready to talk about his feelings instead of acting out in inappropriate ways. It took three hours of silence, periodically broken by episodes of salty language, but he finally opened up. After three hours he began to sob. He reluctantly let me hold his hand. When the sobbing subsided, he began to talk about his anger and his fear of facing life without part of his arm. He was afraid of losing his girlfriend and being unable to have a fulfilling career. The emotion just poured out of him. That was the first of many hours we spent together talking about his future. He became more cooperative with less acting out in negative ways. By the time he was evacuated to the Philippines, he had become a staff favorite.

There was another memorable patient who was in a coma for three weeks. He had a head wound and didn't respond to any stimuli. His condition was much too unstable to evacuate him. One night we were on alert status with all the lights out. We could hear the sound of rockets whistling overhead and the loud booms when they landed. I was under his bed when all of a sudden I heard cussing. The corpsman under the next bed and I scrambled out, and sure enough our comatose patient had awakened to the sounds of incoming rounds. His condition continued to improve, and he was eventually evacuated to the Philippines.

There was one patient that I became way too close to. A few docs, nurses, and other personnel were having a cookout when we heard several incoming medevac choppers. We all ran to the chopper pad, offloaded the patients, carried the litters to the triage area, and began the protocol for handling multiple wounded. Some were so severely wounded that we knew we could not save them. They were moved to an isolated area with a nurse and a corpsman who would administer pain meds and try to keep them as comfortable as possible until they died. Others were prepped for surgery and lined up on gurnies in the hallway in the order they were to be taken into the operating room. We had only six operating tables, so sometimes patients had to wait. Minor wounds were handled in the triage area.

Later that night during my regular shift, I received a patient from the operating room who had multiple wounds from a fragmentation grenade. I later found out he was from North Carolina and had a wife and two children. When we got him cleaned up, the wounds didn't look so bad from the outside. We knew he was in serious trouble, however, because some of his frag wounds were to the chest. Wounds from a high-speed projectile entering the chest cavity frequently resulted in a condition called wet lung, which, in 1968, was usually fatal. The patient's lungs gradually filled with fluid until he could no longer breathe. These patients initially feel very fortunate because they made it to the hospital and through surgery. With pain medication they were comfortable and anticipated recovery. Toward the end of my tour, we had learned to manage wet lung more effectively, but for this soldier that would be too late. We worked as hard as we could to save him, but ultimately we failed.

At first, he was happy and fun to be with. We played games and wrote letters to his family. He loved to talk about life back in North Carolina and what he planned to do when he returned home. His surgeon and I became very close to this patient. As his condition deteriorated, we put in a chest tube. When that was no longer effective, we put in a trach tube. By that time he no longer thought he was going to make it. He would cover his trach tube and talk about never seeing his family again and what it would be like to die. Soon he became incoherent and sometimes combative. He needed arm restraints to keep him from pulling out his trach tube.

One night he succeeded in removing the trach tube and was able to say a few words as I reinserted it. He called me by name and begged me to let him go. Putting that tube back was the most difficult thing I have done in my nursing career. I put the tube back in, and he lived two more days. That decision haunts me to this day. The surgeon and I were sitting with him when he died. Because we were still learning about the pathology of wet lung, the surgeon wanted to do a partial autopsy of the chest. I assisted with that procedure too. It didn't seem right to allow anyone else to do it.

It was around this time that I started taking uppers to stay alert during the long twelve-hour overnight shift. I was already having trouble sleeping, so downers became more and more necessary as time went on. I told myself the drugs were necessary to keep me functioning at a high level. They did not become a habit at that time, and when I was transferred to a malaria ward, I no longer needed them. On the malaria ward I was the head nurse working days in a less stressful environment. Unfortunately, the groundwork had been laid for a more serious problem later on.

It was on the malaria ward that I cared for a very sick little Vietnamese boy. It was a few weeks after Tet (Vietnamese New Year) of 1968. Some marines were delivering clothing to an orphanage. They saw an unconscious child on the floor with a partially eaten rat in his mouth. They picked him up, brought him to the medical ward, and put him in my lap. We didn't think we were going to be able to save him. He was severely malnourished and had multiple medical problems, including intestinal worms. His abdomen was swollen, and his eyes were swollen shut. When the swelling subsided, we discovered he was blind in one eye. He had a very flattened affect, probably due to emotional and psychological problems. We found out later that he spent three days in a hooch with the bodies of his parents, who had been killed during the Tet offensive. The other patients would try to make him smile by blowing up surgical gloves and drawing funny faces on them. We had our Vietnamese workers try to talk with him. We tried everything we could think of to encourage him to interact with us. Nothing worked for several weeks. Gradually his health improved, but he was still withdrawn and uncommunicative. One night the patients and the boy were watching *The Lone Ranger* on TV. There was a lot of gunfire in the show. Suddenly the boy started to act out the gunfight. Other patients joined in, and soon about fifteen guys were running around the ward having a pretend gunfight. Although others were participating, the boy seemed to be in a world of his own. Everyone stopped to watch him because the sight was so mesmerizing.

Apparently, he was able to work out some of the pain through playacting, because from that time on he began to communicate with us. We brought back the Vietnamese interpreter and finally learned about some of the horror he had experienced. His health continued to improve, and he began to speak English. No one wanted to send him back to the orphanage, so we kept him. At that time Americans were not permitted to adopt the children.

He continued to live at the hospital, even though many of the staff had completed their tour of duty and returned home. I was able to keep track of him for a while after returning home. Eventually however, the hospital closed down and I lost track of where he was. I was in graduate school at the time, but I reenlisted to return to Vietnam to find him. Rules had changed by 1970, and adopting Vietnamese orphans was now permitted. I was never able to find him, even with the help of several army units. I hope he was adopted and brought to the United States because, as Americanized as he was, I don't think he would have been allowed to live after the fall of Saigon.

I joined The Church of Jesus Christ of Latter-day Saints a few weeks before I returned to Vietnam for my second tour. I was divorced from my first husband soon after the completion of my first tour and was living with my parents while I awaited my orders. The missionaries were tracting in our neighborhood. They found me working in my mom's flower garden. I told them I was interested in learning about their church, but there was no chance that I would be baptized. I didn't know anything about the "Mormon" Church and was simply curious. When we reached the discussion of the plan of salvation, I was intrigued. It seemed to be what I had always believed, even though I had never heard it before. It just felt right. I had always been active in another church, but I remember sitting in church on Sunday thinking there had to be more to it than what I was hearing. Why did we go to church on Sunday and forget about it the rest of the week? After that lesson with the missionaries, events happened very quickly. I hurried through the remaining discussions and was baptized two weeks before I left for my second tour in Vietnam.

I arrived at my first duty station in Da Nang. There was an LDS congregation in the town, but I had no transportation to get there. For a few weeks I was able to borrow a staff car from one of the officers who was trying to help find my orphan boy. That luxury ended, however, when it was discovered that a nurse was driving a staff car. I was soon asked to play the organ at a nondenominational service on the base. I began to fall further and further away from the LDS Church and the values encompassed within it.

My second tour in Vietnam, which was in 1970, is largely a blur. I was unable to find the boy I was looking for. Many of our patients were being treated for drug overdoses, self-inflicted wounds, and sometimes wounds inflicted by each other. Morale was low in many units. American troops were being withdrawn and the war was being turned over to the South Vietnamese army, with Americans participating only as advisors. The combat-wounded patients that we saw frequently told us they would not have been wounded if South Vietnamese troops had functioned as they had been advised to by their American counterparts. It was a very discouraging time for many of us. Unfortunately, I responded by resuming the abuse of medications. I would write prescriptions to get the drugs I wanted. It was never necessary to take drugs from the wards where I worked. However, my job performance suffered in many ways. Eventually I was sent home to finish my military career at a stateside hospital. As I was being processed out of the army, my discharge physical showed a growth in my right lung. I was hospitalized for tests to determine what was wrong with me.

During the night I would put on my uniform and go to the pharmacy to have prescriptions filled that I wrote for myself. Of course this was very much against regulations, and I was eventually caught. The pharmacist, who noticed the irregularity, sent for me. When confronted with the evidence, I confessed everything. I was astonished that he was kind to me. He seemed to be more concerned about my welfare than about my illegal behavior. We talked for quite a long time. Eventually the conversation turned to spiritual matters and church affiliations. I did not want my behavior to reflect unfavorably on the LDS Church, so I did not tell him I had been baptized. I did tell him, however, that I had taken the missionary discussions and felt a closer affinity to the LDS Church than to any other. It was then that he told me he was a bishop in the LDS Church. It was the most amazing single moment in my life. I don't believe in coincidences of that magnitude. I knew, with certainty, that Heavenly Father had led me to this particular pharmacist. I knew that regardless of the temporal and spiritual laws I had broken, Heavenly Father knew me and still cared about me. It was the moment that began a long and difficult path back to full activity in the Church. I spent many Sundays with this wonderful man and his family. He had several children, a black poodle, and a wonderful wife who welcomed me into their family. They helped me believe that redemption, even for me, was possible through the sacrifice of our Savior, Jesus Christ.

Now, thirty years later, I have a wonderful life. I have been married for twenty-four years to a terrific man. I have a lovely family, including a granddaughter who is heading for college this year and a grandson who brings me great joy during his annual summer visits. The path back was not straight or easy. I have had the help of wonderful bishops and branch presidents along the way. Many visiting teachers have been there to pick me up when I stumbled. Attending the temple is a continuing source of strength and peace. I have been truly blessed by the miracle of this church and the love of my Father in Heaven.

JoAnn Coursey Abegglen

I was actually raised in a military family. My father was in the air force, so my whole life I just kind of traveled around the world and have been a part of that. When I came to BYU, I actually did a first year in dietetics. After that first year I went home for the summer and worked in the local hospital in northern California. They hired me in dietetics so that I could kind of get a feel for that. However, I fell in love with what was going on on the floor. I said to myself, "You know, I'm more interested in the people and not the food they're eating." So I came back to BYU the next fall and because the classes were similar, I just switched my major into nursing. In the fall of 1963 it wasn't difficult to get into nursing. I said, "This is where I want to be." I was always glad that I made that decision a number of years ago. I love nursing. It's where my heart is.

I graduated in 1967, and that fall a friend of mine, Leslie Finehauer, and I were accepted into graduate school at the University of Utah. We went to Salt Lake City to graduate school. We were poor graduate students on a stipend, working during the summer as nurses in California. We worked the night shift in an ICU unit. We decided that we'd never work nights again after working that whole summer on the night shift.

We came back in the fall, and there was a fellow who was the officer in charge of the medevac unit at Hill Air Force Base. He was recruiting flight nurses for his Air Force Reserve medevac unit. He wanted to know if we wanted to join. They would provide us with education and send us off to flight school. The money sounded good, and we thought, "Well, we're adventurous people." So we signed up for the Air Force Reserves. We were commissioned second lieutenants. That year we did a variety of monthly training. The following summer we were accepted into nurses' flight school, a six-week course at Brooks Air Force Base in Texas. The med techs were trained separately. Our classmates in graduate school asked if we were going to spend the summer working on our thesis. We said, "No, we are going to flight school." Once we had been to flight school and were fully qualified as flight nurses, we could be of more service to the unit. We could also be called into work during our two weeks' active duty as flight nurses on the flight teams that were going in and out of Vietnam at that time. We could fly from Travis Air Force Base in California into the Philippines, or from the Philippines taking groups into Japan, and then from Japan back to the United States. We were really well trained. We had six weeks of gruel. Between classes we had practice flights. We practiced everything and flew regularly.

We saw the first Nightingale. This was the very first plane that was designated for use by the military as a hospital plane. We didn't get to fly on it, but we got to go through it before it was deployed into service. They were designed late in the war, about 1969. There were supposed to be three or four of these planes. They actually carried only fifteen or twenty patients, but they had critical care units designed into them. They were really luxurious from a patient care standpoint. We flew in the C-141. It was a huge cargo plane that was transformed by putting in seats and beds or stretcher racks. It then became a hospital because of the equipment brought on board. It had everything—equipment, suction, oxygen—built right into the plane. It was used domestically to fly military patients around the United States. It wasn't really capable of flying overseas. It wasn't big enough, and it couldn't be used as a kind of dual system. Usually the crews on the C-141s went over in the plane, reconfigured it, picked up their patients, and flew out as a hospital ship. It was a huge plane, and we just slid seats in and usually designated some areas for stretchers.

Sometimes we took short trips. If I was just flying between the Philippines and Japan, I might make that run a couple of times and then come back and pick up a group of patients. Usually we flew only one-way with patients, such as into the United States to Travis. I came more into Travis because it had a big military hospital and they could stage patients out of there. Usually another crew would pick patients up and distribute them throughout the country. We had limits on our flying time. The crews could fly only so many hours, and then they would have to have some down time.

The flying team consisted of three nurses and three med techs. We had doctors available to answer questions, but I believe it was primarily the nurses and med techs who made the decisions. We could use the radio over the Pacific to call a physician and say, "By the way, this is what

I have here." We always had a motto that nobody died on our flight. That was possible because the nurse who was responsible for selecting the patients that we were flying out was very careful to select people who were pretty stable. Even though we were careful, we could still have ninety patients with a maximum of ten of those patients who were trached on Bird respirators on the plane at a time. We could have only so many psychiatric patients because it was hard to know how they would respond to the plane and close quarters during the flight.

With three nurses and three med techs, we really moved. We had to be very aware of what was happening to our patients. Some patients had abdominal wounds. The wounds were never sutured but were open, because high altitude changed body cavity pressures and would have disrupted sutures. The Heimlich valve on chest tubes was developed during the Vietnam War in order to allow patients with chest tubes to fly without wreaking havoc with chest pressures. You couldn't have glass bottles or any other kind of bottle attached to the chest tube when you were flying. The Heimlich valve was a one way valve that allowed the air out of the chest with the change of air pressure at high altitude but didn't allow anything else to get sucked back in. As we flew, any air trapped in a cavity could cause a problem. That's why we couldn't have a lot of wounds that were sutured very tight. We packed a lot of neutracaine in the wounds for pain control.

When we checked blood pressures, we had to make sure our stethoscopes were really in our ears because we always had the sound of engines. Listening to breath sounds and making sure that lungs were really expanded or getting vital signs could be a little tricky. Those were the days before we had automatic reading machines and telemetry. We had to be able to hear or palpate it out. We learned these things in flight school. They taught us about the changes that go with altitude changes, the physiological things that take place in patients, and some of the issues that we had to look for and deal with. They taught us how to gather our information. We had a lot of practice listening with stethoscopes because we really didn't have heart monitors.

We did have the Bird respirators—the green machines—from the sixties. We basically set a peak inspiratory pressure on those, hooked the patient up, and hoped our patient was getting enough oxygen. We could blend it and we could humidify some. That was about it. Nothing like the sophisticated machines we have today. There was no such thing as a respiratory tech. Nurses did all the suctioning and made all the changes in the respirators. There were no blood gases. We had to use our assessment skills to decide if the patient was hypoxic and needed more oxygen. We really had to solve all of our own problems in the air. Many times the key to that was doing good assessment and making good selections on the ground.

Assessments on the ground could take several hours. One or two nurses would go out to do all of the assessments. They looked at the patients who were leaving and then went through and carefully checked the patients, gathered the data, and decided who would go. We did a basic assessment, checked out all the injuries, and classified them. We could say, "We've got so many of level-four patient," or level-three or whatever. These were the walking wounded. We divided them up as to how many we could take. "Okay, this is the group. Here's our list." We'd make a list of the patients we would be taking out on our flight, and then the ambulances would collect those patients and bring them out. Then we would load them on and place them where we wanted them. Once we got everybody in place we'd go.

The pilots were great, too. I know that in some of the other crews if they ran into real serious issues they would find a place to land. "We're close, only an hour out of ——." They may have had to divert to Japan and gone in when somebody really went bad on them and was in big trouble. "We'll find you calm air," or "This is what's coming up, so sit down for a while." It was like being a stewardess on the plane. We just laughed about that.

Usually, if you were out on the flight, you were busy. There was no "I'm going to sit down and rest for an hour; I have nothing to do." Between the six of us, we kept moving. We checked everybody, checked vital signs, changed dressings, and reinforced things on a continual basis. We were generally moving the whole flight until we got to point B and signed them off. Then we sat down and rested. Usually the flight nurse—the head nurse—would be the one who was responsible for signing the paper work. If all the patients were going to the same institution, she would check the patients and make the report. We kept brief notes of medications, dressing changes, and IVs. We usually didn't give blood in flight.

I loved the marines. The marine patients who had minor injuries and were ambulatory were always attentive to their marine buddies who needed help or who could possibly get a little out of hand. They would say, "We'll help them out," or "I think that he's really in a lot of pain, but he's not saying anything to you." This would allow one of the med techs to get to them.

We never had anybody die on our flights. I think the toughest flight of all was towards the end of 1970. We were flying a lot of burn patients, taking them to Travis and Brooks, which was a burn center. The burn patients were the hardest. Their burns were caused by napalm. At that time the treatment for burns was to basically just wrap the patient. Our patients were all wrapped up and sedated with morphine in hopes of getting them to the States without too much pain. Some of them were pretty badly burned, some over 50 percent of their body and on respirators. The ones who were super high risk and couldn't really handle the flight all the way back from the Philippines would be staged out from Vietnam. They'd come to the Philippines and then go to Kara, Japan, and then to Travis, and eventually to Brooks.

The burn patients smelled. They had debrided the burns some, but there was still a lot of debridement to do. I can still remember the smell of burned flesh. Five or six hours in the plane with a group of burn patients was hard. We were glad to get them to Travis and off the plane. We kept them sedated and they all had IVs so they weren't hurting. We tried to make them as comfortable as possible, but it was hard on a stretcher where they couldn't turn or move very well.

The med techs were wonderful. I don't think that any flight nurse would have been successful without them. If you had a good one, you knew the flight would go well. You could assign them and say, "Okay, this is your group." We usually broke the assignments down among the three nurses to oversee what the enlisted people were doing. If your medic was on top of things, he would come to you and say, "Such and such is going on. Let's do this and this." It was a wonderful blessing to have these kind of people working with you. If you were splitting ninety patients up among six people, it was important to have staff who were sharp.

There was a lot of drug use in east Asia, and there were a lot of soldiers who were into drug use. Some of them were on the verge of exploding just because of the psychological effects of the war and the pressures of returning home. I didn't have that experience, for which I am grateful. I prayed every trip that this hospital ship would get from point A to point B.

I was never in a situation where I was concerned for my life—no bad storms, mechanical problems, or anything of that type. Sometimes we were grounded because of issues on the ground or things that came up about the plane during the flight checks. In all my flying experience we never had problems with the aircraft. An airplane is really a flying box, so there were few amenities. We had oxygen and oxygen masks. It was kind of rough living because we sat strapped into jump seats. There were two restrooms on board for ninety people. The patients who flew on stretchers were all catheterized. It was just the easiest way to transport people. The guys were kind of used to a few bathrooms for lots of people, and the ladies were sort of outnumbered by the multitudes and just had to take our turn.

Our crews were always really nice to us. If we stayed over, they always made sure we had housing and that we could get around. I don't know if that is typical air force or not, but our flight crews always looked after the flight nurses. The nurses looked after the enlisted, so we really always traveled as a group. I never really had to worry when I was traveling with a crew. Most of them were just great people. They always looked out for the nurses because they really understood what kind of work the crews in the back were doing. I also learned that some days you have to wait a long time for things. Sometimes the weather would ground us, and we'd wait two or three hours before we could fly. If we ran out of flying time, we had to wait overnight. I learned to travel light. The pilots would always say, "Come on with us to the bar and have a beer." We would always answer, "Well, that is really nice. Could I have a Coke?" You could have all the beer you wanted to drink for free, but a soft drink cost a dollar. The crews who were not Mormon got a charge out of teasing us a lot about our not drinking, but they always looked out for us.

I met my husband while I was in the air force. He was in the air force stationed in California. He was a fighter pilot. He says, "My wife picked me up in Vietnam, and she took care of me all the way home. That's how I met her. She was a flight nurse." It is a wonderful story, but not likely. He had graduated from college and had to join the service, so he chose the air force. He was full time. He had gone through pilot training down in Texas and then transferred up to Hamilton Air Force Base in northern California. That was where my father had retired from the air force. My husband came to the same ward, and we met there. He was never injured. He actually ended up never going to Vietnam, though he did have orders. After we were married, he had orders, but it was important for the career of someone in the air force to go, so other people would keep stealing his orders. So after we were married, we were sent to Canada. That was really funny because people who didn't want to participate in the war went to Canada. But we were legitimately going to Canada, to Vancouver Island.

He was responsible for managing the nuclear weapons on Vancouver Island. That duty station was kind of "the eyes" watching Russia, thinking they might come down through Alaska. It was kind of the northern front. There were four young couples sent from Hamilton Air Force Base to Canada for a year after we were married. My husband had about a year and a half left before he was to get out of the service. After we were married and went to Canada, I didn't have a unit I could drill with. I went inactive hoping to find a unit to drill with in the future. It was too far to come down to McCord Air Force Base from up in Canada. I remained inactive and got out of the reserves in 1973. But I loved it. I wear wings that I honestly earned myself. I still have my uniforms at home, flight uniforms and regular uniforms. When we flew we wore nice long navy blue slacks, a light blue shirt with an overwaisted shirt, and a tie. We wore black lace-up shoes and our hat. We wore our names and our wings on our shirt. We dressed really quite nicely even though we were flying. We didn't wear our skirts or formal jackets, and we never wore cammies.

My military experience really did change my life. I found a husband. I had a real appreciation for good assessment skills because so many times we didn't have equipment. Your own skills and knowledge base got you through. I learned a great deal about teamwork and how to depend on other people. I learned how to divide the work up among people and get that work done. I have a real respect for people who provide medical care in the middle of nowhere to keep the patients stable enough to get back to the next point. The dedication of medical people, flight crews, and all of those folks interested in getting all those wounded people back was incredible. I really appreciated that. The politics of war are completely different. But I'll always remember people taking care of the patients and just getting the job done.

Nursing care in the air was a little scary at times, but we also gained a sense of confidence that we could do it. We improvised so many things and solved little problems. We could sit and help people through things. We talked to soldiers so they weren't terrified of flying. If their eyes were covered, their sensory perception would be off. Noises would frighten or startle them. We appreciated each day as it came because we didn't know if it would be our last. We learned to be thankful for everything that we had. If we got another day, that was a gift. I learned to deal with one day at a time and when that was over I would think, "Oh, that's great. I'll go on with the next day." I still do that. When things are stressful and there is a lot going on, I can go back to my military experience and say, "No, this is today. What needs to be done today? Okay, we have to get through this today." I even try to use that with my students at times. In the newborn ICU when things are real busy, I say, "Let's get through this one piece at a time. We'll deal with this issue now and then we'll move on to the next issue." I have always appreciated learning that. If I need to focus for the instant, I can focus and get it done, and then I can move on. I think that is one of the things I learned while I was flying for that short time—to be thankful for the moment.

I think I have a strong testimony, but the war situation certainly puts your faith into practice. I learned a new courage. Sometimes we were out with crews that were not Latter-day Saints, and they would make fun of us. When I was a twenty-two-year-old or twenty-three-year-old woman, it was hard— especially at a time in history when it was not a woman's world. I had to remember who I was and what my values were. I really appreciated having the opportunity to determine my values when those around me had very different ones. I gained a greater understanding of faith. We sometimes flew with some unstable patients, and we had faith to know that we would be sensitive enough to pick up early on what was going on and be able to intervene in a situation. I was always grateful when I got to our destination and got off the plane in one piece. I think that spiritually I was strengthened by patients who just had courage and hope. What were these young people who were missing an arm or a leg and returning to a sometimes unfriendly environment going to do with the rest of their lives? They had girlfriends and wives who they worried might not accept them. They thought that if I would sit and talk with them, maybe their wives and girlfriends would talk to them. We would talk with some of those patients who were actually terrified to get back home for fear that their families would reject them because of the seriousness of their wounds. They were great people. I thought that under those circumstances, you have to have the courage to really go on. The battle was not easy once they got home. They had surgeries and all kinds of things ahead of them. I learned a lot from other people that strengthened my spiritual side.

I had some really great patients who appreciated the little things that we did. We would bring them water or juice, or look at them and say, "You know, you look like you really are in pain. Can I get you something?" At the end of the flight, I was always grateful to those people who got off and said, "Thank you for helping us this far." They were so appreciative, even though they were the ones who were in such misery. Air force nursing was always rewarding. We may have been tired but generally left a flight feeling like we had done a good job. We got everybody to the destination so we could go home and sleep.

Now I am a professor at the Brigham Young University College of Nursing. What I've learned with my own students is to have patience and to believe that we can work through problems. I have learned to spend time listening to people tell their stories. I tell students that they need to get the data correct and look at the history. I explain to them that it is really hard to plan interventions or care if you don't know what is happening to the person. Those are probably the main things that I have brought over into teaching.

Phyllis C. Doxford

Phyllis C. Doxford

My mother had been sickly throughout her life, and I had seen her many times in the hospital and watched people care for her. My grandmother had had some hemorrhages of the stomach as I was growing up, so I watched that. I kept thinking, "You know, if I was a nurse I could take care of them." When I was younger, the books I read always dealt with either nursing or airline stewardesses, and I had a librarian that told me one day, "You know, you're going to go into one of those two fields." At that time a stewardess had to have a nursing background anyway. That was the criteria for being a stewardess. When you flew, you had to be able to take care of any emergency that happened in the air. That got me started, and then afterward, when my family had their illnesses, I decided that I wanted to do nursing.

I chose to go to a hospital school of nursing and not a university program because it was closer to home and didn't take as long. The university was four years; the hospital school was three. I would be able to do more hands-on nursing in the hospital school. I chose St. Mark's School of Nursing. And at that time I could live at home for the first two years. The last year I had to live down at St. Mark's on Third West between Seventh and Eighth North. Today it's on Thirty-ninth South between Tenth and Thirteenth East. The hospital was funded and run by the Episcopalian Church. We had to attend church services on a regular basis. We had our capping ceremony at the Episcopal Cathedral. Nurses don't even wear caps now. I don't know how many times over the years I hit my nursing cap and my hairdo would be askew, particularly when I was bending over to care for the patients in traction. The cap could be a pain at times.

When I first started out at St. Mark's Hospital as a student nurse, we had glass syringes. We would rotate into the central supply, and we had to check the needles for barbs and the gloves for pinholes. We had big jugs of distilled water and a gas stove, and we would boil all of our syringes and everything on the stove. Our morphine came in a tiny, narrow tube that was about a quarter of an inch in diameter with a corked top. We would pop the cork and drop the little morphine tablet into the syringe, draw up the sterile water, shake it to dissolve it, and then give the injection. We didn't have prepared medications for a long, long time. For all my student days, and for the first two years I started working as a registered nurse at St. Mark's hospital, we prepared our own medication. Gradually more packaged supplies were used. Then they stopped having student nurses check the gloves for holes because they had disposable ones.

After graduation in 1962, I worked in Salt Lake City at St. Mark's Hospital for four and a half years. At first I worked pediatrics. I took the older kids. I figured that if I took the older kids, they could tell me what was wrong. I was a beginning nurse then, and I had a lot of fears too.

I took care of a lot of cancer patients. I would see them for the initial therapy and then I would see them back for the chemotherapy. The only chemotherapy drug that we had in those days was 5-FU. Then I would see them for the radiation. They got to be my family. It was a terrible responsibility for a young graduate. They would beg me not to go on my days off. They'd say, "Nobody can take care of patients like you can," and "You can't go. You have to stay here and take care of us." That haunted me when I went home. And I would worry about them and wonder, "Is that person after me going to do their job as good as I was doing it?" I would take these patients through their final stages. The night nurse and I knew when our patients were going to die. I would work seven days and then have two days off, then work another seven and have four off. It was a long schedule. I would say to her if I was approaching my four days off, "Now don't worry about Mr. or Mrs. so and so. She or he is going to wait for me, and I'll be there with them when they go." That worked for me, and it worked for the night nurse because she'd tell me the same. She was LDS, as I was. I think the Lord knew that those people dying needed somebody that they knew. That's the way it went for three and a half years and I got really burned out.

At that time nobody knew what depression was and I just kept getting more and more depressed over the patients who were dying. I had a rose gallery of the dead, and if I was really tired, I'd see them all night long. I got to the point where I couldn't stand that. I didn't want to go anywhere. I just wanted to go home and stay there. I didn't want to go out with my friends. I didn't want to do anything. My mother said I was sitting in a rocker one day and she said, "What's the matter with you? You're so quiet these past days." I said, "I was just sitting here thinking that the good Lord could take me anytime. I'm ready to go." And she said, "What do you mean you're ready to go?" I can still hear her. "You're in your twenties. How can you be ready to go?" I said, "I am. I'm ready to go. He can take me with whatever disease He wants. I'm ready to go." My mother sat down with me, and she said, "You know, you have got to get out of that ward. You've got to do something different. I don't care what you do, but you've got to get away from those patients." And I said, "They're the only patients that I know, and I would come in contact with that if I worked any other floor in nursing." She said, "Well maybe you need to do something different. Maybe you need to go back to pediatrics." I said, "No, pediatrics is not my interest. I don't want to do that."

About that time I was receiving information from the air force. The Vietnam War was going on, and the military needed nurses. The air force was requesting nurses, and they asked if I would like to be a part of that. I quietly thought about it and the more I thought about it, the more I thought that it would be a nice place for me to go. I talked with Mom about it. My mother said, "I think that's a very good idea." And so I went, without telling my father, and took the oath of office to be a nurse in the air force.

My father and I had talked about the military. He was a sergeant in the army, and he would never take a higher rank. He said, "No, I've had enough of the service. I don't want to have anymore." So, anyway, he was very set on things concerning the service. I knew his thoughts on the service. He had once said to me, "Well, Phyllis, you'd never make it in the service because you have too much of a temper. You can't have a temper and go in the service." When my father heard I had joined the air force, he blew his cool. Later he calmed down.

It was a toss-up between the air force and the navy. I liked both of them. But I kept thinking, "I have claustrophobia." In the navy, if you ever had to get off of the hospital ship, your best chances probably would be in a submarine. I kept thinking, "They'd never get me in a submarine.

I'd never be able to do nursing in a submarine because I'd be too claustrophobic. They'd have to sedate me as one of the patients." I decided that I would go into the air force, so that's what I did. I was sent to Mountain Home Air Force Base in Mountain Home, Idaho. My dad finally calmed down. He finally accepted the fact that I was in the service. When we went through basic training in Texas, they had a big celebration for us when graduation came.

Mountain Home was out in the desert. There wasn't a lot to do. The town of Mountain Home had two sidewalks and that was it. It wasn't very big. We were ten miles outside of town, and we had desert all around us. It was a Strategic Air Command (SAC) base. Later it was changed to a tactical command.

I worked four and a half months there, and then they told me that I had orders for the Philippines. I said, "How can I have orders for the Philippines when I haven't been here long enough?" Usually you have to be in active duty for at least two years before you get any change of destination. There was a Filipino nurse at Mountain Home who had orders for England. She came to me one day and said, "Phyllis, I'd like to go home. Would you trade with me and go to England, and I'll go to the Pacific area because that's my home." I said, "Oh sure, I'll do my mother's genealogy there." We were English, Irish, Welsh, and Scottish, and I thought, "No problem, I'll go there." The Air Force said, "Absolutely not." So she went to the cold water fleet in England and I went to the PAC (Pacific Air Command) area, which is where I served the remainder of my time.

I was put on a surgical floor that took all the head injury cases. They would air-evac them out of Nam. They would do enough surgery on the injured in Vietnam to stabilize them and then ship them to us or to Japan. We were the two areas that took care of them if they had to do further reconstructive surgery. If they were not able to go back into active duty after that, they would be sent home. Otherwise they would go back to active duty. That was a sad thing.

I had patients that had leg wounds or arm wounds or different things like that. We would get them sutured and care for them until their sutures were out. As soon as they were able to use their arm or leg, they were sent back into the war zone. I don't know how many patients I had that begged me to intercede for them so that they didn't have to go back. I had to tell them that I didn't have any pull and that there was nothing that I could do. Even the doctors were under orders to send them back if they were capable of fighting another day. That was a sad time for me. I didn't ever see any come back; I'd see them once and that was it. That's not to say that they didn't come back to the hospital.

There was a ward opposite ours on the same floor that was a mirror image of ours. Everything was the same, except they took all the spinal injury cases and we took all of the burn patients. It didn't matter who was admitting that day, we took the head injury cases, and they took the spinal injury cases. The rest of the patients were alternated, depending on whose day it was for admissions.

Since the Koreans were our allies in the war, we also took care of them. We had flip charts to help us speak Korean, and we would speak to them in one syllable or in pantomime. If we wanted them to scrub a certain area, we would pantomime to them to do that. I think that they were probably like our men. If they got well, they were probably sent back out into the war zone. I remember that they were fun-loving. One day we'd had two of them come off the plane. They had head injuries, and one had a plate put in his head. The old hospital beds were really high, and you couldn't raise or lower them. One patient was hopping from his bed to his friend's bed next door, and there was a four-foot space between them. He gave me heart failure. They were having the time of their life, and two other patients were egging them on. I thought, "If you miss that spot and go down and hit your head, then where would we be?" I really chewed them out with facial expressions and hand signals.

They were put out, and they sat there, dumpy-like, looking like they were thinking, "Well, I know I'm in the wrong."

When I began nursing and when I got to the Philippines, they were still using silver nitrate on burn patients. It was messy. We would soak the bandages in it and then wrap the burns. I was taking care of three or four patients. I had a corpsman working with me, and he wasn't paying any attention. It was really hard at that time to get American clothes in my size, and I am five feet five and a half inches. I weighed 165 pounds at that time. I didn't fit into a size 4 shoe, and I didn't fit into a size 28 slip. There I was, dipping and rolling those bandages, and this corpsman wasn't watching what he was doing. He tipped the basin, and the silver nitrate poured right down the side of me. When light hits silver nitrate, it turns black. My shoes, my hose, my uniform, and my unmentionables all turned black. It doesn't come out. I was so mad at him.

Then a short while after that happened, we started using the Silvadene cream. It was all right except that you had to wipe it all off of the burns, and you had to put it on twice a day. Wiping it off was painful. If they had a third-degree burn, they wouldn't feel it, but if they had a second- or a first-degree burn, it was painful to have you wipe that off. They would beg us not to, and it made us feel terrible. By the time I finished my tour, we didn't have to wipe it off. We still had to put it on twice a day, but it was a lot easier on the burn patients.

They usually moved nurses around, but I stayed in surgery that entire time. Taking care of these soldiers wasn't quite as bad as taking care of the cancer patients. We would keep them long enough to get them stable so that they could either go back home or back to the war zone. I didn't become as attached to them as I had to the cancer patients. Yet we had good times with those patients too. I remember playing games, like checkers, that didn't take an awful long time. Those boys really needed that too. There were times when we didn't have as many casualties, and we had a little bit more time to do that.

While I was in the Philippines, we had some earthquakes. That was something. I had corpsman who had never been around earthquakes. They had been in tornadoes and hurricanes, but they had never been in earthquakes. We had been having small earthquakes all along. I kept telling the people who worked with me, "We're having small earthquakes." "Oh, no, no, no—it's the aircraft going over." They just kept pooh-poohing it. But one day I was suctioning a patient, and I was having a hard time getting the suction catheter out. I couldn't figure out why. I looked up and saw that the IV bottle was swinging. I knew then that we were probably having an earthquake. I let my hand drop, and the catheter came out.

The earthquakes went on and off for about a month. One night I was working the midnight shift, and there was one that measured seven on the Richter scale. It hit more in Manila than where we were. My corpsmen had never been in an earthquake, and they didn't know what to do. They were standing out in the corridor, and their eyes were as big as saucers. I said, "You have got to get yourselves into the doorway. Stand in the doorway. That's where you're going to be safe." So that's what they did. Then I remembered that we had a patient in a circle electric bed in the room opposite of me. The top piece wasn't even tucked into its cradle; it was just up against the wall. I realized it was going to start flying and hurt the men. I thought that if I could get in there and stand in the center of the room, I could deflect whatever was going to fly around. I was trying to inch myself in there. It wasn't working very well because the earth was rolling. I only inched my way part way into the room. But I know that the Lord blessed us. The beds rattled and shook but none of those pieces flew anywhere. The patients' beds in the other rooms would move forward and backward, almost touching each other, and then roll back. The circle electric beds never moved.

At the time we had glass IV bottles, and we stored them on high metal racks. We had to use a stool to put the bottles on the top shelf. We would send a corpsman down with a grocery cart, to get his supplies. The quake knocked some of the bottles down into the grocery cart, but not one broke. It rolled other bottles to the edge, but didn't knock them off. We had a big cylinder oxygen tank in the storage room with a file cabinet. It picked up the oxygen tank, tipped over the cabinet, and laid the oxygen tank over the cabinet instead of turning it into a missile or causing it to explode.

The quake made cracks along the baseboard. The corpsmen who ran out onto the lawn said the top half of the hospital was going in the opposite direction from the bottom. It looked like a zigzag. We had a one-thousand-pound air conditioning unit right above us. I kept waiting for all this equipment to come crashing down and kill us all, but it never did.

We had a nurse from Hawaii who disappeared during the earthquake. Later, after I checked everyone out and made sure they were okay, I said to several of the corpsmen, "Where is so-and-so?" "Well, I don't know." She had folded herself up into a corner under the nurse's station. She was so small and was so flat in there, we didn't even see her as we walked around. She came out after a while. She probably did it out of fear and figured that it was the safest place.

The telephone was something else, too. The telephone was set up through the radio operators. If we put in a long distance call to the States, we would get a United States operator. We would be talking along and then we would say "over," and then our parents, or whoever we were calling, would come on. They'd talk, and then they'd say "over." The operator would say, "Now, you realize that you are going through the radio operators, and you have to say 'over' so we make sure that we cut it to the other person." They would rotate it back and forth, so you never knew who else was listening on the telephone. That's what we went through when I first got to the Philippines. Gradually I just put through my own calls. My friend was a captain. She would pay a lot of her own money for some of the men to make telephone calls to their people, especially those that she knew were never going to get home. I really admired her for that. If there is a place for another angel she would be there.

The Vietnam War was an undeclared war. That is my biggest complaint against the government. Those men fought and bled and died there, and they were never recognized. The First World War and the Second World War were different from the Vietnam War. The Vietnamese had women and children that fought right along with the men. They had children who carried bombs and blew people up. They had young girls that claimed to need assistance. The soldiers would go to help them, and they would be blown up. Our men had to worry about pongee sticks, which were six-inch-long bamboo spikes that were guide-wired up into the trees. When the soldiers stepped on the wire, the pongee stick would come down and spear them. The Vietnamese would put feces on the pongee sticks, and our men would immediately get a serious infection. It was hot and humid, and bacteria would grow very quickly. Some of these men, especially the ones that got liver wounds from the pongee sticks, never really got better. There were many of them who died. They would get better, and then they would get worse, and then finally they would die. I didn't work with those patients that had liver wounds, but my friend did. She would tell me about the boys. Most of the time they didn't make it.

It was sad for the men who were in battle. I knew some of the men from our unit at Mountain Home. Two were killed in a battle at an apartment complex. War is a terrible thing. When you join, you have to go where they send you. We were involved in the Tet Offensive. We worked twelve-hour shifts for several months at a time. We would have a full complement of patients, and we knew we were going to get more from the air-evac system. We went in at midnight and started to triage patients to make room for the ones who were coming. We put them onto stretchers and laid them all out in the aisle on the first floor. We put flight tags on them with information about their injuries. As soon as possible, they were moved out to the United States or back to duty, if they were able to go back to duty. I can remember having to pass medications, and my patients were scattered all over the place. I had to go down with a flashlight to administer medications at two and five in the morning. I would be looking at flight tags, praying that it was the right patient with the right name. Doctors had scrawled names and moved patients in such a hurry that I was afraid I would make a mistake. We no sooner got those patients out than we got the beds scrubbed for the incoming patients.

If patients were well enough they would do their own beds, but we didn't have janitors. We worked right alongside the corpsmen. I learned that patients who were active got healthier a lot faster. I think that is why health-care providers decided to get patients up and walking the day after their surgery. I know that came from the service. We didn't have patients with deep vein thrombosis. They didn't have pneumonia. They were up and walking the floors. It was the same when I got home and went back to work at the VA Hospital. They would say, "I'm too sick," and I would say, "I'm sorry, but this is going to help you get well."

I think that my military experience made me more aware of how precious life is. It could be snuffed out at any moment. We treated what we had more lovingly. You figured the good Lord blessed this land. He put all the beauty in it and He put us here, and now it is up to us to take care of it. I never got over the fact of seeing Him. I see the Lord in so much. I see His handiwork in so much around me. I used to come out of the hospital in the Philippines when we had worked so hard and kept the patients alive through our shift, and I would pray that the good Lord would bless and guide them and that they would be able to make it back home, that they would live long enough to get home. I think when you are in situations like that, you see His hand in so many, many things. I saw His hand in saving patients that I didn't think were going to be saved.

There was a small Latter-day Saint group on base in the Philippines. I had been inactive at home before joining the air force. It had been hard to stay active because I worked shifts and weekends as a student and as a registered nurse. I couldn't get off to go to church. You don't say to sick patients, "I'm sorry, I've got to go to church." If you did that you wouldn't have a job. Besides, my conscience wouldn't have let me do that. I just got away from church. When I went in the military, I didn't attend either. I did attend the group on base a couple of times. They just had the sacrament. I still believed in the Lord and I still followed His teachings. I knew the Lord existed and heard my prayers; otherwise, a lot of people could have been hurt or killed during that earthquake. I knew the Lord guided and directed me. I think my military experience strengthened my testimony and helped me return to activity.

One reason I became inactive was that when I cared for the cancer patients, I saw a child with cancer come into the hospital. I used to pray that the Lord would take me instead of the child, but the Lord wasn't ready for me and He would take the child instead. Consequently, I was upset with the Lord and wanted to have no part of Him. But, you know, the Lord lets you have a lot of running room, and then He starts reeling you back in. I began to realize that I wasn't seeing the whole pie. When I finally started reasoning that way, when I came to that realization, I began to understand that the child didn't need all the time I did. He didn't need to spend all the time in the school of hard knocks that I did. All the child needed was that many years, and then he could return to Father in Heaven, where he didn't have to worry about all the stuff I had to worry about. So I came back to the Lord and realized I just didn't know all those things. It wasn't luck that brought me back. It was because the good Lord put me in a place to help me realize I needed to come back. I think all of my experiences have brought me to the Lord and kept me there. You see all kinds of things in nursing—good things, sad things, terrible things. However, you realize that it is part of life, and you grow by those things that make you the strongest and make you better able to know the Lord. The Lord didn't promise us a rose garden without thorns. I have had experiences where I know that He is real, that He is alive.

Jay Nielsen

When I graduated from high school in 1969, I decided I would volunteer for Vietnam. Two days after graduation, I volunteered for the army. I actually counted as being drafted, so, in October I was drafted into the army for two years. On October 8 the group I was drafted with met up in Salt Lake City and found out they would be sending us to Fort Lewis, Washington. I spent two months at Fort Lewis in basic training as a private E1. When you graduate from basic training, you go to specialist training. Out of seventy-five soldiers, two of us were picked to go to medic training.

In early December, I went to Fort Sam Houston in San Antonio where I spent three months being trained as a medic. When I finished my training, I was assigned to the hospital in Fort Leonard Wood, Missouri. Orders came down sending half of my training group to Vietnam. The post commander rejected the orders because we didn't have enough people working in the hospital as it was. We were getting Vietnam casualties and taking care of the veterans in Missouri. When they sent the second order, everyone that wasn't on the first order was on the second order to Vietnam. After joking and laughing and making fun of my friend who was on the first order, I was on the second order. The first order got to stay home, and everyone on the second order was going to Vietnam. They promised me that I would be assigned to the hospital in DaNang and that we didn't have to worry.

I came home for a month and on January 4, 1971, I left to go to Oakland, California. From Oakland, I was shipped to Vietnam. After arriving in Vietnam, I was assigned not to a hospital but to the First Cavalry Division, the First and Twelfth Division Infantry. I would be going into the jungle and riding in helicopters and shooting at people. I ended up just going around in helicopters and being dropped off in the jungle.

We received our first assignment on February 15. Six helicopters placed twenty-seven men ten to twelve miles deep into the jungle. They told us they would be back to pick us up in about twenty days. The stated mission was to find the enemy and kill them. On the way to the destination, the helicopter was shot at by an AK-47. It made an odd sound. I asked what it was and was told it was an AK-47. That was what the bad guys shot. We hiked around in the jungle and looked for the bad guys. It was in the Tainen Province in the highlands of Vietnam. It is very dense, beautiful jungle. We burnt down a village. I thought that was kind of a waste of a beautiful village.

We had a couple of incidents of shooting people, nothing major, but the experience, as far as being a Latter-day Saint in Vietnam, struck home. On March 3, we started hiking along this trail. It was late in the morning and we came to a fork in the trail that was fairly heavily used. As the medic, I would always walk about fifth in line, after the point man, the lieutenant, the man with machine gun, and the man with the radio. I always wanted to be close to the men so that if someone was shot, I could see what was happening. Suddenly there was all this screaming and gunshots. The sound of screaming and M-16s just exploded. I never heard such noise and hollering in my life.

What had happened was that our point man had walked around a curve in the trail, and coming up the other side of the trail was the enemy. So the point man knelt down and shot the bad guy right in the chest. The screaming came from the guy that was hit. He was Viet Cong. We secured the area and went up to the body. My really good friend was there. There was four of us there looking at the body. The dead man had a hole right in the middle of his chest, and when we turned him over we saw he had quite a large hole in his back. He was lying there, and my friend from New York was going to do some things with the body that I didn't think should be done. He got his knife out and was going to cut some things off, ears and things. I was really new in the platoon, but I asked him not to do it. I just really didn't think that was appropriate. So he didn't do it. He did take a big stake and put our patch on it and put the stake right in the hole in his chest. That didn't bother me. He already had the hole in his chest.

The rest of the day was pretty quiet. We saw another Viet Cong and we shot, but we missed. There were a few shots at us from a distance. We heard an AK-47. I was barely twenty years old when this happened, and it really bothered me, all the screaming and the blood and the gore. I thought, "This isn't what I pictured this to be like." This was something that was going to be very difficult for me. I had never shot a gun before I went to Vietnam. I had never killed anything. I don't even believe in deer hunting, so it was really hard for me. I just couldn't get this thing out of my mind. It was really hard for me.

The helicopter came the next day to pick us up and take us back to the fire base. It was the twentieth day. I remember distinctly riding the helicopter back when all the emotion hit me. I was turned away from everybody, but I remember that I had big tears streaming down my face. I thought, "Jay, this is not what you thought it was going to be." I was really having a hard time with the killing and the other stuff that was going with it. We landed on the fire base. The tears had stopped, but I thought, "I have ten months of this, and I just don't know how this is going to go." As I was walking toward the bunker, this man stopped me. He said, "Are you Jay Nielsen?" He said, "My name is Joe Hansen, and I am from Logan, Utah. Jay, I would really like to have a sacrament meeting tonight. I have another person from Utah. Why don't you come to my bunker tonight." It was Sunday.

I showed up. We had this stale bread and some water, and we had the sacrament meeting, and basically the sacrament meeting was exactly what I needed to make it. There was only us three at this meeting. There was no moon; it was pitch black. The best way that I can describe it is to say that there was a presence in that bunker that I cannot deny. There were more than the three of us in that bunker. There was a feeling that I have even to this day. So, as far as a member of the Church in Vietnam, that was a very powerful meeting and it was just what I needed. I was really happy that Joe did that for me. I think he was inspired to look me up and have me come to the meeting.

As far as the rest of my tour in Vietnam, it went similar to that. We would get dropped off, and we would look for the bad people. Sometimes we would shoot at them. Sometimes we would hear an AK-47. For the next few months, it was just kind of like that.

On the 22nd, my two best friends in Vietnam were killed. They were Jerry Davis and Ken Austin. They were really dear friends to me. We were all about the same age. Ken and I were the youngest in the platoon, and Ken was a month younger than me. The thing that struck me with Ken Austin was that he was supposed to be going home in three months. He got engaged to his girlfriend. Her name was Roxanne, and she was from Washington. He was going to get married the first week he got home. They even had the wedding date. I saw Roxanne in her wedding dress. That was sad. It was the wedding dress she never got to wear for my friend.

Jerry Davis was from Michigan, and he had a twin sister. I saw a picture of his twin, and she looked like Jerry. Sometimes I think how incredibly difficult that must have been for his twin. Sometimes I think that she probably knew before. They were very close. I thought that was very sad.

The next month was one that I would never forget a moment of for the rest of my life. It started on August 27, and it ended about fourteen days later. That was a bad time for me and our platoon. We were in a very active area. There was a lot of the North Vietnamese army in this area. Again it was the Tainen area. There was a lot of war things going on, a lot of action, a lot of hit and miss type things. On August 27 we were walking down a trail and up a hill to set our night position. All of a sudden, the jungle opened up with noise. I have never heard so much noise and shooting and screaming. It was like the entire jungle just exploded. We were walking up the one mountain and on the other mountain directly across from us there were about six North Vietnamese army regulars. Another of our platoons was walking up that mountain, but we didn't know they were there. When the Vietnamese started shooting at them, we started shooting at them also. Nobody knew who was shooting at who. There were bullets everywhere. I started hearing a call for "medic" from the other mountain. I ran down our mountain about fifty yards and then up the other mountain because I was hearing this call for "medic." I came to some people I was able to help a little. I bandaged up some shrapnel. With the help of the radio, we realized we were shooting at each other. We all should have been shooting at the bad guys. The bad guys had shot probably three to four hundred rounds and thrown about twenty grenades between us and the people that were climbing up their hill. Our platoon didn't have any wounded, but the other platoon had about five wounded that we were able to medevac.

The next morning they said we would be climbing up the mountain again. We combined platoons and as two platoons, we would climb up the mountain. There was supposed to be a big complex on the top of the mountain. When we got to the top, it was a beautiful village that could probably have fit about a thousand people. It had hutches and a school. So we went in and were kind of sitting there thinking "this is okay." We were setting out our perimeters. Again the entire jungle had just exploded. What had happened was that these six soldiers had climbed up and got on our outskirts and started shooting. They shot about 375 rounds, and they shot about five grenades into the complex. They hit about seven of our soldiers. Our machine gunner had shrapnel all up and down his back. I was able to take care of him.

Our lieutenant basically had half of his face shot off. While the shooting was going on, I was actually able to reach him. I pulled him out from where he was. He had a really small shrapnel or bullet hole in his right chest area. I took care of another soldiers and then came back to the lieutenant, and he was just awful. He was in deep shock. He was obviously dying in front of me. I had never had an experience that serious before. The enemy guy was dead when I got there, and I had seen dead soldiers, but none dying in front of me quite like that. The machine gunner was going into shock, but I was able to raise his feet and got him comfortable. He was okay. That wasn't going to kill him. The guy was hit in the arm. I just put a dressing on it and he was fine. The lieutenant was something else. I realized something was really wrong. I knew that his face could not be causing this. I thought something was real goofy. I rolled him over to see what else was wrong. Beneath him was an enormous amount of blood that had come out of his back. I realized I had to get the blood to his brain.

I elevated his legs to get some blood to his head, put a dressing on his chest, and stopped the bleeding. We called for a medevac helicopter as soon as we started getting shot at. He was there probably for about ten or fifteen minutes. The helicopter came and we got him evacuated, and he got to the hospital and he actually lived. He had lost his jaw; it had just been shattered. He had taken the shrapnel right in his face. I'm sure he had a lot of work done on just that. I was happy that he was saved. I have never seen him since. The funny part is that we hated each other and he never did thank me. He doesn't even know what happened because he was in shock. He doesn't know what I did or what I had to do. It was really quite an interesting medical move that I did. If I elevated his legs, then his jaw was gonna bleed more, but if I didn't elevate his legs, then he wasn't going to get any blood to his brain. If I elevated his legs, his chest wound would bleed more. Finally, I got some packs, and I laid him on his side so his chest was up in the air, and I put him on the hill with his head facing downward, and I was able to get his legs up. The color came back to him a little, enough that it worked. That is what saved him. If I couldn't have got his legs up he would have died. He was about 80 percent gone when I got to him.

From this point, we secured the area and went to a night perimeter. The next day they had another platoon go into this area. They wanted to blow up this complex, but another platoon went up there, and the same thing happened. Their sergeant was shot in the head. It killed him instantly. They had two other people who were wounded very severely. They got those guys out of there.

The colonel was so mad at us. He wanted eight people to go up there the next day and blow up that place, and it was coming from our platoon. We had to get eight volunteers to go in there, so you can imagine how it was to volunteer for that. The next morning I volunteered as one of the eight. Eight of us went up that mountain again and into the complex. I was so mad at those North Vietnamese by this time; I was hoping they would show up. We went up and secured the area. If they would have come up, it would have been just fine; we were all so angry. So we got all the stuff placed, and we blew up the complex. We blew it up very nicely.

Three days later, we set up a perimeter. That morning we sent out a patrol, and I went with the patrol. We were walking into this area, up into this complex, another liveable place for the North Vietnamese, and these six soldiers walked right into where we were. We took cover in the rocks and killed two of them instantly. The third guy we shot up so bad that he left a blood trail, so we figured we killed three of the six. The man that we killed was the sergeant major of these six. He was married and had three children. I saw a picture of his wife in a photo in his wallet. She was beautiful. I felt bad for his wife and those three children. It's the war thing. He was not just a number to me; he became a person. That was kind of sad. He was just like the rest of us. He was there trying to do a job, like the rest of us. Now his wife wouldn't be seeing him again. We secured the area about an hour later. A Viet Cong walked right into our complex, and he was shot and killed. He had all this medical stuff on him. We suspected he was a doctor coming to meet the other six.

Then the scariest moment of my life happened. We were in a rock complex. I didn't want to get into the rocks, so I was behind a tree and was the forward most person. I was about twenty yards in front of anybody, me and John Uloa. We were on the bottom of a hill. John kept whistling and we kept getting an answer from the other side of the hill, so we knew there were bad guys on the other side of the hill. That was about as scary as anything I had ever seen in my life. We thought they would come over the hill and try to kill us. That was what I was preparing for. I was actually preparing to die because I knew there were only eight of us. John kept whistling and I kept telling him to shut up because he was making me so scared. I was behind a tree and the next thing I knew, there was the biggest explosion I have ever seen in my life. The only thing that was standing was my tree. All the limbs were off. All the leaves were off. I was behind it and that was all that was left. Our lieutenant had called in a Cobra gun ship. They popped a flare, and he shot at the flare, and it was right in front of my tree. He lobbed about three or four missiles right in front of my tree. We knew that basically we were kind of surrounded. The Cobras hovered over our head the entire way back to our platoon. There were obviously bad people there who wanted to do us bodily harm, but the Cobras got us back.

Two weeks later, on this major trail, we were setting a night ambush. There were four of us who left our night patrol and walked about one hundred yards to set up a night ambush. We were just going to set up grenades with the trip wires. There was a fork in the road. As those guys were setting up the ambush, I went up about twenty yards from them. I was looking down the one road, and I heard a sound directly behind me. I looked and it was a bad guy. I hit the dirt and I couldn't have crawled any faster. I was on the trail and there were all these other guys behind him. I thought, "If I start shooting, all his guys are going to come up and there are only four of us and they are going to kill us." I sat there for about ten minutes, and then I got up and left, and then he jumped up and went off the other way.

A similar thing happened about a week after this. About ten of us had seen a soldier and shot at him. Later we saw another soldier, and we shot at him. We decided to do a night ambush and we walked down this trail and I was the last person in line. I was walking and I heard a click in the jungle itself. It was a Viet Cong who had taken his AK-47 off safety. It makes a click and I had heard it and I thought, "I'm a dead man. That's it." I think he was waiting to see what I was going to do. He didn't do anything and I certainly wasn't going to do anything and we walked by. And that was about the end of my tour.

On October 2, they got me out of the jungle and sent me home. They had forgotten about me in the jungle. They were suppose to get me out a month before. If they hadn't forgotten me I could have avoided a lot of this. I knew when I was suppose to leave.

I didn't struggle when I got home. When I left to go to Vietnam, I kind of had a feeling that I wouldn't be coming home. I kind of had an idea that I would be killed there. You have guilt feelings because you came home and they stayed. I was so close to my platoon. I really tried to take care of them. That is why I went on every patrol and ambush. I became so attached to them, and if something would have happened to them I just kind of wanted to be there. So I felt kind of guilty coming home. I came home and was a meter reader for nine months, and then I came to the VA to work. I was not particularly active in the Church before I went to Vietnam. The profound effect of that sacrament meeting in Vietnam is the basis of my entire testimony. I have experienced something that I can't deny. I think the presence made me feel that I wasn't alone. I never had the feeling that I couldn't be killed. It was just the feeling that I wasn't alone. The whole time I was there I really had that presence. For all the bad things that were happening, there was a little bit of sanity. It was very comforting. There were a few times that I thought, "this is it." When I was behind that tree, I was sure that I would not leave that tree alive. I was positive that the bad guys were going to come over that hill and kill us. We had killed their friends, and they were going to be mad at us. I was happily surprised that I made it home alive. I was guilty and sad that I was leaving, but I was very happy to be leaving all in one piece. I handled the horror of my time in the service because I was twenty years old and had nothing to lose.

When the shooting started, I never got in a hole. I was never officially wounded, but when I ran up that hill where the two sides were shooting at each other, I had a boot full of blood, totally full of blood. I don't know what happened. It didn't make any sense because I had no wound. I still don't know what happened. I took off the boot and actually poured the blood out, just like pouring out a canteen, and there was no wound.

One night was really scary. I was in my tent, and all of a sudden there were bullets everywhere. I got on the ground and crawled up to where the shooting was. That's just the way it was. I figured if I got killed, nobody was at home that was going to worry about it anyway. I wanted to be a good soldier. When things happened, I kind of went to where it was happening. They kind of joked with me that as a medic I did more shooting than anyone else. When there was shooting, I was there to take care of them, but I kind of wanted to kill somebody. That was something I had to resolve when I got home. I was there, and I did what I was supposed to do. For that I felt like I was a success.

I got involved in the Church as soon as I got home. It was really a good feeling to come home and go to church.

A lot of stories told by people are just stories; they're make-believe. I could sit here and tell you a lot of things, but these kind of verify that what I am telling you is true. I could have played college basketball. I had scholarships from Portland. To play college basketball would have been a great opportunity, but I would not have turned down my year in Vietnam for anything. I am so thankful that I was able to go; I really am. What an experience! The Church helped.

I was my mother's baby, and she said she watched the news every night to see if she could see me. I wrote my brother and told him to tell my mother that I was working in a hospital and that I was fine and that nothing could happen. She never believed it. I sent her this picture showing her where I was in BenHua where I was based out of. On the back of the paper it said, "Seven soldiers killed in ambush." That was on the back of the paper I sent her. She said she cried herself to sleep most nights.

Jay won an Air Medal from the First Cavalry Action for flying more than sixty air missions. Jay also won the Bronze Star for saving the lieutenant's life in the firefight. He also told me that what meant more to him than the medal was the wonderful letter his lieutenant wrote about him when he nominated him for the Bronze Star. On a personal note, I have known Jay for thirty years. When I first met him, he was working as a nurse's aid at the VA Hospital in Salt Lake City. I was a young nurse and I had no knowledge or appreciation for what Jay had been through prior to coming to work at the VA. As far as I knew he was just a nurse's aid. We've both grown up. Jay has grown into a mature man who makes wise decisions, who has married a wonderful woman and raised five fine children, one of which, his son, is currently on a mission in Australia. I am proud to know Jay and am grateful that we are friends.—Patricia Rushton

VaLaine Pack

I always wanted to go into nursing. There was no specific point or incident that happened or anything of that sort. My grandmother on my mother's side was a lay midwife, and I used to be fascinated with the stories my mother would tell about her experiences, driving her surrey to different places in Idaho when we lived up there. And Mother always wanted to be a nurse, but she didn't have the opportunity when she was younger. My mother graduated at the age of fifty-five from the LPN program and worked until she was seventy-three, when she had her first stroke. She and I were both in school at the same time. When the navy sent me back to school in 1959, she was working full-time at the old Salt Lake County General Hospital.

When I decided to go into nursing, I decided to go to University of Utah. I started as a freshman in 1954. I failed chemistry, went to Oregon State College that next summer and took nine months of chemistry in eight weeks, passed it, and came back. I got a D in anatomy. That made me mad because it threw my grade point average down. So I decided to go back to campus and get my general education done and then

VaLaine Pack

concentrate on the nursing stuff. In the meantime my health started to deteriorate because I was working thirty hours a week and going to school full time. I heard about the navy's program where they would select an unenlisted woman and send her to school if she could meet the requirements. I belonged at that time to the Navy Medical Reserve Unit Fort Douglas.

My whole goal was to be qualified for the NENEP. This was the Navy Enlisted Nursing Education Program. It was begun in 1955. If an enlisted woman could qualify and get through the application process, the navy would send her to a four-year school of nursing. It was only for women because at that time the navy didn't accept male nurses. The NENEP Program accepted men in 1965. The army was first, then the air force, and then the navy. The guys had a hard time the first couple of years. There were a lot of the old lieutenant commanders that just didn't like this idea, and they gave them a hard time.

I was one of three women selected for the program. I came back to the University of Utah as a sophomore in 1959. I graduated in 1962 and got my commission. Then I went through Officer Indoctrination in Newport, Rhode Island. Philadelphia Naval Hospital was my first assignment. The Korean War was over. Vietnam was getting started, but it didn't have any prominence yet. This was 1964. We were sending people there; we just didn't know it yet. There were two hospital ships: the *Sanctuary* and the *Repose*.

My first assignment was to work the orthopedic wards for six weeks—3A and 3B. The chief nurse wanted to do an experiment with me. They were just organizing the intensive care unit on 3C as a recovery room intensive care unit. It was the first intensive care unit at Philly. They were getting it organized, and they didn't have any junior officers there at all. They started with lieutenants and went up. The chief nurse decided she wanted to put me there since I'd been in the navy for five years.

When I was in the intensive care unit, we were using the old "green bird" respirator. We didn't have the fancy chest suction units that they have nowadays. We used the bottles. If we had two or three chest patients on them at one time, all of us nurses and corpsmen got to the point where we could tell which "blub blub" belonged to which patient. Everything was in the bottles. Blood products were in bottles. We were just starting to use disposable needles and disposable syringes. We had been using glass ones up until that time. We had to mix the medications. Codeine and morphine came in tiny pills that we put into the little glass tube. It was terrible if we dropped one of those glass tubes on the floor and it broke all over the place. We would carefully put the tube out on a sterile surface and then remove the glass plunger from the glass syringe, which we had already filled with saline, and add the pill. We shook the medication until it dissolved and then administered it. We learned that in nursing school. The saline was sterile. It came in 20-cc vials. It was supplied by Abbott Laboratories.

The main difference between then and now was that we just didn't have all the technology that we have now. We didn't have monitors or oxygen on the wall; it was all in tanks. (Actually, we had oxygen on the wall there because they'd redone the unit that we used, 3C.) It was an open ward, which was handy. I kind of liked that better than the private rooms because you could see everything that was going on. If somebody crashed or something, you could be right there.

I was in Philadelphia two years and then I went to Taiwan. I arrived there in an air-evac plane on New Year's Eve in 1964. My head nurse in recovery room in Philadelphia was my chief nurse in Taiwan. The recovery room and intensive care were combined when I was in Philadelphia. We had about twenty-four beds. Eight were recovery beds, so we had a lot of intensive care patients.

I was in Taiwan for fifteen months. We were general duty nurses there. I worked on the dependents unit. At night, we had one nurse for the whole hospital. We only had a fifty-bed hospital.

I worked both the military and the dependents' ward. The place was staffed with corpsmen and on the women's ward we had local Chinese women that spoke English. They were Chinese nurses who had midwife experience. That was part of the basic program in the Taiwanese nursing schools. They worked for me because I was the only one interested in labor and delivery. I was still young enough that it didn't scare the you-know-what out of me. But on the unit, there were a couple of nurses who would panic when they had to help a woman deliver a baby, even a normal delivery. Of course the doctors were there to help. Some of them hadn't done a delivery either. I trusted the Chinese nurses completely, and they knew it.

At the end of fifteen months, I left Taiwan and went to Great Lakes, Illinois. I started out as a staff nurse. I met the OR supervisor, and she said, "We need OR nurses." So I said, "Well, I can't do a thing about it." She beat tracks to the chief nurse's office. The next week I was down in the OR.

I took over the OR tech school. I ran the school and worked as a staff nurse too. There was a corps school even then. There was a specialty for OR. We needed OR techs in Vietnam. Most of my students went to Nam. The commanding officer called me into his office one day. His name was Alt Britton. He asked if I could change my lesson plans and create an on-the-job training program. I said, "Give me a week, but I do want the privilege of being the one to select the students. Then if I screw up, I've got nobody to blame but myself. I don't want somebody shoving off somebody on me that they don't want around anymore." He said, "You've got free hand."

The corpsmen from the on-the-job training went to Vietnam just as rapidly as the ones that had gone to the school. I was in Great Lakes from May 1966 to the middle of May 1968. It was a two-year tour. Then I got orders to Vietnam. My supervisor called me out of my room and said, "You're wanted in the chief nurse's office." Captain Dirk was the chief nurse at the time. She said, "You've got orders to Vietnam." I came out of that chair and whooped it up, and she looked at me as though I was crazy. She said, "Can I take it from that that you're glad about these orders." I said yes.

I wanted to go to Vietnam out of curiosity and for the adventure. All of us that were there at the time, twenty-nine women and five men, were volunteers in Vietnam. There was one nurse who was given the option of refusing orders, but she said, "No, I'll go." The rest of us asked for it and put it on our preference card in great big red letters. During World War II when I was young, I was fascinated whenever I'd see a woman in uniform. I'm sure that subconsciously, that had something to do with me joining the navy.

In Vietnam I was sent to Da Nang. We had an eight hundred bed land-based hospital there. They called us a dispensary. We used to laugh and say it was the biggest dispensary in the world. We were separate from the other military. The air force had a small unit, but they participated mostly in the air-evac process. The 95th Army Hospital was about a mile and a half down the road from us. Our quarters were air-conditioned Quonset huts. Their quarters were barracks right on the beach. They got a nice breeze off the beach. They wore their fatigues. The drip-dry uniforms were ideal for Nam.

I ran the operating room in Da Nang. Jeannie Higgins was our supervisor. There were only five of us in the OR: two of us on days, one on afternoons, one on nights, and one got a day off. There were eight operating rooms that we could use. We didn't have all of them open at the same time very often, but when we had a sweep going on and a lot of casualties coming in, we did. The corpsmen did the majority of the work. If somebody came in with just one wound, depending on where it was, we didn't pay much attention to him because most of the casualties came in with multiple wounds. The first patient I took care of that came in by helicopter had his arm blown off, his eyeball was hanging down on his cheek, and both his legs were blown off. And he had zits all over in his belly. A zit was where a piece of shrapnel had taken out a chunk of skin. We had to open him up and make sure there wasn't any problem there. A lot of what we did was gross and terrible.

There were some funny things that happened too. On New Year's Eve, two of the corpsmen got drunker than skunks. I was on night duty and I went up to ICU to see if there was anything they needed help with. One of my friends was taking a break, so I went and sat by her and we talked a little bit. We heard a ruckus coming down the sidewalk—somebody singing "Auld Lang Syne." Here came two corpsmen, one tall and dressed like Father Time, with a sheet draped around him, a cardboard staff, and his combat boots. The other guy was potbellied and shorter, wearing a sheet like a diaper and his combat boots. He was the New Year's Baby. He had his combat boots. We laughed and laughed. They went through all the wards waking the patients up singing "Auld Lang Syne." We didn't stop them.

We had four medical wards, four surgical wards, one POW ward, a urology ward, and an ENT ward. The POW ward was for MVA and Vietcong that we captured. I worked there too. We had twenty-two beds on that ward, and they were always full. When they were well enough, we sent them to POW camps. There were camps in Da Nang and then there was a big camp down around Chu Lai.

One of my favorite POWs was a ten-year-old Vietcong. The marines captured him and an older boy and brought them in one night while I was doing the OR. They smelled to high heaven! I think they found them in a manure pile or something. They were not going to enter my operating room like that. In our pre-op area we had a garden hose that we used to hose them off with after we had scrubbed them down with betadine. The Vietcong didn't speak any English. We did surgery on them and took care of their zits. Some of them required sewing up. Mostly we just scrubbed their wounds to get the dirt and everything out so they didn't get infected. We made sure there weren't any internal injuries or anything and sent them up to the ward. We sent the oldest kid out to the POW camp within three or four days because he was really hard core. We were a little bit nervous about keeping him there at the hospital. But we just spoiled the stuffing out of the ten-year-old; he was real cute. I was on the 3:00 to 11:00 shift on four medical wards and the POW ward for two months. One evening I was making rounds and he met me at the door. We had marine guards with their M-16s and sidearms and everything, and they would open the door for me to go into the unit. He was standing there. The corpsmen had taken a paper pajama top and made it up, colored it with marking pens to make it look like a waiter's jacket, and draped one of those green towels across his arm. He handed me an iced Kool-Aid and said, "May I help you?"

He didn't speak English when he came, but he did when he left. The kids taught him. He went to POW camp as well. We don't know what happened to him. That's the sad part. Of course, that was thirty-five years ago.

We had an MVA sergeant who was quite an artist. We went through special services and got him a bunch of paints. He painted murals on all the walls in the unit just to keep busy. He spoke five languages, including Vietnamese, French, and Russian. We taught him English.

Another special patient I had while I was working on the medical wards was an African-American youngster from Detroit. And you know, I made rounds at all hours until 11:30 p.m., and he didn't like me going out in the dark. He said, "You go out to the dark to make rounds, I'm comin' with ya." He was recovering from malaria on the malaria ward. He would make rounds with me. He was my protector. One day when I went on duty they were taking a guy off of the ward out to the ship. He was in a straitjacket and just acting crazier than the devil. They had a psychiatric unit on the ship. They flew him out there and after I took the report from the day nurse, this kid came in and said, "Can I talk to you?" I said, "Sure. Come with me while I make my first rounds." He said, "You know that guy that we saw going out of the ward? He's not crazy. He was high on drugs. There's a drug ring right here on the compound." I said, "Now wait a minute before you tell me anymore. I'm obliged by my commission to pass it on." He said, "I think you should."

So he told me the whole story. I beat tracks right down to that front office. The Medical Service Corps Officer that I'd talked with was named Walt Godfrey. He said, "You know, how can we trust this guy?" I said, "Well, how can I not? Can we afford not to trust him—not to take heed? The problem is now that he's told what's going on, his life is in danger. They're going to kill him."

We got him out of there and sent him back to the States real quick. We broke up the drug ring for a while at least. I was escorted to and from work for about three weeks, to make sure they were gone.

The Vietcong were very close. We had sniper fire coming in all the time. We think they deliberately missed us and were just trying to harass us, because we did take care of some of their people. Our barber was picked up one day. It was discovered that he was Vietcong. We used to hire local Vietnamese to fill sand bags and put the sand bags around everywhere. One of the bag ladies was filling and placing the sand bags. They brought a POW down to x-ray, and it was her cousin, so we got rid of her. So we never knew. We didn't pick anything up off the ground unless you put it there yourself because it could be an explosive of some sort. One of their favorite tricks was to take a soda pop can and cut the bottom out of it. Then they'd pull the pin off a grenade, stuff it in there, and set it down. When someone picked it up, the grenade would fall out and go off. That was one of their favorite tricks. We didn't throw away any of our batteries, portable radios, flashlights, or anything like that in the garbage because they would get them. They'd still have enough juice in them to use for a booby trap. They would rig pencils, so we got kind of paranoid after a while. So I called it my "year of contradictions." We were in a war zone, and our lives were in danger. If I really thought about it, I could drive myself crazy. We'd go up to a place just east of us called Monkey Mountain, which was a communication center for the air force. The view from the mountain top of Da Nang Beach looked like the Riviera. It was gorgeous. We went sailing on Da Nang Bay.

There were Quonset huts on the doctors' quarters. The doctors had built a deck on top, and they would go up there and have cocktails, and the nurses would go join them. But they were perfect targets for somebody to shoot at. One night an anesthesiologist was up there. It was close to midnight, and he was the last one up there. They started shooting rockets over us to try to hit the air base across the road. One of those rockets went awry and came right at him. It didn't hit him, but he dove off of the Quonset hut platform and went head first in the sand! He said, "I didn't care. I didn't want to be blown up by a rocket." We teased him about that all the time.

The watch room was close to the OR office. It had a set of those gray bunk beds. This anesthesiologist had a nice little pot belly. One night when I was on duty, mortar started landing on our helicopter pad, and he dove under the bottom bed to take cover. We went where we could to take cover. I went under the desk. After the attack was over and the all clear sounded, I heard this "Val? Oh Val?" I answered, "What?" The voice said, "I can't get out!" I called my corpsmen's watch room up by the OR and said, "Can you come down and help me get Dr. Aviado out from under his bed?" They had to lift the bed up completely to get him out. That was funny.

One night there was an ammunition dump down by the army hospital that went up in flames, and stuff was going off all over the place. It was like the Fourth of July. One of the guys that administered anesthesia was a dentist, but he'd had a year of anesthesia. We went up on top of the MUST unit, one of those mobile units like the army used in Korea. Everything was portable. You could do surgery in there. I can't remember what MUST stands for, something about trauma. But anyway, it was all steel, so we went up on top of it. I said to Jim, "You know what? We're going to get our butts shot off. We're silhouetted against the fireworks." He scrambled down as fast as he could go, and I was right behind him.

One night I was on duty from 3:00 to 11:00 p.m., and we had just finished some cases in the OR and were cleaning up, and I was doing my paperwork. I heard what sounded like a tank driving up to the triage area. I thought, what in the world is going on? I went down to the triage area and there was a big armored personnel carrier. They had been coming down the road from behind Marble Mountain. The guys who were going in front of it to check the road for mines had stepped on one, and five of them got injured. So the personnel carrier driver and a couple of the other people who didn't get hurt loaded them all in the personnel carrier. They didn't even call for airlift. We were so well-organized. We had those five guys triaged, through x-ray (we did total body x-rays), through pre-op with their IVs started, their NG tubes down, and their foleys in and so forth and into the OR in fifteen minutes. And that's how slick we were organized. The litter bearers carried the litters; that is all they did. One of them was assigned to cut the clothes off. Another was assigned to put the ID tags on. Another one was assigned to take the valuables and put them in a safe—and everybody did their job. Everybody knew what their job was. As soon as I went down and saw what it was, I had my crew out to start setting up the rooms.

I went through the whole year there without any injury. The last week there, I was really paranoid for fear something was going to happen. A lot of people got killed the last day they were there or something like that. So I got over to the air base, and my flight didn't come in until 10:00 p.m., which was really a no-no because they didn't like them to come in after dark. We would always get attacked after dark. This flight was late coming in, so I went out and got on it. One of the general medical officers was flying back on the same flight with me. I looked out the window and some of my friends had come down and see me off. They were standing at the edge the tarmac, where there was a fence. I asked the stewardess, "Do I have time to go say goodbye to my friends?"

She said, "Yeah, but make it quick." So I ran across the tarmac. It was dark and I stumbled across a fuel mine and did a spread eagle on the tarmac, ripped my hose, dislocated my knee cap, and got my uniform filthy. We had the blue Dacron uniforms. I ripped two buttons off and skinned my hands. I got over there, and my friends said, "Well, you're a mess, aren't ya?"

I said, "Yeah. Heck, I didn't get out of here without getting injured!" One of them went into the john and took off her hose and brought them to me, and another one took the buttons out of her uniform and gave them to me so I could have a complete uniform. I got back on the airplane, and the doctor, Paul Titas, said, "What happened to you?" I said, "I'm in a war zone!" The stewardess came along and said, "I don't think I should have let you do that." I said, "Just get me a washcloth." So I washed off my knee as best I could. By the time we got back to the States (it was an eighteen-hour flight), my knee was very swollen.

I went to Indiana University in Indianapolis for graduate school. I got my master's degree, and the navy paid for it. I was one of the fortunate ones who got picked for that.

I went to the reunion in San Francisco in 1990. That's the only one I've been too. I went when we dedicated the Vietnam Women's Memorial in 1993. That was delightful. There were twenty of the thirty-four nurses that I served with at that dedication. It was really poignant. It was almost a spiritual experience. It meant so much to so many people.

The Vietnam War ended in 1975 and then I stayed on another ten years after that. I was able to contribute my nursing skills to subsequent military engagements. It is so important to me to see that our work made a difference. Whenever Congress gets their hackles up about women in combat zones, I just laugh because we've been in combat zones since the Crimean War.

I am a Latter-day Saint. I hadn't been an active member for a number of years before I went to Nam. I became active again in 1976 when I was in Philly. My faith has impacted my whole life. I certainly was protected while I was in the military. I never got injured, except for the fall. Somebody was protecting me.

Patricia Rushton

I have never written about my experiences in the United States Navy, but I have never been reticent to talk about them. I have just never taken the time to write a permanent record. I am sure there is some reference to my navy career in my journals and in pictures I have taken, but it would probably be a good thing to organize my thoughts and experiences into a record that might be understandable and perhaps useful to others. It has been almost forty years now since my relationship with the navy began, so I had better write it down soon or I won't be able to remember it at all.

I entered the University of Utah in fall 1967, declaring my major as nursing. I don't remember there ever being a question that I would have a spot in the program. I don't think anyone ever mentioned a selection process to me in 1967. There just wasn't any question, at least in my mind, that I would not take the required courses and graduate as a nurse. Lately I have learned that only a small number of the applicants were actually admitted.

During the first year of classes, nursing candidates took an Orientation to Nursing course. We got the basic information about what nursing was, what it meant to be a "professional" nurse, ethical behavior, and so forth. Those instructors seemed so mature to me then, but they were probably fairly young and didn't have a lot of years in nursing. In fact, my pediatric nursing instructor was teaching her first nursing class when she taught mine. Little did we know how inexperienced and immature she was. Now she is the associate dean for research at BYU College of Nursing. Nursing as a profession was pretty immature as well. Nurses were still trying to define what appropriate behavior was, what being a professional meant, and what our role was. We have come a long way in forty years. In this class, there was one session where military nurse recruiters came to talk to us and try and get us to enlist. They all came in dress uniform, looking very sharp. However, there wasn't much difference in their stories. They were all going to pay our way through school for a certain length of time and then expect us to serve on active duty for a specific period of time in order to pay back the debt. Salaries and benefits were about the same; after all, the government is the government. The only thing that was really different was the uniform, and I liked the navy's the best.

Patricia Rushton

The information sounded really good to me. I knew it was going to be tough to come up with money for four years of school. My parents were very supportive but not rich, so I knew they couldn't pay the way. I had saved some money, but I knew I didn't have enough to get through four years without working. I wasn't afraid to work; I just didn't know if it would be enough. Besides, even for me, a rather drab, stay-at-home girl, the military sounded kind of exciting. The opportunities for travel and education sounded pretty good, and it felt kind of good to be part of something special like the navy. I talked to my parents, mostly my mother, about it. She never had anything negative to say. She thought it was a good idea, not necessarily from the standpoint of money, but because she thought it would open up opportunities that I might never get any other way. She was right.

I joined the navy the third year of nursing school. The government paid my books and tuition and a salary for those last two years. Because I lived at home, I could bank most of the salary. For the first time, I had money of my own. Though I don't think I was extravagant, I was able to buy some things for myself. I remember that I was able to buy whatever I wanted for Christmas gifts during those last two Christmas seasons under my parents roof. It was a very liberating experience. There have been times when I didn't have much money or I didn't manage it well. The two experiences have taught me that saving money and managing it well can make a person free, and not having money or managing it poorly can make you a prisoner and a slave.

I was commissioned an O-1, or an ensign, six months before I graduated. I don't remember taking anyone with me to the commissioning ceremony. It was short, and it was a means of getting further down the road toward graduation and active duty. My parents would have gone. They were never anything but supportive in all my activities. I think I just didn't realize what an impact that single day was going to have on the rest of my life.

I graduated from the University of Utah College of Nursing in June 1971 and in September went off to Newport, Rhode Island, to Officer Training School. I was there one month. It was the first time I had ever been away from home on my own. It was pretty hard for my mother too. That same week she had sent my brother Delbert off on a mission, and my sister Suzanne had gotten married. She lost three kids in the same week. She said that my brother was going the farthest but that he was the only one she didn't worry about because she knew the Lord was taking care of him. The day Momma took me to the airport, I forgot my coat. Momma insisted on going home to get it so I could take it on the plane. I should have told her to mail it and had her stay to spend those last few minutes with me.

When the cab (my first cab ride) drove into Newport from the airport, I remember seeing those big ships docked in the bay. I had never seen the ocean before, and I had never seen such big ships anywhere but in the movies. The movies don't hold a candle to the real thing.

We were so busy during the month of training that I didn't think too much about being homesick. When I graduated from training in Newport a month later, my parents were not able to come at that time either. Momma wrote and told me how proud they were of me and how sorry they were that they couldn't be with me and how much she and Daddy loved me. I really felt their absence this time around.

I served at the Philadelphia Naval Hospital for three years. At the time, there were five big naval hospitals: Philadelphia, Bethesda, Long Beach, San Diego, and Oak Knoll in Oakland, California. I had purposely asked to go to Philadelphia because it was the East Coast center for orthopedics and amputees. My recruiting nurse had talked so much about working with amputees that I really wanted to do that. I had never been to the East Coast, and I really wanted to see some of the historic sites like Philadelphia, Boston, and Washington DC. At the hospital, I was assigned to work on the orthopedic and amputee wards.

The Philadelphia Naval Hospital, being a rather old facility, consisted of a number of big, open wards with probably twenty beds to a ward but no real walls and sometimes no curtains between beds. The nurses' station was right in the middle and you could see from one end of the ward to the other. The philosophy was that nobody in the service really deserved any privacy, and with the open environment you could really see what was going on everywhere in the ward. The privacy issue was rarely a problem. These young guys were used to a ship space 6 feet by 4 feet and practically sleeping in the next guy's bunk. They didn't have a lot of belongings, so they didn't need a storage space. Their physical closeness helped everyone be a support to everyone else.

These kids, servicemen in their twenties, were usually very supportive and helpful from a physical standpoint and emotionally supportive to the guys who needed that kind of help.

Occasionally, the open ward situation could be a problem. These servicemen were young, often lonesome and homesick, emotionally traumatized by their war experiences, and sometimes not very mature. One young man got upset with something that was happening on the ward one day and just started yelling and screaming. It was very aggravating to other patients, but I knew there was no way I was going to physically control this guy. He was bigger and stronger than I was. I tried to just ignore him, not providing any positive feedback for his behavior. The other patients just put up with him. However, my supervisor was very upset that I wasn't doing anything about the situation. I explained to her that I didn't have any ideas and that if she knew some way to control him, she was welcome to have a try. I honestly can't remember what happened to resolve the problem. I only remember that there wasn't any way to isolate this patient or the situation from anyone else. It was the only time in a year and a half on that ward that I ever remember the open ward being a problem.

During many of the months on the orthopedic floors one of the patients was an older African American navy chief. He had had both legs amputated and was in the process of rehab when one morning he had a heart attack and died. Everyone on the ward, including nursing staff, really respected this man and felt terrible when he died, and all of the other patients were supportive to each other and to the nursing and medical staff while we coped with the loss.

There were five wards in the orthopedic department. On the day shift there was one nurse and two to three corpsmen per ward. On afternoons there was one nurse for all five wards and one to two corpsmen for each ward. On the night shift there was one nurse for all five wards and one corpsman per ward. Ninety percent of the patients, however, were really physically well. They had a broken bone or were limping around and simply couldn't be on board a ship. Since they had to be stationed somewhere, they were stationed at the hospital and would stay there until they were well enough to go back to their regular duty station. A nurse was frequently responsible for the health and welfare of eighty to a hundred patients, but usually less than ten were significantly sick. The other seventy to ninety generally just tried your patience. They were really adolescents who had been sent to do men's work and somehow grew up in the process. But their teenage tricks and lack of common sense frequently got them in trouble and made the nurse wonder if she would survive her naval career. It must be remembered, as well, that the nurses were really youngsters, too. Most of the nurses were right out of nursing school and really didn't know very much. We were all growing up as well. We usually had come from very different backgrounds than the patients we were taking care of or the other nursing staff we worked with, and we really had no experience dealing with military matters or some life matters.

Some examples might be entertaining. One day I was having difficulty getting a locker (closet) door open. I said to the corpsman, a pretty good-sized, burly kind of guy, "I want that door open. I don't care what you have to do to make it happen." He took me at my word and proceeded to take the door off the hinges. The action really amounted to destruction of government property, a felony offense. I never imagined he would go to such lengths—he was just following a senior officer's order. We both really heard it from the supervisor. Fortunately, no one pressed charges. However, I learned to be careful what I said and to be specific in my requests. What would have been casual requests carried out with common sense at home were officers' orders that the enlisted personnel had to carry out to the letter in the navy, regardless of the consequences.

I got so I hated the Friday and Saturday p.m. shift. Friday and Saturday afternoon and evening were the nights that those who were physically able would go on liberty. They would go out in Philadelphia and the surrounding area and often take in the sights and sounds of the nearest bar, showing back up in the hospital pretty drunk. Coming from my Latter-day Saint background, I had no experience with drunks or drinking. One night a fellow came back in and complained about his back hurting. He said he had been drinking, but he seemed to be in pretty good shape and either he didn't tell me or I didn't understand how much he had had to drink. I called the doc about the man's pain, and he ordered Valium, a reasonable dose, as a muscle relaxant. After I had given the medication, this guy's buddies told me how much beer he had had to drink. It was a lot. This kid slept for twenty-four hours straight. Between the beer and the Valium, he had a pretty good hangover. He nearly scared me to death. I was sure that the combination of drugs would kill him. I didn't realize then that it is very rare for anyone to overdose on Valium, certainly not an adult of average size and with the dose I had given him.

The enlisted men, patients, and staff were expected to follow orders. The marines were exceptionally strict about this, and it was sort of ingrained in them to follow orders instinctively without thinking too much about it. One of the patients on the ward was a very young marine who had lost a leg. It was standard policy that patients who were physically able to do so got up at 0600 in the morning, made their own beds, and got washed up before breakfast. I would faithfully go around and shake the patients bed at 0600 and tell them to get up and get going. Instinctively, this marine jumped out of bed when I shook his bunk and crashed on the floor because he forgot he was missing a leg. During a separate incident, another marine told me never to touch him when I woke him in the morning but only to shake the traction bars on the bed and to not get any closer to him than the end of the bed. He let me know that those who had served in Vietnam instinctively would defend themselves if touched by surprise, and he was truly afraid that he would reach out and strike me, or anyone else, if he was surprised.

I was fortunate to get Philadelphia as my duty station, but I had not counted on how far away from home it was or how homesick I was going to be. I had never been away from home for an extended period before, and during that first six months in Philadelphia, I thought I was going to die. Homesickness truly can be a terminal disease, but I coped in several ways. I learned to use the telephone to make long distance calls home on a regular and frequent basis. This was in the days when people didn't make long distance phone calls unless it was an emergency. The first time I called home from Philly, my mother thought something terrible had happened. Then she thought I was being really frivolous with my money. I had to hear her voice and hear what was happening to my family or I would have gone crazy, so I figured it was worth spending the money for it. After a few months, my mother thought I was terrible if I didn't call home at least once a week. It was a habit I maintained for the rest of my life, as long as my mother was alive, except that when I got home I called her at least once a day. She expected it, and I wanted to do it.

While I was on my mission, I wrote every P-day, and she wrote at least once a week.

After a few months I made some friends. One was Kathy Kress. She was from Florida, and she was Catholic. She was a good friend. She never asked me to do anything that she knew was against my faith, and I did the same for her. We did so many things together. From time to time I think about her willingness to take me as I was and let me do the same and think how fortunate I was to have such a friend. I haven't seen Kathy since she left Philadelphia.

Another friend was a member of the Church, Elizabeth Blackwell. She was a convert to the Church and a medical student at Jefferson University. Liz and I became very good friends and good support for each other in the gospel. Liz ended up coming to Utah, marrying a psychologist, and working at the BYU Health Center. She currently remains in that position and is living in Alpine, Utah.

Thank goodness for the gospel. I remained active in the Church in Philadelphia. Attending church was much different in Philly. There wasn't a Latter-day Saint chapel on every corner. It took about a half hour by car through center-city Philadelphia to get to the Philadelphia Ward chapel. I went every week. I was even called to be the Primary president in charge of both an English- and Spanish-speaking Primary. I had no children, of course, and I couldn't speak any Spanish at that time, so I am not sure I was any help to that Primary, but the bishop felt he needed a Utah Mormon to help converts understand what Church organizations were all about. I remember expressing my frustration to my mother. She said, "Don't worry about it. Remember that once the Lord has started something, nothing can stop it. Maybe your job is only to get this started." It was a testimony of how important the gospel is and of how the Lord can and will make important things happen. I have never forgotten what she said.

I spent three years in Philadelphia. Besides my experiences with the amputees, I worked for a year and a half in the hospital's emergency room. My navy experiences taught me a great deal. I learned how to be a nurse. I learned about disease and healing and anatomy and pathophysiology. I learned how to prioritize and organize and face emergencies and work hard and get the work done. I came to appreciate the navy and the financial, psychological, and emotional benefits I received from being a member of that organization.

Mostly, I learned about myself. I learned how strong my testimony was. I learned how important the Church was to me. It was while I was in Philadelphia that the still, small voice came to me and testified that the gospel was true and that The Church of Jesus Christ of Latter-day Saints was the only true and living church on the earth today. I had always known it and behaved like I knew it, but I had never had the Spirit fill my soul as it did one Sunday as I sat in sacrament meeting at the Philadelphia Ward. I learned how important my family was to me, especially my mother. Though that wonderful person no longer lives here on the earth, I think of her daily and hope that my actions would please her.

When I was discharged from active duty in the spring of 1974, I remained in the Navy Reserve in Salt Lake City. I stayed active in the Navy Reserve, extending my navy career for almost twenty-five years. I drilled one weekend every month and went to an active duty site, usually a large naval hospital, for two weeks every year, with only a couple of exceptions. This experience cemented my relationship with the nation's military. Though there were times when the weekend drills were inconvenient and I didn't always like everybody I worked with, for the most part the people were good and the experiences were beneficial. I think that can be said of any work-type relationship experienced in this world. In the process of that twenty-two years in the reserves I bought a house, bought two cars, got a master's degree, and saw a number of places in this nation that I would never have seen if I hadn't been attached to the navy. I met a lot of good people.

I hope I influenced their lives for good. I know that my association with them made my life more pleasant.

In late summer of 1989, Iraq invaded Kuwait in order to control their oil supply. Kuwait yelled for help, and the United States came running. Of course we wanted to maintain the environment of freedom under which the Kuwaitis lived. Of course we wanted to maintain the friendship of peoples in the Middle East that we had previously supported. But the United States was also smart enough to know that if Iraq took over the oil fields of Kuwait, life could get tough for any country dependent on Kuwaiti oil. I personally had no difficulty with this conflict because I think groups of people should have the opportunity to decide for themselves who will govern them and not have another militant leader decide it for them. And, interestingly enough, as American troops went to Kuwait, so did members of the Latter-day Saint Church who impacted the lives of their comrades and possibly those who live in the Middle East. Time will tell.

As reserve forces were mobilized, there were a number of reservists who wanted to avoid being sent to Kuwait or to support sites stateside or overseas. For some reason, there were reservists who didn't seem to think they should serve at a time of national crisis, even though they had already collected the benefits of belonging to the reserves. I didn't have much pity for those who thought they should stay home because of family or work obligations. They knew the deal when they enlisted. My mother had terminal cancer at the time, and I could only pray that I would not be mobilized until she didn't need me anymore. Several people said to me, "You're really going to go?" My response was, "Well, you can't be in this canoe club for twenty years and then tell them you won't go when they really need you." Reservists began to be mobilized in August 1989. My mother died January 11, 1990, and I was mobilized in early February of that year.

I was mobilized to do support duty at Oak Knoll Naval Hospital in Oakland, California. The reservists were sent to take the place of the active duty forces who had been mobilized to the hospital ship *Mercy*, which was sent to the Persian Gulf to take care of active duty troops. Medical personnel were often expected to do types of duty that they were not used to doing. They were often afraid of or very uncomfortable with the new duties that were required of them. Fortunately for me, I'm just an old medical/surgical nurse, and I knew exactly what to do: plain old-fashioned nursing. Interestingly, I was asked to be the night supervisor. This meant I worked from 11 p.m. to 7 a.m., having essentially a four-day weekend because I would get off at 7 a.m. on Friday morning and didn't have to be back to work until 11 p.m. on Monday. This allowed me to come home frequently and to make it to church every Sunday, and since I was in Oakland, the schedule even made it possible for me to attend the temple once a month. I was at Oak Knoll from February until Memorial Day, not long, and then came home.

Again, the gospel was very important to me. It was a strength to me because my mother had just died and only with knowledge of the plan of salvation could I have gone on functioning in a strange situation. When I wasn't sure if I would eventually end up at the front, the gospel gave me a foundation and the understanding of why I was here on this earth and the assurance that I could learn from every situation. My home ward was initially very supportive of my leaving. It was mostly emotional support since I really didn't leave anyone behind for them to take care of. Nobody volunteered to keep an eye on my house. Fortunately, my brother Cory was willing to do that, and fortunately, it was winter, so not much needed to be done. I can't say that the ward in Oakland was particularly helpful. I don't think the bishop spoke to me more than once, and that was when I was handing him the one tithing payment I paid to that ward. No one spoke to me, acknowledged I was there, or even asked who I was. I was just another body taking up a space in the sacrament meeting. It didn't take long to realize that there was no reason to change my membership records to that Oakland Ward, and I just kept sending my tithes and offerings to my home ward. The experience taught me that my testimony was strong enough to survive, even without the support of others. I was pretty certain about that, but this experience just assured it.

The war ended almost as quickly as it started. Those who had been mobilized and who had rearranged their lives completely when called were sent home just as quickly. When they were mobilized, they understood the reason: the United States was at war, even if they didn't agree with it. But when they were sent home, they had to downgrade their emotions from constant tension about their future to feeling unwanted by the military who had so desperately needed them only nine months earlier. Some were ecstatic, but many were disappointed, frustrated, angry, and afraid about going back to real life after being involved in a war. I was fortunate. I had a really good friend, Sherry Brown, who had been mobilized as well, only she went to the "sand" in Saudi Arabia. She had been discharged about a month before me, and she came to Oakland and drove home with me. We were able to talk about our experiences and sort of wind down. Fortunately we both had jobs to go back to. There would still be interesting and difficult experiences for me to go through, but the fact that I am writing this demonstrates that I did a pretty good job of making it through those experiences.

I stayed in the Naval Reserve until 1997. At that time I was a commander and had been passed over three times, once each year, for captain. The navy rule was this: three times passed over and you were out. The officer who told me I had to get out wasn't quite that blunt, but close. I had really wanted to stay in for thirty years, but I had almost twenty-five, which was plenty to collect retirement, so it is probably just as well that I got out when I did. We are facing a new war now, Operation Enduring Freedom, and I don't know about going this time. I am physically, financially, and emotionally able to go. It might be harder to find someone to care for the critters now. However, I would pack my bags and go if I was needed.

— Operation — Desert Storm
The First Gulf War

HISTORICAL BACKGROUND

On August 2, 1990, Iraq invaded Kuwait. Kuwait asked the United States for assistance in defending themselves, and within five days United States F-15 Eagle fighters arrived in the Persian Gulf from Langley Air Force Base in Virginia to begin Operation Desert Shield, an effort to liberate Kuwait from Saddam Hussein, the political leader of Iraq. The United States was able to put together a coalition of more than thirty-five nations who supported the military liberation of Kuwait (moral support, troops, money, and supplies). It was clear that the United States would carry the major burden of the effort. On August 22, 1990, President George Bush authorized the call-up of the reserves. Reservists began to mobilize in preparation to go to the Gulf for combat and to receive casualties. Areas were prepared to receive patients in the Gulf, in Europe, and in the United States. The activities in August began a five-month diplomatic effort to liberate Kuwait and stop the conflict. However, on January 17, 1991, a one-month air war began to try to convince Saddam Hussein to leave Kuwait, with no result. On February 22, President Bush delivered an ultimatum to Hussein demanding that he withdraw from Kuwait by February 23, 1991. When no withdrawal came, United States armed forces moved into Iraq and Kuwait. Though there had been much concern about a substantial resistance from Iraqi forces, little resistance was encountered and on February 26, 1991, Kuwaiti resistance leaders declared that they were again in control of Kuwait. On February 27, President Bush ordered a cease-fire at the end of what is sometimes referred to as the "one hundred hour war." On March 3, 1991, Iraqi leaders accepted the terms of the cease-fire. During the war there were 148 combat deaths out of the 533,608 troops who served in the Gulf War. Another 145 died of non-combat-related conditions. One hundred thousand Iraqi troops died during the conflict and three hundred thousand Iraqis were wounded.

Though it has been over a decade since the first Gulf War, nursing literature is still being generated about lessons learned from that conflict. One registered nurse, Heather Worthington (1995), said of her experience in the Gulf:

> We worked twelve-hour shifts, five days a week. The hospital was thirty minutes away, so bus transportation was important. The buses were always packed. Driving on the Saudi highway was a terrifying experience. I was less afraid of getting killed by a Scud missile than being in a bus accident on the highway. Our young bus drivers didn't have much experience. Also, young soldiers who thought they were "Rambos" rode shotgun. I thought, "Why don't they give the duty to our Vietnam vets who understand that weapons are serious?" We were loaded into buses with our backpacks, gas masks, helmets, and weapons. We learned to live with the gas masks day and night. (18–19)

Worthington (1991) spoke of the short preparation time many military personnel dealt with during mobilization in the Gulf conflict:

> I had only four days to prepare before reporting to my mobilization point, Fort Lewis. This left very little time for family goodbyes. Nothing seemed real through the transition. I felt like I was having a bad dream from which I would soon awake. Tears were always close. Leaving home, I was not even sure of my destination—Germany or Saudi Arabia. (29)
>
> We had twenty-four hours' notice when we left Saudi Arabia. Leaving was another new adjustment, especially for the women. Throughout the entire stay, we had no responsibilities except to our job and to ourselves. We went back to Fort Lewis via Cairo, Ireland, and the Arctic Circle—a striking contrast from the desert. We were warmly welcomed at Fort Lewis. From there, approximately thirty of us flew into San Francisco, where more than five hundred people were waiting for us—members of our units and our families. The emotion and anticipation of seeing loved ones again and of being back in the United States was overwhelming. (34)

Worthington also spoke of her feelings about the combat experience in general:

> As I recount these events, the experience retains a sense of the unreal, as if I had traveled to the "Twilight Zone." My part in the war was an experience filled with contrasts—impoverished apartments, sparse surroundings, and war paraphernalia set against service in a modern hospital with wealthy clients and gourmet food in the cafeteria.
>
> I felt a profound resurgence of patriotism. Homecoming brought tears and a full range of emotions that were different, yet just as intense, as those I felt upon leaving. I felt I had been a part of a much larger group, part of a true international force. Together with persons from many nations, we formed a multinational treatment team, all working toward a common goal. (34)

Kent Dean Blad

Serving in the Persian Gulf War was definitely an interesting experience. My wife and family, we have been truly blessed because of it. We also had many challenges because of it.

Just to give you a little chronological scenario, it was on Saturday before Thanksgiving 1990 that we were at our regularly scheduled monthly drill at the National Guard. I was a member of the 144th Evacuation Hospital out of Salt Lake City, serving in the operating room as an OR nurse. Many units at that time were being activated or put on alert to go to the Persian Gulf to help out with the conflict that was occurring at that time. At lunchtime there was an emergency formation called, at which time our commanding officer informed us that not only had we been put on alert, but we had been activated as of Thanksgiving Day, which was four days following our notice. For me, the reaction was one of fear, mostly because of the unknown. I had four days in which to get our (my family's) lives in order, get our finances taken care of, get our

Kent Dean Blad

shots, insurance—all the technical things that would need to be done in a four-day span to physically leave home—not knowing when we would be back. Even worse than that, we were given four days in which to mentally get ready. I think that was the toughest of the assignments. Thanksgiving Day we did spend at home. They were kind enough to let us spend the morning and the afternoon at home. The buses left in the evening for Fort Carson, Colorado.

We spent approximately the rest of November, all of December, and the first week of January at Fort Carson. In January we were given our station assignment in Saudi Arabia. We flew over on commercial air transportation. We landed at night with the lights on the plane and on the runway dimmed, so as not to be identified. We spent three days, immediately upon arrival in Saudi Arabia, in a makeshift barracks or apartment complex that was sitting empty there until we were to get our exact location to set up our hospital in Saudi Arabia. The place we stayed for those first three days in Dhahran, Saudi Arabia, is the same building that was hit by the Scud missile toward the end of the conflict that took out the majority of our casualties in the Persian Gulf War.

We were assigned to the Riyadh airport, called the King Fahd International Airport, in Saudi Arabia. Our hospital was to be set up at the side of the runway. As casualties occurred, they would be flown in, the planes would stop right on the runway, the doors would open, and they would empty them right into our tent hospital.

We were very fortunate in that we saw no casualties that led to deaths. We only saw one individual with a combat-related injury. The rest of our patients were more or less accident victims—vehicle rollovers, broken limbs—that sort of thing. We did not receive a tremendous number of patients. At any one time we probably averaged ten to twenty patients in our hospital a day. We were very grateful for that. The conflict ended the last day of February, but we were asked to stay on for an additional time period to be medical support for the troops while they were evacuating out of the country. So we did spend a little more time there than a lot of the soldiers who were in the conflict.

But my story today is not about times and dates. It is more about experiences that we had, about feelings that come in such a situation, and about lessons that were learned from that conflict. At the time my wife and I had four children, all under the ages of seven—very dependent children. It was a difficult time. We had a newborn and it was a very difficult time to leave my wife and children. But through the events that happened, there were a lot of blessings that came. It was very difficult leaving small children who did not understand that Dad was going to be gone for an unknown period of time. We did not know if it would be temporary or long-term or if I would even return at all. What do you say to your children when you don't know what the

Kent, left, with a patient

future is going to bring? It was a very difficult thing and one that we certainly do not wish to repeat. It was very difficult leaving a wife right in the middle of raising a family, having had a very wonderful relationship. We were right in the middle of our lives. We were loving life at the time. Things were going great. Things were pretty much turned upside down from this experience.

I would like to share some of the things I learned. Probably the main lesson that I learned was that having four days to get our lives completely in order—physically, mentally, spiritually—was not a lot of time. The lesson learned was that we never know what tomorrow will bring. We should live today as though it might be our last. I don't mean that in a doomsday way but in a very positive way. We should treat others as if this may be the last time we ever see them. We should treat our family members as if this may be the last day that we are with them. Life is very fragile and we never know what tomorrow may bring. I would hope that we would treat others and be kind to others and do it as if tomorrow might not come for us or for them.

I learned also that we should cherish freedom and hold it so close and dear to our hearts that we would be willing to give our lives for it; that we should have wives and husbands who would be willing to sacrifice a spouse for that freedom and children who would be willing to give up a father or mother if need be to protect the freedoms that our country is based on.

What I learned was a great lesson on priorities in our life. All of a sudden, it was not important what kind of car we drove or what kind of a home we possessed. It was not important what kind of sports we played in high school. What we thought was important at times quickly switched to things that really are priorities, such as families and loved ones. I learned very quickly and in a big way that where your heart is, there also will be your treasure, and that is what we should focus on in life.

I also promised myself that if I made it through this conflict, that in the future if I ever had to choose between time and money, I would always choose time—time to be with my family, friends, and associates—time to be with those that I love.

We may find times in our lives when we are totally helpless. No matter how much control we think we have over our lives, we must always remember that we have to have faith and trust in the Lord. We are not in control of things. There is a higher power beyond us that controls the big scheme of things. That was brought home ever so emphatically in this situation.

In addition to what I said about cherishing freedom, we should always cherish the things that we love the most, and not take them for granted: our families, our friends, and those around us that we care about so much. We should not think that they will always be here for us, no matter what, because that may not always be true.

The next thing I learned is that the gospel and the family are everything. Without those two things, our lives would be pretty empty. I cherish them even more now. I thought I did before, but I do even more since this happened. Those two things became the main focus of my life.

Another thing I learned was that the time we spend on things should equal the priorities that we have. The things that are lowest on our priority list should not be the things that get the majority of our time. The time spent in our lives should be equal to the importance of our priorities, whatever they may be.

I learned that there are great rewards in service. How many times are we told in the scriptures or asked to provide service and commanded to be of service and to love like Christ did? Even though each individual soldier who went to that conflict may not feel like they alone made a great impact, collectively there was a great impact by all the individuals that were involved. Having an opportunity to serve and to love those things that I cherish so dearly was a great blessing in my life.

I learned to always be positive. Too often in life we focus on the negative aspects of life. We spend a lot of time and attention thinking and talking about negative things, when in essence, life is so short and fragile, it should be just the reverse. Our time should be spent with positive things and our attitudes should be positive. We should approach things always in a positive manner. We should treat others positively.

I learned that you should treat people you love as if you really love them. Don't just go through the motions. Show with your time, energy, and actions that you really do love them. Being kind to others is a good insurance policy. We never know when we are going to need others to be kind to us. I am thinking specifically that when I left that Thanksgiving night, I left my family not knowing if I was going to return. Knowing that I would be gone, I prayed so hard that people that we had tried to be kind to would show generosity and kindness toward my wife and children in the absence of their husband and father. I prayed that I would now be the recipient of that 100 percent home teaching that I had tried to do for so many years. The day before I left, the bishop came over and met with us in our home. He asked us, as kind as he was, what he could do specifically to help us while I was gone. It was not the need of food, it was not the need of money, and in fact, it was not any physical need that we had at that time. I begged the bishop to please be sure that my wife received the best home teachers that he had in the entire ward, someone that could be dependable, somebody that may come on another day besides the last day of the month. He assigned himself and his wife as our family's home teachers. According to my wife, there was not a week that went by without him checking in. I'm sure it was probably closer to daily visits. The children's birthdays were not missed; special events in our family were attended to in a great way by this great man and his good wife. So we should remember that if we are kind to others, we may end up being a recipient of that kindness from them. We should always treat others with kindness.

The next lesson learned is that righteousness always prevails. Sometimes it takes a little time for that to happen, but righteousness, goodness, and honesty—the best thing that could happen will always prevail.

One of the last things, but certainly one of the most important things, was my gratitude to my Savior for many things—for protecting me and for protecting my family. Over in Saudi Arabia, in the Arabian Peninsula, close to the birthplace of our Savior, there were many nights that I was very lonely. Even though we were surrounded by many people, there were many nights that loneliness and missing our families set in. That is the worst feeling that anyone could experience. On those nights of loneliness, I would go outside and stare into that sky, that eastern sky that held that star on the day that our Savior was born. That was a great comfort. It was a great feeling and a great thought to know that for the first time in my life. I was able to stare at the same sky that the wisemen and the people around the time of the Savior's birth had stared at. I was grateful to my Savior for my wife's sake. My only prayer, the whole time that I was gone, was not that I would be protected, but that my wife and children would be well cared for in my absence. My wife relates experiences that are very sacred and very private, particularly of protection and help that she did receive. She said that at no other time in her life had she felt so secure. She felt protected to the point that she would not hesitate to leave the windows open at night in our home, which for her is a major breakthrough. She is very security seeking. We did not live in a great area of town at that time. She said that she felt that there was a shield, a protection that was over our home at all times. That meant a lot to me.

My oldest child at the time was seven, and his name is Matthew. He was the only child we had at the time that could even remotely understand that his dad had to leave and that it was not necessarily Dad's choice, even though I was grateful for the opportunity to serve. I sat each of the children down and said goodbye to them. As I specifically said goodbye to him, not knowing his level of maturity or sensitivity, I said to him, "Son, I'm going to have to go now. I don't know when and I don't know if I will be able to return. Since Dad is going to be gone, I need you to be the man of this house. Mom is going to need a lot of help and Dad will not be here to help Mom like he wants to. I would ask that you would now take over as the man of the house." The day I arrived at the Salt Lake Airport, where we were released from duty, he ran to me with his arms out. We embraced for a long period of time, as fathers and sons often do. He said, "Dad, I'm so glad that you are home because I am tired of being the man of the house." And I saw a physical release come over him. Little did I realize that he had taken me so literally that day when I asked him to be the man of the house at seven years old. He was physically exhausted from trying to help his mother. There were many lessons that I learned from that experience about children and about human nature in general and about being a father in a family. I have been ever so grateful to him for the valuable lessons that he taught me with those one or two sentences that he muttered that day. I was anguished and pained that I had put that burden upon his shoulders but grateful for the seriousness with which he took it and grateful for the lessons that he taught a mom and a dad that day.

Even though we did not experience great numbers of casualties through the Persian Gulf conflict, there were many valuable lessons that were learned. My wife and I feel like that was a turning point in our marriage, which was very good at the time but became even better. There was a bond that occurred there that could never be broken. There was a newfound love for my country. Ever since that very day that I returned home, I cannot see a flag or hear "The Star-Spangled Banner" without privately coming to attention and paying respect for the symbol that flag represents. I am deeply offended by those who choose to talk negatively or unfavorably about our country and our flag, especially those who have never had to pay a price or who are so willing to be the benefactors of those who have fought for their freedoms. Yet they bad-mouth those very freedoms that have been protected over the years. I am grateful for the opportunity that I had. I feel like it was a huge blessing in my life. In a lot of ways it was an answer to many prayers and in six months time I surely grew many years beyond my age. I will ever be so grateful. We have benefitted financially, physically, and most importantly, our family has benefitted spiritually from that experience. I am ever so grateful to my Heavenly Father for that.

Paul Levi Blad

In 1981 I was doing pre-med courses at Snow College and decided I needed some financial help. That is when I joined the army. After joining the Army National Guard, I trained to work in the operating room as a technician. I did that at LDS Hospital while I attended the University of Utah College of Nursing, plus I did weekend drills for the 144th Evacuation Hospital. After my four years of nursing school, I decided I just wanted a break before I went into a graduate program. I joined the Air Force as an active-duty member and was stationed in Northern California at Beale Air Force Base. It was there that I had a major life event.

My first wife passed away—a sudden, unexpected death. I got off of active duty because of my family situation. I had three small children—one a baby daughter. I came back to Utah and joined up with the original Army National Guard unit that I had previously belonged to. That was the 144th Evacuation Hospital out of Salt Lake City. I had invested enough in the military that I knew I didn't want to get out completely. Within a year of going from active-duty status to National Guardsman, Desert Storm broke out and I was activated as a reservist. The active duty unit I had belonged to never was activated. Here, I got out of being an active duty member to be Mom and Dad to my children. Then the war breaks out, and of course they don't take hardship cases. They need you for your specialty, and that is what I trained for.

I had just gotten remarried when I was activated for Desert Storm. It was about a year after my first wife had passed away. I thought, "How could my poor new wife take on my three children and her two children—five children into this new marriage?" It was a hard time. Basically, we had just come off our honeymoon. We began our marriage with me leaving to go to a war. I did not try to get a waiver. It was my responsibility, and I went. I didn't see my hardship as any worse than anyone else's. Basically, my life had stabilized because I had gotten married and my children had a support system. Also, my brother, Kent, was activated and left a large family.

Right before Thanksgiving we had a weekend drill. They notified us that right after Thanksgiving we would be leaving. It was a hard, emotional, and sad time of my life because we did not know what we were getting into. We had the impression that Iraq was almost a world power when it came to military equipment. We had heard about the Russian-made equipment and how efficient it was. If we went over, we really did not know if we would be coming back. Of course, that is the situation with any war. It was a very emotional time. And having survived it and looking back, I have to say that a major bond formed between me, my wife, and my family. We survived it together. We feel like we went through a hard time and survived it. We did our best.

I live in the small community of Kanosh, Utah, total population of just under five hundred. In the entire Millard County, only two people were activated to the war. I pretty much represented the east side of Millard County. I got more support than I could have imagined, but I didn't realize it until after I got home. It was a good thing for my wife to be in a place where she received a lot of support. It was a time when home teachers and visiting teachers and the whole ward really kicked in. I have extended family in the area, and they really helped out. It means more than I can ever say.

We went over to Saudi as a whole unit, about three hundred members. They supplemented our unit with members from all over the nation. Most units have vacancies, and in a war situation vacancies are filled. We received physicians and nurses from all over the nation who were put into basically an LDS unit. At least 90 percent of our unit was LDS with about 60 percent activity. We functioned as a branch during the war. It was really fun to be a part of something like that. Bonding came with it. We were all kept together as a unit when we got to Saudi. It was interesting watching our medical unit function as a branch. Many of the leaders of our unit were bishops or stake presidents back in Utah. Important people in society were taken to a war zone, leaving their comfort zones. We were all so humbled. I can't tell you the spirit that was there in our sacrament meetings. It was always so strong. Usually the theme was how much we appreciate the gospel, our families, everything we had previously taken for granted. There was a great spirit, and we became very close because of it. We held positions in the branch. Everyone was at least a home teacher or a visiting teacher. We took turns teaching, and we had a lot of testimony meetings. The leadership was already established because we functioned as a branch during weekends before mobilization. Our branch leader was also our commanding officer. We had a chaplain who was part of the branch presidency. There were a lot of inactive people that became very active during that period. However, there were a few people that you would have assumed were strong and active who went the other way. It was interesting to stand back and watch how people cope with the stress of such situations. For the most part, people usually bonded together and made the most of it.

We were warned not to bring up religion to the Arabs. We befriended many Arabs and some of them actually invited us into their homes and explained their way of life and actually asked us questions about our religion and what we believed in. We were told that if we were asked about our faith, we could respond, but it was not okay to proselyte. I have heard it said that war usually opens up doors of missionary work, so who knows what seeds were planted during this war.

Our unit was designated as an evacuation unit, like a MASH unit. We are supposed to be able to pick up and set up our hospital anywhere in twenty-four hours. We set up our hospital right next to the International Airport in Riyadh, where we could receive the heavy casualties. It was a five-hundred-bed hospital, covering just about every specialty you can imagine in a wartime setting. Some of our physicians were actually plastic surgeons. That wasn't their title in the war, but that's what they were in the civilian world. We had sixty physicians, three hundred plus nurses, and all the ancillary support and equipment that went with it. I was associated with the operating room section. All of our operating rooms were huge mobile boxes. They popped out to be these incredible two-bed operating rooms. The OR suits were interconnected to the hospital so that we have the same air-conditioning and heating systems and air control.

We were activated and we went to Fort Carson to do our pre-war training, most of which was nuclear and biochemical warfare training. That took two or three weeks. Once we were done with that, it became a waiting game—waiting for our turn to go over. Of course, all of our equipment had to precede us. It was kind of a logistics nightmare. It was over Christmas and we couldn't decide whether we should bring our families to Fort Carson and have a little Christmas or whether we should we go meet them somewhere. We were told we really couldn't leave because we could be sent off at any time. That's why Fort Carson was difficult for families.

I spent a lot of time on the phone. My phone bills got as high as $800 a month. We were lucky to even have access. To be able to call home during the war situation was fortunate. We had to hike several miles to a phone in Saudi, at least at the beginning of the war. Later, as technology came in, we did get phones closer to us. You would have to wait hours sometimes to get to the phone. I don't remember anyone having cell phones. There were several ways to call home. One was like a ham radio where you say, "Hi honey, I love you, over," and then she would have to give her message and everybody in the camp could hear you. I really felt that as a newlywed I needed to call home, and I wanted to call as often as I could. I was promoted during Desert Storm from first lieutenant to captain. So the pay raise all went toward phone bills. That was how I justified the phone calls.

They took us from Fort Carson to Saudi in a very large commercial airliner. We didn't fly right into Riyadh. We flew into Bahrain. It was frightening. There were certain instructions given to every unit coming to Saudi. When the airplane got close to the city, it had to turn off all of its lights, and we landed on a very dim airstrip. Lights were out. We were going into a war zone and we did not want to enter conspicuously. When we got out of that plane and walked onto the runway, we were dead silent. The feeling was very eerie. We had just walked into a war. Everyone kept the noise level down. We didn't turn on our flashlights. Fear of the unknown dominated our thoughts.

They put us up in Bahrain in an apartment complex while we waited for our final assignment as to where we were going to set up our hospital. The apartments that we stayed in are the very apartments that ended up getting bombed at the end of the war. It was hit by the one Scud missile that did get through and ended up killing thirty servicemen. Speaking of the Scud missiles that had come into Riyadh, after it was all over, they sent each of the units a copy of the trajectory of each of those Scud missiles, where they would have hit had they made it through. There were four of those that were projected to hit the complex where we resided. So we were grateful for the Patriot missiles and modern technology.

We had a Patriot missile battery right next to where we were stationed. They were set up right next to our hospital, right there by the international airport. Whenever a Scud missile would come close, a Patriot missile would go off. They sent two Patriot missiles at each Scud missile. They did that in case the first one missed, which they rarely did. Sometimes one would hit the warhead of the Scud and the other one would come by and hit the rest of the missile.

We were in Saudi a few weeks before the war actually started. Our hospital was already set up and we had already started to work shifts in the hospital. The hospital was twenty or thirty miles away from the apartments that the Saudi Arabian government gave us to stay in. We would be shipped in for our shifts, which were twelve-hour shifts. The first night of the war they sent thirty-eight Scud missiles. We medical types had no idea what was happening. All we knew was that there were a lot of explosions, a lot of earthshaking, and we thought we were right in the middle of it. I was not on shift at the hospital on the night the war began. My brother and I and our little group had actually gone to watch the football playoffs at about 1:00 in the morning. We had to walk several miles to where we knew there was a TV. I remember it was half-time. We decided we would leave and go get some breakfast. They had mess halls set up everywhere, and we were in the mess hall eating breakfast about 1:30 or 2:00 in the morning when Iraq started sending the Scud missiles. When the first one hit, the lights went out. We basically just took cover. None of us carried weapons, and we didn't know what to do anyway. We were in the mess hall, took cover under the tables, and just listened over the next few hours to one explosion after another. When this all happened, there were a lot of people in there. It was pitch dark. The attack lasted two to three hours. We did have our gas masks and chemical suits, and we were trained to get into those immediately. So there we were, all decked out in our chemical gear, and it was very hot. Eventually, we high-tailed it back to our apartment complex.

Being stationed next door to a Patriot missile battery, we experienced the power of such technology. Each Patriot missile being launched felt like a double earthquake, one explosion from the concussion of the launch and another as it broke the sound barrier right out of the launchpad. The biggest explosion of all was when it would connect with the Scud, and then everything would just shake. Pieces would come flying down around us. In the daytime we could go around picking up shrapnel. At home I have pieces of Raytheon circuit boards from the missiles. Fortunately, none of us got hit with any of the debris. It was a bewildering situation. We were trained not to panic, but fear of the unknown and not really knowing what your place is in such a situation was just different.

During this war we treated many more non-war casualties than war casualties. We were next to their freeway, and we treated civilians involved in accidents. We were willing to take any patient we could as we had ample medical gear and personnel waiting to do something, not wanting to lose their skills. As far as war casualties, the few that we did get had already been seen by front-line medical units and so they had been treated and triaged to the point that they were stable. We performed some surgeries: appendectomies, exploratory laps, on-the-job injuries, heavy-duty lacerations, sandstorm accidents.

About half our unit was male and half female. While we were waiting for the war to start, we befriended the Saudi medical personnel. We actually went to their hospitals and worked alongside them in a teaching/learning situation. Some of the male members of the unit got to spend time in the homes of the Arabs we befriended, but the women were not welcome. When the women would go into town, they would get pinched by the Arab men, not because they were trying to be fresh, but because they disapproved of women who were not veiled. Some of the women continued to try and go unveiled. Others didn't go into town. Some actually bought a veil and wore it over their battle dress utilities (BDUs) to go into town.

The physicians were so concerned about losing their skills. We were seven months over there. We arrived there the first part of January 1990, and we left the end of May or first part of June. We were one of the last units to get there and get set up. Because we were set up so well and had a reputation of efficiency, they decided to keep us behind to support the troops. We were the designated medical support for the exiting troops.

By the time we got home, the ticker tape and parades had pretty much ended except for my little community. When I came into town, they were waiting outside with the town fire engine, and they made me and my family get on and ride down the only street in town. Folks were waiting and welcoming me home. At the Fourth of July parade in Fillmore, I was designated the grand marshal. While I was gone, the staff at the hospital doubled up and covered for me, so when I got back I tried to pay them back by working some extra shifts, but they were so supportive. I received several letters and postcards from them. The support was just incredible.

In retrospect, from a family standpoint, the war turned out to be one of the biggest blessings of my life. While I was gone for seven months, my three children learned to love their new mother. When I came home, she was their mother. There was no stepmother/stepchild barrier. There was love and bonding. It was incredible. I just stood back and admired and cried and thanked the Lord. It was a great blessing. You just never know. My wife went through a lot more than I did in the war, trying to make the family stick together. Once we were there and set up, there wasn't much stress involved. We weren't getting casualties. It was a waiting game.

We learned to entertain ourselves and keep busy. We had Olympics between us and other countries, like the Swiss unit right next to us. We would have get-togethers and entertainment shows. My brother Kent and I had the unwritten assignment as entertainment specialists and tour guides. We took tours into downtown to the perfume and gold shops. These activities appeared to aid in building morale during such stressful times.

None of our people were hurt in action. Some of the ladies were sent home because of pregnancy. We had a couple of on-the-job heavy-equipment accidents, but no one was sent home because of them.

One of the great lessons I learned during the war was how important our freedoms are as Americans. When Iraq left Kuwait and the war was basically over, we were allowed to go in and help where needed. We would go into Kuwait, only as small groups as a security measure, because there was always the threat of terrorism and a few bands of Iraqis left behind that weren't

Susan Herron with a flag that her unit kept in their plane

very predictable. The streets of Kuwait City were pretty empty, but the Kuwaitis would come up to us and thank us and cry at our feet and do anything they could think of to show their appreciation for what we had done. When we left Kuwait, all the oil fields were burning and that was a really eerie feeling. We went to the freeway that leads to Iraq, Thunder Hill. During the conflict, all the tanks and Iraqi troops were trying to get back to Iraq by that route. Our air force just bombed it all. The sky was black and the sun looked like blood from the burning oil, and there was a feeling of death and destruction and darkness. I can't tell you what it felt like. It penetrated to the bone. It has had an everlasting effect on me. It certainly felt like a sign of the times.

I learned three lessons from my combat experience. First, I am so grateful to be a member of the Church and to have the gospel and the blessings and security of the plan of salvation. Second, the strength of family and their love and support through prayers and letters meant everything. Finally, love of country. Having experienced firsthand what it would be like to be stripped of your freedoms by a neighboring country, I would defend our nation at all costs.

Susan Herron

I have been in the air force reserves since December 1988, when I was commissioned. It was one of those things where I was reading one of my nursing magazines, and it said, "If you want to see the world, join the air force." They were right because I've been all over. I knew that I didn't want to spend my weekends in the hospital, that's what I did during the week, so the air force offered the opportunity to be a flight nurse and to fly around. The army uses rotary aircraft, like helicopters, for medevac. They'll go in and get the sick and wounded and bring them to us. We fly in a large cargo plane to do the long haul.

For Iraqi Freedom, we had a very complicated thing to start with. We started out in England, then we would fly down to Sicily. We would sit alert in Sicily, then we would go to Kuwait and pick the patients up and fly them to either Germany or Spain. It was a huge circle. As the war progressed, they eliminated some of these spots. Pretty soon we ended up going from Germany to the desert, Germany to the desert, and so forth.

The planes that we mostly flew on were the C-141s, and they are capable of transporting 103 litter patients and then a mixture if you have ambulatory patients. We had a combination of patients. Some of the patients would come on the plane and they had an abnormal pap smear. Other patients would come to us on ventilators with head injuries or blast wounds or burns. You saw everything. We had Landstuhl, which was a big hospital in Germany that had the capability for everything. They could handle trauma and all kinds of stuff.

After we took care of the service members, we never really knew what happened to them. What we did know is that we took them to Germany, and then occasionally we would do a mission to the States and we would bring some of the more serious ones stateside. We never really saw them after that. Now I'm assuming that there were many that returned to duty. We were deployed from February 2003 until August, so about six or seven months later.

We never seemed to stay in one place for more than two days. We were in England for two days, and then we would fly to Sicily. Then we would crew rest, get ready for a mission, and stay there for two days before going to Kuwait. In the initial part of the war, we would just land in Kuwait and go on, and that made a twenty-four-hour workday for us. We would be dead after that. Then they decided that they were killing the aerovac crews, so they decided to allow for crew rest. Even then when we hit Kuwait, we had to off-load all the cargo that they put on the plane and set up everything for air evacuation. By that time, we were twelve hours into our day, and we were dead tired already. It was also 120 degrees outside, and we were in a metal tube. We would pick up all our patients and then fly to Germany. That was another overwhelming thing. When we were in Sicily, we would get a basic initial report of how many patients we were going to get. They would tell us that we would get twenty to thirty patients, and that in itself was kind of overwhelming because we had three nurses on the plane. So then we land in Kuwait and they come on the plane and say, "Oh, you're getting seventy patients today." Seventy patients! It was crazy.

Our patients were mostly active duty. We did have a couple of Iraqi nationals. Most of them were humanitarians. I remember one was a sixteen-year-old girl who had burns. Another one was an Iraqi freedom fighter. There were a couple others interspersed in there. Most of the time they had an interpreter with them. That really helped. Otherwise, we used body language. You have to be very careful, especially if you're dealing with the males, because females couldn't touch them or even approach them. You really had to keep that in mind. We Americans are very touchy-feely. That's how nursing is.

There were three nurses on the flight crew. One nurse would be the medical crew director, who was in charge of paperwork and coordination and all that kind of stuff. The other two nurses would split the plane in half. One nurse would take one side of the plane, and the other nurse would take the other side of the plane. So you started at one end of the plane and you just worked your way down. You gave medicines and bandages, started IVs, gave morphine pushes, charted when you could, and did whatever else you had to do. By the time you finished and got down one side of the plane, you had to start all over again. We have very strict guidelines and regulations on narcotics. When a client comes on a plane with narcotics, you do a double count and chart that. Well, when you have seventy patients and at least half of those are coming on with tons of morphine, there's no way to count it and no way to account for it. So you're just pushing morphine and hopefully charting it because there are so many that you're doing. Everything took so much time because we were mixing all of our IV antibiotics since nothing came premixed. It was overwhelming.

One of the things I realized when I got back here into the urgent care emergency room here at the VA was that there were some days that I really enjoyed my job here and other days where I felt this stressful feeling. I realized that I was having some feelings, I don't want to call them flashbacks, because that just sounds so veteranish, but it was that overwhelming feeling, the feeling of being overwhelmed and being out of control and not knowing if you could do it because there are so many things that needed to be done. When we have fifty patients out in our waiting area and they all need to be seen now and you can't get to them all, it's just like seventy patients being on your plane and each one of them needs something, but you can't do everything. Again it was that overwhelming feeling that I felt during the war and I didn't like that, so I started to think that it was time to go on to a more structured environment, so that's why I was looking for another job position.

I'm going to have to word this carefully because this was one of our difficulties. They tell you to train the way you're going to go to war, so we train a certain way. We have our medical supplies packaged a certain way. We go on training missions. Like this weekend, I have a training mission coming up. We're going to bring our supplies and set up the plane, and we're going to have people playing patients and people playing crew members. We will have diagnoses for these patients, and we will have to go get supplies out of our kits to take care of these patients. That's how we train.

Well, I don't know when it was, whether it was the week we left before the war or the week after we got to the war, but they changed the packaging guidelines. It was great in theory because the theory was if you have between ten and twenty patients, you're going to take bags one through three, so you only have to take three bags. If you have between twenty and fifty patients, you're going to take two extra bags. Okay, now that's five to seven bags we're up to, but it was still manageable. That was the theory. If you have fewer patients, you'll take fewer bags. So that was great. However, like I say, when we got to Sicily, we were told we were going to have twenty to thirty patients, but by the time we get to Kuwait we were told we have seventy. So we ended up bringing every single piece of equipment and every package of bags full of all our stuff on each and every mission. So now that the packaging guidelines are different, we don't know where to go or which bag is what. It didn't really help, because we had to take everything anyway. So when you're looking for IV tubing, it used to be in bag number three, but you'd have to look through the packaging guideline. Then you would have to look through sixteen pages of the packaging guideline to figure out which bag it was in, and your patients are screaming in pain. You don't have time to be looking for stuff like that. It was very frustrating to have things change right before we went to war.

Initially, we had enough stuff because we were only carrying twenty to thirty patients during the first couple of weeks of war. After that is when we started getting our missions of fifty, sixty, seventy, and sometimes up to eighty patients. Then we started running out of things like saline flushes, piggy backs, tubing, needles, syringes, or other things you were using all the time for a lot of patients. What we as individual flight nurses started doing after every mission was repacking our kits. We all had our own little kits, our own personal bags that we would throw a bunch of extra stuff in, the stuff we knew we were going to be using so much of, so we all had extra supplies with us. It happens to you once and you learn, and then the rest of the time you're prepared.

I was deployed three times. I went on Operation Restore Hope. That started in 1992. I was deployed in 1993 for it. It was the famine relief effort in Somalia. You might remember it from the movie *Black Hawk Down*. It started out being a humanitarian effort. We went there to feed the hungry people, but it didn't turn out like that. I was a flight nurse then too, and we spent half of our time in Cairo, Egypt, where our base was. We would do rotations down into Mogadishu. We spent two weeks in Cairo, two weeks in Mogadishu, two weeks in Cairo, and again two weeks in Mogadishu. Our plane would take off from Cairo, come down, pick up the patients, and fly back to Cairo and then on to Germany. That was our ultimate destination. If we had a really sick patient who couldn't tolerate a stop in Cairo, we would go all the way on to Germany, which was a ten-hour flight. It was really hard on the patient and hard on the crew. But sometimes you just have to do it.

It was a United Nations effort. On the flight line in Somalia, you had the different countries camped all the way around the flight line. You had Americans here, Pakistanis there, Egyptians

Susan caring for casualties on an aerovac mission

here, Romanians here, Germans there, and Italians here—every country you could imagine. It turned out really well. If you had some connections, you could go to dinner at a different country every night. We carried a lot of American military, but we also did a lot of humanitarian missions. The Pakistanis got ambushed, and there were fifty patients. We regulated those to go to Pakistan, so we actually sent one of our aircrafts into Pakistan. It was the first time in I don't know how long. We did not have good relations with Pakistan back then. We sent fifty of their soldiers back with our medical crew taking care of them. That was really cool. We never took any Somalis out. They pretty much stayed in country. I don't remember any of them going out.

There were nurses on the ground as part of the humanitarian mission. The army was there as the ground unit. They initially were at the flight line as well. They got bombed a couple of times, so they decided it wasn't a good place for the hospital to be. They moved into town, which didn't seem much better either, because then they were right in the thick of things. So we would have to convoy initially to go up to the hospital to see patients or to do whatever we needed to do preflight because there are things you've got to tell patients or make sure they have before they get on your airplane. Initially we would just get in convoys and go up to the hospital, but pretty soon that became too dangerous because people were getting either sniped or bombed or whatever. So the army had the helicopters there, Blackhawks, and we would just ride the Blackhawk to the hospital. That was really cool because you don't get to fly in a Blackhawk helicopter all that much. That was a lot of fun. Pretty soon that too became very dangerous.

Did I feel like I was threatened? You know it's funny because people ask that, especially when you get back. They always want to know how close you were to being shot at or something like that. For me, I must always have a false sense of security or I just know that I'm being protected and watched over and that whatever happens is going to happen no matter what. I know I have to be careful, but when I was deployed and doing my job, thank goodness for me that was always way back in my mind. I'm not so concerned with safety or things like that.

We did have a couple of instances. We had gone in a convoy to the hospital and there were several of us in the convoy and we were done with whatever we had to do. It was me, one other flight nurse, and the SP. We were in a Humvee and we were done with our task, so we just thought we would go ahead and drive back. The convoy was still doing their stuff, so they stayed. Well, I won't mention names. The marine that was our SP escort asked if we wanted to take a different way home, because we would always take the same path back and forth. So we said, "Sure!"

We went through a district called K-4. The day after we went through there, we were banned from going through that area because it was so dangerous. We were going down this street and there was a car accident in front of us, so that blocked all the traffic. I don't know how it happened, but all of a sudden there were two or three hundred Somalis coming out into the street. Whenever we drove in a convoy, we always carried a stick because people reach into your vehicle and try to steal things. As they were reaching in you'd swat them, and that was basically your protection. We all had to carry guns. That was the first time nurses had ever had to carry guns. You always had your weapon strapped to your chest.

On this particular day, the accident, Somalis surrounding us, the marine was in the front seat of the Humvee and the other flight nurse and I were in the back seat. As this swarm of people started to approach our vehicle—and it wasn't just our vehicle, there were several vehicles—thank goodness there was a UN vehicle behind us with a turret gun. The other flight nurse and I ended up back to back in the vehicle facing our respective window with our sticks because these people were just converging on our vehicle and they were grabbing at anything that wasn't tied down, especially our sunglasses. So we're beating people out of the vehicle. They popped the back of the vehicle and start scrambling in and stealing. It's like you're just beating people right and left. This whole time I kept thinking, "Please don't let me have to pull this gun off my chest and start using it." Then next thing I hear is the nurse who's got her back to me and she says, "That guy over there has a knife." I kind of looked around and this guy lifted up his shirt to show that he's got this huge machete stuck down his pants. He was just showing us to let us know that he had a weapon.

The next thing I hear is the marine, our driver, with his M-16 locking up. I was like, "Oh my goodness, please please just let us get through here." My first thought was, "I wish I had a little piece of paper to write a note to my mom and tell her that I loved her so I could stick it down my shirt, and hopefully somebody would find it." Then I realized, "That's so stupid, my mom knows I love her and I don't need to write a note to tell her." But it's one of those crazy thoughts that passes through your mind when you don't know what's going to happen next. Anyway, the traffic finally cleared. What seemed like an eternity was probably only about ten minutes. So we get back to the base and I had that incredible adrenaline surge and thought, "We made it. That was the weirdest experience, and I'm so glad we're here. I will never do it again." But I'm so glad I had that experience because it was so incredible.

Another time one of the army pilots and I had gotten to be friends. He was going through a hard time at home with his wife and everything. He just needed someone he could talk to. We had concertina wire all around the camp, and we were told never to go outside of that. Well, there was this fuel truck with a bench beside it. It was parked just right outside the concertina wire because, of course, you can't maneuver the truck inside of it, so we just walked right outside the concertina wire. We were just sitting on the bench chatting. All of a sudden we heard gunfire and we could see the tracer bullets going right over our camp and right over the fuel truck. So we're like, "Oh, crap." Here it is. It's dark outside. We can't run into camp because camp doesn't know what's going on and all they hear is the gunfire, so if they see people running, they're probably going to shoot us. So we just kind of stayed there waiting to see what was going to happen because there were reports that the Somalis were trying to come over the wall of the camp. So we we're just sitting there and didn't hear anything after that.

We probably waited half an hour and still nothing, so we thought we needed to do something because we didn't know what was going on inside camp either, and they were probably looking for us because they must be doing head counts. It was probably about forty-five minutes after the incident. We kind of nice and slowly walked into camp talking so they could hear our voices and know that we were coming. They had blackout conditions in the camp, so we made our way to our individual tents. I got into my cot, and the person next to me said, "Susan, is that you?" And I said, "Yeah, what happened?" She said that evidently some Somalis tried to come over the fence, and the Egyptian guard went crazy and was just shooting randomly all over the place. She said, "I knew where you were, I knew who you were with, so when they came in to do the head count and called your name, I just said 'Here.'" So I thanked her.

Everything turned out fine, but it's times like that that you don't know what's going on. You don't know how threatened you really are. I guess the different countries took turns posting guards on the wall, and he must have seen people coming up. I don't know if he was shooting directly at them or firing warning shots or had too much to drink. Who knows?

I think if you thought about these kinds of experiences and knew that they were going to happen, it would be something that you wouldn't want to go into or do. My mom always used to say that I was looking for adventure, and maybe that's it. But I don't focus on the danger of the experience. I think I always have to ask, "Why am I doing this?" Well, I'm doing this for a reason. "Am I willing to do whatever it takes?" Well, yeah, because I've already made that commitment and taken that oath, and that's what's asked of me. Like I say, if you knew it beforehand, you probably wouldn't do it, but you don't know the individual experience that might be the one or the one that comes close. Sure, if we had known that we were going to have our vehicle surrounded and that we would have to beat people out of it, we wouldn't have gone that way, but you never know.

When I was young, I always used to think I would die at an early age. Don't ask me why. But that early age I thought was more close to my twenties, and here I am at forty-three years old and I'm thinking I haven't had that feeling or thought for a long time. I guess I'm not destined to die at a young age. I had another experience after my mom died. She died in 1997. I had this feeling after she died like, "My mission on earth is complete. I have eased my mother out of this world and have helped to take care of her until she could die. Now I feel like my mission is done." Then I realized I still had my own mission to complete. I guess I just have this innate sense that I'm protected and taken care of and that my Father in Heaven is with me and that whatever is going to happen is going to happen because of the experience that I need to have or the growth I need. I don't think everyone experiences that, because I've had friends in the past who seemed to be afraid of everyday life. Part of me, when I sit and listen to them, has a really hard time. "What's the matter with you? That's not right." And maybe it's the way they were brought up or they didn't have that religious background. To live in fear everyday—that's got to be hard.

Absolutely, I think being in the air force is part of what I'm supposed to be. I became a nurse by accident. My very first job when I was sixteen was in a nursing home, and my job was to wash the wheelchairs, pass ice water, and feed patients. I considered myself an assistant to a nursing assistant. Then I graduated to be a nursing assistant. After high school I was working at this convalescent hospital full time, there was a group of people who were going to go down to the city college and take the entrance exams for the LPN program. I thought, "Hey, I'll go with you," so we went. There were probably six or seven of us that went down. I was the only one that passed. I had to ask myself if I was doing this because everyone else was doing it or because I really want to become a nurse. So I thought, "Well, I'm not doing anything right now." So I went to the LVN program and of course that led to the RN program, which just continued on.

I guess for so long I had been working and going to school, doing both at the same time. When I graduated from my RN program, I found myself just working for the first time. Then that's when I got interested in the law, so I went to law school, and I was working and going to school again. When I got finished with that, boom, all of a sudden I was just working again. I was working at the law firm, and call it boredom or whatever, I guess I just don't know how to not be busy. It was then that I was looking through my nursing magazines and saw the ad. I went through the interview and said, "Hey, this sounds great."

Susan with the marines in Somalia, 1993

Now that I'm not working and going to school all the time, I'm working and doing the reserves. I've got at least those two things going still. When I joined the military, I think I just became a different person. It caused whatever was in me to sprout and grow because I was forced into different situations (like leadership positions), and I hated that. Initially I hated being put in a leadership position. Once I did it several times and started to become comfortable with it, I realized I kind of liked it because now I could set the tone. I could not do things my way, but I could make sure things ran smoothly and got done efficiently. I think that's the part of the leadership position that I liked, so I knew I was destined for the military. If I had known it was going to be like this, I would have joined years ago, and I would have been able to retire by now.

I graduated from nursing school in 1983, and I didn't join the air force until 1988. I was married at that time. I got divorced and then joined the air force. When I was married, we had some friends, and the wife was in the navy. They had been to the Philippines and lived in all these places. She was active duty. I thought, "Oh, I wouldn't like being told where I had to live and having to move to someplace that I might not like." I knew that active duty wasn't really for me, so I thought, "Hey, the reserves, that's great because I can live where I want and work where I want. I don't have to be at Balboa. I don't have to be in a tent with the army. I can go on a plane and fly and I can stay in hotels." I chose the air force over the other services because of what I could do with them.

I think that until we have certain experiences in life, we don't know what we're capable of doing. It's the same no matter what you do. If you're challenged, you're going to rise to the opportunity. It's like our callings at Church. My first calling was a Primary instructor, and I thought, "Holy cow!" Number one, I don't do kids. I'm forty-three and I don't have children. I'm not exposed to children. I don't know how to deal with children all the time. Sure I have fun with them and laugh and joke, but to know how to control them and to make them listen and discipline, I don't know how to do that, so it was really hard for me. But I learned how through trial and error. My next calling was camp director. Well now I had the teenage girls. Oh my goodness, teenagers! They're harder than the kids. I had a lot to learn. I remember the stake leader said, "If you're ever in doubt, just keep loving them. No matter what they do, just keep loving them." So that was a real growing experience because you want to say, "No, you need to be over here and not over there!" Then again, going right into the military and being in charge of your crew and being responsible, that's something that they really can't teach you. They can teach you the principles, but then it's up to you to figure out how to apply them through trial and error. You don't always do it right, but at least the job gets done.

I remember my mom asking me, when I first became a nurse, "Susan, how do you do it? How do you deal with all the stuff you deal with during the day and then come home and be like a normal person?" And I said, "One day as I walked in the hospital and came through the front door, it was like a feeling. I could feel that I became another person." I must have put up that protective wall or whatever it is that you do in order to deal with the patient who has cancer or the child who is dying or the family member who is going through all the grief or whatever it is you do during the day. I think we all have our own protective mechanisms that we put up.

I was inactive for a very long period of time, about fifteen years, from my early twenties to my mid thirties. During that time of my inactivity, my coping mechanism was going out and partying with my girlfriends. We'd get drunk almost every night. I look back now and I see that that was a coping mechanism for nursing and for the stress of the day and for the crazy things I had to do or see, especially during deployments and wartime. You get done with your flight, and the first place everybody goes to is the bar. Then in my thirties, when I started going back to church and stopped the drinking and other things, I realized, "Uh oh, what am I going to use for my coping now?" Then it became chocolate for a while. Then it was exercise for a while. Sometimes it's a book. My escape during the war was a book—to be able to totally focus on one thing and be in another world. That was just an escape. So home life as opposed to professional life during the various years of my life have been a little different. I just did what I had to do. I now know that I need to concentrate on being a social person because as I've gotten older, I've realized that I'm involved in fewer social activities. When I was younger, we were out all the time socializing. Now that I'm older, I prefer to stay home, and it's just nice to have the peace and quiet.

I would do it all over again. If there was another war, I would volunteer for that one too. It's kind of funny because we knew that the war was coming up, we didn't know when, and they were asking for volunteer lists because we have a squadron of 150 people. In an air evac squadron, they usually don't deploy your whole squadron. They usually take bits and pieces and make their own squadron with a bunch of different people. So when we knew that the war was coming up, boy I was like, "Are you sure I'm on the volunteer list? I want to see it." Then when we got the call, it was like, "Uh-oh. This is really going to happen now." But I knew that because I have over fifteen years in that this might be my last chance for a war and my last chance to do what I've been trained to do. Maybe you get psyched up your whole career because this is what you're trained to do and then finally you're able to do it. There are several people in our squadron like me.

Then there are several people like, "Hey you know what, I joined to go to school and to get benefits, and I've got a family now." I totally understand that. I can't even imagine being a regular reservist and having children and being gone one weekend a month, let alone being deployed away from your home when you have kids. So I'm so thankful that my life worked out to where I've been single and I can just float around and go wherever I'm asked to go. But I remember thinking, "This might be my last chance for war, so I'll go."

Each deployment is different. For Desert Storm, I was in England. It was a party time. We never saw a patient. We never got on an airplane, never flew. Operation Restore Hope was half party, half scary. When we were in Cairo, we were in five-star hotels and were catered to. It was just wonderful. Then when we were in Somalia, we were in a tent in the middle of a desert, but still that was great. Then with this war, it was totally different because there was no fun-and-games time. There was none of that party time or that let down and relax time. In that seven months, I would venture to say I had five days off. On those five days, if you were in England, you went down into London, and that was your day off. Once we were in Sicily and we went to Mount Etna. Two more times I had days off in Germany, and that was pretty much it. Your other days were spent getting ready for the mission, doing the mission, or recovering from the mission. Then you started up that whole cycle again. I don't think of myself as being an adventurer. I think of myself as having a pretty mundane life that every once in a while has these blips on the screen of excitement. I would do it again. Maybe that's a personal thing, but I would do it again in a heartbeat.

When we got back, they were asking for volunteers who wanted to stay on active duty and probably go out again soon, and I said no to that. I was dead when I got back—mentally, physically, psychologically, spiritually, and emotionally. I felt like my sense of joy had been taken away, and it was so hard to integrate back into normal life, back into my family, friends, and home life. I don't remember it being that hard before with other deployments or coming home from my mission or other stretches of time of being gone, so right when I came back I said I was never going anywhere again. But I've recovered and am back to normal life, and, oh yeah, I would go back again.

In comparison to other times, when I was deployed for Desert Storm, we were only gone for three months, so that wasn't a big issue. We didn't see anything there. We heard about it on the news, but CNN was as close to the war as we got. In Somalia, it was such a great time that that's why it was hard to come home, because I didn't want to come home. It was an intense experience and I loved it. It's kind of like you leave the stress of your normal life and take on the stress of different life, but this stress is different. It's easier to take initially because it's a different stress. Then this time, I didn't really have any preconceived ideas of what it was going to be like because I just had no clue. I knew it was going to be totally different. When we got there, we were separated into crews, so I knew who I was going to be flying with. I had a great crew, people who I flew with all the time at home. Well I do one mission and then they split the crews up. My second crew was a crew that was at each other constantly—fighting, bickering, and having power struggles. It was horrible. I flew with them for a month on other deployments. I never ever remembered feeling like, "I can't wait to go home." But that's the way I felt during that time.

We were on one-year orders with an opportunity to extend for a year, so we didn't know when we were going to go home. I thought,

Susan in a casualty receiving area, 2003

"This is going to last forever and it's going to kill me." Thank goodness at the end of that month the crew I was with was in a special group and they got to go. That was hard too, seeing other people go home, especially after this difficult time I had been through with this crew. Plus, the guy who I had been dating sent me a "dear John," and it was right at the height of the war. All of these things were hitting me during this one period of time. The next crew, which was my last crew, I spent the most time with, probably two and a half or almost three months with them. They were a great crew, so then I thought, "Maybe I can make it now."

This whole time I kept thinking, "I can't wait to go home," and I had never felt like that on deployments before. Then I get home and it was like, "I can't wait to go back," because life is so hard now. It's hard to get back into a schedule and routine. I don't know what normal life is like. I don't have a job—well, I'm still on active duty. I had three weeks off. I was commuting back and forth from Riverside to the base. We get home, we have three weeks off. That was the hardest three weeks of my life. I had people living in my home who were moving out since I was moving back in. I wanted my house back. Then finally I got to live in my house. I woke up every morning and wondered, "What do I do?" There are so many things to do and you're overwhelmed, so you don't do anything. Then I found out that I had to start going back up to the base. It was such a relief and it felt so good to be around people who I had been deployed with, people who had been through the same thing that I had and understood the stressors. And they were all going through the same thing too. It was so good to get back to our family, our military family. It's weird now to be uncomfortable with your own family and to be very comfortable with your military family. That was my life. With my own family now, I have more of a level of comfort. When I first got back, I stayed with my brother for a week because people were still in my house. I didn't feel comfortable there because it wasn't my home. People always want to know how it was and what I did, and if they don't ask, you wonder why they're not. You're uncomfortable sometimes when they do. And now there are some who say, "I didn't know what to ask or what to say, so I just didn't."

You had such a structured life being on active duty for so long, and then all of a sudden there's no structure whatsoever. You felt overwhelmed, so you just didn't do anything because it was easier than having to tackle all these things. I guess for me, I felt like I needed to give myself permission to take a break. I've been through all this; it's okay to just sit on the couch and do nothing. My favorite thing was just flipping through the channels not watching anything because while I was deployed, we didn't have TV that we could understand. In Italy it was all in

Italian. In Germany we did have some TV, but nothing was familiar. So once I got home, it was like, "I have ninety-six channels that I can flip through." I wouldn't concentrate on any of them; I just wanted to see what they were.

The three weeks were hard, but I did feel like I needed them physically, especially because your sleep cycle is weird. It takes time just to get your sleep cycle back on track. When you're deployed, you slept, but you were always one step ahead of yourself. Alert days were hard because you were always in a state of "What's going to happen today?" You just never knew. It got to the point after a while where you just got so used to it that it wasn't a big deal any more.

When I got back, I did not want to share anything. Part of you feels like it's a very personal experience and if somebody hasn't been there, they can't understand it. When they do ask you specifically or they invite you to talk about it, you tend to be very superficial. You tell them pretty much what they already know—what they've seen on the news. Every once in a while you'll interject something like, "The seventy patients . . ." or something like that. But you never talk about how scared you were when you flew into the desert because of the intelligence briefing you got beforehand about how you might get shot and where the RPGs are located and what they're aiming at and the chemical possibilities and how you're having to strap on all your chem gear when you land in the desert. All this kind of stuff.

The first several weeks when we flew in, we were getting these intelligence briefings, and that was enough to scare the crap out of us. So that was hard. You don't talk a lot about that stuff. When we got back, unfortunately, it wasn't until about three or four months after we got back that our squadron had a debriefer. We didn't get debriefed until everybody was pretty much getting over it. We had already talked amongst ourselves. We went through about a month where everybody in our squadron didn't really say anything until one person said, "Are you having any difficulties now that we're back?" And I said, "Yeah!" Then we asked a couple of other people, and it turns out that everybody is having some sense of difficulty. Maybe not the same but in some facet of their life they're having some difficulty. We all talked about it, and then all of a sudden we're getting a debriefer.

I still keep in touch with the people in my squadron that were deployed at the same time. I see them every month. That's very nice because we all have a bond. The other people, we have bonds with them too, but it's a little different, not as strong. There are a couple of other people from different squadrons that I ended up flying with that I still keep in touch with. That's really neat to see what they're going through now. I got an e-mail from one of the guys I flew with the longest, and he talked about some of the difficulties he'd been through, so I wrote him back. He wrote me back and said, "I don't know if you knew this, but every time something happened or something came up that was difficult on the mission, I always kind of turned to you for validation or to make sure it was okay or what I did was right." I thought that was so sweet. I never realized that. But it's nice to hear stuff like that, especially with him, because I looked at him as being the guy in charge. He was the strong man, but he never showed his fear. The sign of a good leader is not showing how scared you really are.

I had been e-mailing the guy who sent me a "dear John." We only started dating two or three months before I left, but we were talking to each other every day and going out every other night before I left. We were pretty close. I had been gone about two months, and looking back I can tell that his e-mails had slipped off a little bit. Then I remember the day that I got the e-mail. We were able to go check our e-mails at either the library or tent or wherever the computers were set up. Like I say, it was that time when I was on that really hard crew, and when I got the e-mail, it was something I couldn't share with anybody.

I didn't feel close enough with anybody on my crew that I could share that, so I kept it inside. The other nurse who was very difficult was my roommate at the time. After I got the e-mail, I just remember I was walking home in the dark and went in between two buildings where I knew no one would see me, and I just leaned up against the wall and slid down to ground and was just bawling. I had to let it out and that was the only way I could then. That was really hard.

Through the Church, I had really great support. I had been the Relief Society president before I left, so the ward knew me. That was really nice. I would get a lot of e-mails. Every week the Achievement Day girls would get together and spend the last five minutes of their meeting writing to me. Their leader would then send all their cards to me. That was really special. Every week I would get a packet.

I have two big brothers; neither one has been in the military. My dad was actually in the navy for four years during Korea. They didn't call them this back then, but he was a SEAL. He did underwater demolition and all that good stuff. UDT is what they called them then. It's funny because once I joined the military, he started opening up and telling me a couple of stories. Then when I would go on deployments, especially after Somalia because I would write back all the time, he would open up a lot more. Especially now, after this one, I got back in August. My dad was a fireman, and he got emphysema really bad because he was a smoker, plus all the smoke from the fires, so he just moved in with me in November. He lives with me now, and we have more opportunity to talk. It's nice to talk about things with my dad, especially about things that he's kept in for so many years.

He worries a lot, especially now. When he was living in Georgia, he didn't know when I would go off on the weekends or whatever, but now that he's living with me, he knows. This weekend I'm going to be gone on a three-day mission, and he worries now because our planes are old and they're falling apart. He would never tell me how much he worried, but when I got home I could tell by some of the things he said that he was definitely worried. But he didn't want to let on to that, because he wanted to support me. He didn't want me to worry about him worrying.

He was very supportive and wrote me a lot. Most of the time when I received his letters, it was great. He had a very difficult living situation back home. That is one of the reasons he lives with me now, because life back there got so dangerous. So when he would write me about how he almost ended up in the hospital or how he did go to the hospital because he couldn't breathe. I was like, "There's no one taking care of him!" But thank goodness the Church was there and they were looking after him, so I knew that for the most part someone was looking out after him. But it was hard getting the bad news because, being the daughter, I'm the caretaker of the family. When something happens, that's my job. Being that far away, you have to just trust the rest of your family. I would write my brothers and tell them they need to call Dad once a week without fail. For the most part, it's good to hear from home.

After a while, it's like, "I hope no one else writes me, because I don't feel like writing back." I felt obligated to write back if someone wrote to me, but that got so hard. To a certain extent, I wanted to forget about life back home. When I first left—and maybe this was one of the reasons I got a dear John—I did not call my boyfriend. I would e-mail him, but I did not call him. I needed to make a break with home, and that's the way I did it, by not calling home. I e-mailed everybody, but I didn't maintain telephone contact. So you do need to break it off to a certain extent. I didn't want to know if my cat had to go the vet. I didn't want to know if my plumbing broke. But I'd still hear about all this stuff and it got to be hard, so I would tell my brother to just take care of things.

We have rotations right now. There's one going out in March. There are enough volunteers for that. There's another one going out in June sometime. I haven't heard if they have enough volunteers for that or not. Now normally I would say that I would go in June, but right now, now that my dad just moved in with me, I'm kind of in a different living situation with different responsibilities, so I have to think more about what I need to do versus what I would like to do. Right when I first started back here in my job, I wanted to go back because it was hard being integrated back into work again. But now I'm getting used to that.

On our airplane, we had three flight nurses and four medical technicians on every flight. Occasionally, but it got to be almost every flight, we would have a CCAT (Critical Care Air Transport) team. That consisted of a doctor, a critical care nurse, and a respiratory therapist. They would take no more than three patients. They could take three critical patients, but no more than that. We would give them our three worst patients, and we would do the rest. That was usually the ventilator and the cardiac monitor guy and somebody else who required suctioning or stuff that required hands-on every so often.

The form has a patient's name, their diagnosis, doctor's orders, and a place for nurse's charting. Half of the time it's old because they've been in the system for at least twenty-four to forty-eight hours. Sometimes you'd have patients puking their guts out because they're airsick, but you have no orders for Compazine or Phenergan or anything. Those were the times that we were thankful for the CCAT doc to write an order. We do have a couple of standing orders. Sometimes the doctors would be good about writing standing orders, or PRNs, but if they did not, in our regulations we have certain drugs that we can give as one-time doses. Nothing push or nothing IM, it's all PO. If they're vomiting, they're not going to be able to keep POs down. You just do what you can and hope you don't run out of barf bags.

I got to the point where I would carry around Dramamine everywhere because I never get airsick, but on these missions, probably because of the length of your day, once that fatigue hits, you're susceptible to everything. I remember two missions specifically where there was something wrong with the autopilot and we were just listing from side to side the whole time and everyone was throwing up. We were pushing Phenergan like crazy. The crew members would go in the corners and throw up in the barf bags and then go about their duties, then go and throw up again. We had no pharmacy support. For the really sick patients, we'd get either a bag or a box with all their medicines. You made sure during training missions that you had the right supplies requested. But during the war you hoped you had what you needed and you just made do.

I would say during the height of the war, we did a lot of putting out fires, because you came upon situations that you hadn't encountered before that you can't anticipate, so we were reacting. As we learned the kinds of things that were happening, and we knew that we were still going to be facing a lot of this stuff, we learned to be more prepared and to be able to act. After every mission, our entire crew would get together and debrief. We would actually have to do a written debrief for our commander about the problems we encountered and the solutions we implemented and the things we wanted to have change. We would give as many suggestions as possible.

We got along well with the other services. We worked a lot with the army. The navy, I don't think we had a whole lot of interaction with them other than as patients. They mostly got flown out on a helicopter and put on the boat because the boat was right off the land there. We had lots of patients from the marines, especially eighteen- or nineteen-year-old kids. That was hard. There were kids who now had no arms, legs, or eyes. I remember one kid who was sitting next to me.

He came on the plane and took off his helmet, and he was looking at the inside. I glanced over to see that he had a picture of his little baby girl with his wife. That was enough to break my heart. He turned to me and said, "I just missed her first birthday."

That was hard because all of a sudden they became human. They became real. They weren't just patients. They weren't just the belly wound or the burn. They were people and they had families and they were just like us. You try to always have a smile on your face. You always greet them. You always talk to them. They had been eating MREs for months and months. So what we as a crew used to do is take up a collection and we would all donate between five and ten dollars. This particular mission, we would do it once a week. We would take the money and go to the commissary and buy hot dogs, cookies, and french fries. We had these little ovens on the plane, so we could cook the food. These guys must have thought they had died and gone to heaven, because they had not had real food in so long. It was the coolest thing. We had a fireman on our crew for most of my flights, and somebody sent him this huge American flag that we hung inside the aircraft. When the patients saw this, they knew they were going to get some food. You always had to think of their morale because we knew that they had been through the worst of it. It wasn't us. We still got to stay in a bed and shower and go eat at restaurants. We had those things, but they didn't.

In the beginning when they came on the plane, you could tell they had been through something because of their affect and the look on their face. You could smile and do whatever, but they wouldn't respond as much. Some would but some wouldn't. Then they all seemed to be in a phase where they were much happier and much less stressed. Then I remember when we started doing the mission straight into Iraq. What would happen was we would pick up the patients in Kuwait, they had a 130 unit, a smaller plane, and they would go to Baghdad and Tikrit and Kirkuk and bring them down to Kuwait, and that's where we would pick them up. We started doing missions directly into Iraq and into Baghdad and bringing them straight to Germany. This was probably after the major fighting had gone on and I was ground support in Germany, so we recovered this plane that had just come in from Baghdad. These people had the flat affect and no energy, and they were quiet. It was weird to see that again. You knew that they had been through some stuff. It's hard because you can't talk on the plane. You can't hear. You have ear plugs in because the plane is so noisy, and you have to yell even at a close distance. Sometimes you could carry on conversations on the rare occasion that you had a lull in what you were doing because you had an eight-hour flight. The techs were able to chat more because they had fewer duties than the nurses. I would see the techs going up and down the aisle talking to people. Most of the time, the patients just slept. They were exhausted.

Who knows now at this point when I'll go. I'm kind of waiting for my dad to stabilize with his emphysema. If it was just selfish me, I would go with the next wave. It's a responsibility issue now. I have two brothers, but guys just don't see things the same way. Maybe guy nurses are different, but my brothers—we'll be all in the same room and none of them would see how my dad was suffering with his breathing. My brothers are more unifocal, whereas women can be doing something and know what's going on other places.

The Association of Military Surgeons of the United States has a conference every November, and I was fortunate enough to be one of the presenters this past November. There were around five thousand people there. At the time I presented, there were probably only two hundred because it was one of the breakout sessions. But one of the speakers talked about how he had just gotten back from Iraq and how misleading the news is. All we see is how all these Americans are being shot and killed and how we're spending all the money and how the Iraqis are still shooting at us and hating us. He said, "When we go to Iraq, when they see an American, they run up and hug us and thank us, and they are so grateful to us. They now have clean water, they now have food to eat, and they now have medical systems. They now have an infrastructure." He's talking about how all these people are so grateful for the things that they have now and the change that has happened. I think now's the time when they need to have the reporters embedded in these units so they can see what's really going on and the good that we're doing instead of getting the negative aspect from the news. So every opportunity I get, I tell people about that.

STEVEN MCCOLLEY

Steven McColley

I started off with a bachelor's degree in respiratory therapy, but I wanted to become a nurse anesthetist. I needed a degree in nursing and a license to do this, so I decided to attend the nursing program at Weber State University. In 1984, after two years of schooling, I graduated with my associate's degree in nursing. Afterwards, I began my anesthesia training program in Kansas City at the Truman Medical Center School of Nurse Anesthesia. When I went there, I was automatically enrolled in the University of Missouri Kansas City School of Biology for a master's degree. At the same time that I was receiving my anesthesia training, I was also going to graduate school at nights to work on my master's degree in biology. In 1987, after thirty months in my program, I was finally finished with my education.

After graduation I worked for a bit. In June 1990, I became a part of the Army Reserves, not to be mistaken for the Army National Guard. The difference between the two is that the Army National Guard is under the control of the governor, whereas the Army Reserves is under the control of the president.

There was no obligation for me to enter the military, but I've always felt at some point that I wanted to enter. My father was a marine. He joined the Marine Corps Reserves in 1950 and was immediately called up to go to Korea. My brother was active duty military in the army for about twelve years, but he never saw any combat. In June 1990, he gave up his command of the 24th Mechanized Infantry of Stewart, Georgia. Unfortunately, just a few months later in August, his unit was called up after Saddam Hussein's invasion. I think he was quite upset with the fact that he had given up his command to someone else right before his unit got tagged. After ten years of infantry, I think he would have wanted to be there. There were people he knew who were going, yet he wasn't going with them. I was relieved that he wasn't going, but then a few months later I got tagged and called up with the 328th General Hospital in West Germany during Operation Desert Storm.

In February 1990, I was working at the Ogden Regional Medical Center (St. Benedict's Hospital) in Ogden, Utah. Later that November, I received my first call. At that time I was single, so it wasn't a big deal for me to leave. My parents were even living in Germany then. They were serving a mission for The Church of Jesus Christ of Latter-day Saints in Frankfurt, Germany. I had just been visiting them in October when I told them it was a possibility for me to come back to Germany. It was ironic that three days before my parents were to leave their mission to come home, I landed at the Frankfurt International Airport. I was able to meet with my parents and speak to them for half an hour before I was rushed off to Rhein-Main Air Force Base. I was then sent off from Frankfurt to Nuremberg, where the Nazi trials were. I got to Nuremberg in December 1990.

I didn't know many people in my unit because I first started with the NAAD, the National Army Medical Department's Augmentation Detachment. The NAAD is essentially a float pool where we were assigned to a unit but didn't have to drill with that unit if we were more than a certain number of miles away from our home unit. Physicians, nurse anesthetists, and such were assigned to one unit but drilled somewhere else with a different unit. At the time I was actually drilling up in Ogden, so I was close enough to meet with them for my drills. But at the same time, the headquarters were up in Salt Lake City, which was a ways away from where I was actually living.

I only drilled with the unit in Ogden twice before I got tagged. I hadn't even put on my uniform yet, nor did I know where things went. It is a requirement for everyone in a unit to go through officer basic course before being shipped out, but when my unit got called up, not everyone had fulfilled this requirement. There were twenty-six of us who had to go to a two-week course in San Antonio, Texas, to complete our training. When we came home, we were immediately shipped to Germany after completing our in-processing at Fort Carson, Colorado. The rest of our unit had already flown to Germany by the time the twenty-six of us were ready.

My unit and I were at the 98th General Hospital in Nuremberg. We were set up for four operating rooms so we could run twenty-four hours a day. We did all kinds of surgeries there, especially orthopedic and amputations. Before the ground war there were many football, volleyball, and jeep injuries. But soon after the war started, it became bullet, tank, or shrapnel wounds that brought patients to us.

Our patients were mostly casualties from combat rather than friendly fire. The ground war ended abruptly one hundred hours after it began. Many causalities were brought to us then. Most of those casualties came from the Gulf and were actually treated in places like Saudi or Kuwait before being flown to us on a C-130 or C-141. We were getting around fifty patients a day for about a week an a half, so we saw approximately three hundred to three hundred and fifty patients total. This was certainly fewer than we had anticipated.

For the most part we tried our best to keep from being shot by terrorists, so our involvement with the community was limited. I tried to blend in and not let the Germans know that I was an American. I even bought some German clothes for when I went outside, and my hair was longer than the usual military standard.

I guess you can say I was quite familiar with the language and country of Germany. I took German in junior high, high school, and college, so I was able to speak the language well enough to get by. My brother and parents also spoke German after serving their missions for the Church there. I went to Germany a couple of times during my high school years and afterward. It was helpful to know the language and culture, especially when going out to eat. I always had to help my friends with the menu and the customs. In Nuremberg, if customers left a 15 percent tip, the Germans would go crazy on them because the tip is included in the meal. The people in Nuremburg didn't speak English, so I usually did all the ordering and paying.

The Germans weren't too friendly. When we first got to Germany, we rode the subways and street cars everywhere. One time there was a transit worker who was giving us trouble, so I took everyone's money and gave it to the man and told him I needed twenty-four passes to start the same day. We had a little conversation, and I insisted that I needed all twenty-four passes. For those transit workers, their job is one of the greatest in the world. They just sit there and don't do anything. If someone wanted a rail pass, they would take a whole hour just to get one pass done.

So when I came in there with a request for twenty-four passes all at once, the guy wasn't too happy. I could see the disgruntled look on his face as he had to stamp out all those cards. Once I got the passes, I went back out and distributed them to everybody and told them how to get new ones when they needed to get them replaced. Word spread quickly throughout the unit that I could speak German, and I was happy to help others out.

The war ended sometime in March, but we still took care of many patients until there weren't many to deal with. Once our patient load reduced, the army saw that they didn't need the medical reserves or any other reserve units, so they packed us up and shipped us back to the States. We left Germany, and I came back to North Ogden, Utah.

Serving overseas was kind of like serving a mission for the Church. I had served my mission in Toronto, Canada, before joining the reserves. Once again, I was in a small area where there weren't many Latter-day Saints, so I appreciated the opportunities I had to spend time with other Saints. We Latter-day Saint soldiers didn't receive any Church callings. Our main and usually only responsibility was just to go to church on Sundays. We had to stay in the hospital if we were on call, but otherwise, we always went to church on Sundays.

There was an English-speaking branch in Germany that met right after the German branch. While they had sacrament meeting, we would have our priesthood meeting. We walked to the chapel since it wasn't too far away. The members who attended the English-speaking branch were mostly military people or people connected with military. The leadership of the branch was military people too. We were only in that location for a short time, so I don't really remember what the structure was like. I couldn't even tell you who the bishop was or anything else. I just know where the elders quorum met and where the chapel was located. I don't really remember going to Sunday School while I was there. We usually just had priesthood class and sacrament meeting.

During my time in Germany, I didn't see any other cities, because we had tight limitations. Our commander drew a very small circle around Nuremberg on a map and said we couldn't go outside that circle. He didn't want people to be absent in the event of mass casualties; otherwise there would have been big problems. This was a huge possibility because we were expecting many casualties, but overall we got far fewer casualties than we thought we would get.

Anytime people go to war, they get the chance to have many experiences and be with different people. It's a nice thing because it provides opportunities for strengthening testimonies. If Latter-day Saints become complacent in their Church activity and do nothing but the regular grind every day, they may have a greater tendency to slip a little bit. But when someone gets to experience different opportunities, it helps to strengthen them because they're in a new environment with new challenges. I'm not a person who is tempted by coffee, cigarettes, or any of that kind of stuff, so being away from home where no one would have seen me was not a big challenge for me.

After I came back from Germany, I continued to drill with the 328th unit over the next seven years. Around 1997 or 1998, I received a letter in the mail saying I'd been transferred from the 328th unit to the 934th Forward Surgical Team. I didn't know what a forward surgical team was, but I knew what the word *forward* meant. I didn't want anything to do with it. It was a brand-new team and a brand-new concept that the army was putting together. The team had a rocky start because they started with only two nurse anesthetists. I was the fourth nurse anesthetist by the time they brought me on. We had two local guys, two NAAD people, and one unit administrator. The unit administrator was not a friendly person, but he was still the full-time administrator for the unit. He felt that he already had the two people he needed with the two local guys. Later that unit became short-staffed when two of the CRNAs left. At that time the unit was supposed to do their first two-week assignment, where they actually put the hospital together. Since they were short-staffed, the unit administrator was just begging me to come. From then on, things were friendlier each time I went to drill with them.

I chose not to drill often with that unit since I had that option, but I did do my summer camps with them. We did one at Fort Polk at the Joint Readiness Training Center (JRTC) in Fort Polk, Louisiana. Training at that site was supposed to be the closest to combat we would ever get. It was, for those of us who didn't know anything, but we already knew how to put together a hospital and take it down.

Essentially there were twenty people in my unit, including two nurse anesthetists and four surgeons. Three of those surgeons were general surgeons, and the other was an orthopedic surgeon. We also had an emergency room nurse, a recovery nurse, an executive officer, a commander, three scrub technicians, and medics. Everybody and everything fit in our six Humvees with trailers. We would take all of our equipment, ammunition, generators, gas, food, water, and other supplies into the Humvees and trailers, and then we would be off. All together we were an FST unit, which was a forward surgical team, also called a "fast team."

This past December there was a change in command. The new commander was a nurse anesthetist, and he called a friend of his and invited him to join the unit. This meant we now had three nurse anesthetists. Two of them were full-time and drilled with the unit, and I was the NAAD person. When the unit got called up in February, the new commander was slotted to go, and he slotted his nurse anesthetist friend to go as well. While the commander was fulfilling command obligations and trying to get our unit ready, the rest of us met together for one week in February. The commander's friend had only drilled with the unit once and was just getting back into the military after being out of it for a while, so he was scrambling to get his paperwork in order so he could get privileges and go with us. This meant that there was no one taking care of the anesthesia supplies and business, so I was called and asked to go and help out.

I ended up packing everything that was going to be available to the unit. I talked to a real transplant surgeon from LDS Hospital in Salt Lake City, Utah. He had been in Afghanistan with a forward surgical team, so I kind of pumped him for information on what things I should pack. I asked for information from anyone who had ever been deployed.

For some reason, I always felt there was a good chance that we would be going somewhere soon. I felt it could be to Afghanistan, Bosnia, or Kosovo, because those were places that were still rotating people. Iraq was not on my mind at that time, but when people were suddenly being sent to Iraq, I felt there was a good chance that we would be going there as well.

Before departing, I put all the equipment and supplies together for our hospital. I found out that neither of our anesthesia machines were working and needed to be replaced. The whole fast team centers around the operating room. If there were no anesthesia machines that worked, then nothing would have worked at all. When I called the people in the army, they didn't argue with me about replacing major equipment like the anesthesia machines, because they knew the fast team was dead without them. The machines weren't replaced until we went to Fort Lewis, Washington. Interestingly enough, the two anesthesia machines came from Hill Air Force Base in Ogden, where we had just come from. We could have just driven up the street and gotten them, but the army usually gave us the roundabout way with things.

My unit was at Fort Lewis a few weeks for our in-processing. We were supposed to have only been slotted for twenty people, but there were twenty-eight people in the 934th Surgical Team unit. One enlisted woman was pregnant, so she wasn't going to go. Then there were two others who had just barely joined the unit, and their slots were taken up by someone else, like me. So there were about eight of us who weren't able to go, but we still went in during that time to help out as much as we could getting the unit ready to go.

They spent a week in Salt Lake City, Utah, before going to Fort Lewis for their in-processing. After they left, I came back to Utah to work at the VA Hospital. In the meantime, while the unit was up in Fort Lewis, I was calling up the NAAD to see if anyone needed a nurse anesthetist to go over to Iraq. To my surprise, they just weren't short of nurse anesthetists. Nobody could find a slot for me. I said it was okay, but I let it be known that I was a free entity and could be taken.

The unit then went to Ryder Trauma Training Center in Miami, Florida. The Ryder Trucking Company donated money to build that hospital. The army has a contract with them, so they rotate these forward surgical teams down there so they can work with trauma and improve their skills. When the unit got to Florida, they found out that neither of the nurse anesthetists were prepared for the job that lay ahead. One nurse anesthetist worked in an outpatient surgical center for more than twenty years doing only office surgeries. The other nurse anesthetist had been working for eight years, but he had been in a small community and hadn't had any experience with trauma. Since these two nurse anesthetists weren't used to being around trauma cases, they didn't feel comfortable.

The unit knew I had experience in hospitals doing emergency and trauma work, so they wanted me to join them. They felt more comfortable having someone who was up to date on trauma surgeries than having only those two other nurse anesthetists. So on March 6, when the unit was coming back, my orders came in to Salt Lake City, and I received twenty-four hours' notice. My unit wanted to go to war, so we essentially volunteered to go. We were the only reserve forward surgical team in the theater during the war.

I had gotten married in 1994. I had three sons and one little daughter. My second oldest son and baby daughter had just celebrated their birthdays in January and February when I got tagged. My other two children's birthdays were in April and May, but I was in Iraq for both of those. My wife had no previous military experience. Her father had served twenty years in the navy, but he was out of the navy by the time he married her mother. My wife did pretty well in my absence. We also had a really good ward that geared up for this kind of stuff. Once I knew I had only a few hours to leave, I called my bishop to inform him and ask him to watch out for my family. He and the whole ward geared up to help. They were the kind of people who live to serve and help others.

I could have passed on the opportunity to go to Iraq, but I wanted to make it known that I was volunteering. My wife was not happy with this. I felt I was going to go either way. There was no doubt in my mind that I would have been going somewhere sometime. It was easier for me to make the decision to go then rather than wait and get called during a bad time. I didn't want to be on a family vacation and get a twenty-four-hour notice and have to cancel everything. There was one guy who was on his honeymoon when he got called and had to come back early. I didn't want that sort of thing to happen to me and my family. I wanted the word out that I was ready so I could go soon, have my obligation taken care of, and have some control over my enlistment.

Our unit flew over to Kuwait in March, and then we went a couple of days across the berm border and into Iraq. We crossed as a unit with our six Humvees and trailers. There was a convoy that was going north to the same place that we needed to go, so we went along with them. March was the beginning of spring. The sun would be down by 5:30 p.m., so we'd put on our night vision goggles. I usually rode on the back of the Humvee. Sometimes we'd stop along the way at a couple of places to get gas from U.S. military supply lines.

Early one morning around 1:30, someone realized that we were completely lost. So about 2:00 a.m., we turned around and went back to the refueling point, where we felt we were safe. We threw out our cots near the Humvees and slept right there. We woke up at 6:00 that morning and hooked up with the convoy again. Less than a week before, the 507th Main Force Company had gotten lost in essentially the same place and had gotten shot at, resulting in nine deaths. That was a little unnerving.

The same thing happened again the next night, but this time we got lost further north. We were traveling with an MP group that was supposed to be leading us. They got us lost, so we had to turn around. As we were turning around, we got separated, and a Humvee right behind me hit a dune and flipped its trailer over. We didn't want to stop too long, so we got out and unhooked the trailer from the Humvee, then took off without the trailer. We went back to another refueling point at 2:00 a.m. We woke up at 6:00 a.m. and went back to get the trailer. When we got to the trailer, it was empty. There was nothing on it; even the tires were gone. If we had stayed there during the night, we surely would have been attacked.

We continued to travel up north until we hit a place called Camp Spartan. As soon as we got there, we were told, "Hurry up, get going, and put your hospital together! We've got casualties coming within half an hour!" Casualties were coming as we were still setting up the hospital. It took about an hour and a half to two hours to get the hospital set up, put together, and ready to go. The hospital was made out of a general-purpose tent with no heating or air-conditioning. We had four beds in the intensive care unit. We also had monitors and ventilators. In fact, the first patient I worked on ended up on a ventilator, and we did surgery on her again the next morning. Our hospital seemed to be full most of the time. We would do surgery at night because that's when we usually received casualties. Between surgeries, we would walk out the back of the tent and watch the 3rd Infantry Division bomb the Karbala Gap. We would sit and watch the rockets before going back in for more surgeries. Then we would come back out and watch more rockets.

Instead of just packing supplies for U.S. military men, which was what we expected to get for casualties, I followed the advice of others and also packed supplies for women and children. Sure enough, the first two patients we had were women. They were local civilians who had been hit and brought to us. During our time at Camp Spartan, we operated on a lot of prisoners of war. There was even a prisoner of war camp right next to us. People would bring us civilians who had been shot, we'd work on them, and then they would go to the prisoner's camp for interrogation and be released if they were not a threat.

My unit decided early on that we would help anyone who came to our doors. The army told us that we would have to take care of them as if they were Americans. We all thought, "You don't have to tell us that, we're reservists. We're essentially private practitioners over here. We don't turn people away!" It was primarily our motto, "Whatsoever you have done unto the least of these, you have done unto me." We heard that other units had told their staff that they were not going to take kids or civilians because they were active duty. Not all units were like us. We worked on anyone that came through the door, many of whom were children of various ages. One time we had a set of brothers younger than nine years old. Another time, we had a fourteen-year-old come in with thirty wounds all up and down his back and legs. We also had a lot of women and some of our own guys as patients.

As soon as we were done working on patients in one place, we'd move on to another place. Once during our travels with the convoy, my unit ended up between the 3rd ID and an enemy tank battalion, so instead of being behind the lines, we were actually in front of the lines!

The next place we set up was Camp Dogwood. We actually found a building there where we were able to do surgeries. From Camp Dogwood we drove north to Baghdad. At one point during this time, we saw and heard AK-47s shooting at us. The Humvee right behind me got shot at and picked up a bullet hole. No one got hurt, but we knew that we were being shot at. We got through and continued north to Balad, where we stayed for a few weeks doing more surgeries. While we were there, our base was attacked. We were just a few hundred yards from the firefight, up on top of a cement airplane hanger with our weapons loaded and drawn. If the enemy had gotten through the first line of defense, we would have been the next in line. The next day was Saddam Hussein's birthday, and we felt that we would be attacked again. Because we had such a huge perimeter around us, volunteers were needed to help cover it. I volunteered with some other officers to go and guard part of the perimeter in case of another attack.

An interesting thing happened while at Camp Dogwood. One of my old buddies, a CRNA (nurse anesthetist) got called up to join us. We then had twenty-one members in the unit. Usually I would trade off cases with the commander, but I ended up with the most cases since the commander was very busy. After my old buddy Mitch came, he and I traded cases. Sometimes we would do anywhere from five to eight cases per day, depending on how busy the 3rd ID was. The 3rd ID were the guys who did pretty much all the fighting. Since we were right with them the whole time, everyone in our unit was awarded the Combat Medical Badge for our work with the 3rd ID. After staying in Balad for a while, we went on to Tikrit, Saddam's home town. By the time we got to Tikrit, the war had ended.

We called it "jumping" whenever we would move from one area to another. While we were jumping from Balad to Tikrit, Secretary of Defense Donald Rumsfeld was scheduled to speak at the Baghdad International Airport. I was chosen from my unit to go and represent the 30th Medical Brigade. I flew in a Chinook from Balad down to Baghdad and back, which was about a forty-five-minute to one-hour flight. The next day, after listening to Secretary Rumsfeld's talk, I flew back in a Blackhawk. The crew that I was with treated me very well. I was given MREs to eat and a place to sleep. I was supposed to have flown to Tikrit, but there was a full-bird colonel that had "hijacked" the bird. The crew was going to leave me in Balad, but I opted to stay with the crew since I hated Balad. We ended up flying to Mosul while we dropped off the colonel and his crew. Eventually they dropped me back off at Tikrit, where I had to find my unit, but they had actually dropped me off at the wrong place! Just as they started taking off, the chief warrant officer, who was also a pilot, said, "Man, you're in the wrong place!" He grabbed my stuff and I grabbed my weapons, and we started running after the helicopter. The helicopter came down and I got back in; then we flew to the right place.

Although the war had ended by the time we got to Tikrit, we stayed there to work on patients. We set up our operating room on an army post's airbase north of Tikrit. For five weeks we were going in and out of that place. We had to drive from the airbase to Tikrit and back, and from the airbase to Balad and back. Each time we did so, we had to be armed and told what to avoid. One day we had to go downtown to Saddam's palace where the engineers were and take some water with us. Our hospital in Tikrit was so bad that the army kept over-flying us. The hospital building had no windows, so dirt would get in and cover everything. We only did one case during our whole five week stay because casualties were taken to other places. While we were there, we would help out the 566th Area Support Medical Company (ASMC) that we were assigned with. They would call us up if they had a trauma that they couldn't handle. We would get in there, move their people off to the side, and then take over their emergency room during the trauma. After we took care of and stabilized the patient, we would turn the care back over to the company.

By this time, we had worked on more than one hundred patients and had done about fifty or sixty surgeries. The only time we ever came close to having someone die was when we worked at Camp Dogwood on a fourteen-year-old civilian boy who came to us after being operated on somewhere else. When we received him, he had a hematocrit of less than ten and had already crashed before crashing again hemodynamically. I was called over to put an endotracheal tube in him while the others were trying to stop his profuse bleeding. They ended up having to amputate his leg to keep him from dying. In the meantime, his blood pressure had crashed.

Our commander announced that anyone with type O blood needed to help out. Our blood refrigerator had broken earlier because it was so old, so we kept all of the stored blood up the street with the med log. I sat three volunteers down and stuck each of them with an intravenous line (IV). The IV was a 14- or 16-gauge that had a little tubing with a three-way stopcock on the end of it. I taped it down to each volunteer, drew blood out of each arm, turned off the stop cock, then turned and infused their blood right into the patient. I was able to administer a total of 750 cc of blood from those three volunteers. After forty-five minutes of requesting the blood from our blood refrigerator, it finally came. I stopped drawing blood from those guys and started administering the blood from our blood bank. As soon as I started pumping all that blood into the kid, he regained hemodynamic stability and survived.

The next day the captain in charge of the blood bank hassled me about why I gave whole blood without having done a type and cross test. Let me tell you, he just took on the wrong person. I ate him alive. We all knew about Jamie Smith, who died in Mogadishu in 1993. The unit couldn't ship him out fast enough, so they just gave him fluids until he eventually bled to death. There was also Jason Cunningham, who died from a gunshot wound in Afghanistan almost two years ago. The unit couldn't evacuate him fast enough, so they gave him IV fluids until he bled to death as well. We knew this fourteen-year-old boy was going through the same thing. We were pouring fluids into him, but he kept bleeding. My unit and I decided we were not going to let another incident happen again, so we drew blood. The decision was immediately made. We didn't want to watch this kid die in front of us when we had blood that could save him. It was the policy to use a walking blood bank, so I didn't care that this captain didn't like the fact that I didn't type and cross, especially when it was O-positive blood. I knew the kid could take it. And I only took blood from people who were O-positive. The kid had no reaction to the blood, and within two to three weeks, he went home. His leg was amputated, but he went home.

We were running in between having things like that and being shot at in Balad and Baghdad. We tried our best to survive on MREs. Heat often bothered us throughout the day. If we worked on patients early in the morning, they would be freezing to death because we had no way to keep them warm. But when we did surgeries later in the day, everyone had a temperature of 102 degrees. It was hot, and there were flies landing everywhere and dust blowing around. We tried to clean up as best as we could, but we could only do so much when there was a sandstorm going on and dust flying everywhere. I don't know if any infections resulted from this because we didn't keep patients around for very long. My unit had to be able to quickly take apart the hospital and move, so our patients didn't stay long. We usually kept a patient for only a couple of days before we shipped them out to a place like Kuwait. If the patient was an Iraqi, we shipped him to southern Iraq. Most of our patients went on a Blackhawk to the Navy's USS *Comfort* ship, which was anchored in the Gulf.

Since my unit went wherever the 3rd ID went, we spent a lot of time sitting around and waiting. If we saw an MEK, (a kitchen on wheels that dished out hot foods) we knew we would be jumping soon. We came to this conclusion because oftentimes the MEK would be around one day for one meal, and then we'd get the word to jump the next day. Afterwards, we would be back to eating cold MREs. It was as if the MEK was there to kind of boost our spirits before a jump.

Our unit would move to wherever there was a battle, and usually it would end just a couple of hours before we arrived. In fact, there were a couple of times that the other unit pulled a Bradley tank right in front of our convoy. If a battle was still going on in front of us, we would have to wait for it to end. When we got to an area, there was no guarantee that it was enemy free. It just meant that our army had cleared out active opposition, but there was still the possibility of the enemy being there to shoot at us.

Because of the threat of something like that happening, all of us carried weapons and knew how to use them. The army trained us for this. In order to be deployed, we had to qualify on our weapon. To do this, we had to have twenty-three out of forty hits on our targets test. I did thirty-six out of forty using an M-16 when I was at Fort Lewis. I had used a rifle before and shot blanks from an M-16, but I had never had an M-16 with live rounds. My time in Fort Lewis was really the first time I had ever been in a target range with an M-16. During our testing, I had to get in and set my site and adjustments. It was winter then, so it was raining and freezing everyday. I would shake so bad, it's amazing that I was able to even hold my weapon at all. When my group and I went to our first testing, we ended up quitting because it was unbearably cold. Later I got smart and went to a clothing store to pick up some neoprene underwear and gloves. I was nice and toasty the next time I went to the qualifying range.

All of us Latter-day Saints who wore garments had special brown garments because we used desert camouflage uniforms (DCUs). The Church issued these garments to people with military identification. Most of the time it was so hot that I wouldn't wear a shirt, just my garment top. In our unit, a lot of us would write our blood type on our garment or undershirt tops, helmet, and the back of our boots. When I came back to the States and visited Hill Air Force Base, one of the officers thought it was quite unique of me to have my blood type on my boots. He came up to me and asked, "Is that your blood type on the back of your boots?" "Oh, yes it is," I replied. He just said, "Oh," and turned around and walked away after realizing where I had been. The air force guys didn't get around combat too much, so they found this type of labeling unusual. However, most people who were in combat did the same, so it wasn't unusual for me or my unit.

We were in the Gulf for a total of three months, and during that time we held church every Sunday. There were many of us who were made group leaders before we were deployed. We were set up as group leaders so we would be able to hold sacrament meetings. My stake president interviewed me and set me apart, like many other guys, so a lot of us had these cards that said we were ordained and set apart as group leaders to hold sacrament meetings. Most of the time we had sacrament meeting and a Sunday School lesson. We tried our best to also have priesthood lessons. The military even issued us our scriptures.

When we were in Camp Dogwood, just outside of Babylon, we held church on top of a building right next to an enemy prisoner of war (EPW) camp. The first time we had church there we sang the hymn "Ye Elders of Israel." It was funny because we would be singing Church hymns right next to the EPW camp. I'm pretty sure the EPWs just heard a bunch of men singing, but they didn't know we were holding our own church services. In our sacrament meetings, we would have talks as well as the sacrament.

Whoever was the group leader was also in charge of assigning talks.

We didn't have trouble keeping track of the days since we all had calendars and watches, but we still had very little information and news coming in to us. The *Stars and Stripes* magazines were always three to four weeks old by the time we got them. We never got any Church magazines or any mail from home because we were moving so much. About a week before I went back home, I finally received a package my wife had mailed two months earlier. Luckily someone had a satellite phone, so we would have three to four minutes once a week to call home.

When I was in Camp Dogwood, there were three kids that had been hurt by a hand grenade. One of them ended up with a very badly damaged arm. When I called home on my buddy's satellite phone and spoke to my wife, I learned that our five-year-old son had fallen and broken his arm and needed to have surgery. It was ironic that I was taking care of those little kids at Camp Dogwood when I knew that my own son was going through surgery. It was a pretty tough time, but it was nice to call and say hi on my children's birthdays and on Mother's Day. Calls usually lasted only a few minutes on that phone because I did have to reimburse my buddy who owned the phone. Beforehand, we were told not to bring any phones, because the army didn't want us communicating with others. They told us never to tell anyone about our location. This sometimes bothered my wife, but she didn't need to know where I was for her own well-being. I didn't want her to turn on the television to see the 3rd ID lined up at the Karbala Gap, being shot at and injured, and know that I was in that dangerous situation. I would usually tell her every time that I was safe and out of harm's way, when in fact I was right at the front line. I didn't want her to know any of that until later.

When I got home, I told her all about our close calls, how we got shot at, and how we were just one mile away from an enemy tank battalion. I told her about the time there was a firefight just outside our hospital and how I stood at the guard tower and watched the tracer bullets. I also told her about the time I was driving a Humvee and had to force a man off the side of the road. The rule was that we weren't to let people get between us and the convoy. The lieutenant in the back of the Humvee drew a bead on this civilian, who was in a taxi cab. The civilian decided that he was going to come over, so I had to bump him and take him out of our way. He had to know that he couldn't get in there. If he had gotten in and shot a weapon or done anything weird, the lieutenant would have taken him out. Most stunning for me was the fact that I had my weapon loaded and the safety off. There were several times that I had taken a bead, and if it had been necessary, I would have squeezed the trigger and killed someone. It bothered me to know that, but luckily it didn't happen.

There were many times that we didn't know what would happen, so we had to be ready to go because people were being shot all the time. Even though we were noncombatants, the enemy didn't know that, nor did they care. People asked me what to do if they saw someone with a weapon. I told them to take a bead on them. Then somebody else said, "Yeah, but they have a right to have a weapon too." But I said, "They don't have the right to have a weapon if it's pointing at me. If they pull out a weapon, you take a bead on them. And if they look like they're even remotely going to turn that weapon on you, you put 'em down. If you can't do that, then you get behind me and I'll do it." Then I told the guys, "This is the way it works; you have to do it." There were a couple guys who had trouble with this, but most guys were ready to do what they had to do.

All in all, I had some spiritually enlightening experiences having church in places like Iraq, Babylon, the place where Abraham lived, and near the location of the Tower of Babel. Those were nice experiences. When we held church services, people from all over would attend.

Some guys would travel for miles because they couldn't have a meeting on their own since none of them were set apart to be group leaders. Some of them were the only Latter-day Saints in their unit, and not everyone knew about the position of a group leader. I remember a Major Wells from Missouri who was on active duty. He was sent to Iraq from Fort Hood, Texas. Every Sunday he would pray to meet up with other Latter-day Saints. Then suddenly, out of the sky fell the 934th Forward Surgical Team from Salt Lake City. He found out we were having church and came running. During the next week, some military intelligence guys from another unit also came. Then the next week, another man from a combat support hospital heard about us and came. Our group would grow and grow, but then we would have to jump and try to find another place to have church. If people knew about it, they would come. Like I said before, we had church pretty much every Sunday. We even had a sunrise Easter service at Camp Dogwood.

The last two places that I served were Balad and Tikrit, two extremely dangerous places. Despite the risks, I somehow felt protected, and I don't know why. We had many close calls. We could have been picked off easily during the time we were shot at with AK-47s. There was also the time with the tank battalion. If they had come over that little ridge, they would have seen us and taken us out in a heartbeat. During the big firefight in Balad, we sent guys out who actually had to discharge their weapons. Then there were the nights when I had to be part of the first line of defense as a guard on duty to protect the perimeter. I even saw many tracer rounds going off that were directed towards us. Officers do not do guard duty, but we did it out of self-preservation.

Balad was a very bad place, but for some reason I felt very protected. We didn't have anybody get injured. Just before the whole unit flew out, one guy playing volleyball tore a whole bunch of tendons in his leg. Then an officer had a sudden flare-up of carpal tunnel syndrome. We had a whole bunch of weird little medical things like that, but nobody in my unit got shot at or was seriously injured. In fact, we only had one guy leave early because he had some family issues to deal with back at home. He had a son with some medical problems that kept worsening. When his baby was only three months old, the little guy had already been through three surgeries. After everything was done and when we were at the point where we weren't doing anything else, the commander laid down the law and told this guy, "You have to go home, your wife needs you. We want you to stay. We love to have you here and realize this is your only shot at combat, but you have to go home." He reluctantly went home to help his wife and take care of his baby. When he was sent home, we were back to twenty in the unit.

While I was in Balad, I broke my right wrist. I was coming down a rope when I fell and landed on my right side. We didn't have an x-ray machine, so I didn't know I had a broken wrist. I went around the next couple days as usual until my wrist hurt so bad that I had to do my push-ups on my knuckles. When we got to Tikrit where there was an x-ray machine, I found out that my wrist was indeed fractured. I had to put on a cast that drove me nuts. The unit knew if we had problems, I wouldn't be able to work with the cast on, so I had them bivalve out the cast so I could use it as a splint. I told them that if we got into problems, I could easily take it off and work. I had already done cases with the broken wrist for a month, so I knew I could take off the cast in a heartbeat and still work efficiently. Luckily we didn't have to deal with it that much, but I still had to carry my weapon around with a broken wrist, which was a bit difficult.

We were able to bring home souvenirs but only what was allowed. Nobody in our unit tried to sneak anything back. If the army said we couldn't use it or take it, we dumped it. At first they told us we could take certain things like gas masks, but later they told us we couldn't take them. We grabbed all the gas masks we had and dumped them in the amnesty barrel. We knew we couldn't take any of the weapons, but none of us wanted to take those anyway.

My experiences during my years of service did have an impact on my testimony. During those times, I wasn't in a huge group of Latter-day Saints. Even though we were in a war during our time in Germany, it was still a little different from Iraq. We were told to watch out for terrorists because there had been a bombing earlier in Berlin that killed some servicemen. It was far more dangerous in Iraq than in Germany, but for some reason I felt protected. It was as if there was something good going on for me. The days spent in Tikrit were long, so when we weren't operating and we had nothing to do, a couple of us would whip our scriptures out and have scripture study. One of the two CRNAs was a high priest, and the other was a first counselor in the bishopric. Since there were three of us CRNAs, we spent a lot of time studying the scriptures and discussing questions we had about different doctrines. But it had to be something we could look up or find in the references. Each time we went to church in Tikrit, we thought it would be our last. But five Sundays later, we were still there.

We went back to Balad after being in Tikrit, and I hated it there. We would have church in a tent on a Sunday afternoon. It had to be at least 130 degrees in that tent because it was 118 degrees in the shade and 125 degrees outside. We had no air conditioning inside of the tent. I remember leaning forward and watching the sweat drip off my head about every second. Fortunately, by this time we had big bottles of water that we were able to take everywhere with us. No one wanted to sit in church and get dehydrated. There would also be weapons lying all over the floor, so church was different because everyone had a weapon and a big bottle of water at their side.

We did have trays for the sacrament. If we were a group leader, we could buy trays beforehand. Sometimes we ran out of water cups, but we would just bring up our caps from our water bottles and fill those. We didn't have any regular bread, but we used pound cake from the MREs or other kinds of bread stuff. The regular bread was so horrible that it was much more satisfying to eat the pound cake. Plus the regular bread usually ran out by the end of the week.

When we came back to the United States, I had to stay at Fort Lewis to do rehab on my broken wrist. I ended up spending a total of six months away from my family on active duty, and my being gone did impact my family. My wife had to learn how to do a lot of things that she didn't like doing. She had to do things on her own and rely on other people, which she didn't like doing, even though they were members of our ward.

During the Gulf War, we were told that the army needed to rotate nurse anesthetists, dentists, physicians, and others more often because many guys would either lose their practice or get killed. They said people in those positions would serve ninety days and then rotate. Our surgeons assumed this to be true, which meant they would be called up in February and released by May. This turned out to be false. We had a general who came to us and said, "Let me let you in on a secret. We're at war. This ninety days policy does not apply during war." There were some guys who were pretty miffed by this, but I wasn't. I just figured my orders said that I would serve at least 365 days, and I accepted that. In the end, two surgeons were able to leave by the end of May, but the rest of us didn't leave till June.

I got home on a Saturday morning. It was interesting that when I came home, both my son and I had broken arms. My ward was supposed to have a Primary activity that day, but they found out I was coming home and changed the Primary activity into a parade for me. They lined the streets to my house. As I pulled into my driveway and got out of the car, everyone from the ward was congregated at my house to welcome me. I gave a little talk, and then we all sang "God Bless America." It was nice to finally be home.

It is now my fourteenth year with the military, and I plan to continue with them. I have at least one more chance for deployment, so hopefully my children will be much older the next time around. It's easier when the kids are older than when they are young.

My experiences were really spiritual because I was forced to make sure my prayers were more fervent. Most of my prayers were not for my protection but for the protection of my family. My biggest concern while I was away was my family. I was more concerned that something was going to happen to my family than to me.

Deanna Nielsen

I joined the military in 1975 as an enlisted person. I received my commission to be an officer when I graduated from nursing school in 1976. In 1977 I became an officer. I was an enlisted person in another unit, but I had been with the 328th General Hospital after I transferred over as an officer. I was in the 328th when they called us to Desert Storm.

We had our drill in November 1990, and there was a lot of talk going around because the 144th had been activated. They got activated the first part of November. This was an exercise for us in getting our paper work in order, and I was a little concerned because this was highly unusual. Unit administration was saying, "Oh, we are just doing this in case we have to send our group out." We all figured that with the 144th being gone, there was no way they were going to take another medical unit because that would pull all the medical people out of the local hospitals. Lo and behold, that wasn't the case. We got called up on December 3. They said, "You are activated. We will be sending you to Fort Carson to prepare you to go to Europe." It was fortunate that we were going to Germany and not Saudi Arabia. I felt blessed in that fact because I love Europe and Germany. My ancestry goes back to Germany and Sweden.

Deanna Nielsen

It was a very stressful week. I had four children ranging in ages from eleven down to three. I was more concerned about having Christmas ready for them because my husband Jay isn't much of a shopper. I don't know what it was, but this was the first year I had all of my shopping totally done. I had no clue we were going to be activated. I was glad that I had gotten all my Christmas shopping done.

We were going to have a family portrait that year, and I was making the girls all the same dresses. I knew that it was probably the last year that Natalie would wear the same dress her younger sisters were wearing. I really wanted to have a picture like that. So I was in the middle of that and I received the news. Of course, I was crying. I couldn't think of being separated from my children and my husband. It's not that I didn't want to go and serve my country, but a lot of emotions were raging through me. I was questioning our purpose in going over there a little bit because of all of the political things that were going on. I was concerned that people were going to give their lives for something that was not sensible. That week was probably the shortest week of my life. I had to get everything done and prepared for Jay before my departure. I've got to say that I couldn't have received better support. My ward came to my rescue. My good friend came over that Sunday, and she said, "Deanna, what can I do to help?" I was crying and I said, "I don't know. We are suppose to have our family picture taken this Thursday and I don't have these dresses done and I've got to get all this other stuff done." She said, "Give me the material and the patterns," and I said, "There is no way you can make these dresses." She said, "I'll take them. I can handle them." I said, "Okay." So I gave it to her. She called up a day later. She said, "Deanna, I'm in a bind. I don't know where you got the thread for this." I know this sounds silly, but it was really important to me at the time. I said, "I will go get the thread and bring it to you." I got in the car, raced down and got the thread, and ran it back to her house. Her daughter opened the door and said for me to come in. I went into this huge kitchen and here were all these people working on these dresses to have them done before I left. It just really touched me. It made me so happy. We got everything done and we had our picture taken.

The week flew by. We had to go up to Fort Douglas for grouping. Governor Bangerter spoke at that time. He said, "We will take care of the families. We will make sure that everything is provided for your families. We will make sure there aren't any problems here. We give you our full support from the state of Utah."

We left on December 9, which was a Sunday. It was a very cold day. It was bitterly cold. I was serving in the Primary presidency, and that day the children sang my favorite song, gave me some roses, and wished me well. The bishop came over and said, "I don't like to do this, but I have to release you from your position because we don't know how long you will be gone." I felt like during that week an end was coming to every part of my life. The hospital closed me out. I had to turn in everything. So that door was shut. The next door came when they released me from my position. I just felt like all these doors were being shut behind me.

That Sunday we had all the family over who were living in Utah. My sister was out of state at the time. They came for a little Christmas celebration. I had started putting up some Christmas things. We always starting putting up things the weekend after Thanksgiving. Jay said, "You better not put up the expensive things, because I am afraid they will get broken." We put up the tree and a few decorations. It was a good thing, because when I came home and saw how he had just tossed all of the decorations into a box without putting them in their individual boxes, I was amazed nothing got broken. But when I realized how many things he had to deal with while I was gone, I forgave him. So we had our little Christmas dinner and farewell. My mother was having a very difficult time with all of this. She always worries about her kids, and it was very hard to see her. I felt very good, very calm inside even with all the stress of the previous week. I had prayed earnestly that I could get through this and not have it affect my kids. I went into the garage, and Jay put my bags in the car. All my kids stood at the door and waved good-bye, and that was the last thing I saw. Jay took me up to Fort Douglas. All the buses were lined up. You chose a bus that had an empty seat and you got on it. They gave us a few last-minute instructions, and we left as a group. There were six hundred-plus members in our unit. Because of the large size of our unit, we were going to placed in different cities in Germany and in Vicenza, Italy. Some went to Belgium and then the rest of us to Germany.

In Fort Carson, Colorado, we had to go through all these stations to make sure all of our finances and medical care and legal affairs were taken care of. The hardest thing about Fort Carson was that it wasn't a fun place to be. They put us in barracks without any window coverings. We had to use brown paper as drapery. It was like a condemned area, but not quite. They weren't that bad, but they weren't clean. We had to use our cots to sleep on. I refused to unwrap my sleeping bag because I knew I wouldn't be able to get it rolled back up. So I slept in my thermals, robe, and my ski warm-ups. I threw on my army jacket on top to cover me. It was a mess.

The hardest thing about Fort Carson was that they were coming to our unit wanting people to go with the 144th. The 144th had left before us. The reason I knew the 144th was there was because when we went to the movie, I heard these people calling "Deanna." I turned and I said, "Oh my gosh," and I ran and we hugged each other. My one friend who worked on the same floor as I did was on the 144th. We chatted and we all went to dinner.

The 144th was short on some people with certain skills and they wanted to take some of our people. The way they went about it was not in the kindest manner. It was a great sacrifice for someone to go with the 144th to Saudi. Our active duty chief nurse gathered all of us together and said, "We need to have a couple of volunteers go over to the other unit. They are short and they need to fill their ranks. If no one volunteers, we will just draw names out of a hat, so we are hoping that someone will volunteer." In our unit we had satellite units who met in Idaho, St. George, Provo, and some other outlying areas. We didn't often see these people. Grace Jacobson and Beth Taylor volunteered. We were so happy. I said to these women, "Thank you so much for doing this." They said, "That's okay. We don't mind." They had to relocate across the base from where we were. They asked one of the commanding officers of the 144th how they were supposed to get their duffle bags over to the new barracks. He said, "Well, that is your problem, but you need to be over here by such and such a time." She started crying when she was telling me that. It was like, "What have I gotten myself into?" The rest of us decided we wanted to get out of there before they start plucking more people. I was really upset with what had happened.

Luckily the rest of the week passed quickly, and we were on our way to Germany. I was with people I knew. We arrived in Germany early in the morning, and we were all tired. We were waiting in a big room at the terminal. Finally, the chief nurse called me and told me that I would be going to Landstuhl. I had put down the name of a friend and Nuremburg as the place I wanted to go, and I got neither. It was late at night, and we got on buses to go to our duty station. I was glad it was dark because as we went along, we could see homes with Christmas lights on them. I started to cry. Tears were streaming down my face. I didn't want to be gone for Christmas, although I had dreamt of being in Germany for Christmas sometime in my life.

We arrived in Landstuhl. We were tired and dragging. All we wanted was a place to lay down. We got to stay in the air force barracks. These were a lot nicer than the army could provide. I was given the option of a private room because of my rank. At that very moment I knew it wasn't a good idea to be alone, so I said I wanted to be with someone. I roomed with this one gal that I knew and we just collapsed. The next day we met with the nursing personnel at the Regional Army Medical Center in Landstuhl, Germany. There is also a Regional Army Medical Center in England. We met with the nursing personnel, who told us how wonderful it was to have us there, because so many of their active duty people had left for the front. I have a shirt that shows how many units supported that area, and that shirt really means a lot to me. We were given our assignments according to our rank, and I was assigned to the neurosurgery unit.

The hospital was made up of wings, with half the wing for inpatient and half for outpatient. Now, because they had to anticipate casualties, they were turning that hospital into a thousand-bed hospital. They were having to remodel, with new wiring and everything, and the Germans were coming in to do that work. I met with my head nurse, and she told me there wasn't much going on right now. We were to come in and go over the paperwork and learn the routine, but there wasn't much to do. We arrived there on the 18th, and the holidays were coming up, which meant that the hospital would be virtually closed.

They were planning to have their Christmas party for the children, and I got involved in planning that. It was hard because I wasn't in the mood, but it was good to be involved in this activity. We prepared little bags of goodies for the children to receive from Santa Claus. It was actually a pediatrician there at the hospital who was organizing this activity, and she was just wonderful. Everybody had a good time. We had entertainment and we made snowflakes to put on the stage and decorated trees. It was a lot of fun. A little girl at the party resembled my youngest so much that I just watched her for the longest time.

The Sunday before Christmas I went to church. I was sitting there with my two friends Mike Gorzitze and Lynn Birrell. At the end of the meeting, they asked everyone to stay seated. The bishop got up and said, "We know this is a difficult time for everyone. We ourselves have family members who are serving in Saudi, so we don't have complete families. You have been pulled away from your family. We want to make Christmas the best Christmas we can possibly make, so we have some members here who would like to take some of you in for Christmas. If you don't have a place to go on Christmas, we would like you to raise your hand." This was an American ward held in Keiserslautern. The three of us looked at each other, and I said, "I'm not going. It is bad enough being away from my family, but I don't think I can take it being with somebody else celebrating Christmas." We didn't raise our hands. They approached us, wanting to know if we had a place to go, and we just said, "No, but that's just fine." We decided we would just do our own thing. I was walking out and this woman came up to me and said, "I noticed that you didn't raise your hand. Do you have someplace to go?" I said, "No, but that's okay." She said, "I really want to have you at my house for dinner. I need to have you come to my house for dinner on Christmas. My husband is in Saudi. I have four children at home and I want you to come."

I told her I was going to be with my two other friends. She told me to bring them along. She said she would pick me up. I told my friends, and they wanted to know what I was getting them into. I told them I wasn't going alone. If I was going, they were going. She picked us up. She lived out in this cute little German town miles away from our base. I just loved the German countryside. I was excited from that respect. This sister and her children knew how to speak German. Well, we got to her house and those kids were so excited to see us. They welcomed us, and they never stopped talking. We played games and we had a nice dinner, and she gave us little gifts. She was very hospitable. I had the time of my life. I forgot about everything for a while and had a lot of fun playing German games. We really had a fun time. At the end of it she said, "Thank you so much for making this a special day." I realized at that time that we fulfilled the needs for each other. It really turned out to be a positive experience.

We became really good friends throughout the rest of my time there. She liked to do *volksmarches* (6 or 10 K walks or runs through the German countryside). People of every age do these *volksmarches*, and at the end you get a patch or a medal. I got something from each place. You walk through the wooded areas and through the towns. You can usually buy some juice along the way. At the end you go into this big room, and they have all the German food. It probably saved my sanity because I love nature. I love the out-of-doors. We would drive to all these places, and some were quite a ways a way. It probably saved her sanity, too.

I was only gone for four months total. We ended up being in the hospital. We did receive casualties, usually freak accidents, things like a shooting in the foot. I don't think they realized there would be so many problems with the shifting sand. There would be pockets under the sand. There was a deuce and a half (a semi) that was covered over and had the troops in the back. It drove into a hole and flipped the deuce and a half. One of the people that I took care of that had been hurt in the accident was a physician. He was the saddest case. He had a head injury. He couldn't remember anything. He had amnesia. I don't know how he recovered. While we were taking care of him a doctor went in to evaluate him. He came out of there saying, "I can't handle this. This man was with me during medical school. It is just too difficult to see him like this." The patient was in a wheelchair and couldn't remember anything. He could talk, but he couldn't remember anything.

I took care of a lot of nice people. A lot of soldiers would say it was so good to come to this hospital and get rid of the sand and have clean sheets and no bugs. It was like living at the Hilton. A lot of injuries were minor, but the soldiers were so grateful for whatever you did. I didn't have even one disgruntled soldier. We took care of one soldier who was close to a fire that started. He was burned and lost part of his vision. He ended up receiving a purple heart at our hospital.

I was glad I was able to take care of patients instead of just sitting and twiddling my thumbs. There were some people who were deployed who had nothing to do. Even so, I told people it was like being on vacation. I was relieved of all responsibilities at home. It was almost like being single again. I couldn't worry about home because there wasn't anything I could do about it. All I had to care about was me, and I hadn't been in that mode since I got married. We pulled a seven twelve-hour-day tour when the war started. After that first week, we would find time to go over the Ramstein Air Force base and go to the movies and go shopping. I would go shopping in the little towns close by.

The children did well overall. It was a hardship for Natalie because at eleven years old, she had to become the mother figure. She went grocery shopping with Jay. She watched the kids. They reached the point after a few weeks that Natalie said, "I don't want anyone coming over here. I'll watch the kids." Natalie has always been a very responsible person. I know that it was a hardship on her because when the World Trade Center thing happened, we were at lunch with my cousin. My cousin asked if the event was going to impact me. Natalie had this look on her face. I said, "We don't discuss this at our house." Natalie said it was the saddest Christmas, with no spark on Christmas Eve or Christmas Day. Jay said Nathan cried himself to sleep every night. I'm glad he didn't tell me, because I just burst into tears when I heard that. I don't think I could have taken that. Adrienne thought I was in an airplane just flying around the whole time. She had no concept. I talked to her on the phone, but she still didn't understand. Lindsie had her sixth birthday. She was not forgotten. She received five cakes on her birthday. Jay turned forty that year in February. We had planned on going on a cruise. The day that we were called up I was calling to start the reservation process. He didn't get to go on his cruise. My family had a little party complete with black balloons. Jay received a lot of support from my really good friend who I have known since sixth grade. She even gave piano lessons to Natalie.

I can honestly say I received wonderful support from the ward. They wanted to bring meals in every day, but Jay said, "Absolutely not." Jay is not one who feels comfortable with people doing things. He was on the stake men's athletic committee, so he did consent to someone from the Young Women's coming in to stay with the children one night a month and someone from the Relief Society bringing food in on that night.

On the other hand, a captain who was serving with me was upset because his bishop never called to inquire about the status of anything. He never talked to the wife. She had two little kids, and he was very disappointed. I felt really bad that he was experiencing that. One gal who was not a Latter-day Saint wanted to know how I managed to stay in such good spirits. She said, "You have left your family at home. You have four little children. How come you can be in such a good mood?" I told her that it made a big difference when your family is being taken care of and that my church was providing this support. I had an inner calm come over me when I came over here and I have felt that the entire time." She said I was one lucky person. She only had one little baby at home. She was really struggling.

I can say that overall I had very positive experience over there. It isn't something I would wish on anyone, but I developed an appreciation for so many things, so many aspects of my life. The gospel has taught me what matters most in life. And now it came to light. At the time I was packing my bags, I was very limited in my space. I could only pack a small amount because my uniforms and my gear took up most of the space. I took my scriptures, which I hold dear to my heart, and a few other books that were meaningful for me and had been given to me before I left. I wrote in my journal that I knew I could leave everything behind, my house and all my material things, but if I didn't have my family, which is the number one thing, my life would be nothing.

Having the ward members and the Church in Germany involve me in Church activities really gave me strength. It made me feel a part of something I could identify with. It gave me the strength I needed to increase my faith and my testimony. It helped me to know that the Church wherever you go in the world is there to support and sustain you and that the feelings and faith of the members in Germany were as strong as that of the members of my own ward.

I am so thankful for the tiniest things, the freedoms, having a warm bed and hot water. I got to take a bath at a friend's house, and she told me they only turned the heat on in the rooms they are using. I was shivering by the time I got done with that bath because it was so terribly cold. It was so cold in that room you could almost see your breath. I thought, "This is not fun." I had a chill the rest of the evening. I was so glad to get back to my place where we had a water heater. My head nurse had me come over and spend a weekend with her. She told me I could go in and take a bath, and she kept her whole house warm. She told me to go in and just have the time of my life, and she had this bath stuff, and I did. To think that people who were basically strangers would take you in and provide for you and try and make it a nice situation for you. It was wonderful.

When I came home, it was hard because we had that mind-set of being there for a long time. It was the two hundredth anniversary of the death of Mozart, and they were having this big concert in Salzburg. I said to my friend, "We are here in Germany, let's go." We were getting ready to buy the tickets, and they called the meeting and said, "You are going home." It was just like shifting gears to an abrupt halt. "Home! I can't go home! I'm going to that concert in a week." I guess Governor Bangerter put in a word that he wanted his people home because they were having such a terrible time with the medical personnel shortage. We were pulled out first.

When I got back to the VA, my head nurse acted like I had hardly been gone and that it didn't matter that I was back. But Mike Harwood, the nursing assistant, came up to me and said, "It's so nice to have you back." It made all the difference.

Kim Walkowski

Back in high school, when I was seventeen, the Vietnam War was hot and heavy. And my friends knew that as soon as they got out of high school, they would be eighteen and going over to Nam. So I started thinking, "What can I do? I don't want to go to Sweden. I don't want to go to Canada. I support this country. I don't know if I really support this cause." I thought,

"What could I do as a seventeen-year-old to avoid getting killed? I will join the National Guard."

Across the street from where I was, on Sunny Side Avenue, was the 144th Evacuation Hospital. I was seventeen, and I had a close friend of mine with me who was my magic friend, my magic buddy whom I grew up with. We were both magicians. As we were growing up I told him, "We gotta do something, so let's go try to join the National Guard." On April 1, 1969, April Fool's Day, we went over to the 144th and signed up. They said for us to call them every week until we were actually accepted because their waiting list was so long. It took almost a year to get to the top of that list.

Right after I graduated from high school, I was all of a sudden zipped off to Fort Bliss, Texas. When I got there, they asked me what I wanted to do. I never thought I was going to go into the medical field at all, but I thought that was a safe bet. If I was in the medical field, I was not packing around a gun. I would not be shooting people, and I don't believe in weapons, especially in a war that didn't make sense. So I thought, "If I'm in a medical unit, I'm helping people, I'm fixing people, I'm going to make them better, and I'm going to do something good." Because I was just a little grunt without any rank or seniority, they said, "Okay, we're going to make you a medic and start you at the bottom." And I was okay with that. They taught me how to patch people up, and they still handed me a rifle and taught me how to throw hand grenades.

Then I went on to Fort Sam, Houston. On the day that basic training ended, they started calling out the names of everybody and where they were going. With every name they would say Vietnam. They got down the list, and there were only two of us that came back to Salt Lake City: me and my friend. All the people who we trained with got sent over to Vietnam. I missed that by the hair of my chin.

So then I was back in Salt Lake as a young high school graduate and I thought, "Well, I need to get a little job. What can I do? I have a little medical training." I went up to the University Hospital. They needed orderlies at the time. They had an opening in the operating room and also in the psychiatric ward. My friend grabbed the psychiatric ward, and I thought I'd go to the operating room. I thought it was kind of interesting working in an operating room, and I started thinking also that I didn't want to stay at the bottom of the ladder, so I thought about what I could do. I ended up going to Trade Tech, which is now Salt Lake Community College, and became an operating room technician. While I was doing that, I started thinking of staying in the military and keeping my military career.

I was twenty-seven when I got married, so I waited a long time. By now I was an officer in the military. I hung in there lots of years and finally got to the point where I could almost qualify for retirement. You have to have twenty years to qualify for retirement. All of a sudden, Desert Storm broke out. I was about forty years old when the war broke out. So the next thing I knew I was telling my wife. She saw the writing on the wall and told me, "You need to call it quits. You're a captain in the military." I had done this for twenty-seven years. I had tolerated all the little drills, and I knew all the military games and everything, and I had gone to those different schools. She told me I needed to get out.

But I told her, "I need to hang in there to get this retirement, I'm so close." She said, "Get out!" The next thing I knew, right before Thanksgiving 1990, I got a call that said I was going over to Saudi Arabia. And the army said, "We need to ask you a favor. We know you're a magician. You've performed in a lot of our shows. There's no entertainment in Saudi Arabia. There are no movie theaters. There are no operas. There's not even a TV. The people there say their prayers seven times a day. They're not allowing us to bring in any of the entertainers over there. We're bringing Bob Hope, Steve Martin, and a couple others, but the Saudis are watching them closely and they'll only let them shake their hands. We want to make a little U.S. host show if you'll entertain the troops over there." And I was thinking, "You're asking me to perform in a war? I'm scared to death because Saddam said this is the mother of all wars." I honestly didn't believe I was coming back. I really thought I was done for. When my wife found out, she was really upset that I didn't get out. She was rather mad and very scared. I think a lot of it was that we had a little daughter who was in kindergarten or first grade, and this was all new to her.

The army said they wanted me to perform for the troops if things worked out. So I agreed to do whatever I could do to help. They boxed up all of my magic props in these crates that they had me take down to the armory. They told me they would send them off on ships, and I thought, "Well how are you going to find me out in the middle of the desert?" And they said, "Well, we'll do our best." So right away I started calling my insurance agent. They said, "Sorry, we don't insure anything going into a war zone." And I said, "Can't I get a home owner's policy or anything like that?" So I called insurance company after insurance company and nobody would insure me for anything that was going to a war zone. In my mind I was thinking, "Not only am I never coming back, but I'm also never going to see my magic again. I'll probably never see it over there in the war to begin with, to entertain the troops."

I went to Fort Carson, Colorado, with the 144th, which was really a good experience because our unit—and I've known these people for years—are nice people. It is good to go with friends. It is good to go with compadres. I would say 50 percent of the unit were Latter-day Saints. We had a strong bond. We had people that weren't going to be rabble-rousers. We were going to stick by each other. I was going with people that I really felt good with, that I could trust if things got bad. I would be protecting them at the same time that they'd be protecting me. But at the same time, I still didn't think I was coming back. I kept this to myself. My unit didn't know my thinking. My wife didn't know that either, but I think secretly she didn't think I was coming back because she wanted me to take out the biggest insurance policy on myself that I could get.

Before they shipped us off, my wife was in such a state of sadness and shock that she couldn't see me off on the buses. So I was sitting down at the armory, and all these other spouses are hugging and crying and stuff, but she was in so much pain that we had our little moment at home before I drove myself down to the armory. At the same time, to make matters worse, my brother was activated in the same unit as me. He is two years younger than me. He is also a nurse, but at the time, he was enlisted. He became a nurse and paramedic with the county fire department. Now my parents were losing two kids, two boys. We have another brother, but he was dropped on his head and had to get a metal plate. The army doesn't take people like that. My sister-in-law and my wife were able to console each other, and that was very helpful for them.

So I went to the VA and they said, "Normally we don't do this. We only do this during open season, but under this situation, we'll go ahead and raise you up a little bit." Fortunately, I was luckier than a lot of my friends because nurses are brought in as officers. I was a captain at the time, and a lot of my friends were attorneys and accountants. They were enlisted, but they had private jobs on the outside, making three times the money I was making. But the VA was nice because they were helping me out and they let me use my annual vacation time to help offset things. Also, the loan officers helped us with the mortgages and things like that, so I felt pretty good about that. I was working as a dialysis nurse at the VA. The only thing is, they didn't need a dialysis nurse out in the middle of a war zone. If someone is in renal failure, they get triaged out. So I was with this little group in the operating room.

So we were shipped off, but I was kind of separated from my brother because he is enlisted and I am an officer. Even though he was over there, which was kind of nice, we were separated. We drove out to Fort Carson, Colorado, and we were there for several weeks until they figured out when to ship us off. We did get a break for Christmas. We were not supposed to leave the base, but several of us got in a car or went on a plane or whatever to get home for a couple of days. I came home disguised in a little hat and dark glasses so no one would recognize me. For three or four days during Christmas, we all got to be with our families before we snuck back. They shipped us out right after Christmas.

We arrived in Saudi Arabia in January. We took off in this big, beautiful 747 decorated all nice and patriotic for us, and they landed in some remote makeshift airport out in the middle of the desert; it was pitch black. They shuffled us all off and pushed us into these buses with other people. I don't know if they were Saudi Arabians or what, but they couldn't speak English. We couldn't talk to them. We did not know where we were going. So we were sitting on this bus and I remember looking out at the pitch blackness, going across the sands hour after hour. There were both men and women mixed all together, officers and everything. There was no way to communicate to these guys for a rest stop or anything. We needed to go to the bathroom, but there were no bathrooms. They gave us bottles of water as we boarded the bus because there is no water over there. We got to the point where everyone had to go to the bathroom. Everybody was kind of numb. We had been awake all night. We used our water bottles as pee bottles. People respected each other's privacy on this bus, plus it was pitch black. The girls did it too. We couldn't talk to these guys because they couldn't speak English. They just knew they were supposed to drive their bus wherever, and I was looking out into the darkness thinking, "What in the world am I doing here? How did I get myself into this mess?"

I was going across the desert with everyone else, and by now people were so tired that they were falling asleep, and I remember looking out in the blackness at nothing. They took us to a place called Dhahran, to a little holding area in the bottom of some carports, and they just dumped us off and laid our things on the concrete. That was where we slept the first night, not knowing what was happening. The next day we got up, and the officers were saying that they needed people on the front lines and they were going to send our unit right to the front lines. These were our officers, and they had gotten the information from someone else. And I was thinking, "Why are we going to the front lines? I thought we were a hospital. I just wanted to go home to my family.

So they kept us in this carport for several days while they tried to get information. We were eating MREs (meals ready to eat), but it was so hot that we could throw one of those MREs on the hood of a truck and five minutes later we had a hot meal. After that our troop commanders came back and told us that they didn't have enough people in their hospital. We had to wait and get an attachment from other hospitals so we could fill all of those spots and have a fully functional hospital. We spent a couple more days in this carport, which was bombed near the end of the war. Then we were loaded into these old planes in the middle of the night, wondering what it was all about. They sent us over to a place called Eskan Village, which is a place that the Saudis had built for the Bedouins, nomads who roam the deserts. It was seven to twelve miles outside of the capital, Riyadh. It was really nice that the Saudis built this place for the Bedouins, but the Bedouins insisted they needed to bring their camels and sheep. The Saudis said that the housing was for them and not their camels, so the housing never got used.

We were put in this "Ashcan" Village, as we called it, while they were finding us a place for us to build our hospital and set up our tents. We were there for several weeks while they shipped us back and forth to build our hospital. I don't remember the date, but all of a sudden these sirens started wailing. The next thing I knew, the ground started shaking, bombs started blowing up, and the sky was just echoing with Scud missiles going off. My heart was pounding a hundred miles an hour. We grabbed our chemical suits and put our masks on, and we were thinking, "What is happening?" Every time the Iraqis would send up a Scud missile towards us, we would shoot two Patriot missiles at that one Scud in case one of the Patriots would miss. Each missile cost two million bucks. So every time they shot up one Scud missile towards us, we shot up four million dollars to shoot that thing down. I'd never heard of a Patriot missile in my life, but I was so thankful that they were there. I was so thankful because we would feel this big explosion and the sky would just echo and shake, but at the same time we didn't know if it was chemicals or what in these missiles. So for twenty-four hours we lived in our chemical suits, hyperventilating with our masks on. The next day when we took them off, we were black because the charcoal would leach through the chemical suits.

For the next several weeks, these missile attacks would come constantly, whether we were building our hospital or filling up sand bags to build walls around it. These Scud attacks would go on for weeks and weeks to the point where we would hear the sirens and know that we had seven minutes from the time that missile left Iraq to when it would reach us. So for seven minutes we would sit and meditate and pray. During those seven minutes, we knew that those chemicals were coming to us, and we would sit in our chemical suits trying to find something to be under. A lot of times we were out in a tent. Seven minutes we spent just meditating and praying that we were going to be okay. And this whole time, I would be praying for our guys to shoot the Patriots and waiting for the explosion in the sky.

That turned my life around. I had never really been a spiritual person. I believed in our Father in Heaven and all that stuff like that, but something changed my life when I was out there, to the point that I would attend every single service they offered. It was something to be sitting in a group in the middle of a war zone in our battle fatigues having a sermon about our Savior; it really touched me. I wasn't going to take life for granted anymore. I was going to appreciate every day and every moment that I have. I was going to come back a different person.

Well, the ground war flared up near the end of January and went through the whole month of February. During that time, there weren't as many Scuds going off. Around our compound we'd be out in the desert many times, and I'd go out and meditate. I would have my pockets full of little magic tricks. I'd see bunkers out there where they would put enlisted guys with their M-16s, and I thought, "Oh, these poor guys stand here all day long and can't go anywhere, guarding perimeters and stuff." I, being an officer, had a little more clout; I could come and go. So I'd pick out a bunker maybe a mile away, and I would walk out there with my pockets full of magic tricks. I'd see two little rifles aimed at me as I'd start coming closer and closer. They were American bunkers to guard perimeters in case there were tanks or terrorists out there. They'd call out for me to halt and say who I was. I would say, "I'm one of you guys. Come here; I want to show you something."

Now, they wondered, "Why in the world is an officer coming out here?" Most of them would be scared because they were just enlisted guys, and they'd be saluting me, and I would say, "Take it easy. It's okay. I want to show you something." Then I would reach in and do a couple of little tricks for them. I would always, even to this day, carry two little rubber bands around my wrists. They didn't know what I was doing. I would take a rubber band and another rubber band and I would show them that the rubber doesn't stretch, but right then it would stretch right through, and then I made the rubber bands pass through each other. Something simple like that, and it would bring a spark to their eyes. Here was some officer out in the middle of the desert coming out and pulling out a couple of rubber bands. I'd then reach in and do a few little card tricks for them, and after a while those two guys in the bunker were just laughing and happy like, "Wow, this made our day!" Well, it didn't really make their day as much as it made mine because I was giving something to somebody else.

I'd wander to another little bunker, and this gave me time to meditate. In the meantime, I took a little tape recorder and I would make little recordings to my wife of my thoughts and feelings. The more I meditated, the more I realized that life is valuable and precious. You have the chance to do something for somebody. Then one day someone said, "Hey, we got a video camera. Do you want to send a videotape home to your wife?" And I thought, "Well, my wife is a schoolteacher. I'm going to make the kids a video." I did it eating a packet of MREs and talking to the little kids at a low level explaining my situation. Then I sent it off. When I got home eight months later, I found that this little video had made the rounds to a majority of the elementary schools. The schools liked this video so much that they made copies to share. Several of my friends said, "Man, we need to send that to *America's Funniest Videos*." The video was of me eating a dehydrated MRE hamburger and telling the kids what life was like. Even to this day my friend Stan says, "I guarantee you can win ten thousand dollars if you send that video." But someone had this little video that I didn't even know preceded me.

In the meantime, the war was still going on. Then by the end of February, the ground war was wrapping up. And guess what arrived at our hospital? A truck. And guess what was in that truck? All these crates of magic props. And the army says, "Okay, we want to put together a little U.S. social. We're going to be sending our troops home. Can you travel around and perform for our troops?" So they got me and another guy named Gaylin Young to team up, with Gaylin playing the guitar and me doing magic. He is now a nurse, but I don't think he was at the time. We were about six miles from a Swedish hospital, so they got a troupe of Swedish girls, and we would travel around from unit to unit, performing for these people. It was so much fun. We had a captive audience. They had a little entertainment, and most of them had a big feast. They all knew they were going home. It was one of the neatest experiences once again to be able to share something, a special talent that you have.

The funniest part of the whole thing is that I packed my tuxedo in one of those trucks. Here performing in front of these troops was a guy dressed in a tuxedo in a war zone. People came in, and they just couldn't believe that here was someone who packed his tuxedo in the middle of war. Sometimes when I wore my white tuxedo, I would get a Saudi Arabian white scarf to wear around my head for my magic show. Gaylin would play guitar and folk songs. The Swedish girls would dress in their cut-off, beady uniforms with their legs showing. It was really a fun time. And many times my friend Kent Blad would come around and be my right-hand man. He was a good friend of mine.

What kept me longer is that when it was time to go home, they needed what they called a rear party for units being shipped off. They needed a group to stay behind for people getting hurt. I was in one of the small groups. So when our unit, including my brother, went home, my wife just couldn't believe I had to stay. It was kind of a rough. One person out of every section had to stay. There had to be an OR nurse or an OR tech, enough to make a little surgical team so they could stay while all the rest of the teams were processed out. I was one that was chosen.

Kathryn Ray Hiersche Walther

I was about fifteen years old when I came across a flyer at an army recruiting booth at a county fair for a full-ride four-year scholarship at the Walter Reed Army Institute of Nursing. I held onto that piece of paper throughout high school. When I was a graduating senior in 1969, I applied for that scholarship. At that point I wasn't even that sure I wanted to be a nurse, but I decided, "Well, if they're going to pay for me to get my university education, then that's what I'll do." I did receive the scholarship, and that is how the decision was made that certainly affected the rest of my life in a very dramatic way.

The way Walter Reed's nursing program worked was that students went for their first two years to any university in the country. I spent my first two years at the University of Oregon, which was about 120 miles away from my home. All of the students accepted in 1969 (all girls except for one male student) moved to Walter Reed Army Medical Center in Washington DC, where we then became students of the University of Maryland. For eleven years, the University of Maryland had two campuses. One was in Baltimore, and the other was at Walter Reed Army Medical Center. The Baltimore campus is where our diplomas say we graduated from, where we physically registered for school for the first time, and where we went for graduation ceremonies, but we lived at and attended all of our classes for our last two years right there on the compound of Walter Reed Medical Center.

There were about one hundred students per year accepted into the Walter Reed Army Institute of Nursing (WRAIN). All of our instructors were Vietnam veterans with master's degrees in nursing. That was really amazing in those days because at that point there were still a lot of diploma schools out there; an MS in nursing was very impressive. Baccalaureate nurses, nurses with their BSN were made first lieutenants after they graduated, while diploma nurses were made second lieutenants. That did not make for really good feelings between the new graduate lieutenants.

Kathryn Ray Hiersche Walther

The first graduating class of WRAIN was in 1968. The purpose of the program was to produce army nurses to meet the needs of the Vietnam War. There were about one hundred of us in each class, and we were from all over the country. By the time I graduated in 1973, the WRAIN graduates were no longer going to Vietnam. This was the pull-out time, so none of my class ever served in that war. But we did have a three-year obligation to serve on active duty. It was very interesting because some of the previous graduating classes went straight to Vietnam. As the war progressed, the graduating classes were required to do a couple of years in country before they went to Vietnam. The last WRAIN class to graduate was in 1978, since the Army Nurse Corps realized that they did not need as many army nurses during peacetime.

After graduation, I went to Fort Sam Houston in San Antonio, Texas, and then did my active duty at Fort Leavenworth, Kansas. This is where the Command and General Staff College is for all army officers, which is a type of military graduate school. There were tons of majors there, while the only lieutenants were a few nurses and support staff, so to be a lieutenant on that post was the lowly of lowlies. The hospital of Fort Leavenworth was very small. It had four small wards. One was obstetrics, another was considered an intensive care unit, another was a medical-surgical ward, and the last was a prisoner ward. If prisoners from the army's prisons at Fort Leavenworth found themselves ill or injured, they would end up in that ward, which had bars on the doors. It usually had only fifteen patients. I worked on all wards at one time or another, but I did the biggest block of my time in obstetrics, which was one year.

While I was in the army, I got pregnant. I was married to a marine officer who at the time was stationed in Kansas City, Missouri. I had met him in Washington DC when he was at the Naval Academy and I was at WRAIN. It was an interesting time in the army for women starting families. Previously, a woman was given a discharge if she got pregnant. At the time I became pregnant, the pendulum did a really fast swing, and women were no longer allowed to get out of the military if they got pregnant. By the time the baby was born, I had done about two years of a three-year active duty obligation, but the army still told me I could not get out. Things were rough during my pregnancy. I had to drive about an hour to work. Since I was the lowest ranking person on my ward, I was chosen to do everyone's days off. I was working two nights, two evenings, and two days, and it was a horrible schedule. They would not give me a permanent shift. My husband was on active duty. And to top it off, I was also very ill during the pregnancy.

At the time I had an old-fashioned army chief nurse. She had never married. She still lived in the hospital compound, and she saw nursing as a calling. I mean to say, the army was her life. She was a nice lady, but having a pregnant nurse was really more than she wanted to deal with. It was as if she thought, "Well, how annoying. Why would you do something like that? How dare you get pregnant!"

I had a friend who was also a lieutenant. She got pregnant a couple of months before I got pregnant. She wanted to stay in the army, but the army was trying to force her out. While my friend was fighting to stay in, I was trying to figure a way to get out or to at least be given a decent schedule that would allow for daycare. I went and spoke to our hospital chaplain, and he suggested that I request a hardship discharge. When the hardship discharge went in, it requested the army give me a permanent shift to allow me to plan appropriate child care, but the army just gave the hardship discharge instead, and I joined an Army 325th General Hospital Army Reserve Unit in Kansas City.

The decision to join the reserves was the result of a bit of a guilty conscience. I knew the army paid for me to go to school for four years and I had not completed the three-year active duty obligation payback. The reserves was my own way to fulfill the obligation. I drilled one weekend per month and did one two-week tour of duty at Fort Sill, Oklahoma.

I observed an interesting historical event in the army that first year of my reserve duty (1975). A woman who was in her forties joined the army and even became my chief nurse. What made this so special was that the army had to give her a special waiver for her to join. The reason she had never joined before was that she was a nun. At that point, nuns had not served in the military or had not been allowed to do so by their church. She became our chief nurse. Not only was she a nun, but she was also a reservist. It was a time for many changes in the military as you can see, especially for women. First we couldn't be married, then we couldn't have children, then we had to stay in no matter what. Of course now, even to be in the military, parents have to have a care plan on file identifying the individuals who have agreed to take care of their children should they be deployed overseas. Having children and a husband does not keep a woman out of the military. Women just have to plan ahead on how children will be cared for in the event of war.

After being in Kansas City for about a year, my family and I moved to San Diego, California, where I affiliated with the 67th Combat Support Hospital. A combat support hospital was one that ended up on the front when there was a war. It was similar to a MASH unit, only it was more inflatable and better equipped. We drilled at the Naval Regional Medical Center, also known as Balboa. There we did our military training on the weekends. I also did some army-nurse recruiting at colleges and recruiting days while in San Diego.

After San Diego, my family and I moved to Las Vegas, Nevada, where I was in the 125th Combat Support Hospital. Although it was out of Phoenix, Arizona, a detachment was in Las Vegas, so we drilled there at the county hospital. I worked in the emergency room, where I supervised the corpsmen and the medics that we had in the detachment. I was there almost two years, and I even did one army reserve two-week tour of duty at Fort Lewis, Washington. Some years I did not do my two weeks because I was either having a baby or nursing.

I had another baby in Las Vegas, so again I had time off. In fall 1979, my family and I left Las Vegas and moved to Federal Way, Washington, and that area became my home for the next nineteen years. During that time I affiliated with the 50th General Hospital, which was based in Seattle. The hospital also had a detachment in Tacoma, and since I lived halfway in between, I spent my last eight years in the reserves drilling with the detachment in Tacoma.

The 50th General Hospital was a very large reserve unit with the potential for six hundred members. It was while I was in the position of training officer in the 50th that I was called to active duty for the first Gulf War in 1990. The entire 50th General Hospital was mobilized. We were the largest unit mobilized for the Gulf War. That was in November 1990.

It is interesting to me as I look back on the experience that I was pretty realistic about it. I never thought, "I'm in the army and I'm never going to care for anyone that has been in combat." For one thing, when training at Walter Reed, the majority of the patients we took care of were Vietnam veterans. Not Vietnam veterans that had been wounded years ago but Vietnam veterans who were coming back directly from Vietnam for treatment. So even though we certainly were not in the theaters of operation, we did care for patients who had become ill or injured in the course of the war. I saw war as a realistic possibility. Also, as the unit training officer, I trained people and designed training with the idea of mobilization. I heard someone compare it once to working in an emergency room. You never ever want to see trauma. You have compassion as a human being, and you do not wish a car accident on any of your fellowmen. You don't want any kind of a mass casualty or anything like that, but there are times when you are there saying, "This is really boring. I wish something good would happen," but you don't really mean "good." I think that's true in the military. If you're a realist and you're training people all the time, you do think sometimes, "I wonder if we'll ever use this training?"

I was never so naive that I thought, "Oh, I won't have to go," or, "I have a bunch of kids, so I don't have to go." I always felt that by belonging to the military, my responsibility was to be prepared to go. My husband was also in the reserves. We had pretty elaborate family care plans should either one of us be mobilized or certainly in case both of us were mobilized. Family care plans involve everything from powers of attorney to who will care for the children while you're gone to who's going to take care of them until the designated caretakers get there. It didn't include who's going to take care of your children if you don't come back; that would be in your will. The military's family care plan was designed to determine who will take care of your family if the military requires your services. There is no point in having people in the military that say, "Oh I'd like to go, but gee I can't go; I have little children."

Because I had gone to the Walter Reed Army Institute of Nursing, all four years of my college counted as active duty. I went onto active duty on September 11, 1969, which never had much significance to anyone but me until the events of the recent September 11 happened. Not everyone knows that date. But I had my own special reason to remember September 11—that is when I was first sworn into the military.

In 1989 I was eligible for my twenty-year letter. My plan had been that at twenty years I would get out of the military. I had invested twenty years so that when I was sixty years old I would receive a retirement benefit. In September 1989 I hit twenty years. I was warned by several people, "Don't get out until they actually give you your twenty-year letter," because everybody knew a horror story of someone who had thought they had their twenty years in, but when it was really figured, they were missing two months or something like that. So I said, "Okay I'll wait until I get my letter." It took the army until the following August to get my letter issued. When I received it in August 1990, I went to my unit administrator and said, "Well, I'm really done. I'm ready to check out." I was thirty-eight years old when I hit twenty years and thirty-nine when I got my twenty-year letter. I was excited to say to my commander, "You know, I'm really going to retire?" He looked at me and said, "You can't retire! There is a war going on." I said, "Yes, I can. Here is my twenty-year letter. There is always a war going on." Even though Desert Shield had started, I thought, "What's the difference with this and any other involvements we've had in the military?" But I was told I really could not get out at that time.

I drilled in August, September, and October. Sometime in November 1990, we received an alert and were called to the unit headquarters in Seattle. This is when we began to feel like we were participating in a dark comedy. They told us that we would go through what was called a premobilization drill. They said to us, "We don't have the word that we're being mobilized yet, but we're going to do all the paperwork and immunizations." At the end of the two days, there were at least four hundred of us standing in formation with our commander on an outdoor staircase. He was up a couple of floors, so it kind of reminded me of King Benjamin. He had a bullhorn or some sort of PA system, and he was talking to us and congratulating us on a good two days and saying that we had done such a good job. Then he said, "I know you haven't believed us, but we do not have any orders. We have not been mobilized. This has been a premobilization exercise. We are on alert, and you will remain on alert when you return to your families." As he was going on trying to convince and comfort us, we saw a sergeant come running up the stairs while the commander was telling us this, and we knew what he had in his hand. He got up there and, sure enough, it was our orders. The commander was in shock.

We had Thanksgiving with our families and said good-bye. We were put on buses with police escorts, and we went to Fort Lewis, Washington, which is about an hour and a half south. We drove through the town I live in and went back down to Fort Lewis, where we were put up. Fort Lewis was just bursting to the gills because there were so many people being mobilized, so we were assigned to an area of Fort Lewis that had some old Bachelor Officer Quarters (BOQs). That is where we stayed. We went into the BOQ building to see our new "home." I had a roommate I knew well and respected, and I knew we would get along well. We went into the room assigned to us, and of course it was absolutely bare. I'm not even sure it was a BOQ. It might have been an office building. There was a bathroom attached to our room. When we went into the bathroom, the toilet was stopped up. I had done really well emotionally until this point. I just burst into tears. It was like, "You can send me to war. You can rip me from my family, but don't give me a stopped-up toilet." I just lost it.

For the first night or so, we slept on very thin foam pads. We had sleeping bags at first. Eventually they got us bedding. We were at Fort Lewis for two months, which was only an hour from my home, but we were not allowed to go home. Of course I snuck home and got caught in a snowstorm coming back and thought, "Oh great, I'm going to be in jail or something."

During those two months it was all training and preparation, but we still did not know where our final destination was going to be. We didn't know if we would end up going to the East Coast to augment some hospital that had lost all their active-duty medical folks to the war early on. We did know that it looked like we were going to the theater of operations. While we were at Fort Lewis, we would see other reserve units come and go. They would come to Fort Lewis and leave for Germany, or they would come in and go to other places in Southwest Asia. It was just weird. We couldn't get real empathetic. I had a friend come through who had been at WRAIN with me, and she was with a unit out of Vancouver, Washington. She was extremely upset because they were going to Germany. She was upset to be leaving her family, which I could empathize with. But her destination was Germany, so I just could not feel much sympathy for her. It was like, "I like Germany. I'll go to Germany," because of course all the while we were thinking we were going somewhere much closer to the action.

We were given a couple days at Christmas and New Year's to go home. Our families also got to come and visit us on a few occasions. After the holidays, we came back and received our orders. We knew we were going to Saudi Arabia. Our families were able to come down and say good bye. My five children and my husband came to visit. He was actually in an army reserve unit at the time. He was in an army reserve unit that was the unit that mobilized everybody else. My husband was never mobilized, but he had volunteered to work full time for the army during the mobilization phase.

Though I didn't keep a journal most of the time I was mobilized, I did a little bit at Fort Lewis. On January 7 I wrote, "Still at Fort Lewis. Said good-bye to the kids tonight. Molly said (she was almost three when she said this), 'But this is Saudi Arabia.' She thought I was at Saudi Arabia the whole time that I was at Fort Lewis because everyone talked about how Mom's going to Saudi Arabia." Since she saw me every couple of weeks while I was in "Saudi Arabia," she was very upset that she could not come and visit me anymore. I cried with the kids and felt sad and very lost.

Fort Lewis was an interesting experience for me. This big group of four or five hundred members was divided into several companies. My roommate and I became the co-commanders of a hundred-member company that was made up of the Army Nurse Corps and Medical Service Corps officers. The MSA is made up of the dieticians, physical therapists, and occupational therapists. I was supposed to keep them busy and trained.

It was one of the worst winters the Northwest had had in years. We were outside in the wet Northwest snow many times. Snow is not real typical for up there, so this was very unusual for late November or December. We tried to do things that would help the unit members not feel so alone. We were at least on familiar territory. A lot of us had been on active duty or done reserve duty at Fort Lewis, so we didn't feel lost in that respect. Most of us lived nearby. We were not that far from home, but there was the business of feeling very locked in because at any minute we could be told, "The plane's ready. We're out of here." We got to the point that we just wanted to get moving. You would think that we felt good and safe at Fort Lewis, but that wasn't the feeling. It was like, "Oh please, let's hurry up and go to where we are supposed to serve!"

People were learning to take apart their M-16s and their .45s and put them back together, and for the first time, having to shoot for a score.

Before mobilization, nurses were just expected to familiarize themselves with the weapons, but this time we were actually being graded and lying on our stomachs in the mud and shooting. We weren't twenty-year-old recruits anymore. I was thirty-nine, and I would say that the majority of people were in their late thirties or early forties.

We tried to make things work, and we'd say, "Okay, this is your assignment should you choose to accept it. You have to go out and find two Christmas trees for the two lobbies of the two BOQs, but we can't tell you where to get them or how to get them or whatever, and we're not even going to say we sent you if you get caught." They loved it. Those folks actually recruited another lieutenant, and the three of them went out and got these gorgeous Christmas trees for our lobbies. We decorated them with homemade decorations and things that we had.

The other thing we did was put up signs. I had a really talented psychiatric nurse in my group, and he and I did some planning together. I had done my master's degree in psychology, not psychiatric nursing, at Antioch University. I had my emphasis in holistic health and had completed it in 1983. Now it is 1990 and Jim and I decided that we needed to do something to help people vent because there was a lot of unhealthy venting going on. So we put three large newsprint signs up in the day room of the BOQ. One was titled "Stress Management Techniques That Work for You," one was "Thanks and Acknowledgments," and one was "Bi— List." We then encouraged them to write down all the things that they wanted on these posters. You would see people all the time reading them and laughing and having a bit of fun. There were lots of humorous comments, but at the same time it helped to let it out because life was truly scary.

If someone had said to me, "Will you go four months and spend a couple of months at Fort Lewis and a couple months in Saudi Arabia and participate in this war and take care of anyone that needs to be taken care of? I'll ensure you that no one will be killed among your group of friends and none of your unit is going to lose their lives. Then you're going to come home in only four months and you will have had this amazing experience." I would have said, "Well, yes, I will do that! I'll figure a way for me to get those four months to get away." But that's not the way it was. It's the uncertainty and the feeling of, "Is this the last time I'm going to see my family? Is this the last time I'm going to touch ground here? Is this the last time I'm going to be in this airplane? Is this the last time I'm going to see my friends and family at home?" And then of course when you're a mom, you also worry that something will happen to your kids while you're gone. Even if you come back in one piece, will they be in one piece? That was the most stressful thing, not knowing. I really believe that about the type of experience I had, and certainly many people are having it now.

When I came back from the Gulf, I think I spoke about my experience fifty times in the first three or four years, and it was very therapeutic for me. I would always start by showing a picture of my family whom I had left behind. That was my reality. That was my real world. Then I showed them that my world became the pictures taken from the hospital where I was assigned to work—the pictures of Patriot missiles in the process of intercepting Scud missiles. My reality changed extremely fast, and that was a disturbing part of going to war.

My dad, who served in World War II, was gone for months and even years. Being a child of the generation whose parents and relatives lived through the events of World War II made me realize that war might also take me away for a long period. There was a part of me that thought, "I could be gone a really long time." I think many of us felt that it could be at least a year because we were the generation that sent our young people to Vietnam, where soldiers typically served a one-year tour of duty and sometimes went back for more. Most of us felt that our tour of duty would be about a year, but we really didn't know.

Information changed often, so when we finally knew we were leaving Fort Lewis, we had this goodbye time with families. It says in my journal that my family was there around January 7, and I think we left Fort Lewis the next day. We definitely knew we were saying goodbye for real.

There is a test called the Holme's Stress Scale developed by a researcher from the University of Washington, where you give yourself points for all the stressful things that have gone on in the past year of your life. If you hit over a certain number, you are at higher risk for accident, injury, or illness. One of the things that is not on the list is going to war, and I've decided that that automatically gives you the three hundred points or whatever you need to hit the high risk level. The morning we left, I did something really stupid. I woke up, and I was trying to be so organized. I went to the mess hall for breakfast, took an apple, and went back to my BOQ room. I had finished packing, and I had a certain amount of time to finish up my last-minute tasks, but first I decided I would give myself a break to eat my apple. I took out my brand-new pocketknife that I had bought to take with me to go to war. I had probably only used a pocketknife twice in my life, and I decided that I would cut the apple, but in the process I managed to stick the knife through my hand. It was really a sharp little knife, and it went right through my hand. Of course everybody said, "You're supposed to shoot yourself in the foot to get out of going to war, Katie. Stabbing yourself in the hand doesn't work." My best-laid plans for having a restful and organized preparation day were ruined. I got to spend my time running over to the clinic to get a couple of stitches in my hand before getting back on the bus. My hand was fine but sore, and I still had to carry a big duffle bag and a pack and all my army paraphernalia. I can't believe I made my trip more stressful by trying to plan a stress-free moment.

We flew Pan Am Airlines to Saudi Arabia. If you remember, the civilian airlines that had contracts with the military turned their airplanes and staff over to the military during the war. We had flight attendants and Pan Am captains and the whole bit, even snacks and drinks. Now in a general hospital unit like this you have a commander, and one of the people on his staff is the company commander, who is actually over all the enlisted people. The company commander also has a say in things. He was a good friend of mine, so when I got on board, my roommate and I found ourselves sitting in first class. It wasn't the highest ranking people that were sitting in first class, but the friends of the guy who was in charge. I was in a very comfortable seat that was right in the nose of the plane. I've never been on a plane like that since.

We flew over and I think we refueled in Spain. Then we arrived in Riyadh, the capital of Saudi Arabia. Riyadh, although it's not Mecca or Medina, which are the holy cities, is considered one of the most religious cities in the Arab world. The veils of the women covered their entire faces. It was as if they were wearing a black sack over their heads. We arrived in Saudi Arabia and were taken out to what is called by the military Eskan Village. *Eskan* evidently means "village," but the Americans had always called it Eskan Village. The air force had been out there for months, probably since August or September, and they had used it as a base of operations. It was a huge village. A story was told to us about the village. The Saudi Arabian government decided that they needed to do something about the number of nomadic people they had and that they should give them a more stable life and get them educated. They built two Eskan villages, huge ones, in the kingdom of Saudi Arabia. One was on the outskirts of Riyadh, and it had fire stations, schools, and clinics. All these buildings were built plus many living quarters, which were usually high-rise apartment buildings that were five to seven stories high. Each apartment had balconies, an entryway, a formal dining room, a living room, a kitchen, a kind of open area like a family room, and then anywhere from two to four bedrooms. They moved the nomadic people into these living spaces, but they refused to live there because their camels had to be separated from them. Their camels were important to their culture. I don't know how you get a camel up seven flights of marble staircases or into an elevator. The staircases were marble, and it looked beautiful but dusty when we moved in, but the balconies were full of pigeon droppings.

The only trouble was the apartments themselves were like cinder block walls; you couldn't get a nail in them for anything. There were no closets, nothing to hang anything on, and no furniture. Ten of us were assigned to an apartment, so there would be two people in the dining room, two in the parlor/living room, and then two people in each of the three bedrooms, and I believe we did have two bathrooms. There were ten of us in this kind of a common living area. When we moved in we had one-quarter-inch pads to put on marble floors to sleep on and no place to hang anything. Some of the doctors, while we were at Fort Lewis, had formed a "construction company," they called it, and they had brought some power tools. They had taken power tools with them thinking they were going to need them when we got over there. It took them a while, but they eventually figured out ways to drill into some of these walls.

One day I walked into my room and there was a closet, like a wardrobe! One of my friends had his sister order it through the Sears catalog and got it delivered. It was one of those things that you put together out of heavy cardboard, and this was a true luxury. We still had nothing to sleep on and we hadn't received a medical assignment yet, so one of my good friends got an idea. She was our infection control nurse and had brought thousands of condoms with her because that was the one infection she was the most concerned about. She told me one day, "I have an idea. Let's go out and see if what we heard is true." Well, we went out into the Eskan and found out that there was the army side of town and the air force side of town. The air force people had been there for several months. They had been there so long that they now had little beds, metal framed twin beds, but they originally had been cots, which were now being used to lie in the sun. We would have given our teeth for a cot at that point, so she called it her "cots for condoms" program. She would trade condoms for cots, and usually it would either embarrass them enough that they would just give us their extra cot or they'd take her up on the offer. Through this barter system we slowly started getting cots into our living areas.

We were absolutely forbidden to have anything to do with the local community, so whatever socializing we were doing was with each other. This had to be just among the Americans. There was absolutely no socializing with the Saudis. The army did give us quite a few culture classes before we left Fort Lewis. If this didn't cure people, I don't know what would have. They said, "Okay, we need to explain to you that in Saudi Arabia, if somebody steals something and is found guilty, they will cut off their hand. We don't even want to imagine what they would do to you if they found you sleeping with one of their women." Right there the guys' eyes got real big, and that comment effectively cured them of any desire to fraternize with the women in Saudi.

I think the military did a good job of explaining that there were specific rules for living in Saudi Arabia. We could see how strict this country was once we started working in the hospital. The hospital we took over was what they called a Saudi Arabian military hospital. But by military they meant that if anyone you have ever been related to had ever served in the Saudi military, you could go to their military hospitals. There were not many military people in these hospitals because they had started clearing them out before contracting with the American government to come in and superimpose our structure onto theirs. I would say that over half of their employees had already left.

In Saudi Arabia there were no Saudi citizens, at least at that time, that worked in any medical profession except as physicians. It was considered low and horrible, and nursing was looked down on as a degrading occupation. None of their people would be nurses, nor would they allow any of their children to ever be nurses. Nursing was considered a really evil thing. The majority of the nurses in the hospital that we were assigned to were Filipinos. Many of the original Filipino staff had returned home, but some of them stayed and worked alongside of us. There were also Canadians and American civilian nurses, and it was run on a British system. The hospitals in Saudi were either run on an American system or a British system. We had this lovely old-fashioned Irish nurse who wore one of those blue capes. She was the chief nurse and ran the hospital before our arrival. When we started to work and convert the hospital to the 50th General, we met many expatriates because those were the people who had been hired to work there during peace time.

I personally believe that the Saudi Arabians allowed the Americans in during the war because if the war had continued all of their expatriates would leave the country, and the country could not survive without outside help. They would not have nurses, they would not have physical therapists, and they would not have plumbers or construction workers if their expatriates evacuated completely. All of those roles are performed by expatriates. It was interesting because certain countries provided certain types of workers. The Philippines provided nursing and medical people. The United States provided the hospital administrators. England and Canada provided nurses and administrators. In addition, there were all of the people who did our laundry, who seemed to be all from Pakistan. All of the repairmen were from other countries as well. Saudi Arabia was just run that way. The natives held "positions," but they did not hold "jobs." I talked to a young man who was actually in an OR tech program, the first of its kind, and he literally said that they were training only three Saudi citizens to be OR techs.

I asked him what his family thought about this and he said, "Oh, they're so embarrassed. They're embarrassed, they're ashamed, and they don't know why I would want to do this. They ask me why don't I want to hold a position and why do I have to have a job." The citizens got paid for holding positions, and they were the people who serve as the figurehead of any concern. Sometimes they knew what they were doing and were good engineers or good whatever, but other times they were not. They would be the head and the one that signed for everything. It wouldn't matter that it was the Canadian or English or German or American person working under the figurehead that wielded the power, those who held a "position" had the authority.

We learned more about the customs and culture once we got out among the expatriates who had been living there for a long time. They usually chose to work in Saudi because the money was good. Filipinos told me they could live there for ten years and then retire. While they lived in Saudi Arabia and worked, they would have their children cared for in the Philippines. They were given two one-month vacations per year when they would go home and see their families. They would work for ten years and then they would retire, and their families in the Philippines lived wonderfully with maids, and they owned homes. Now, the salaries that they were being paid were not grand by American standards, but they were wonderful by Philippine standards.

At the Eskan, we finally started getting livable conditions. We ate in a mess tent, and eventually they even started serving us underneath our high rise, where there was a big parking garage. Of course we didn't have cars, so they turned that into our mess hall. We started working at the hospital within a few days of our arrival. When we started at the hospital we would work ten-hour shifts, but it really meant a twelve-hour shift because it took an hour for our buses to transport us. We had to leave an hour before our shift started. We would have twelve hours on and twelve hours off. It seemed like we were working five days a week most of the time, five or six days, but we worked different days.

The Sabbath in Saudi Arabia is on Friday, from sundown on Thursday to sundown on Friday. We didn't work what we thought was our traditional five-day work week. We just worked whenever. We did observe Christian Sabbath on Friday. The expatriates who were members of the Church in Saudi Arabia always had held church on Friday, since that is the Muslim Sabbath. A Latter-day Saint group leader was called for our unit who was set apart by the stake president of the geographical area when our unit headquarters was located in Seattle. He was called our group leader, and he had been a bishop in his ward in Tacoma before mobilization. There were about ten of us in any of our Church meetings.

I can remember that when we first met as a group, the decision was made as to how we would hold our meetings. We decided that we would hold them on Fridays because that was the day the church had the expatriates meet in Saudi and the day when more of us would be available to attend. Our group leader said we would have priesthood meeting and sacrament meeting. I was the only woman at this meeting.

The group leader asked, "How should we go about teaching priesthood meeting? I'm thinking we should just maybe take turns." The group agreed, "Yes, we should take turns." I immediately raised my hand and said, "I want to be first! I want to be able to say that I came to war and I was a priesthood teacher." They thought that was great, and so I taught them the first priesthood lesson. And so I can say, "Yes, I was called to be a priesthood teacher!"

We had an interesting experience as members of the Church. We had a unit from Salt Lake City that moved across the street from us in the Eskan village. We all heard ahead of time that they were moving in, but they were a full hospital unit. They arrived, and of course I was excited and so were the other Latter-day Saints. The unit was welcomed by everyone because they had something our unit didn't have, and that was a Catholic chaplain. Somehow we had ended up with three Protestant chaplains. We had had a Latter-day Saint chaplain, but because of his medical history of kidney stones, he wasn't allowed to be deployed with us, which he was quite torn up about. When the Salt Lake City unit came, we decided that we would attend services with them. Someone in our group contacted them and found out that they were going to have Church service on Sunday morning and try to stick to their tradition. They didn't know yet where they were going to go to be assigned to work.

On Sunday morning three or four of us from our Latter-day Saint group were free to go to their meetings, which were held in the garage under their unit's building. Oh my, there were lots of them in attendance. We were just amazed. There must have been about 150 of them. It was just a huge portion of the unit. The only way I could analyze our experience was it was like I was visiting another ward. It wasn't as we expected. We expected them to be the long-lost brothers joining the fold, but it was more a case of, "We're our group, and now you're coming to visit." They were holding a testimony meeting, and a couple of men bore their testimonies. There were a few women in the group, but largely men were in attendance. The testimonies ranged about how glad they were that their wives weren't there and that they were really glad that the women were at home so that they could be protected. There were only a few women in the group. I was coming as a visitor with another woman, and I was like, "Well, what am I, chopped liver? Am I invisible? What is the deal here?" No one in attendance addressed the issue that there were women there alongside the men at war.

Now in looking back, I think they might have all known each other in the same way I knew the people in my unit, and my unit wouldn't have taken offense at things I might say because they knew the context from which it was coming. But here we were, the little orphans from Seattle, coming over to the big Salt Lake

City church. First of all, we thought it was really crazy they were having their meeting on Sunday, because the whole country celebrates the Sabbath on Friday. They had their meeting on Sunday, and then on top of it all, it was not like, "Oh good! You can join our group and be a part of us." And, "Oh, I'm so glad we moved in because there's only how many of you? You can be a part of our group." We returned to our unit across the street, and we voted to stay as our own group. We didn't join their ward or their branch, whatever it was, which we could have easily done. We also talked to some of the people who went to visit the Latter-day Saints on the air force side, and people said that they were a very friendly group made up of people from all different groups and were very welcoming.

Of course that Latter-day Saint unit was brand-new in the country. We had been in the country a week or two, they had only been there a day or two, and maybe the day-to-day life hadn't hit them yet. In retrospect, I can think of all kinds of perspectives they were coming from, but I will tell you, when we had fewer than ten members and we saw this whole big Latter-day Saint group move in, we thought, "Oh good, I'm going to have all this support and all these brothers and sisters," yet we were treated as visitors and we knew we were not part of their group. I guess I can look back now and say, "Oh well, it's good that they had a group identity." But when anyone showed up at our little meetings, we were thrilled to death. We were so pleased to have them; it was wonderful. Because of our schedules, I know a meeting was held every Friday. I know I went every Friday that I was able to, but it was not always possible.

When I was first on active duty as a young lieutenant at Fort Leavenworth, I knew there was one other member who worked in the hospital. He was in administration. I also knew a wonderful Christian woman who loved the Savior with all her heart. I had an experience where I had an ovarian cyst rupture. I was at work when I had this attack of incredible pain and ended up on a gurney headed for OR. They asked me, "Well, do you want us to call anyone?" I said "Get Robin for me." I had known Robin in nursing school. When she came, I told her she must get the Latter-day Saint brother from administration. I told her to tell him that I needed a blessing and that it was important to me. I knew she would follow through even though she didn't understand it. After I had made that request, I was given anesthesia and had my surgery. When I woke up, the doctor came in and spoke with me. He said that by the time the "guys from your church" had shown up, we were already in the OR. The doctor let them scrub in and get masked and gowned and come in and give me a blessing while I was on the operating table. I asked him, "Well, what was it? What had happened to cause that pain?" And he said, "You know what? When I got in, all I could find was a teaspoon of something. Whatever was there was gone, and there was just this residue." Then he said, "Somebody up there really likes you, Katie." This OB surgeon had a friend who was a Latter-day Saint, and because of his love and respect for his friend, I believe he was open to allowing the priesthood to give me that blessing.

This is how the military usually is. You know every other Latter-day Saint, and they are really supportive. We probably thought we had hit the jackpot with this unit from Salt Lake City. It was not like they were mean or antagonistic or anything, but it was like they had their own way of thinking. They were a closed group. That was a very interesting experience, but we had a good experience with our unit's Latter-day Saint group, which is what I believe was meant to happen. How else could I have been a priesthood teacher!

The first day we went to the hospital in Saudi I received my assignment. I was to be the head nurse of what was going to be a medical-surgical ward. There was a Canadian head nurse there who had not left the country, and it was great because I had a knowledgeable, experienced nurse to lead with. We also had a few civilian nurses who were still there, plus I had my army medics, so we were well staffed. It was a very nice facility. My infection control friend went nuts the whole time she was there because their ideas of infection control were so different from ours. I was also given the small ward next to ours that did not have a civilian head nurse.

On our first day there, we went through a little orientation and we were all introduced to this little lovely Irish chief nurse. I said to her, "You know, I have very dear friends from the United States, and one of them is a hospital administrator. In the last card that we exchanged, he was here in Saudi Arabia in a place called Al Khari, which I can't even find in the map. How would I go about writing to them from here?" She asked me for his name and I said, "Ken Smith." She said, "Just a minute." Then she dialed four numbers and handed me the phone, and it was Ken. This hospital where Ken was working was a satellite of the hospital that I was now assigned to. The coincidence was just unbelievable. These were not just very dear friends of mine. Ken's wife, Ludona, is the person who brought me into the Church. And now we find ourselves at war together! Ken was an expatriate hired to work in administration, and even their three kids were there with them. As soon as Ken was able to tell Ludona, she came over to our hospital on the shuttle bus. There was a shuttle that ran daily between the two hospitals. Ludona came regularly on that bus and visited me while I was on duty at the hospital. She was not allowed to visit the Eskan.

We decided that Ludona must have been the first hospital volunteer ever in the Kingdom of Saudi Arabia because the concept of volunteers in a hospital was unheard of, since they don't even allow their people to work in the hospitals. Although Ludona could not work on my ward, she was able to do volunteer work on the orthopedics ward where there were American soldiers with broken bones. She would read to them and write letters for them and cheer them up with fun conversations. She would even take my laundry home and bring it back on the next shuttle trip! The army had a laundry run by the Pakistanis. We dropped off our laundry but were never sure whose laundry we would get back. We did our underclothes in our bathtub in the apartment. Anything we needed, Ludona would go and find because she could go out into the economy when we were not allowed to. In her little town, she visited the market and found all kinds of things for us.

I think it was a Friday when the war was officially over, and we figured that we would be going home in a few weeks. I don't remember how I pulled off my next adventure. I must have ridden the shuttle myself, but I went out to Ken and Ludona's town and slipped into civilian clothes. I wore American clothes, but I had to wear the abaya and the scarf, without the veil. The expatriates don't wear veils. I had it explained to me that the reason we did not have to wear veils or the reason our faces were not covered is that the Saudi Arabians consider all Western women whores. I thought that could not be true. I mentioned before that I had a student in the OR who was a Saudi citizen. We got to chatting, and I innocently asked, "How do the Saudis feel about American women? I've heard that they think of us as kind of whores." He looked directly at me and said, "Yes." It was as if he were saying, "Yes, so what's your point?" So that's really the way it was. We're so below them we don't have to wear veils.

I spent the night with Ken and Ludona in their compound. The next day I attended church with them, which was back in Riyadh. It was really interesting because the government had a lot of stipulations on what Latter-day Saints could and could not do. They could meet in groups of a certain size, but they could never tell anyone they were Christian. They could never tell anyone what religion they belonged to. They could not show their scriptures, so when they went to meetings they would carry a brief case or a shoulder bag with their scriptures hidden in them. They were basically on their honor to not ever tell anyone anything about the Church. As a member of the military, I was not under that obligation. I was not even aware at the time I arrived in Saudi Arabia that members of the Church were under any kind of censorship. Ludona was with me one day at the hospital and we were having a conversation with the young Saudi Arabian OR tech. As we were talking, I started telling him what church I belong to. I brought it up and told him about the Church and asked him questions. When we were done with our little discussion, he walked away and Ludona about fainted. She said, "I never thought I'd ever hear that conversation take place in this country. I just can't believe it happened. I'm just amazed!"

Expatriates would go back to the United States on vacation and return to Saudi with Church videos for their kids and Church literature. As long as they did not have a lot of the same item, they usually got through the checkpoints. I do know that one of Ludona and Ken's Church leaders had a really bad experience. Evidently, the story was that maybe he had made some enemies at work or there were Saudis who were jealous of him. When he and his family returned from a trip to the United States, they went through his suitcase. When they found a Christian video, they wouldn't allow him to reenter the country, so he had to go back the United States, thereby losing his job.

Medically speaking, as far as nursing goes, we were preparing and waiting around for the war to start. Right away we started to get soldiers coming in that had medical problems with sudden onset diabetes, car accidents, broken bones, or things like that. We still had a few patients that had been in the hospital before the war had broken out, but they had not been transferred to a nonmilitary hospital. The hospital we were in was a Saudi military hospital that used to be a transplant hospital before the military took over. I had one little boy who was waiting for a transplant, but since the hospital had switched leadership, he could not get his transplant. He had to be transferred to another hospital.

We had an eclectic patient load, and I decided I would work a couple of nights to see how everything was functioning. While I was working nights, we had two Saudi Arabian female doctors who were working with the patients on our ward. One doctor wore the complete veil and black abaya and scarf, so it was difficult to communicate. She spoke English with a thick accent, and she had the ever-present veil covering her face. You can imagine how difficult it was to understand her English. It was very frustrating working with her.

Once she examined a soldier from Mississippi who had diabetes. I will never forget the absurdity of this conversation. She was talking to another doctor in front of the patient, as if he were ignorant. They were talking about how the patient had high blood sugar, and then the doctor turned to the soldier and asked through her veil, "Do you have a family history of diabetes?" It was truly impossible for the soldier to understand her. The patient replied, "No." She said to the other doctor, "No, there's no family history of diabetes." I jumped right in and said to the patient, "Sergeant, is there any member of your family that has ever had diabetes?" And he said, "Well, my mama has diabetes, and my granddad has diabetes, and my brother's got diabetes, and, well, my cousin got diabetes . . ." And he just went on and on and on.

Well, I guess that was worth the trip because at least somebody will believe that this guy had a family history of diabetes. Who knows if the doctor was offended at my interruption because of course her face was covered. After the war, when people would ask me what I did in Saudi Arabia, I would say I was an interpreter. Then they would ask, "Really? What would you interpret?" I said, "I interpreted for people in Saudi Arabia who thought they spoke English to Americans from different parts of the country like New York or Mississippi."

The other female doctor was very interesting. She wore all white, which was very unusual. She wore a long white lab coat that went nearly to the ground, but I could see a skirt and heels under it. She also wore nylons and a white head scarf so her hair did not show. She never wore a veil. We were working together one night and I said to her, "Why do you dress in white? Why no veil?" She replied, "My father dictates what I wear since I will never be married." I asked, "What do you mean you'll never be married?" She replied, "No one would ever marry a doctor." Like, "I'm the lowest of lows because I'm a female doctor." I asked her why, because I am so naive. She said, "It's because we have to take care of people and touch people." Since she is not going to have a husband, her father decides what she is allowed to do. Since she is not ever going to have a husband and because she is considered lower than low, he does not make her wear a veil.

I couldn't let it go, and I said, "Wow, that's interesting. How does that work? Do you ever get in trouble when you're in public?" She said that sometimes she is approached by the Matawa, which is the religious police who carry sticks and hit people if they are not dressed modestly, but when she explains to them that she is a physician and that her father has given her permission, they leave her alone. I asked her if this was her father's way of punishing her, thinking he will make life miserable for her because she chose to be a doctor. I almost felt like it was some kind of religious order, like the father was saying, "You're stuck. You're not ever going to ever have a family or be married, so I'm going to give you privileges that other women do not have." I don't know.

We were still sitting there at the nurses' station and we were having this fairly intimate conversation. I was the naive Mormon who read *National Geographic*, and I brought up an article that I read in the *National Geographic* before I came to Saudi. I told her how I read about this woman who had gone to school in Oxford, England, and had dressed in Western clothes. In the interview she said that when she came back to Saudi Arabia, she realized she really missed her abaya and veil and was happy to get back to it. This doctor and I were sitting in chairs with rollers on the legs. All of a sudden she rolled her chair across the length of this nursing station right up to me and put her face within six inches of my nose. Under her breath she said, "She lies." Then she rolled her chair back, resumed writing, and didn't say anything else to me. I think the women of Saudi Arabia will be interesting to hear from someday.

I got called into my chief nurse's area while on my off time in the Eskan village. (Wait, what am I thinking? We didn't have off time. Who am I kidding?) During the time that I wasn't at the hospital, I got called to go to a meeting. When I arrived, our chief nurse had a few of her supervisors there whom I highly respected. They were probably all in their mid- to late forties, and some of them were Vietnam veterans. It was interesting because they were kind of all there to give me support, so it made me think, "Okay, has something gone wrong at home? What are they calling me in for?" It turned out that they called me in to inform me that my ward had been chosen to receive all the enemy prisoners of war (Iraqis) that were going to be captured, and that I would be the head nurse of that ward.

Now here's the difference. If you see the word EPW, that means enemy prisoners of war; that's the other side. If you see POW, that's a prisoner of war, and that can be an American. But an enemy prisoner of war would be Iraqi.

Colonel D'Allesandro, who was a Vietnam veteran and one of the assistant chiefs, sat down next to me. She was very forthright when she said, "This is not a good situation to be in. I need to tell you what experiences from the Vietnam War taught us. If you take care of the EPWs, then there are some Americans who will see you as helping the enemy. Even the people at home whom you tell may wonder why you're risking your life to take care of enemies. Your staff and the people that are working for you, some of them will not be able to handle this, and you need to think through this." They did say to me, "If this is something that you will not accept, then we will find a replacement for you, but it's the ward you're familiar with and we chose your ward." They chose it more for security reasons, not because of me. My ward was located at the end of the hospital complex, so it was easier to have it a locked area. I did feel that they were expressing a lot of confidence in me as well.

From the minute they told me about this, I felt that it was the right thing. I felt like I was one of the few people there that understood that Iraqis were my brothers. I may have not liked the war. I may have been very upset about the Iraqis. I may have hated Saddam Hussein with a passion. But at the same time, I did understand the need to offer care to those people, and I knew that I could do so in a positive way.

So we talked some more, and I went back and held a staff meeting with all of the personnel assigned to our ward. I explained our assignment and tried to prime them with the same philosophy that I had. I also told them that if any of them wanted to be replaced, they could request a transfer, and that I did not believe we were short handed. I did believe that I would be able to get other people in the unit who were willing to help. In my whole group I only had one enlisted person who was very apologetic but very honest and willing to acknowledge that this was not a place where she felt comfortable serving. It just wasn't what she came to do, to take care of the enemy. She did mention her family at home and how she would feel awkward to say that she was there taking care of the Iraqis. That was fine with me. She was transferred off our unit and we got somebody else in.

My ward master was very supportive and also really good about the whole thing. The highest-ranking enlisted person who works on each ward serves as the ward master, and they supervise all of the enlisted people, including all the LPNs and orderlies. They also order all of the supplies. They are really fabulous. In my opinion, there should be an equivalent role in civilian hospitals. My ward master and I met with the expatriates so that they would also understand what was happening.

While the rest of the hospital was waiting for patients (some wards never did get any patients) our ward was full. And this was before the war started. It was all during what are called "skirmishes." It is interesting because maybe in Gulf War II (Iraqi Freedom), with the embedded reporters, they would have had a better handle on this. But when you would read in the newspaper that there was a skirmish here or we dropped a bomb there, the real war hadn't started yet and certainly the ground war hadn't started. But I was getting patients with bullet holes through their bodies and amputated limbs. These were casualties that had been taken previously to a mobile hospital or an American combat support hospital and stabilized. It was not as if we were getting them right off the battlefield.

Remember that this was a Saudi Arabian hospital to begin with. The Saudis still owned the place, and therefore all of the enemy prisoners of war belonged to Saudi Arabian doctors or physicians. It put us into a very difficult position because the Saudi Arabians do not practice medicine the way we do. I will be the first to say that it was not unusual for us to call on our American doctors to sneak up and write an order that we requested and then sneak out. We did it because the Saudis practiced medicine in a way that we found unethical at times. I think the main difference is that they did not believe in pain management. They had pain medication, but not pain management. For example, I had a patient who had a bullet hole through his calf. You could see daylight through it. When he was to have his dressing changed (it was a packed dressing), he was to have two Tylenol if it hurt. So like I said, it was not unusual to grab an American doctor from our unit and say, "I realize this isn't your patient, but you've got to write this order for me." And they knew it. The Saudi doctors never asked us any questions; I don't even know if they read the records or saw the difference.

The second difference was that since the EPWs belonged to the host country—that is a fact in any war—I wasn't allowed to use our MPs; I had to use Saudi MPs. I had these guards with loaded weapons sitting around my ward to supposedly guard the patients who were all in bad shape. Believe me, none of us were worried about the patients, but we still had to deal with the Saudi guards. Before we received EPWs, I made an appointment with the captain of the guards. Now think about this. I outranked him and was a decade older. In his office he offered me tea, but I had to tell him I don't drink tea because of my religious beliefs. The Saudis do seem to be respectful of people who will live their religious principles. I had been told ahead of time by my expatriate friends that if I get in that situation, I should tell them that it's my religion and they will stop at that because their religion says no alcohol. So I told him that I would like a glass of water.

So we talked, and the first word I learned in Arabic was "lieutenant colonel." The idea was that I did have a rank and they didn't have to think of me as a woman. The media did say later that was how the Saudis eventually coped with the women in the military, by seeing them by rank rather than gender. I read one article that said we were gender neutral, and they did see us that way.

Their concept of security was just so different from ours. My friend, the infection control nurse, Kathy, was so funny. Now I had the locked ward with the EPWs and my other little ward that still had a few patients, a couple of Saudis and a French soldier. One day Kathy and I were coming back through the locked door. She was coming to look at something related to infection control in my ward, and here was a Saudi guard sitting kind of slumped over in a chair with his weapon pointed at us! I mean, he was just leaning forward asleep and cradling his gun in his arms. American MPs would not do that. What happened next was kind of funny in retrospect. You have to remember that an American military person would never let anyone touch their weapon. Nobody would walk up and grab your rifle from you or even touch it.

Kathy, with that in her little American mind, decided that we had to teach this guy. We woke him up and tried to explain to him that he must have his weapon pointing up, not at staff members coming through the door. Of course we weren't touching the weapon, but we were trying to explain this to him. The interpreter wasn't there yet, so we were using sign language and acting it out. Then Kathy grabbed his arm to show him what we were talking about. It was as if she had touched him with a hot iron, because in his mind, here was this Western woman, who was obviously a whore, touching him. At that point, he jerked back and started yelling and was very upset. Then she took his weapon and put it in the right position, and he was fine with that! Cultural differences within the military brought an entirely different perspective.

Back to the second ward I oversaw. One of the things we were told by the expatriates was that the Saudis were possibly being told that there were no such things as HIV or AIDS, just as there was officially no spousal abuse or child abuse in Saudi Arabia. These were all Western diseases and problems that did not exist in the Kingdom of Saudi Arabia. I had one Saudi patient who was there for pneumonia when we first took over the hospital. I was going through his chart one day to look up his diagnosis and treatment and to see how soon could we transfer him out, because we needed to make room for the wounded that were predicted to come in. I went through his whole chart and when I read his lab reports, what do you know, he was HIV positive.

I had an opportunity to go to the hospital in Al Khari where Ken worked to see if it could handle overflow just in case the war got bigger. I was sent with a delegation of about half a dozen nurses to look it over and see what we could set up. Our tour guide was an American nurse. She was an expatriate who was working in pediatrics. We divided up, and she took three of us into a pediatric room. There were a couple of kids running around while their mothers sat with their faces completely veiled and their hands covered with black gloves. So I asked the American nurse who they were, and she said they were the mothers. I asked her, "Why are they veiled in here? It's just their children." And she explained, "Oh, they have to stay veiled because a man might walk by, and they cannot be seen." I asked, "How long have these kids been here?" She replied, "Oh these kids have been here their whole lives." The children were about twelve to eighteen months old.

I said to her, "Well the first thing is, you're telling me that these mothers are in here and they've never felt their babies skin?" She says, "That's right." And then I asked, "Why have these kids been in here for so long?" She answered, "The mothers will not take care of them at home." A child in the United States would have gone home with a breathing treatment that the mom could do at home or that a home health nurse could help with, but in Saudi Arabia the families would not learn to do it. Then the nurse said, "That's nothing, come and look at this."

We went to another pediatric room where a mother was holding a child that was a couple of years old, and she said, "I want you to see this one. This child is in and out of the hospital all the time with asthma and has been in the hospital with us more than he's been in the home with the family. But look at this." She pulled the child's shirt up to show the scars all over his back. The scars were at different stages and all about one-half to three-quarters of an inch long and about the thickness of a line. The newer ones were long blisters that had liquid in them. I asked what happened.

I was thinking it was some sort of weird chicken pox because nothing that I have ever seen could have given me an idea of what this was. The nurse told me, "This is the way that they treat the children when they go home. It's to drive out the evil spirits that are causing the illness. They take a wire, like a paper clip or the edge of a coin, heat it, and then touch it to the child's skin."

On that same visit we had a chance to ask a lot of questions on health care. What did they do for public health? Did they have public health? And the answer was basically no. Because the country has plenty of money, the money goes to treatment. They have these little stores—there was even one in the hospital compound—that are like our convenience stores, or the old "mom and pop" store. They are literally one little room with two of the four walls holding a variety of odds and ends for sale, like canned goods. On the other two walls would be sugar cubes. People would buy sugar cubes and hold them between their front teeth and drink their tea through the sugar cube. Needless to say, there's a lot of missing front teeth in Saudi. There is also a high rate of diabetes, according to the Americans who lived there. They said that it wasn't unusual for Saudis to have their own dialysis machines. The government would pay for the technology to treat diabetes but not for diabetes education or prevention.

Saudi Arabia was the most closed country imaginable. The expatriates there could not have anyone come visit them except immediate family members. They could have brothers, sisters, parents, or children come, but no one else. When their children reached high-school age, they had to leave the country for school. Expatriates were not allowed to attend high school in Saudi Arabia because the government did not want foreign teenagers there. If the expatriates stayed there while their kids were teenagers, most Americans would send them to boarding schools in Europe or back to the Untied States for high school. They were allowed to come home for Christmas and summer vacations, but they were not allowed to live with their families anymore.

When the Scud missiles would land in Saudi Arabia, there were never any casualties according to the Saudi media. Those Scud missiles never killed anybody. They would land on "empty houses." At least that was what the news reported. What the government didn't want in the news didn't go in the news. They were very absolute.

I have saved the stories about the patients for last. The Iraqis came to the ward, and they were absolutely terrified. We had an interpreter assigned to us from Kenya who was very good. He spoke Arabic (the language for the whole Gulf area) and very good English. He would go with me when I visited each patient as they were admitted. I usually introduced myself and made sure they understood that I was the highest-ranking military person there, that I was their nurse, and that while they were there, they were patients and we were health-care providers. They were not soldiers and we were not soldiers, and we were there to take care of them and give them the very best care that we could. That was our way of thinking.

The Saudi Arabians really didn't feel that way, because we were in their hospital. I had a burn patient who should have been down in a burn ward, and I had orthopedic patients who should have been in orthopedic wards, but they were not allowed anywhere but on our EPW ward. I could speak for us as a staff and tell the patients, "We respect you as patients. What has happened before and what will happen in the future, we have no control over. But while you are here, you will be given the best medical care that we can possibly give you." Eventually we heard things like how they were told that they should never be taken alive and that if they were taken alive, the Americans would torture them and kill them. I guess they thought they were there for medical experiments, because they were scared, so we reassured them. Of course a lot of my medics were their age. They were young too, and so they would develop a rapport with the patients. My staff was excellent. They were very good with the patients. It was kind of the old-fashioned open wards where you might have six patients in a room. It took a while to gain their trust, but we did a good job taking care of them. They were then sent to specialists all over the city for eye or limb repair or whatever was needed.

They had some interesting things to teach us. When the truce was called, the Iraqi patients would say, "You must kill Saddam Hussein. You must kill him!" We replied, "We can't do that. The war is over, and we're not going to do that." But they kept on insisting that we do it. I asked them why they said that, and they answered, "Because we can never go home again. We cannot go back to Iraq because if we do, Saddam Hussein will kill us!" When I asked why, they said, "Because we were told not to be captured." I told them, "You guys are not the ones that surrendered. You didn't surrender. You were unconscious when you got picked up." These severely wounded men replied with desperation in their voices, "It won't matter. We were told not to be taken alive, so we will not be allowed to return to our families."

I don't know what happened to them. I've looked in the papers at different times trying to find out what happened to them. Did the Saudis keep them as EPWs? Did the Saudis allow them to stay in their country? I can't imagine that, but did they get sent back to Iraq? If they did, what happened to them then? I don't know. When we said to them, "We can't kill Saddam Hussein. The war is over, and we're at peace now," they told us, "Well, get the Israelis to do it."

When I first got there, I talked to one of the little boys that I told you about who needed a transplant. He was not sure how he felt about the war. He was not against the allies but he kind of thought that it wasn't good to fight against the Iraqis because Iraqis were Arabs too. This was very confusing for him. We were always trying to convince him that we were the good guys and that Saddam Hussein was really evil. Now at the time, Israel was not a part of this conflict. They were affiliated with the allies and were even suppliers for the war effort. The night came when the Scud missiles hit Israel completely unprovoked. I went in the next day, and I said to our boy, "Well, now what do you think? Aren't we right about Saddam Hussein? Look at that bombing. What do you think of that missile attack on Israel?" And he looked at me, completely serious, and said, "Well, at least Saddam Hussein did something right." The hatred in that part of the world is just unbelievable.

Anyone who was Jewish was counseled to have their religious affiliation taken off their dog tags in case they were captured. I had a friend there whose brother was studying in Israel through the University of Michigan. We were able to call the United States easily, so she would call Michigan and then they could then put her through to her brother. She did that, but as soon as the operator answered in Israel and it was obvious that was where it was, the call was cut off and she could never make that call again. Somehow the Saudis knew, and there was no contact allowed with Israel. It was interesting because if you had Israel stamped on your passport, you weren't able to enter into an Arab country. The expatriates who were there and wanted to visit Israel only visited on their final trip home.

All the Christian chaplains who wore a cross as their military insignia were told they had to remove it while in Saudi Arabia. The International Red Cross symbol is a red crescent there because of the Crusades. Those people do not forget. If they do not allow crosses because of the Crusades, why are they going to forget what happened in 1946? They're not going to. All of the American Red Cross and the navy hospital ships that went to the Gulf wore a red crescent, not a red cross. The international organization's name is the International Red Cross and Red Crescent, and the reason is that they will not forget the injustices that were done during the Crusades. So they are not likely to forget something that happened a mere fifty or sixty years ago. When people think there will be peace in the Middle East, I'm a fatalist. I just say, "I'm sorry, I don't see that happening because these people never ever let go of a grudge. They cannot forgive."

As far as taking care of the patients, they were very cooperative. Most of them were very low-ranking foot soldiers. We asked them why they had joined the military and they explained that the soldiers had come to their homes and asked them if they would like to join the military. Then they explained that they would kill their wife and children if they didn't want to come, so they joined. And that's how they told it.

There was one gentleman who might have been an officer or a higher ranking enlisted Iraqi who actually had scars from wars with Iran. He was a career military person, probably the only one we had, and he had this strange wound. Now I've taken graduate-level anatomy and physiology, and I never could imagine what caused this strange wound. It didn't affect his organs, but it was all in his muscle tissue. It was as if somebody had taken a scythe to the side of his body. It was some kind of shrapnel injury. We had a lot of those kinds of wounds that we had to pack and take care of, and I hadn't done bedside nursing for years. I did some there, but my staff worked extremely hard, and they did a good job.

We also had one Iraqi civilian who had been a taxi driver. He said he was driving his taxi in Baghdad with his sister when they were hit by some sort of mortar or missile or shell. His sister was killed, his taxi was destroyed, and he was burned terribly. He found himself lying on the road and was picked up by Americans and put into the American medical system, which he was sure saved his life. He became an enemy prisoner of war, even though he was not a soldier, because there was no place else to put him. I have to hand it to the GIs who picked him up and put him into the system and to the people who kept taking care of him too. At some point they could have shipped him back or just left him on the road. He was terribly burned to the point where it took four of us at least two hours to change his dressings every day, and that was only after we got good at it.

I did not take a patient load, because I tried to help with all the patients so I would know what was going on with all of them. The first time we changed his dressing, I chose to be a part of that team, and I got the interpreter to come into the room. I told the interpreter that it was important that he be there for a good share of the procedure to explain to the patient what we were doing and why and try to get his cooperation as much as possible. Again, the pain management was horrendous, and we medicated him with whatever we could get, but it was not enough. It was a bad situation. We were changing his dressings, and partway through this incredibly painful procedure he said, "You take better care of me than my family would." When we finished his dressings, he offered me his son in marriage! He also said that I could come to Baghdad where he would give me a ride in his taxi and give me pork. We thought that was the funniest thing, but because they don't eat pork or pork products and they know we do, so they somehow think that pork is very special to us. He would go out illegally to get pork to give us.

On this same day, partway through changing the dressings, one of the other medics came in and said, "Colonel Walther, this patient that you changed the dressing on this morning is really complaining, and I don't know what he's saying. I don't know how to help him, and I don't know if it's the dressing or if something else is going on." I was kind of feeling bad because I was the who changed his dressing. I was working on another case, but I told the medic that I would be there as soon as I was done. Evidently the patient kept complaining, and nobody could quite figure out what he needed, and of course I was tying up our only interpreter.

The interpreter that day was not the one from Kenya. He happened to be a Kuwaiti citizen who was married to an American. He was visiting his in-laws in North Dakota when the war broke out that summer, and he could not return to Kuwait because of the war. He did not know what had happened to his family, his business, his home, or anything, but evidently the American government made a deal with the Kuwaiti government. The American government said, "Let us put your citizens into our military to serve. We'll give them a high enlisted rank, and we'll pay them." We all suspected that they were making as much as an American general by working as interpreters, since the Kuwaiti government also paid them. They could be used in any place because they were very fluent in Arabic, and since they were in the United States when the war broke out, most were very fluent in English.

This interpreter was a great guy, and he wore an American uniform. His name was Abdul, but he went by Abe in his American life. Abe went with me to see the complaining patient. It would always confuse the patients when they would see an Arab in an American uniform, so I told Abe to explain who he was and what he was doing and ask the patient what was wrong. So Abe started talking, and even though I did not know the language, I could still hear familiar words. I could hear him say his name and my name, and I could hear him ask questions.

Then Abe gets into a discussion, and all of a sudden the patient starts shaking his head, saying, "No, no, no, no!" The patient started to weep. So I said, "Whoa, what's going on?" And Abe said to me, "Well, when I told him that I was from Kuwait and that I was here to help him, he said he just cannot let me help him because the Iraqis have done terrible things to my country and to my people and to my land, and he can't accept this help from me." Here was a man who in the morning had to bite on a towel for pain management when I changed his dressing, and now he was weeping because his enemy is offering to help him.

I had to shift into army mode and say to the interpreter, "Look, you tell him that we're here to help him and I'm your commanding officer in this situation and you have to do what I say, so you're going to do it." So the interpreter got this different voice and said it, and we found out that the patient wanted his bandage adjusted, which we did, and all was fine. We walked out of the room, and I said, "Abe, how do you feel about that? You don't know where your parents are, you don't know what's happened to your business, you don't know what your life's going to be like, how do you feel about helping these Iraqi patients?" And he said, "You know, the Iraqi soldiers don't know what's really happening. It wasn't their choice. They hardly have an opinion about it. They're not like American soldiers. American soldiers all want to tell Schwarzkopf what to do. American soldiers all think they know exactly what's going on and exactly how it should be done, but the Iraqis aren't like that. They're victims just like I am, and so I have no problem helping them. It's true that when I took this job I thought I would be interrogating prisoners at war. I didn't know I would be working at their bedside, but it's okay, I can do this."

When I came home, I told a really dear friend of mine that story, and she said it reminded her of Romans 12:20: "Therefore if thine enemy hunger, feed him; if he thirst, give him drink; for in so doing thou shalt heap coals of fire on his head." Now I'm not saying this is vengeance, but at the same time it doesn't say if you do kind things to your enemy, he'll do kind things to you. Or if you do kind things to the enemy, you'll be blessed. It says, "for in so doing, thou shalt heap coals of fire upon his head." And I saw the coals of fire heaped on this guy's head when he was weeping. He had been wounded, I saw daylight through the calf of his leg, and I could change that dressing with him literally biting on a towel and taking Tylenol, but when the Kuwaiti citizen offered to help him in his pain, he wept. So dramatic! That was probably one of my biggest learning moments. There was a lot of learning that happened gradually during those four months, but that one was a dramatic lesson in five minutes.

The Saudi Arabian doctors would determine when the patients had to return to the prisoner of war camp. We developed a wonderful relationship with these patients. Now remember, I had only been there a couple of months, and these guys were treated and evacuated while we were still there. When the first group left, they were lined up and handcuffed to be transported to an EPW camp. As they were leaving, they shook our hands, including mine. A few of them shed tears as they left us. I couldn't help but feel that maybe they were tears of fear for where they were going, but that wasn't the moment for those kind of tears. I realized that they were actually saying good-bye and crying.

I can't help but think that one benefit of war is getting to know people. When I was a child, my father worked for the federal government, and we lived for two years in Milan, Italy. Our maid was married to a man who had fought in World War II, and of course my father had fought in World War II. And I thought, even as an eleven-year-old, how odd it was. Here these men had fought on different sides of the war. The husband, Gildo, was an enemy, but he just loved Americans. It was so obvious. He loved us, and he would come and talk to my parents about America. He had been a prisoner of war and at the time had eaten better than his family who had been left behind. He was actually taken to the United States as a POW and had been left to work on a farm. He loved America, he loved Americans, and he had nothing but positive things to say about being a POW.

What was the reason I was chosen to be the head nurse of the EPW ward? It was an incredible experience for me because I was allowed some wisdom to help my staff cope, and I was blessed with truly excellent staff members who were willing to work with a "brotherhood of man" attitude. When I look back, I can say, "I know there were forty prisoners of war that left loving Americans. I know there are forty Iraqis that knew Americans loved them." I know that the whole experience that we had was for a reason. I preached the gospel in my own little way in a country where the expatriates couldn't believe that I didn't get sent out of the country for doing so.

Well, I'm divorced. I came back from the Gulf in 1991, and my divorce did not take place until 1999. I'm not going to say that the war was a direct cause of my divorce, but it certainly added to the stress of the relationship. I think one of the most difficult things is it changes the family dynamics completely when someone is mobilized. It happens especially when you're a reservist. Even though you know that the potential is there, it's not like Mom or Dad are on active duty and they regularly and routinely go six months to Okinawa or they get deployed for short terms on a regular basis as an expected thing. When a reservist who has been in the reserves for twenty years and has never been mobilized is finally mobilized, there is no practice for that scenario.

So now we had a change in our family dynamics. I can remember sitting at the dinner table after we were told of our mobilization. We were talking to our children, who ranged in ages from three to fifteen years at the time, and one of the school-aged children said, "Well, Mom, [we were reassuring them that Dad was going to stay at home to take care of them] who is going to make money if Dad's staying at home to take care of us?" When I told her that I would be paid, she asked, "Can you make enough money?" I replied, "I make more money in the reserves than your dad makes in his job." It was a foreign idea that Mom could make money too. Our dynamics changed immensely because now I was making the money and Dad was at home. He wasn't as good with money as I was. Financially, things didn't go as well as they could have. I think my husband did a good job, and I think his heart was in the right place. I do believe that he really loved his children, and I think he tried very hard to stay organized and make sure that they had the care that they needed. Physically he took good care of them.

My then-fifteen-year-old is now working on her doctorate in sociology, so she has all kinds of interesting insights into family dynamics. I think that as a child she felt a huge burden, especially spiritually because she took all the kids to church then by herself. Their father did promise to make sure that they got to the church, so he would drive them to the church, but he didn't go with them. She had this role then at this very young age to get these kids to church, and I'm assuming she was also making sure they were dressed appropriately.

The second daughter found time to rebel. She would sneak out and do some of those petty shenanigans that adolescents do since I wasn't there to keep a close eye and to be as strict as usual. My husband did write me a letter while I was over there, and he said, "I will tell you the area that has gone down. I've been able to keep track of everything, but I cannot keep control of four kids at school and still take care of this three-year-old at home. I just have to accept that I have my limitations." So that was tough. He did realize what a hard job it was and that he was not super good at it. I think in some ways when I look back, he had some of the same reactions that housewives have, like, "Why don't I get more recognition for what I'm doing?" I got all the glory. I came back and I got the homecoming and the kudos and that sort of thing. I'm sure there were people who said to him, "Well, what a good husband you were to do that. What a good dad you were." But it wasn't as visible. Nobody asked him to give talks or speeches. Because he wasn't a member of the Church, he was very negative about receiving offers made by the ward to help bring in food. I think he felt that it was like they were saying that he couldn't do it, whereas he could have just kicked back and taken some of the help that was there for him. He wasn't comfortable letting people serve the family, and I'm sure it had something to do with his own relationship to the Church as well.

Before I left, the ward had let me know they would be supportive. I think it was more of my friends in the ward that were supportive because it wasn't an organized effort. There was a member of the bishopric who gave me the counsel and advice that I needed. Back then, the Church didn't make brown garments for women, but they did for men. So that meant I was going to have to either wear my white garments and a brown t-shirt on top of it and then my army long sleeve jacket in the desert, or do something else. Additionally, because the military didn't know where we were going initially, we were told that white was not a good color to take because that was the color reserved for royalty. We might be hanging our clothes out to dry in a village or someplace where that would not be seen as appropriate.

When I talked to the member of the bishopric about this, he said, "Let's use common sense. First of all, there is nothing wrong with you using a man's shirt." As far as the pants, he said, "Why don't you go ahead and dye them if it's a matter of not being able to wear white." So I went ahead and dyed them. He was a very smart man, and I thought that was very good counsel. I truly don't know what all the military women in the Church do about these things. I don't know what the percentage is of the female members of the Church in the military. I do feel like I had plenty of support from individual people in the Church acting in official and unofficial capacities such as the group leader who took care of our spiritual well-being, the counselor in the bishopric who gave me good counsel, and the Relief Society officers and presidency who wrote to me. In fact, they sent me taped Relief Society lessons. My children had good teachers at church, so that was all in place.

I think I felt a little forgotten by the Church as a whole; that is why this project is exciting. There is so little written about women in the military. There is so little counsel given to the women in the military. It's like the guys from the Salt Lake unit who were bearing their testimonies in Saudi Arabia. Women in the military were invisible to them.

I have had people say odd things to me in relationship to the Church and the military. In the military, I had people who got to know me and would say, "I've known Mormons before, but you're not a regular Mormon, are you?" It made me want to say, "What have I done that would make you think I'm not a regular Mormon?" I said no to the coffee at lunch, and I said no to the beer that was passed around the officers club, and yet they were saying that I wasn't like the rest of the Church members they've known. What does that mean? I am a card-carrying member. I have my temple recommend with me at all times. I am as doctrinally sound a member as you will ever find. But maybe what they were thinking was that I am not as culturally a Mormon as other people whom they may have met, perhaps because I'm not from a member family. When I talk about my parents or my extended family, maybe there are things that I say that aren't what someone who had grown up in the Church would say. And I don't have pioneer ancestors. I am the pioneer. So maybe there is something about Latter-day Saint women in the military that creates a doublethink for some people. I think it has to do with the cultural perceptions about what a woman should be or what she should not be. Perhaps a Latter-day Saint woman in the military seems incongruous to people.

There's another thing that is really weird. I used to always dye my hair. When I got to Saudi Arabia, I found the same color, but my hair became lighter than ash brown. I was using the same color on my hair just to cover the gray. When I came back, I had someone say to me something about being a blonde, and I said, "I'm not a blonde." And they said, "Yes, you are." I guess I was blonde by then. Before I left, the Miss Clairol shade that I was using kept my hair very dark, but when I came back, people would say I was a light ash blonde. I guess my hair got lighter from the stress or situation.

One day I saw one of my interpreters from Kenya walking across the compound, and his wife was completely covered like an Islamic woman in Riyadh would be. She was totally covered in black, and she was walking about six steps behind him. When I saw him on the ward, I said, "I saw you walking across the compound with your wife. Why did you move here from Kenya?" He said, "So we could live the religion in a more pure form." "How does your wife feel about that?" I asked. His response was, "Oh, she's fine. This is a good place for us to be."

Then I said, "You know, the hard thing for me would be that I would not be able to have any male acquaintances. I wouldn't be able to have any men that were just my friends. I wouldn't be able to work with men. That just seems so odd to me." And he said, "Well, that's the way it should be. Men and women should not be friends because that's not appropriate. You should only be friends with your spouse. That's the only person of the opposite sex that you should have anything to do with." But I said, "Look at us. We're friends." And, oh my word, you would have thought by the look on his face that I had just made some horrible sexual innuendo because he just looked at me and said nothing. We were interrupted then, and we never returned to that topic. I would have loved to know what he would have said. He gave me a big, beautiful Koran before I left, he spoke with me, and he talked to me about his family, so he did consider me a friend. But maybe a part of it was that I was gender neutral. I had a uniform on.

When I came back, I went to work up at the army for a couple of weeks. We got out in such a hurry that we weren't going to have medical coverage, so I said I'd work up there day to day as much as I could since my husband didn't have a job. He quit his job because we thought I was going to be gone for a year. I asked for as many duty days as I could. One of the things I did was put together and file all the clippings that had come in and made copies for myself.

I got there on the night of the 13th, and then I had my vaccination, which was the anthrax vaccine. They didn't tell us that at the time, but we knew what it was. When the military wanted to give us an immunization while we were at war in a foreign country that threatened biological warfare, we didn't really care what was in it, we just wanted to get it. If they tried not to give it to me, I would have thrown a fit.

One day we had four Scud missile attacks, and I never wrote another thing on this calendar. I just said, "This is too depressing." I wasn't going to write down things that I didn't want to remind myself of. I didn't want to deal with that.

A young man from the air force brought us some leaflets. What would happen was they would send the pilots up with these leaflets and drop them. It would say, "This is your first and last warning. The 20th Infantry Division will be bombed. Leave this location now." I mean they actually sent these out to warn the people. This was the craziest thing—the most humane war in the world. I had a problem with that because it was like our air force guys would go up, and some of them would get shot down when they were trying to warn the people that the guys with the bombs were coming the next day.

One day one of my roommates was sitting in this common area, painting her toenails, when a guy walked in and asked what she was doing. She told him she was painting her toenails, and so he asked her why. She told him, "Because when you have to dress like this all day it's nice to take off your boots and look down and see that you've got painted toenails." And he said, "Is it hard to do? What does it feel like?" Then he asked her if she could paint his toenails. So she talked to me and we decided that we would have a toenail painting party. Anyone could come that wanted to have their toenails painted. I asked Ludona to bring us a bunch of nail polish. We thought we had better invite a couple more girls because there might be a lot of guys. All these folks showed up, and we painted all of the guys' toenails, and what was so funny was that men's toenails are huge. You can draw pictures on them. So we painted all those toenails. The guys were so crazy about it. About a week later, we found out that we were going home, and one of the guys came to me, and these are grown men in their forties, and he said, "You know, when we go home, I just might have a hard time explaining my toenails to my wife. How do I get it off?" With a totally straight face, I said, "Oh, it just has to wear off." I never did tell him how to take it off.

But I think that was a real typical kind of activity that you would find because there weren't movies to go to and there weren't companionships. We knew that we should be in a group and that we shouldn't be one on one, yet what were we going to do? Other companies would all just be sitting around on the floor trying to read a training manual because that's what they were told to do. I do think that you have to go into something like this thinking, "Okay, we all agree on one thing. We all agree that we're going to go out and give the best medical care possible under whatever circumstances we find ourselves in. We're not going to have it as bad as some people or we're going to have it worse than others." I think that even at the young age of thirty-nine, most of us were fairly philosophical about that.

The one scare that I truly had was with a medic who was about nineteen years old. He worked with me on the ward, and I had known him for a long time because he was in the reserve detachment a year before, but he wasn't that much older than my own kids. My oldest was fifteen. He was a 91B, which is a field medic. Now when the military came through and asked for volunteers for field medics, he asked me, "Do you think that I should do that?" And I said, "No, I don't think you should do that because that means you go out into the fields with the troops, and I don't know if you're well-trained for that and you are needed here, so I think you should stay here and help me."

Well, he passed it up then, but they came back again when they needed more volunteers. This time he decided that he really wanted to go. And I said to him, "You don't want to do this. They're not giving you orders. They're just asking for volunteers." And he said, "I really think I should do this." Now here was this young man who probably wanted to do what was right and wanted some glory and thought that since everyone else was going, he shouldn't be the wimp and not go. So he went out with the people in the field, and I think that was my most maternal moment. I felt the most nervous about that.

They came back about a week later, and he came to me and said, "I will do anything, *anything*, if you get me out of this." So I told him, "From now on, you will take all my advice and never doubt me again." And he said, "Yes, ma'am." So I went to the company commander and told him that if anyone else volunteered, they could take my medic's place because he was ready to come back and work with the EPWs. And he said okay because he knew we were a lead group, and he wanted to keep my people happy. If somebody wanted to work with me, they helped with that sort of thing. This young medic of mine said it was a grueling experience. I don't think he saw action, and I don't think that was an issue for him, but I think it was the tension, the dirt, and the heat that did it. I cannot describe to you what the desert is like. Of course I haven't spent much time in a desert, and maybe this is common, but I thought it was going to be sand. I'm from the beaches of the Oregon coast, and I'm thinking sand, but the desert was like talcum powder. It was the same consistency as talcum powder, and it was everywhere. It would get in our mouths, our eyes, and in our ears, and that was just while standing and waiting for a bus. We had a place to shower every day, but we had to be like that for many hours.

The other thing we did over there was a mass-casualty exercise. We did moulage with whatever we could find: ketchup, toilet paper, or Vaseline. We made it incredible. I felt like a real moulage artist because we did it without the goodies that are usually in a moulage kit. These mass-casualty exercises were really good training for people because we didn't know how long we were going to be there or what kinds of things we were going to see. Even though we would be on duty for twelve hours and then off twelve hours, there was still time to do training and give people things to do. When the helicopters came in for the training exercises, our surroundings became black. We couldn't see our hands in front of our face because of the dust rising in the air. We could hear them, but we could not see even our hands. We didn't dare move for fear of getting mowed down by the helicopter blades.

THE TRAGEDY OF
— SEPTEMBER 11 —

HISTORICAL BACKGROUND

On September 11, 2001, two American Airlines jumbo jets, hijacked by terrorists, flew into the twin towers of the World Trade Center in New York City. A third airliner crashed into the Pentagon, and a fourth, forced to the ground by its passengers, crashed in a field near Shanksville, Pennsylvania, before it reached a possible fourth target. Within a week of the event that took the lives of nearly three thousand people, President George W. Bush, son of former president George Bush—who had declared war on Iraq—declared war on terrorism throughout the world.

A. ELAINE BOND

On the morning of September 11, 2001, I was frantically getting ready to go to Amman, Jordan, to be co-chair of an international nursing conference. I had at least four days' worth of material to compile for the conference, and I only had two days to do it and be on the plane. I went out for a run. All was well in the world because I almost thought I could pull off the preparation for the conference. When I walked in the house, my husband had the television on and said, "There are two planes that have just gone into the World Trade Center." Before we saw what happened to the Pentagon, I knew that our lives would never be the same. The ramifications of 9/11 would continue to unfold over a period of time. I stayed home to watch television instead of going to my office, which meant I was home when I got the first call from Red Cross. It came from General Headquarters. The caller asked if I would please be available, even though they had no way to get me there, because there was no air traffic. I said yes, I would be available. I thought I probably would not be going to Jordan. That, of course, turned out to be true. Initially, the Red Cross only drew from those on the East Coast who could drive to either New York or Washington DC. As the days progressed and they decided that they could open airports, I got another call on Friday that said, "Can you go today?" I said, "No, I need until morning to be able to go." So I made all the arrangements, left first thing Saturday morning, and was on one of the first flights that flew into Dulles Airport. I thought I was going to New York City. When I got my orders, they said DC.

Dulles is one of the airports from which the terrorists launched their attacks. The scary thing about going was questioning all of the security and what might happen next. I was at the Salt Lake Airport three hours before departure time. Passengers were already lined up outside the door of the terminal and clear down the entire length of the sidewalk, because the airport was using very few check-in points, and everyone who was flying Delta had to go at once. All flights were mixed together. There were zillions of people, but everyone was patient and considerate of others. Those of us who were standing in line recognized that we were going through increased security and that it had to be that way. We moved fairly quickly. It only took about an hour and a half to get through the line up to the ticket area. Then we had to go through a couple more security points. They had to open everything and look at everything. We had to show personal identification and a ticket everywhere to be able to get in. There were absolutely no problems. Everyone worked together very well.

When I got to Dulles, I expected to have difficulty in that there would be even more security. But they weren't as concerned about those getting off the planes as those getting on. I got a rental car without incident. When I got to Red Cross Headquarters, I found I was one of the very first people to arrive from outside the area. The local Red Cross chapters had handled things up to that point and done an excellent job, but they were absolutely overwhelmed.

I had five hundred pairs of boots from the Salt Lake Red Cross chapter for the rescue dogs in New York City. Their feet were being badly torn up and burned, and there was even a dog that died from heat exhaustion. When I got to DC, the Red Cross arranged to transport the boots with someone who was going to New York. The boots made a big difference for the dogs that were there. I don't know who donated them, but it was someone in the Salt Lake area.

There was a lot of work for us to do in Washington DC. The first day I went to the Pentagon. At that time there wasn't as much security. We helped with small wound dressings and mostly mental health support for the relief workers there—the firemen, the military, anybody who was there helping out. I only spent that one day actually at the site. There wasn't that much that needed to be done there. There were other people who could fill those roles as well as I could, and I was needed other places.

The next day I spent checking health records of the volunteers who were arriving. There were two hundred fifty of them who showed up that day. Out of that bunch, I had to send two people home. Some of them were just overzealous and were not quite ready to return to Red Cross service after having surgery or some other kind of condition. They were not very happy about that, but you just can't be at a disaster and not be in the best of health.

As far as our individual positions, I don't think we ever felt threatened. I think we felt like we were safe enough doing what we were doing. It was traumatic and emotionally taxing to work with the people who were there. We worked with rescuers. We worked with firemen. We worked with all of the branches of the military, Secret Service, CIA, FBI, the local fire department, and all of the volunteers, and everyone worked together really well. Even though they were the big tough guys on the front lines, the Red Cross could help in ways they could not. As one fireman put it, "I hadn't been there very many minutes when I knew I couldn't make this all better. The Red Cross is the one who really makes it all better." As they came out, absolutely exhausted, they didn't really want to talk about some of the things they were seeing. It is just that they needed to, and as they would sit down and start to talk, it was like opening a floodgate. They would give us a lot of information. This was especially true of military people because even though there were mental health workers there for the military, the rescuers didn't want to talk to their official people, because it would go on their record. They were happy to talk to the Red Cross people because then they could unload the things that were bothering them. Many times all it took was someone to talk to.

After those two days I developed several Integrated Care Teams. Some of the teams worked with patients who had been treated and released from local hospitals. The people I spent the most time with were those who were hospitalized or discharged, along with their families. There were other groups, whom we all joined at the end, who worked with the families. We also worked with the families of the deceased: American Airlines passengers' families as well as family members of all those at the Pentagon who were killed.

There were one hundred eighty-five people who were killed in Washington DC, some of those from the airlines, the majority from the Pentagon. A lot of community nursing techniques were needed for working with the hospitalized people and those who were discharged. I learned that you always look in the least obvious places. The two hospitals that I originally had under my direction were Arlington Hospital and Walter Reed Hospital. When we arrived at Arlington to visit the two patients who we knew were still in the hospital, we discovered that there were more than twenty-two patients who we did not have on our records. That is where those detective pieces helped us to get information. There was a military liaison person there. When we told him the two people we were to visit, he took us to them. One was about to be released, and she said she had lots of help from neighbors and friends and family who would take care of her. The other person was badly burned, though the hospital did not think she needed to be in a burn center. While we were waiting for her to get out of dressing changes to her burns, we met with the admitting office and the emergency department. They willingly shared all the names, addresses, and telephone numbers of all those who were not on our list. So it was a wonderful communication-negotiation-networking kind of thing.

When we visited with the second woman who had the burns, she was so distressed. She had not come to terms with it. By now, it had been approximately five days since the disaster. The realization of what had really happened was sinking in. She was a civilian Department of Defense worker. She was extremely traumatized by the things that she had seen. The person who was sitting at the desk next to her went for coffee and never came back. They were good associates and had worked together for a long time. She realized that she had survived and her associate had not. We discovered those feelings of guilt were common among survivors. We found that over and over because they would say, "Why would someone die and another wouldn't?"

As we talked with her, she expressed that the most important thing to her would be to see her family. Her family was from Louisiana. We were able to make arrangements for them to fly up. Her father had never been in an airplane. It took some work to be able to make the arrangements, but she was so ecstatic to have her family come. She wanted to have all of her nieces and nephews and brothers and sisters come, which was a little bit out of our range. They couldn't come anyhow. It made it so we didn't have to resolve the issue. She and her husband were extremely grateful for the care they received. Every time we interacted with them, we watched them come from a terrible shell-shocked position, where they were just scared, to having happy eyes and being happy to see us. They lived in DC because of her work, and he worked somewhere in the city as well. They were an example of everybody who we worked with. It was extremely worthwhile even though we were thoroughly exhausted.

Each night when we went home, we would be totally ready for bed. I would call my husband, talk to him for a few minutes, and sit there to watch the news. I would wake up about two or three in the morning. The TV was still on and I had been sound asleep. I would turn off the TV and sleep a couple of hours before I was ready to go again. One of the things that helped with my mental health while I was there was that I continued my practice of running every morning. We were in Virginia in Falls Church, and they had wonderful running paths there. I was able to go running every morning before it was time to go down to headquarters to begin our day's work.

After I had done the majority of the work at Arlington and was able to get into Walter Reed, we began to work with some terribly devastated people. Getting into Walter Reed was a choice experience because it was a military hospital and there was always the regular security. But because of the disaster, there was even more. We had to have our FBI identification. We had that to be able to get into the Pentagon, and it was the identification we used everywhere else as well. We could go anywhere. They just had to check us along with anyone else who happened to be there and see that we had the proper credentials. I went through checkpoint after checkpoint after checkpoint just to get into Walter Reed. One of the people we saw at Walter Reed had saved several other people in her area. She had tremendous burns as well, but not bad enough to be in a burn unit. She is an example of what we see anytime there is a disaster. Nobody gets up in the morning and says "I think I'm going to have a disaster" or "I think I'm going to start a war." We think we are going to carry out our everyday activities, and we often have a dozen items on our calendars that we haven't finished yet or that need to be worked on or that need to be resolved. If we have dysfunctional family relationships, they hang over whatever else we are doing. And this particular patient was dealing with several of these issues. She was recently divorced, and all of the details of that were not yet worked out. Her mother had some mental health problems and lived in South Carolina. Working out the arrangements with the mom was taxing, to say the least, but we did help her. The mother came on a couple of occasions. The client did not want her mom there when she went home from the hospital, and it didn't take us long to understand why. It took a lot of PR skills to be able to deal with people. We had their fears from the disaster and all of the other odds and ends and quirks that all of us have.

Another person at Walter Reed was in the process of moving. She had only been on the job for two days. Her family was still in upstate New York. She was staying with her father in DC, trying to care for her husband, who was going back and forth; her children; and her mother, who was also going back and forth taking care of the children and the patient's needs. It was quite a challenge to help arrange the moving and to make sure everything was coordinated on both ends. In the meantime, her mother had a heart attack while she was in New York. There was no one to take care of the children. We were finally able to work it out.

People from the Red Cross came and went, and as some people on our team left, we integrated two of our care teams. I took on the responsibility for the worst patients that were at Washington General, where the burn unit was. Once again, it was terribly devastating to watch the effects of the disaster on families. We didn't have much association with these patients. The majority of them were still in critical care in the burn unit. There were some who were out of the burn unit, and we were able to talk to those individuals. For the most part, we worked with their families. Those families with education, access to resources, and knowledge about how to access the system did fairly well. Those families who did not know how to access the system, those who had struggled their entire lives, and those who did not have a good education were absolutely devastated. I would go home and want to adopt them and help them to have some positive experiences in their lives. One husband was absolutely overwhelmed by his experience. His wife was severely burned. I am not sure that she survived. I talked to the charge nurse in the burn ICU. It was obvious to her and me that we were talking multisystem failure. Each day the patient would have surgery to remove necrotic tissue, and each day there would be less of her. The poor husband was just beside himself. Very poor, very nice people, but so deprived when it comes to the things of this life. Those experiences wore on us, dealing with them all the time. It was really hard for us, but not nearly as hard as it was for them.

The one who got to my heart the most was a developmentally delayed gentleman. I think he was forty-three. I doubt that he worked at all before he started working at the Pentagon as a janitor. The mental health person on our team was wonderful with him. At first we were not able to find him. That happened often. Names didn't match the telephone numbers or the addresses. Sometimes there was a telephone number or address at the Pentagon, and obviously we couldn't access that. But in his case we just couldn't track him down, and it was his mother who called us. He lived at home with his mother in a modest subsidized apartment. He was not sleeping at night and he would hold his head and shake it and say, "Make it go away. Make it go away." His mother told us that he didn't talk very much, and for him to say even that much was something he didn't normally do.

When we arrived, he was so agitated; he just couldn't sit still. He had been in the hospital but had been released. The reason they had taken him to the hospital was that he had been seizing when they found him on the floor in one of the halls at the Pentagon. They assumed that he had a seizure disorder. He went to Arlington and then went to Walter Reed and was released from there. He was at home when we found him. His mother told us that he had never had a seizure disorder and had never taken any medication. He had been in two healthcare systems, and they had never picked up on that. They didn't believe it. When we have these underprivileged people who won't speak up for themselves, they are just so accepting. It was one of those times when I just wanted to tear out my hair at the failings of our society. Even as enlightened as we think we are, we are missing the needs of so many people. He just sat there so agitated and rocked back and forth in his chair.

He was jumping from side to side and our healthcare worker said to him, "You don't have to talk to us about this. You don't have to tell us anything you don't want to tell us. We'll find somebody who you can talk to, and they will come and see you lots of times, and you don't have to tell them anything until you are very comfortable with them." That comforted him a little bit, and he calmed down. I think he was probably worse because he thought somehow we were associated with what he had gone through. He functioned on such a low level that he was not able to verbalize a lot of things. He said, "No, no, don't talk about it, no, no, not talk about it, not remember. Never going back there, bad place, never going back." When we went that first time, we took him a card from a school child. School children all over the United States made get-well cards and sympathy cards, and we delivered them by the thousands to patients and clients. When we gave him the card, he looked at it from beginning to end, over and over and over. He clutched it tightly in both hands and just looked at it and continued to rock as we talked to his mother.

One of the things the Red Cross does is provide financial help, but the mother said, "We don't need it. We want someone to get it who needs it more than we do." There I was, sitting there dying! Their apartment was maybe seven hundred to nine hundred square feet total. They lived on her social security and his minimum wage check. They lived from day to day, but she didn't want any financial help from us. There were people who needed it more. The Red Cross was handing out thousands to people who could go out and get another job, who could take care of themselves in short order. Here was this woman who needed it more than anyone I had talked to except the one lady we discussed who was at the hospital. This woman just continued to say "We are blessed." I thought, "How blessed you really are because you've got that sense of self-worth and the attitude that 'We'll take care of ourselves.'" Eventually we found a way to get her some money, but it took some real convincing on our part. She needed to have surgery, but she was the sole caregiver of her developmentally delayed son, so she didn't feel comfortable going to have the surgery and leaving him on his own. He had never been alone.

The next time we went to visit, he was happier to see us and was not quite so agitated. We took him a basket of fruit, the kind of thing that anybody would want, but we also took some coloring books, some simple objects, and another card from the children. He loved it. He just sat there and smiled and looked at it over and over and then he said, "Were these children in kindergarten?" It was a full sentence not related to anything we said, and he initiated it. The mother looked surprised, and we were very surprised as well. He did talk to us in short sentences, and his mother was absolutely overwhelmed.

When we went shopping to get the goodies for his bags and especially to get the coloring books, we were in our Red Cross vests with our Red Cross nametags on, and the stores would not take our money. Whatever we wanted, they just provided. They would say, "No, you need it. It's our contribution, because we want to be of help." We found that all over Washington DC. It was like living in a Zion society. Everybody considered each other their brothers and sisters. Everybody worked together. Even though there was tight security, everybody was kind and considerate and thoughtful. It was magnificent to experience. Everyplace we went, it was the same thing. When we walked down the street wearing our Red Cross vests, everybody said, "Yes! We are so glad you are here. What can we do to help you? Where can I go to give blood? Can I give you money?" We would say, "No, no, you can't give us the money. It has to go through the proper channels." Everybody was so cooperative. In light of the horrid experiences that our patients and clients told us and the emotional strain it was on us, overall, it was a positive experience. It was very positive to see how everyone worked together.

At the last, we all moved to the Marriot Hotel, which was across from the Sheraton. The Sheraton was where all of the families from the deceased victims were staying. Between the government and American Airlines, they brought all of those families together. The families didn't pay anything for staying there. Red Cross helped transport them so that everyone could get there and then the government, military, and the airlines paid for their hotel rooms, all of their meals, and all of their needs. All of the organizations that they needed to see, such as the Social Security Administration, the branches of military service, and the American Red Cross were on one floor of the Sheraton. There was a casualty officer, a military person, assigned to each family. The casualty officer would make the appointments and then go with the family to make sure everything was done for them. They didn't have to chase to a lot of offices, and they didn't have to worry about whether they had forgotten anything because they were so distraught. The casualty officer would see to that. I said that the government and American Airlines paid all of the hotel costs, but Sheraton, Marriott, and Holiday Inn all donated lots of rooms. For example, Holiday Inn provided rooms for all of the families who had members at Walter Reed, Arlington, and Washington General. All of those families could stay at no cost for as long as they needed to be there. There were lots of other organizations that donated a tremendous amount of services.

During Red Cross disasters, you usually sleep in a sleeping bag, and if you get a shower every so often, you are lucky. Because of the nature of this one, we each had our own hotel room. We slept in a nice clean bed and had our own shower, and if we could stay awake, we could watch television. Local businesses brought meals in every day. It was unbelievable. One night we had prime rib and everything that goes with it. Then we had a pork dinner and several chicken dinners and wonderful sandwiches and salads. So every night a different restaurant brought the dinner, and they served one hundred forty-five people at Red Cross Headquarters besides all of those who were out. There was always tons of food. Everybody kept saying, "This is not like any disaster we have ever been in." This was the first disaster that I had ever been out of town for. The Salt Lake tornado counted as a disaster, so this was the second one I have been on, but it was the first one I had ever been able to go to away from Salt Lake. The Red Cross expects a three-week commitment from volunteers when they go. I can understand why, because it takes a while to pick up the pieces. The fewer times you have to report off and change people, the less likely you are to lose people between the cracks. I was there for three weeks. The reason I was able to be there for three weeks was that I was on leave of absence from BYU, since I was supposed to be in Jordan for the conference and then for research work.

The highlight of my experience was the unity—the working together. There were a couple of events that were absolutely remarkable. One was a candlelight vigil on the steps of the Lincoln Memorial. It was organized by the local Afghanis, but there were all kinds of religious groups there: Christians, Jews, Hindus, Muslims, and numerous others. Everyone was there together, and it was a tremendously powerful spiritual experience to share. We did a candlelight ceremony at the end of the talks, and the flag came down the steps of the Lincoln Memorial. It looked like it just floated down there by itself, even though it was being carried by people. I just don't have the words for it. We lit each other's candles, and there was a sense of unity there.

The name of the whole operation while we were there at the Pentagon was called Camp Unity. Each of us has a tee-shirt that has that emblem: hands holding the Pentagon in a circle with a flag in the background and then underneath it says "Camp Unity." We really felt that.

We were able to go to the Kennedy Center for a concert. The National Symphony and Orchestra put on a concert, along with other performers from across the United States, as a benefit for the families and the Red Cross workers. We had six hundred family members there along with the Red Cross workers. We had the National Symphony in the Kennedy Center hosted by First Lady Laura Bush and Senator Ted Kennedy, and we sat seven rows away from them. We all sang "God Bless America" and stood while they played the National Anthem. There were other tributes that were paid. It was an extremely powerful, unifying force. This is the way we need to live together, and it is unfortunate that we have to have a war to be able to bring us together. I understand that it happened with World War II as well. We were not so good for Vietnam and the Korean conflict, but for World War II and this present conflict, it has brought us together as a nation, and we really needed that at this time. We have been struggling. It has just been a horrible experience for us, but the big thing that came out of that for me was the unity and the brotherhood that was shown by all.

I went to the temple while I was there and that was a wonderful experience. I had not been to the Washington DC Temple before. I accidentally found it when I first got there because I always have to take the scenic route! I did not go to Church on Sunday, because that was my day to work, but we did have interfaith church services at Red Cross Headquarters almost every evening. Out of that we had many interesting religious experiences. We had a mixture of people, and I said, "I am not acquainted with doing a service that way. Tell me how that works." For instance, on our care team there was a Protestant and a Catholic. We talked about some of the differences and similarities between Latter-day Saints, Protestants, and Catholics. It opened up the conversation. It was a spiritual discussion. As we would go to the candlelight services and listen to those speakers from each of those religions, underneath it all was the brotherhood of man and the love of our Heavenly Father. They may call Him by different names, but the same concept is there. If we can build on those similarities, on those strengths, then we are so much better off. There will come a day when we all are one church, but those relationships we build in the meantime are the unifying, strengthening, spiritual experiences that make it easier for people to come into the gospel.

It has been interesting to listen to the debate going on across the country. It is a bad thing that anyone is questioning how the Red Cross money is being used. The money that goes to Red Cross is not meant specifically to hand over to people. It is meant to provide relief. Well, there are lots of ways that people need relief. All of the supplies that we did purchase cost money, though we didn't have to purchase a lot of things. Getting that many volunteers to the site cost money. Each volunteer provides thousands of dollars' worth of relief. They're not paid for it, but their expenses are paid. Red Cross has arrangements with airlines so that the cost of airline tickets are very low. Each of the families involved got a blanket amount of three months' worth of their living expenses: rent, groceries, credit card statements, car payments, transportation, whatever they have as ordinary expenses. Then there were also grants that paid for additional food so that they have a supply on hand.

People who have lost personal items have those items replaced. One lady lost both pairs of glasses in the Pentagon. She had to have them. Those didn't come out of the Red Cross funds, because I made a telephone call to Lenscrafters in her small New York town, told them that her prescription was less than one year old, and asked them if they would please donate her glasses. In less than an hour I had a call from Lenscrafters in DC. They had received a call from the Lenscrafters in New York, and they were FedExing the glasses over to the lady at that very moment. In less than two hours from the time I made the call, she had two pair of glasses. The Red Cross will take care of lost medications, lost glasses, or any lost things that make a difference in people's lives. All of those things cost a tremendous amount of money. In addition to that, these people are not going to be free and clear in three months. They are going to have long-term needs and there will continue to be funds paid out.

There is a little bit of criticism that you have to prove that you qualify to be a recipient, but I'm sorry, I dealt with ex-husbands and ex-wives who wanted their three months' worth when they hadn't had anything to do with the family for two or three years. Those kind of people come out of the woodwork in a disaster, the same way the goodness and the sharing and the brotherhood come out. There are always people who want to take advantage, so you do need to have rules and regulations. The Red Cross rules specify that the funds must be spent for the purpose for which they were gathered. The money will go into the disaster fund over a period of time. You don't just automatically put it all out there and say, "Here, come take all this money." That is not helpful. We ask, "What are your needs, and how can we meet your needs?" rather than say, "Here's money, go do it yourself."

I think there will be enough money because there are a lot of people who are donating to a lot of causes: United Way, Salvation Army, relief funds for firemen and policemen, and pension funds for all of the organizations. Most people have life insurance and social security benefits to survivors, so children will always have that kind of money. The idea is to meet people's needs without paying out a lot of money unnecessarily. If you are getting college tuition paid from one fund, there is no need for another fund to duplicate this. It takes a long time for those things to be worked out.

OPERATION IRAQI FREEDOM
THE SECOND GULF WAR

HISTORICAL BACKGROUND

On January 29, 2002, President George W. Bush, in his State of the Union address, named Iraq as part of the axis of evil that threatened world peace. Inspection teams had been in Iraq looking for weapons of mass destruction but failed to find the expected large caches of such weapons. One theory for the failure was that Iraqi officials were successfully hiding the weapons by moving them from one place to another, just ahead of the inspectors. The United States was so convinced of their existence that they convinced the United Nations Security Council to publish Resolution 144 in October 2002. This resolution held Iraq in material breach of previous resolutions that stated that Iraq was to be inspected and existing weapons of mass destruction were to be destroyed. Inspections continued, but no weapons were found. In March 2003, Britain submitted March 17, 2003, as the deadline for Iraqi compliance with inspectors looking for weapons of mass destruction. When compliance with inspections did not become a reality, the United States issued a forty-eight-hour ultimatum for the leadership of the Iraqi regime to leave Iraq. Hussein and his administration did not leave Iraq, and on March 19, 2003, United States special operations forces began to enter Iraq. The air attack on Iraq and the push of U.S. ground forces into that country ended twenty-six days later, on April 14, 2003. U.S. forces remain in Iraq at this printing.

CHARLOTTA LEADER

My name is Captain Charlotta Leader. I am a nurse in the United States Air Force. Currently, I am stationed at Spangdahlem Air Force Base, Germany. This week I will be deployed to an unnamed location in Southwest Asia for three to six months in support of Operation Enduring Freedom, providing medical services for our troops in the desert.

Deployments are not new to me. I am grateful for the opportunity to serve my country in whatever capacity I can. As a reservist, I was called up as a medical-surgical nurse at Nocton

Hall, England, during Operation Desert Storm. When obstetrical nurses were needed at Lakenheath Air Force Base in England, I went to help the staff there. This was during the ground war of that campaign. In 1995, I spent three months in Guantanamo Bay, Cuba, providing health care for the Cuban and Haitian migrants during Operation Sea Signal.

As a single mother of four, there have definitely been sacrifices, especially by my children. But this time will be the hardest sacrifice of all. My youngest son will be returning from his mission next month and our reunion will be postponed for the better part of this coming year.

My son's name is Nathan Leader. He has been serving in the New Jersey Morristown Mission. He watched the Twin Towers fall on September 11 and wrote, "Mom, I had front row seats to the beginning of World War III." Nathan is a young man not entirely unaccustomed to tragedies. During his high school years, our town and our home flooded, mountains of snow caused roofs to cave in, and the extent of forest fire damage set records. Through it all he has been strong and optimistic, but the towers definitely shook him up. Thankfully, the Lord protected him and the other missionaries of the New York and New Jersey Missions.

After returning from my humanitarian services in Cuba, I incorporated a segment of my journal into my Relief Society lesson about the celestial kingdom and exaltation. Some sisters thought I should have my story published. I will share it now.

I went to Guantanamo [Gitmo] Bay, Cuba, this summer in support of a humanitarian mission to give medical aid to the migrant Cuban population en route to the United States. When I arrived, there were approximately twenty thousand migrants. When I left, that number had been reduced to just fewer than fourteen thousand people. I was assigned to work as an emergency room nurse at Camp Buckley and to do triage in Echo, Foxtrot, and Golf villages.

I loved the sunshine, warm weather, and going to the beaches after each duty day to look for seashells. I was privileged to live and work with some wonderful people. But I also had a very sobering experience while in Cuba that caused me to take stock of my life and where I was going. I think that this particular spiritual living lesson has been evolving in my head all summer. I hope you can see the analogy that I'm trying to make.

Guantanamo Bay is the oldest military post outside of the United States. It encompasses forty-five square miles of Cuba, including the bay. Guard towers and armed military personnel, both United States Marines and Cuban infantry, surround it. In addition, the border is surrounded with concertina wire and mine fields. If you wander too far out in the bay, the coast guard will escort you back to the naval base.

In 1994 all the American spouses and children were sent back to the United States for their safety due to the large number of migrants pouring into Gitmo as they tried to escape Cuba. There were homes, but no families; playgrounds and an elementary school, but no children.

I missed the children. Two out of the three months I was there, I never saw a child. The few Cuban children that were left were in different camps than the one I attended. (On my return trip back home, we landed in Jacksonville, Florida. I saw children waiting for their military fathers. It brought tears to my eyes as they reached through the chain link fence trying to touch their fathers' fingers and hands.)

Many of the Cuban migrants were hardworking people who displayed a great deal of patience and endurance as they waited their turn to go to the United States. But some of them had never been exposed to the concept of God and His teachings. They did not seem to know how to live the Ten Commandments.

During my first few weeks there, I was unable to locate anyone from the Church. I inquired at the base chapel, asking if anyone knew about services for The Church of Jesus Christ of

Latter-day Saints. I was told that the little group that had met together had left. Wrong information. I later discovered that the most senior-ranking chaplain on base was a Latter-day Saint army colonel from Utah. I appreciated his insight and direction. He was in contact with the Kingston Jamaican Mission president, whose goal it was to visit our small group that met each Sunday on a regular basis. Special permission had to be granted by the base officials for him to come to Gitmo.

As a military person you speak in terms of "day in" and "day out." When it was time for the air force nurses to leave, we all wanted to leave together.

So how does all of this relate to exaltation and the celestial kingdom? Just like Guantanamo Bay, once assigned to the telestial or terrestrial kingdoms, you won't be able to leave. There will be no family structure as we know it, and there will be no children to watch grow and develop. It's hard to imagine a world without children. People in the telestial kingdom will not be accustomed to obeying God's commandments. That sweet spirit that comes in the presence of righteous living will not be there or on the faces of those who live there. Like the Kingston Jamaica Mission president, who could not freely come to Guantanamo Bay, Jesus and Heavenly Father will not be able to visit members of the telestial kingdom because the people there will not be able to behold Their presence. Only Christ can visit those who dwell in their terrestrial kingdom.

In this world, which we know is after a telestial order, we speak of birthdays and the day we die—kind of like our "day in" and "day out" of Guantanamo Bay. And if we have developed strong relationships, I think we wanted to come into this world with friends, and I think we want to exit with friends and family.

I know that these experiences are not unique to me. Many have had similar situations in their lives. It's just that this experience helped me get a little better focus on what the celestial kingdom is all about. It may be a beautiful place, beyond anything that we can imagine, but what is most important is who will be there. There will be families and children, our heavenly parents, and our Savior—and I want to be there with my family, too.

It is a privilege and honor to serve my country. My father was a member of the American forces in Europe during World War II. I feel blessed to walk where he walked and see some of the same German countryside that he saw. Because of the increased fighting in Afghanistan this past week, I believe I may be busy during my deployment down south. I pray I will do my job well, as my father did before me.

I was part of the 320th Expeditionary Medical Support Group in a classified location in the desert. We received and treated military troops and contract civilians at an air evac hub. Most of our patients arrived at night via C-130s. Those who needed more definitive care were stabilized and sent on to Landstuhl, Germany.

Two things really impressed me about this experience. First, most of our American soldiers did not complain when they arrived from Afghanistan or Pakistan. They were extremely grateful for everything that we did for them or gave them: cold water, hot meals, showers, clean clothes, and air conditioning. As I settled one young man on a narrow medical cot one night, he remarked how good his bed felt. I never thought of our cots as feeling very comfortable. Curious, I asked him where he had been sleeping. He replied that he and his unit had been sleeping on rocks for two months. He was so very tired, as were many of the troops that came to us.

The second thing that impressed me was the outpouring of supportive letters, cards, and food items that we received from the citizens of the United States. Many grade-school children wrote to us, thanking us for what we were doing. I am grateful to the teachers who are trying to instill patriotism in the next generation of Americans. Living in Germany at the time of September 11, I did not fully comprehend the spark of liberty and freedom that was ignited that day. What a legacy to live up to!

Jared Scott

During a period of two weeks during the winter of 2003, our inpatient ward at Naval Medical Center San Diego took care of over 150 recruits from the Marine Corps Recruiting Depot (MCRD) in San Diego, California. These recruits had developed pneumonia. Our work began when three recruits were transferred to the ICU after their pneumonia turned into empyema and pleural effusion. After those first three recruits, the MCRD began screening all of their recruits for pneumonia.

Multiple factors make such epidemics possible. Along with the physical, mental, and emotional stress of boot camp, the close quarters allow virulent strains to spread quickly. Recruits are never alone: they eat, sleep, drink, run, and study together. They go to the dentist together and have medical examinations together. All of these risk factors also support the spread of infectious GI disease. Breakouts are common.

It took four days to screen all of the recruits. Thousands of throat cultures, blood cultures, and x-rays were processed. The laboratory and radiology departments of our hospital received two weeks' worth of work in four days, and they performed well.

I was going off shift when the director of nursing service determined to turn our med-surg ward into a recruit pneumonia ward. We transferred all of our regular patients off the ward. At 1800 hours the recruits started pouring in. We admitted forty patients that night to our floor. All were eighteen- to twenty-year-old young men with pneumonia contracted while at MCRD. That same day the surgery ward was also converted into a pneumonia ward. I stayed until midnight.

I volunteered to stay a few extra hours to help track the admission process. Working with the ward clerk under my direction, we processed physician orders for forty new admissions. The six phones available were just barely enough to coordinate services with all the various hospital departments.

Recruits were still expected to act like recruits. They have to be told everything to do and are not to speak unless spoken to. On one occasion, a recruit did not go to the bathroom all day because he had not been told to do so. As our caregiver numbers became low, we had able recruits change their own linens and empty their own trash. If I took time to empty trash, a recruit might not get his IV antibiotics before my day was over.

Sunday morning, as the pneumonia ward began to adjust to the routine and marines began to be discharged, we were informed that a recruit had died from complications of pneumonia. Many staff had worked relentlessly to save him from the disease. Everything possible was done to save him. The nurses grew solemn. A young, strong, capable, healthy servant of our country lay motionless. He never made it to the battlefield. Never fought an enemy. His mom and dad were no doubt proud that he had volunteered to serve his country as we were waging a terrible conflict in Afghanistan with rumors of a conflict in Iraq. I don't know his name. Probably never will. Like the many hundreds of thousands that gave their lives down through the centuries for our country, this young recruit stands as testimony to the Savior's teaching, "Greater love hath no man than this, than a man lay down his life for his friends."

I have been with many people near death and stood close as others left this world. On many occasions, death is a relief from pain and struggle caused by years of disease. This case was different. Death was not a relief for this young recruit, but a wall. He had been struggling to create his dreams and live his passions and was stopped short. He had given his life for us.

We decided not to tell the marines that one of their shipmates would not be returning to MCRD with them. For good or bad, we did not feel right that it should come from us. It did not take long for them to hear the news. A shipmate had died from the same disease for which they were being treated. They took it in stride. At least they didn't show that it bothered them. They were strong. It was an honor to care for them.

Death is just a doorway. Time that these young men miss out on will be given to them in an ever better place. Time continues. Their lives will continue. I take comfort in knowing that even as lives here are cut short, there is a far better life beyond this veil of sorrow. Those who give their lives for others have felt as the Savior felt and will feel the joy of love that He felt.

— CONCLUSION —

WE, THE EDITORS of this book, sincerely hope you have enjoyed the work and have gained an appreciation for the contribution of nurses during wartime situations. The *Nurses at War* project is an ongoing project. The hope of the editors is to collect the accounts of as many nurses as possible and to have them permanently archived in the L. Tom Perry Special Collections Section of the Harold B. Library at Brigham Young University. The project has been expanded to include not only nurses who are members of The Church of Jesus Christ of Latter-day Saints but any nurse or physician who has served during a wartime situation. The project would welcome accounts from nurses and physicians who have served during any wartime situation for any country. Accounts may be contributed by the nurse or physician or by family or friends if veterans are unable to make the contribution themselves. For more information, Dr. Patricia Rushton may be contacted at 801-422-5375 or by e-mail at patricia_rushton@byu.edu.

— References —

Baer, E. D. 1987. Letters to Miss Sanborn: St. Vincent's Hospital nurses' accounts of World War I. *Journal of the American Association for the History of Nursing* 2 (2): 17–31.

Barger, J. 1991. Coping behaviors of U.S. Army flight nurses in World War II: An oral history. *Aviation, Space, and Environmental Medicine*, February, 155–57.

Beebe, L. S. 1996. To be one of the boys: Aftershocks of the World War I nursing experience. *Journal of Nursing and Military Research*, Spring.

Bledsoe, H. W. 1997. American nurses for American men: A World War I diary. *N&HC: Perspectives on Community* 18 (1): 11–14.

Breakiron, M. 1995. A salute to the nurses of World War II. *AORN Journal* 62 (5): 710–22.

Fosburgh, L. C. 1995. Nurse anesthetists remembering a world at war—Part 2: My assignment as a Red Cross nurse. *Journal of the American Association of Nurse Anesthetists* 63 (6): 501–7.

Fosburgh, L. C. 1995. Nurse anesthetists remembering a world at war—Part 1: Nurse anesthetists prepare for war, 1939–41. *Journal of the American Association of Nurse Anesthetists* 63 (5): 385–87.

Hoskins, R. 1998. Lest we forget. *Nursing Times* 94 (45): 15.

Mosley, M. T. April 30, 2003. Operation Iraqi Freedom. By the numbers: Assessment and Analysis Division. USCENTAF. 1–16.

Nurses in the Vietnam War. 1995. *Nebraska Nurse: The Official Publication of the Nebraska Nurses Association* 28 (2): 1, 4.

Norman, E. M., and S. Eifriend. 1995. How did they all survive? An analysis of American nurses' experiences in Japanese prisoner-of-war camps. *Nursing History Review* 3:105–27.

Norman, E. M. 1992. Women at war: The story of fifty military nurses who served in Vietnam. *New Jersey Nurse* (March/April): 15.

Norman, E. M. 1999. *We band of angels: The untold story of American nurses trapped on Bataan by the Japanese*. New York: Random House.

Roark, J. L., M. P. Johnson, P. C. Cohen, S. Stage, A. Lawson, and S. M. Hartmann. 1998. *The American promise: A history of the United States: Volume 2: From 1865*. Boston: Bedford Books.

Robinson, T. M., and P. M. Perry. 2001. *Cadet nurse stories: The call for and response of women during*

World War II. Indianapolis: Center for Nursing Publishing.

Sarnecky, M. T. 1999. *A history of the U.S. Army Nurse Corps*. Philadelphia: University of Pennsylvania Press, 286, 301–20.

Scott, M. 2001. Focusing on the "forgotten war." *DAV Magazine* (Sept/Oct.), 26–27.

Sterner, D. M. 1996. *In and out of harm's way: A history of the Navy Nurse Corps*. Portland: Peanut Butter Publishing, 229–54.

Worthington, H., and S. Titus. 1995. A nurse's role in Operation Desert Storm: Psychosocial nursing in a war. *Journal of Military Nursing and Research* (Winter), 18–23.

Worthington, H., and S. Titus. 1991. A nurse's role in Operation Desert Storm: Psychosocial nursing in a war. *Journal of Psychological Nursing* 29 (9): 29–34.

INDEX